Onward to Victory

JAMES E. ARMSTRONG
1902-1974

Onward to Victory

A CHRONICLE OF THE ALUMNI OF THE UNIVERSITY
OF NOTRE DAME DU LAC
1842 – 1973

by

JAMES E. ARMSTRONG

A.B. '25, LL.D. '67

THE UNIVERSITY OF NOTRE DAME

Notre Dame, Indiana

Acknowledgments: The Alumni Board, for their constructive efforts, and abiding confidence in me. Jim Cooney, for starting the alumni world again when I stopped it to get off. To the thousands of alumni who, over the years, nourished their alma mater and their association, so that the dreams of the old men and the visions of the young were continuously coming closer to the reality of the University. And, before coeducation acquires roots and stature, to the women—the mothers, wives, daughters, nuns and friends—who shared with Our Lady the generous gifts of grace and graciousness in "La Vie Intime."

1973 -

the 131st year of the University of Notre Dame. . . . .
the 106th year of the Alumni Association. . . . .
the 50th year of the Alumni Office of the Association. . . . .
the 50th year of the Notre Dame (Alumnus) Magazine. . . . .
the 6th year of lay governance. . . . .
the 1st year of coeducation. . . . .

ONWARD TO VICTORY
A STORY WITH 50,000 HEROES

Is dedicated
To the alumni of the University of Notre Dame
Who have been dedicated to the University of Notre Dame
Which has been dedicated to Our Lady, Notre Dame

NOTRE DAME VICTORY MARCH

Rally sons of Notre Dame
Sing her glory and sound her fame,
Raise her Gold and Blue
And cheer with voices true:
Rah, rah, for Notre Dame.

We will fight in every game,
Strong of heart and true to her name
We will ne'er forget her
And will cheer her ever
Loyal to Notre Dame.

CHORUS:
Cheer, cheer for old Notre Dame.
Wake up the echoes cheering her name,
Send a volley cheer on high,
Shake down the thunder from the sky.
What though the odds be great or small?
Old Notre Dame will win over all,
While her loyal sons are marching
Onward to Victory.

Music by Rev. Michael Shea, '04
Words by John F. Shea, '06

THE OFFICERS AND DIRECTORS
OF THE ALUMNI ASSOCIATION
OF THE UNIVERSITY OF NOTRE DAME
1973

Dr. John C. Lungren '38, honorary president
William K. McGowan, Jr. '57, president
Joseph G. Bertrand '54, vice president
Paul J. Doyle '36, vice president
Peter F. Flaherty '51, vice president
Charles F. Osborn '38, vice president
James D. Cooney '59, executive director
Michael E. Jordan '68, assistant director

Directors to 1974

  Joseph G. Bertrand '54, Chicago, Illinois
  Paul J. Doyle '36, Houston, Texas
  Peter F. Flaherty '51, Pittsburgh, Pennsylvania
  William K. McGowan, Jr. '57, Indianapolis, Indiana
  Charles F. Osborn '38, Seattle, Washington

Directors to 1975

  Peter J. Cannon '56, Reston, Virginia
  Patrick H. Meenan '49, Casper, Wyoming
  Robert J. Metzler '44, Kansas City, Missouri
  Richard W. Murphy '58, Canton, Massachusetts
  Coleman O'Brien '69, McLean, Virginia
  Martin R. O'Connor '51, Fort Myers, Florida

Directors to 1976

  Edward A. Bracken, Jr. '35, Detroit, Michigan
  Eugene C. Calhoun '33, Los Angeles, California
  Thomas R. Curtin '68, Kinnelon, New Jersey
  Thomas L. Mulcahy, Jr. '57, Milwaukee, Wisconsin
  John R. Mullen '53, New Brunswick, New Jersey
  John A. O'Brien '51, Birmingham, Alabama

CONTENTS

Foreword
Rev. Theodore M. Hesburgh, c.s.c.

FOREWORD

The late Jim Armstrong made many contributions to Notre Dame during his lifetime. Now, several months after his death, comes this book, his final labor of love for his alma mater and his fellow alumni. It is not a history of the University although there is a lot of Notre Dame lore in it. Rather it is a warm and often witty account of the role alumni have played in the development of Notre Dame from an obscure frontier school to an internationally celebrated university. It is a chronicle of Notre Dame alumni through the years—from Neal Gillespie, of Lancaster, Ohio, the first alumnus, to Roberto Martino Salvo, of Managua, Nicaragua, who was the last degree recipient at the August, 1974, commencement.

Between Gillespie, who became a Holy Cross priest, and Salvo whose career is just commencing lies Jim Armstrong's chronicle. He calls it "a story with 50,000 heroes," both the celebrated and the unsung. Notre Dame has had more than its share of heroes in the combat of war and the gridiron, and we have been inspired, too, by the way Notre Dame men like Fred Snite and Van Wallace and Tom Dooley have met adversity. But the quiet and unheralded heroism of tens of thousands of others in their family life and in their life's work is also Notre Dame's glory.

Jim Armstrong was that kind of man, and because he was, there was no one in the Notre Dame family who was loved so much by so many people. His was a wonderful example of fidelity to Marion and their five sons but also to Our Lady and her sons. He was able to roll with the punches, to accept change, whether on the campus or in the Church, and yet be faithful to basic truths. Smoothing the way during his forty-two years of service to Notre Dame was his unfailing sense of humor. If you believe deeply enough of things eternal, you can make light of the things of time. Finally, his was a great vision. He saw Notre Dame as a very special place melding the human and the divine, a place that accepted youngsters and turned out men and women. He, as much as any man, enriched this place and its vision, and he helped it come true.

Jim Armstrong's book has a beginning because Notre Dame and its Alumni Association began in time. But there is as yet no end to the Notre Dame story, and, therefore, there is no real conclusion to this book. We believe that Providence touches the lives of institutions no less than the lives of men. The same Providence that brought Father Sorin and the Holy Cross Brothers here in 1842 and which has led tens of thousands of others here since then will surely lead Notre Dame to its rendezvous with destiny beyond the present horizon. Whether as individuals or as a university, we must press onward to victory. Many of those whose names fill this book have already won their victory. The rest of us must carry on.

Theodore M. Hesburgh, C.S.C.

I

Course Outline

Alumni are an American phenomenon. Like tobacco and tomatoes, in their introduction to the scene they were sometimes considered poisonous. In subsequent years, like tomatoes, this fear of them is commonly held to have been an intellectual error. And even where, like tobacco, some stigma may remain, they have nevertheless become a habit hard to break.

Johnny Appleseed is a national legend, a folk hero. It is true that we are indebted to him for much of the fruit, juice and sauce in our heritage. Father Edward Sorin, who, at the age of 26, in a clearing of less than ten acres with a log chapel its only structure, planted seeds of education is another. In the rich valley from which the Potawatomi Indians had only lately been displaced, and in the settlement still dominated by the twilight of the fur traders, he started his work whose fruition is an increasing phenomenon in a widening world.

It is into this vacuum of values that the present story of the men of Notre Dame intends to bring understanding and balance. Throughout, as in its beginning, its purpose is, to a large degree, the singing of the unsung.

The Alumni Board has asked me to undertake the story of the role of alumni of Notre Dame in the history of the University. The request impaled me on two prongs. First, as the executive secretary of the Alumni Association—actually its first full-time director, and editor of the *Alumnus* magazine—from 1926 to 1967 I was on the kaleidoscopic scene for 42 of the 50 years of actual association function. This began with the establishment of the Alumni office and the *Alumnus* magazine in 1923. There is much that predated this crystallization of program and which shaped it. But it is in the functioning of the

1

office and the editing of the magazine that both a review of its
past and a study of its future became essential.

There is no lack of modesty in accepting the assignment.
Primarily, because there were few records, quick developments
in the pace of progress, and a continuing overlap with areas of
the University itself—all working against constitutional procedures and clear understanding—I am left as the inevitable nomi-
nee for this long overdue commentary.

The second prong, by the way, stems from my association
with other alumni associations in the colleges and universities of
America. The American Alumni Council, of which I was president in 1962, embraced at that time 1,600 institutions and
some 2,200 executives and editors of their alumni associations.
They were public, private, coeducational, church oriented,
men's, women's, junior colleges and even a few secondary
boarding schools. The panorama of this field of higher education in America widened my personal horizon far beyond Notre
Dame, but at the same time did much to provide many of the
comparisons which brought increasing conviction of the unique
values inherent in the University of Notre Dame and its alumni.

In this broader frame of alumni reference, as well as in my
own programs, I believed that alumni were unidentified and
underrated by their alma maters but not by design or as offense.
The academic oasis that was labeled faculty-administration-
student turned its eyes inward to the ultimate illusion of its
own self-sufficiency. And alumni, because their talents were
many and their paths went to the four corners of the world,
were categorized in the misleading, unjust and costly areas (for
the male alumni particularly) reflected in exuberance over athletics, or exuberance stemming from very non-academic spirits.

I urged the American campus, and I repeat this conviction as
often as I can, to point to the contributions of professional
competence, of business and civic leadership, of scientific exploration, of cultural advancements and of the military strength
which in two wars protected all these essentials of our democracy against overwhelming odds of traditional power. These all
were accomplishments of our alumni.

True, Notre Dame alumni were concerned with the great
common denominator of sports, especially the football tradition. They clamored for tickets. And on game week ends they
gathered on the campus for relaxation and reminiscence. And at
commencement (originally) or reunion time (separated in recent
years from commencement because of growth in numbers),

they again relaxed, reminisced and enjoyed the various stimulants of the occasion—of which beverages were the least.

It was to our loss that we did not have them wear placards that gave their true identities—Christian, gentleman, husband and father, lawyer, doctor, corporate executive, scientist, priest and brother, teacher, legislator, inventor or coach.

This brings me to another of my concerns which led to my involvement with this pleasant assignment and one which will explain the personal overtone of its presentation. Our neglect of past and present was not due over these many years to a failure to appreciate alumni contributions. Rather it stemmed from the relentless pull of a future for the University and its alumni which was always so visible on the horizon that it never permitted any confusion with mirage but demanded our full attention and our efforts for its realization.

So with what I hope this story becomes—it will indeed remind us of our past and our debt to it. But more importantly it is written as a contribution which should provide a path to the future of Notre Dame, a path which can be straighter and broader through an understanding of the tortuous routes by which the University and our alumni have arrived at the impressive plateau on which we stand now.

There is still another personal observation which I hope you will indulge, because it affects vitally the nature and the purpose of this story. A history of Notre Dame could be voluminous. It would be of interest and value. But it would leave out two non-historical factors which to me are perhaps the real essence of a proper history. The lesser of these is opinion—the facts of history judged by a fallible commentator, but nevertheless interpreting facts as they affect the institution indirectly and perhaps out of time and place. The second and more difficult factor to treat, but possibly the ultimate explanation of Notre Dame, is the conviction which I have always had—and find shared by many in the past—that the University of Notre Dame, from its origin, reflects a supernatural influence, an arrangement of large and small miracles, a common denominator among its people of a destiny beyond the academic. From the three petals of the fleur-de-lis of the France of its founder, and the three leaves of the shamrock that for so many years was associated with its Irish domination, it should not be considered too great an imaginative stretch to come upon this three-pillared foundation, fact, opinion, and miracle.

For example—if I were just a historian, I would launch this

account with 1868, when the first Alumni Association constitution marked the organization of Notre Dame men to celebrate the silver jubilee of their alma mater. This was indeed a milestone.

But in reading the history that led to this vital step, I believe I have uncovered, for myself at least and I hope for you, a sort of Rosetta Stone which has explained to my satisfaction many of the mysteries of the long history of this University of Our Lady.

It explains the bond between the French and the Irish at its inception.

It makes believable the fact that from its opening, students came from far beyond the immediate area. In fact the far have consistently outnumbered the near.

It unravels the relative absence of complications that should have stemmed from bigotry in the neighborhood.

It reveals a thread of philanthropy that became evident in the warp and woof of Notre Dame 100 years before the Notre Dame Foundation was organized.

It makes reasonable the difficult but ultimate dedication and conviction reflected in the gravestones of the Community Cemetery where administrators, faculty, priests, brothers, French, Irish, Germans, Poles, Americans and even a row of the immortal laymen—Lyons, Stace and Corby (Michael) among them—rest among modest and uniform markers in the democracy of death.

But most of all and most significant in this effort, I found in that first era what I believe can be the continuing life and future growth of a Notre Dame which, by a change of governance (1967) and by the introduction of full coeducation (1972), seemed to be moving away from its nature and purpose.

You should enjoy reading this story of Notre Dame alumni. There will be many omissions. If I were to devote only five words to each of our present alumni (hardly enough for name and class and home town, and not enough for occupation) the book would be twice as big as it is projected to be. There are reassuring circumstances.

There seems, for example, to be no good reason for gilding the lilies that already comprise a brilliant bouquet of history. Professor Joseph A. Lyons, himself an alumnus, wrote a memorable Silver Jubilee history with the aid of two well remembered colleagues, Professors Timothy Howard and Arthur Stace, and two outstanding alumni-priests of those pioneer years, Fathers

Neil Gillespie and Michael Brown. The same Professor Howard, then Judge Howard of great civic stature, prepared a thorough and valuable *Golden Jubilee History*. For the University Centennial, the excellent *Notre Dame: One Hundred Years*, by Father Arthur J. Hope C.S.C. '20, brought the progress of the University during its first 100 years vividly and informatively to the attention of its alumni and friends.

In 1951, Professor Richard T. Sullivan '30, teacher of writing and a prominent figure in American fiction, wrote probably the most literate comments on Notre Dame history in *Notre Dame: Reminiscences of An Era*. He updated the book for paperback in 1961. In 1969, Francis Wallace '23, who had written of Notre Dame in many sports channels of fact and fiction, wrote a book *Notre Dame: Its People and Its Legends*. The late Father Thomas T. McAvoy, C.S.C. '25, wrote a scholarly and beautifully expressed biography of Cardinal John F. O'Hara, C.S.C. '11, whose life for so many years affected the lives of Notre Dame alumni. The legend of Knute Rockne '13, and the sagas of his successors, have been recounted in most of the media of our age. D. C. "Chet" Grant '22, authored a most important contribution to Notre Dame's history in *Before Rockne at Notre Dame*. (1968).

And in preparing what must, for any of us, be a compilation of highlights based on our purposes and aspirations, the bound volumes of the *Scholastic*, founded in 1867 and the oldest continuous student news magazine in campus journalism in this country, the bound volumes of the *Dome* yearbook, suspended only for one year in World War I (1919) and for two years during World War II (1943 and 1944) and the bound volumes of the *Alumnus*, established in 1923, are invaluable references. The *Alumnus* is in 1972 suffering an eclipse of its traditional title, but not its traditional function. The new general publication called simply *Notre Dame Magazine* now serves the dual purpose of the *Alumnus* and *Insight*. The latter was a name which had replaced the simply titled "Notre Dame" that had been launched in 1948 by the Alumni Association, (with the editor of the *Alumnus* as its first editor also) to serve the growing numbers of non-alumni which the University's postwar needs dictated as necessary for an adequate program of financial support.

These are the burgeoning accounts in which the academic, the religious, the athletic, the traditional stories of Notre Dame have found eloquent telling. My own purpose suggests the

limitation of this account to the part that Notre Dame alumni
have played in the development of the University.

Highlights of that story will be the first organization, in
1868, the reorganization in 1908, and the establishment of the
Alumni Office and the *Alumnus* magazine in 1923.

But to get to those highlights, it is intensely interesting and
important to trace their roots.

II

La Vie Intime

"La Vie Intime."

Remember this simple phrase, one of the few French expressions which appear in the account of Notre Dame's origins reverting to a vivid French appreciation of a way of life.

I believe that it was then, and has remained, the key to the unique development of Notre Dame. I believe it holds the key to the University's future.

Those first years at Notre Dame were indeed "the intimate life."

In actuality, Notre Dame was established on Nov. 26, 1842. Father Edward Sorin, C.S.C., stood in a clearing of less than 10 acres of land. One log chapel-and-cabin combination was the sole building. Snow covered the water called Ste. Marie des Lacs by the French missionaries who had earlier ministered to the Potawatomis.

He declared then that this was the chosen site of his college which would be dedicated to Notre Dame. Snow symbolized the purity of the Mother of God, long a patron of Father Sorin. The blue sky was her mantle of glory. And the bright sun was the gold that clothed Her. In writing to France, he said:

"Oh, may this new Eden be ever the home of innocence and virtue."

Many have mistaken this piety of Sorin, even as a 26-year old missionary, as his sole and satisfying goal.

On the contrary, he was on this site in Northern Indiana that day because he intended to establish a college. This intention he had proposed for his original site in the new world, St. Peter's near Vincennes, Ind. Bishop Hailandiere had refused permission for this academic extension of the mission. It was Sorin's determination, which sacrificed a year of accomplishment to make a fresh start in new wilderness.

So, while the first college was a log building in a small clearing in actuality, in a broader reality it was already the University of Notre Dame du Lac. This was the superstructure of purpose, of vision, of dedication, of faith.

It is when we contemplate the difference between the real structure of that little clearing and the superstructure that was in the mind of Sorin that we begin to understand the mystery of Notre Dame.

For 23 years Father Sorin was the founder-president of his University.

His dream had become a reality. It was not from the beginning founded on completely spiritual foundations. The first spark had come when Bishop Bruté, first Bishop of Vincennes, had spoken to Sorin's class in the French seminary where he was two years away from ordination.

The second stage had come when he discovered the missionary priests and the Brothers of St. Joseph, gathering at Le Mans under the direction of Father Basil Moreau.

The third stage was his assignment by Father Moreau to Vincennes to form a mission and a school near that city.

The fourth stage came when, in his college controversy with the new bishop of Vincennes he heard of the land in Northern Indiana which had been a mission in an area hallowed by Marquette and Allouez, and which had recently been bought by Father Stephen Theodore Badin, the first priest ordained in the United States. Father Badin had in turn been directed to this dormant mission by Father Gabriel Richard of Detroit, who acted on a plea from the Potawatomi Indians, once served by this northern outpost. There Father Badin had renewed mission service to an area extending from Coldwater and Kalamazoo, Mich., on the east to the Calumet area of Northwest Indiana.

The seeds of religion at Notre Dame were old and deep. Father Sorin brought to the site the related seeds of education.

Another factor which to me explains some of the unique thrust of this little frontier University, among many others which were springing up in the paths of progress, is the background of its founders.

The French and the Irish—the major blend of the founding and pioneer eras—had a rich heritage of religion. Both had suffered persecution, which had toughened their spiritual fibers.

And both the French and Irish were fervent in their appreciation of education. The French were fresh from the disruption of their schools by the Revolution but the heritage of teaching and culture remained vivid. The Irish were long-standing victims of oppression. Their education had been necessarily pursued in the clandestine efforts of the Church and in the hedge schools of the scholars.

To French and Irish alike, therefore, this venture combining a mission of the spiritual and the intellectual was one to which they could wholeheartedly dedicate their lives.

When there was added to this a factor which Father Sorin immediately recognized and harnessed to his goal, a new and powerful dimension was provided. This was the pull of education which America could see as the essential implementation of its national future. It was the factor, along with morality, upon which the nation's founding fathers had predicated its success as a democracy, a broad base of educated citizenship.

Between these pushes of academic heritage and the pull of opportunity encouraged by the young nation, Notre Dame du Lac grew "in wisdom and in strength, in the eyes of God and man."

The charter of the University, granted by the Indiana legislature in 1844, has to be one of the near miracles of its being. (This was in 1844, with one small brick building.)

"Be it enacted by the General Assembly of the State of Indiana that Edward Frederick Sorin, Francis Louis Cointet, Theophilus Jerome Marivault, Francis Gouesse and their associates and successors in office be, and are hereby constituted and declared to be, a body corporate and politic, by the name and style of the 'University of Notre Dame du Lac' and by that name shall have perpetual succession with full power and authority to confer and grant, or cause to be conferred and granted, such degrees and diplomas in the liberal arts and sciences, and in law and medicine as are usually conferred and granted in other universities of the United States, provided, however, that no degrees shall be conferred and diplomas granted except to students who have acquired the same proficiency in the liberal arts and sciences, and in law and medicine as is customary in other universities in the United States."

This was eight years before the railroad came to South Bend.

It was in the same year that the telegraph was invented, and years before the telephone.

It was before the states of Iowa, Wisconsin, Minnesota, California, Texas or Florida were admitted to the Union.

It was before Purdue, Illinois, Michigan State, Northwestern, Cornell, M.I.T. or the U.S. Naval Academy were founded.

It was before Boston College, LaSalle and St. Joseph's of Philadelphia, Loyola of Baltimore, Manhattan College, Santa Clara, the University of San Francisco, St. Benedict's in Kansas, St. John's in Minnesota, St. Vincent's in Latrobe or Seton Hall had appeared on the horizon of Catholic higher education.

These things may seem fragmented and irrelevant but they illuminate the vision and the faith which became the heritage of the Notre Dame man. They contained the indomitable quality of the pioneer and the dedication of competent men, for life, to principles in which they believed. These also became hallmarks of our alumni.

Through the presidencies of Tyler, Polk, Taylor, Pierce, Fillmore, Buchanan and Abraham Lincoln, Father Edward Sorin, President of Notre Dame du Lac from 1842 to 1865, pursued his direction of his University, through vicissitudes that were in many ways a microcosm of the catastrophes of much of his country. It is in the survival despite these adversities that the facts of history must add a dimension of miracle to explain the continuity and growth of Notre Dame.

And it is among the catastrophes that afflicted men and buildings that we find the seeds of future greatness manifesting themselves. It is in the weaknesses that beset the structure that we find the great and lasting strength of the superstructure.

For example, in 1849, a new structure used as the apprentices building burned to ground taking with it "the tailor shop, bakery, kitchen and all its provisions, shoemaker's shop, the sacristan's room with all the altar linens, and the stables." For Notre Dame it was a catastrophe indeed.

But note this, in 1849: "Nothing had been saved. In this crisis two women from South Bend, Mrs. Coquillard and Mrs. Woodworth, came to the rescue. Not only from their own larders did they bring food but they went begging for help among the citizenry. They begged all week. Protestants as well as Catholics came to the assistance of the hard-pressed University. Later—Mrs. Coquillard and Mrs. Woodworth went to Detroit and Cincinnati for the same purpose. . . ."

Here we see the involvement of the community, the enlistment of women leaders as active friends of the University and the reaching out to non-Catholics for support. The practical pursuits of Father Sorin provided a rich reference of works with which he supplemented his faith. He and Father Marivault contributed their patrimonies. And as they visited families in St. Joseph, Niles, Bertrand and Plymouth " . . . they give me what they can. It is little enough, for they are poor, and like us, they are making sacrifices, too . . . . . but if all men fail me, there is one treasury that is always full, and from which, when all else is exhausted, I can draw. That is the treasury of Our Most Holy Lady." Here was the confidence in his cause that became a part of the alumni heritage. I know the truth of his practices, because my grandparents were among the Catholic families in Niles.

Cholera, malaria and dissension with his Congregation in France provided human hurdles sometimes more dire than the fires. From the desperation of the deaths from disease, caused by nearby swamps, came the unexpected acquisition of the land at fault which, drained, has subsequently provided health, expansion of Notre Dame and the campus of Saint Mary's.

Disagreement with Father Moreau stemmed from the long delays entailed in communication with the mother house in France. Sorin was impatient and impetuous. When fire razed buildings, he started immediately to replace them. This was not in the procedures of religious community life, but it brought to the University the tradition of decision and of progress that grew stronger in the face of adversity. These were early seeds of the familiar "When the going gets tough, Notre Dame men get tougher."

Father Sorin, like religious non-conformists before and since, found his achievements and his convictions threatening his career. An effort was made to move him from his controversial rule of Notre Dame to the more remote missions of Bengal. He secured a dispensation from his religious vows through the Bishop of Vincennes, and refused to accept the assignment from Father Moreau. But just as he withdrew his rebellion and submitted to Moreau, Moreau reconsidered the circumstances and reassigned Sorin to Notre Dame. Are there simple human reasons for this? I do not believe it for a minute. Our Lady had to have whispered in Moreau's ear.

But from all of these early evidences of ferment on the frontier we have inherited the lack of fear of ferment and the respect on many later occasions for political resistance to organizational inequities.

Possibly the greatest event to test the persisting purposes and policies of the University was the Civil War. The national character of Notre Dame's enrollment was already in evidence.

What would happen when the Southern States seceded, and war was declared? In spite of unswerving loyalty to the United States, and the presence on campus during the war of the family of General Sherman, the student body actually increased. Alumni Union Generals Robert Healy and William Lynch, the magnificent Holy Cross chaplains, including the dramatic service of Father William Corby at Gettysburg, and the heroic services of the Sisters of St. Mary's in the hospitals and prison camps, instead of alienating the Southern States seems in the long run to have won their respect. Certainly the war put an indelible stamp on patriotism on the University and its alumni.

In 1865 Father Sorin was summoned to the higher councils of the Congregation of Holy Cross. He relinquished the presidency to the young and dynamic Irish priest, Father Patrick Dillon.

From then on, alumni presidents have guided without interruption the continuing progress of Sorin's Notre Dame. It was an act of faith in the values of his own University by its founder.

And this brings us to a consideration of the quality of "La Vie Intime."

The early physical conditions, a single large room, a single stove and the bitter cold, combined to bring together into a most intimate community the priests, the brothers, the lay teachers, the college students, the preparatory students, the elementary students and the students of the manual labor school. The latter was the first Catholic trade school in the United States.

In this "vie intime" there is explanation of the lasting sense of both democracy and family which has transcended all the growth of Notre Dame. The orphans who huddled with the son of a Miami chief and young American students from comfortable homes provided a lasting heritage free from caste. The religious and lay faculty, many with educational and cultural roots in the intellectual capitals of the Old World, found easy common cause with the less privileged but equally principled colleagues, some whose only weakness was in being retarded by persecutions.

Father Sorin has been described by critics as having had no great scholarly aspirations for his University. Even a modest program of sound education of young men for the Christian life would command respect.

But I suggest the greater thesis implicit in "La Vie Intime" that Sorin saw that even the education and aspirations of orphan boys and the very young would be enhanced by association with and inspiration from the intimate company of scholars.

III

The Two Faces of Success

The alumni office over the years has periodically received requests for a "list of successful alumni." Most of these queries were honest, many in fact directed to the glorification of the American Catholic.

But for the 42 years of my tenure I have never supplied such a list without the accompanying reservation that "success," in the judgment of Notre Dame and the Alumni Association, was often a different "success" than that usually heralded in the secular world.

Just as Father Sorin had a dual treasury of resources—one material, which was usually straining at its dregs, the other spiritual, constantly overflowing with the graces of God and his Mother—so the University, in its preparation, sought an alumnus who achieved dual successes. One was success in the world. The other was success in the spirit. If one had to be sacrificed, it was to be that of the world.

Several other factors modified the American concept of success as Notre Dame men achieved it.

Until the early '20s, very few American Catholics of Notre Dame's pioneer era had enjoyed higher education themselves. Neither were they endowed with worldly goods. As a consequence, their sons came to Notre Dame rich in purpose but poor in pocket. The young alumnus inherited only the admiration and encouragement of his family. Few inherited wealth that could provide instant business or professional advantage.

There was another obstacle to the easy path toward success in the accepted sense. Father Sorin, from the opening of the University, admired and sought talent. Much of this talent he

14

found, as it continues to be found, in young men who needed help to attend Notre Dame. And as a result, resources needed for the University were diverted to the encouragement of this segment of the student body. It was academically profitable, but in the alumni pattern it produced an even larger number of young graduates beginning their lives with education as their only asset. And it reduced at Notre Dame the potential philanthropy that had already begun to advance contemporary American campus developments.

The result of this was a very unfortunate fallacy which attended Notre Dame alumni for many years. They were generally considered "unsuccessful." This produced a corollary error. The University must be inferior, to produce unsuccessful alumni. Too many people who should know better either believed these myths or kept silent and allowed them to persist.

It has never been clear to me why the Catholic Church, whose scholars and whose monks preserved for the Western World most of the intellectual heritage of civilization during the Dark Ages and whose missionary scholars had established a University on the North American continent many years before John Harvard's modest library became the first university in the United States is considered essentially unable to produce a major institution of higher learning.

What prompts me to present the above comment on "success" is the promise that as success story after success story unfolds, you will note that one may be founded on the American norm, whereas another may be built upon the yardstick of the spirit.

The "whole man" and his education have come under recent criticism, with the charge that he too often represented a mediocre man. The compartmentalized man, and more lately the computerized man, seem to me not to have eliminated mediocrity but simply to have transferred it in more complex forms to their more mechanized lives. Confusion seems most probably when the duality of life, the life temporal and the life eternal, is not clearly defined and pursued in the preparation man must undergo for both. The ability to encompass this dual process was always one of the major strengths of Catholic education.

The caliber of the Notre Dame alumnus, from his first emergence, was, in my judgment, indicative of a high quality of education. It reflected the inculcation of a competence which contributed from the start not only to the Church, but to the broad American society of which it was a proud part and to which it was willingly dedicated.

The opening of the University to non-Catholics from its founding, with assurance of the integrity of other student religious persuasions, was a hallmark of Notre Dame and Notre Dame alumni, and remains so. I say in simple truth that in my many years I never knew whether some of our alumni were Catholic or not. It was never allowed to affect their alumni status.

The second President of the University is eloquent testimony of alumni competence. Father Sorin, called to administrative duties in the Congregation, must certainly have cast a critical eye on the first successor to his post.

Irish-born Father Patrick Dillon had come to Notre Dame from Chicago. His administration talent asserted itself in the small community and he was made steward of Notre Dame even before his ordination. He showed such ability that he was made president of Saint Mary's College in Chicago, only to be recalled as vice president of Notre Dame under Father Sorin from 1862 to 1865, during years when the Civil War created new problems and placed extra burdens on the young campus. Father Dillon also acted as director of the Commercial Department during those years. He was still only 33 years old when he became the second President in 1865. During the single year, plus three months, that he served in this capacity he and Father Sorin remodeled and enlarged the buildings on the campus at a cost of $100,000 or more, then a major expenditure. He also directed the building of the large academy structure at Saint Mary's.

In 1866, Father Dillon was summoned to the general chapter of the Congregation in France, where for two years he served as secretary and assistant to the Superior General. He returned to Notre Dame in 1868 with Father Sorin, then the Superior General. Father William Corby had been made President of Notre Dame, its third, and Father Dillon asked a dispensation from the Congregation to attend to the care of members of his immediate family. Death took him at the age of 35 but the caliber of the Notre Dame alumnus seems evident in his brief but brilliant career.

Another convincing case for quality takes us no farther than the first alumnus to receive a degree in course, Neil Gillespie, Lancaster, O., A.B., June, 1849. Gillespie remained to become Father Neil Gillespie, C.S.C., director of studies, later vice president. He studied in Rome and served the Congregation in Le Mans and in Paris. He returned to Notre Dame in 1866 and succeeded Father Sorin as editor of the *Ave Maria* magazine. This was accompanied by his appointment to act as editor of the student paper, the *Scholastic*, pursuing his earlier interest in a paper called *Progress* started by the seniors.

Richard Shortis, who received his A.B. at the same time as Father Gillespie, also chose priesthood in the Congregation and later became a vice president of Notre Dame.

Father Augustus Lemonnier, a nephew of Father Sorin, was graduated into the Congregation of Holy Cross. He remained to become not only vice president and President of Notre Dame but the pioneer in encouraging its library. He enlisted the enthusiasm of a lay professor, James F. Edwards, in the collection of books. When Father Lemonnier died at the age of 35 during his presidency, Professor Edwards had already embarked on the 40 years of effort that would create a major library at Notre Dame and make it one of the great depositories of Catholic archives in the United States. These were alumni of stature, in any age.

One of the most convincing tributes to the quality of Notre Dame education was Professor Joseph A. Lyons who had entered the Manual Training School as a boy. He showed such promise that he was made director of the juniors and the minims in 1858. One of 13 children, he gave thought to the priesthood, but decided he did not have a vocation. Notre Dame appointed him a lay professor. So popular was he with students that at his death they erected a major monument to his memory in the Community Cemetery, usually reserved for religious.

Timothy E. Howard, who had studied for a time at the University of Michigan, was one of the great alumni. He remained at Notre Dame as a member of the faculty. Even while studying at Notre Dame, he taught the Minims. He enlisted during the Civil War and was seriously wounded. Upon his return to Notre Dame he became a professor of rhetoric and the English language. He was made a member of the faculty of the first Catholic law school in the United States in 1869 when Notre Dame instituted it. Professor Howard later became an eminent jurist in Indiana and the Chief Justice of its Supreme Court. As evidence of his continuing literary competence we are indebted to him for the *Golden Jubilee History* of Notre Dame. So continues evidence of the high quality of education of Notre Dame men.

We deal with a very small numerical group of alumni in those
early years of the University but this only enhances the significance of their achievements as a tribute to the quality of their
preparation for life.

Father James Dillon, a brother of Father Patrick Dillon, was
another example of great ability. He, also, served as president of
Saint Mary's College in Chicago, and was later one of the
memorable chaplains of the Civil War. Ordained on the same
day as his brother, his death came only a month after that of his
brother, brought about by disease contracted in the rigors of
service with the famed "Irish Brigade."

Justice in recognition of these early alumni would require
inordinate space, and the point to be made seems adequately
demonstrated. Professor Arthur Stace, the popular teacher of
mathematics and surveying who evidenced the first great sense
of humor among early faculty and alumni, kept the campus
publications lively with his humor and his poems. Like Professor Lyons, his unselfish devotion and his close ties to "la vie
intime" of Notre Dame are reflected in his tombstone in the
Community Cemetery adjacent to those of Lyons and Professor
Michael Corby, another layman of great dedication and talent,
especially in voice and the broader field of music.

Perhaps nothing testifies to the qualitative nature of the
Notre Dame environment more than the extra-curricular activities. These reflect not only the academic and broad expressions
of the formal courses, but the dedication of administration,
faculty and students to pursuits which joined the classroom in
the creation of character and competence. At the time of the
silver jubilee, in 1869, there were already these diverse campus
groups, most of them organized much earlier, and already with
flourishing memberships and program achievements:

The Archconfraternity of the Blessed Virgin Mary, organized
by the College students in 1845, strengthened the spiritual fiber
of its members;

The Holy Angels provided spiritual outlet for the preparatory
and Minim departments;

The Sodality of Our Lady of the Sacred Heart and the *Holy
Childhood* groups were further booster activities for religion.

St. Aloysius Philodemic Literary Society began in 1851 the
cultivation of the study of history by its members, and an
accompanying program to encourage their eloquence in writing
and speech.

St. Edward's Literary Association provided the younger students with stimuli for their practice of elocution and their study of literature.

The St. Cecilia Philomathean Society was one of the oldest of the campus organizations and made signal contributions to the arts of debate, dramatics and music.

In 1868 the *United Scientific Association* reflected the rise of the interest and study in the developing areas of science.

The Thespian Society devoted itself almost exclusively to dramatic productions, primarily for celebrations on the campus adapted especially to all-male casts.

The Philharmonic Society provided expanding attention to the musical programs which increasing campus festivals indicated, and to study of the fields of sacred, secular, and vocal music, including theory and practice. Specialization was reflected in the Choral Union, the Cornet Band, the University Orchestra and in the St. Joseph Orchestra (the latter formed within the membership of the Band).

A Chess Club offered its combination of recreation and study. There was a *Social Rowing Club* and the *St. Joseph's Boating Club*.

Baseball's popularity was evident in the existence of four baseball Clubs—the *Juanita*, the *Enterprise*, the *Star of the East* and the *Star of the West*.

In rowing and baseball, the competitive urges of excellence and victory had their roots, and made the campus a fertile field for the arrival some 20 years later of the budding sport of football.

There is one item which dictates a brief comment—the presence in 1854 of a student from California, which had been a state only since 1850. In 1849, Father Sorin, always alert to the material opportunities of America, is reported to have sent a brother of his Congregation to California to join the gold seekers of that tumultuous discovery. The legend reports failure. It seems to me that the brother may have found one of the most valuable nuggets of the era in this early student. From that time on, California, in obvious surmounting of geographical and financial obstacles, sent to Notre Dame a growing number of bright young men, many of whom became leaders in the later development of their state.

There is another explanation of the persistence of "la vie intime." I am dwelling on this quality at length because it continues to assume for me the key to the distinctiveness of the University, a part of that superstructure which has provided

canopy and continuity for the century which followed this first
quarter.

The new element is found in the items on "conduct" contained in the several University catalogues, bulletins or registers,
as they were called in various epochs.

The 1867 catalog says: "Whether in class or in recreation,
when permitted to converse at table, or during their walks,
students should endeavor to improve the purity of their language and cultivate urbanity of manners. A few years in college
would be profitably employed if nothing else were learned than
to converse and behave with the dignity and propriety of
gentlemen . . ." This passage predates a similar statement attributed in my generation to Father John W. Cavanaugh, "that a
student could obtain a good education at Notre Dame even if he
never attended class."

Twenty-five years later, in 1892, the catalogue says: "Although the rules made and enforced with this intention (a
thorough college course) are more stringent than is usual in
American colleges, there is nothing required by them in which
any earnest student can reasonably object. Other than earnest
students are out of place in the University."

Administration and faculty joined the students in all the
departments in the pursuits of both curricular and extra-curricular education. Living and boarding facilities contained an essential unity of the small community, from its founder to the
littlest orphan in the Minims.

This "vie intime" has remained a hallmark of Notre Dame
through the years of its growth in spite of the changing circumstances of those who make it up. The development of departments and colleges on the academic level has remained a part of
the continuing total education goal of the University. The
expansion of the residence halls from the revolutionary introduction of Sorin Hall with its private rooms—a first in United
States Catholic higher education—actually helped to preserve
"la vie intime." With the housing of small groups of students,
from different colleges and departments of the University and
from the many states and countries—even, in more recent years,
from different classes within the University—this feeling of a
universal family continues. Residence of administrators, faculty,
and, on special occasions, visiting alumni in the halls preserves
the tradition of community.

It was in this atmosphere that the fraternity of the recreation
hall, the front porch, the chapel and the playground assumed a

strength and a spirit that made the introduction of the conventional or "Greek letter" fraternities as unneeded as it was unwanted.

This was the growing phenomenon of the University of Notre Dame as it moved toward its silver jubilee. This was the period in history when the tide of empire in the United States was sweeping westward as the tragedy of the American Indian opened new opportunities.

In the list of student origins in the 1851 *Catalog*, Michigan leads in number. Indiana, Illinois, Louisiana, Ohio, New York and Mexico are there. Three years later in 1854, 10 years after its charter and three years after the railroad reached South Bend, Wisconsin, Kentucky, Missouri, California, Rhode Island, and Ireland were added. "La vie intime" was not without its rich sources of internal interests and development.

In the catalog of 1917 we read: "The faculty maintains that an education which gives little attention to the development of the moral part of a youth's character is pernicious and that it is impossible to bring about this development where students are granted absolute relaxation from all faculty government while outside the classroom."

In 1942 the *Bulletin* of the 100th year of the University of Notre Dame, the statement above is repeated verbatim as continuing University policy.

In 1972 the *Register* states in part: "A Catholic University is a society composed of faculty and students whose primary purpose is the pursuit of Christian wisdom. This society can exist only in an atmosphere of responsibility and good order. The University seeks, therefore, to provide those conditions and opportunities best suited for educating the student. . . . The University reserves the right to place a student on disciplinary probation, suspension or dismissal. The University also reserves the right to deny the privilege of enrollment to any student whose conduct or attitude is believed to be detrimental to the welfare of the institution."

Thus, for 130 years, the University of Notre Dame has pursued the dual goal of temporal and spiritual education within a dual discipline which retained some of the rigors of its French origins, yet added the American freedoms as circumstances dictated. But to administer this changing structure, it drew on "la vie intime," the transcending integration of religion and morality specified in the Northwest Ordinance and by Cardinal Newman. It was the best of *in loco parentis*, using love and concern, adult guidance and good example rather than penalty or corporal punishment. The shadow of the super-structure, the great spirit of the founder and the near miracle of this long rule of law hovers over the picture of the ever-changing campus and its generations of young men.

Like the reign of Queen Victoria, which this first quarter century paralleled, the University grew in stature and significance, and in its relations with the world. Oddly enough, like its Victorian contemporary, its critics seem to dwell more on its discipline and its morality standards than on its achievements.

IV

Bridge, Beacon, and Crossroad

One more chapter is indicated before we come to the beginning of the actual chronology of the Alumni Association. It is important because it provides a dimension of Notre Dame which explains a great part of its early success before there was any alumni organization.

It indicates a part of education at Notre Dame which is not found in the curricula but which is peculiarly adapted to the cosmopolitan nature of its campus population and has always been reflected in Notre Dame alumni.

And, most importantly in my personal judgment, it has been specifically advanced in the dynamic administration of Father Theodore Hesburgh as an essential of the modern university, and is the keystone of his greatest contribution to American higher education, his concept of "mediation" as a functional obligation for our colleges and universities. This makes it a milestone of the present and future University.

In brief, the principle defines the campus not only in its traditional role as a depository of knowledge and a teacher of the young. It also strengthens its growing role as a proper agency in the search for new knowledge. But its distinctive major contribution lies in its definition of the campus as a present part of present problems, singularly endowed with the intellectual resources of the past and the trained manpower to direct them toward present and future solutions. And further, it considers this application of present strengths to present problems of the whole social strata as an added and constructive dimension to the education of the young who will soon be face to face with the responsibilities attending these problems.

This concept makes the campus not a vacuum between the

past and the future but a bridge on which the present traffic should be constant.

It makes the campus a beacon where the traditional lamp of learning is not in an ivory tower but is raised like a lighthouse so that the theologian, the politician, the teacher, the professional people, the scientists and the sociologists, can know that where the light is there is enlightenment for them also.

And there follows, of course, the concept of the campus as a crossroads, where all those who need the bridge and who see the beacon join in the crossing of paths that will bring quick solutions and accelerated progress to all mankind.

Interpreting Notre Dame is an amazingly complex task. I was about to record simply one of the earliest instances of beacon and crossroad.

This was the visit of Miss Eliza Gillespie, a sister of Notre Dame's first alumnus in course, Neil, and later Father, Gillespie. She was on her way to Chicago to become a Sister of Mercy. A brilliant young woman, she had been in Washington in the household of a relative, Thomas Ewing, then Secretary of State under President Harrison. Father Sorin, seizing upon the opportunity, used what must have been unusual persuasive powers to induce Miss Gillespie to go to France and become a member of the young Order of Sisters of the Holy Cross, which was also under the direction of Father Basil Moreau. After receiving her veil from Father Moreau, Miss Gillespie returned to the Notre Dame community and later became Mother Angela, director of Saint Mary's and Superior of the Sisters. It was Mother Angela who led the heroic "nuns of the battlefields" to permanence in American history during the Civil War.

This memorable incident in early Notre Dame history could flourish in its own direct channel. But it also adds an immediate dimension to an already great man. Father Sorin was, from the beginning, an advocate of the education of women, and appreciated the constructive values of the proximity of Notre Dame and Saint Mary's which could cultivate social values in both.

The insistence on Saint Mary's as an academic institution, which placed it first in Bertrand because of the opposition of the bishop of Vincennes, seems to be to nullify an idea too often implied, that Father Sorin was interested in the sisters and brothers only as they formed a work force for Notre Dame. Generations of alumni and their Saint Mary's wives provide living rebuttal. Saint Mary's was moved in 1855 from Bertrand to its present location as soon as two major obstacles were eliminated—one the purchase of the land from a somewhat reluctant owner in South Bend, and the other the division of the Vincennes diocese and accompanying removal of Northern Indiana from the jurisdiction of its bishop.

So beacon and crossroad, which brought Miss Gillespie to her unexpected direction of vocation, added at the same time a magnificent bridge between the isolation of education for men and the broader future.

The beacon brought another early and significant visitor. Father Stephen Badin, the proto-priest who had first bought this land, saw the young University in 1845, and made one of the many financial "deals" which in Father Sorin's regime (and many times since) have assisted the Holy Ghost in survival determinations. It was to provide him residence and income on the campus, in exchange for property in Louisville. Father Badin lived longer than expected. The property was worth less than claimed. The natural result was some chagrin on Father Sorin's part. But the supernatural result was probably a great profit, derived from ensuing caution in annuity commitments. Certainly the presence of Father Badin in his old mission area improved Catholic contacts in the adjoining states. And certainly it brought the attention of the American hierarchy and clergy to the young University.

In 1857, the enrollment (of all students in all departments) was 140. In that same year the Vatican, which had had many representations from the young Indiana branch of the Congregation of Holy Cross, approved the rules and constitutions of the Congregation. And the first Superior General and founder, Father Basil Anthony Moreau, C.S.C., veteran of numerous and sometimes turbulent misunderstandings with the dynamic Father Sorin, first visited personally the American university which was bringing attention to his missions in the New World. The new ecclesiastical structure of the C.S.C. brought many further disagreements in years to follow between Notre Dame and the Superior General in France. But it was only a decade later that the progress of Father Sorin placed him at the head of the world organization of Holy Cross, the first American to achieve world leadership of a Catholic religious congregation. Again, the beacon and the crossroad bring with them a bridge— between the Catholic higher education of the New World and the centuries-old traditions of this faltering system as it struggled with the Church's adversities in the Old World.

In 1851, Notre Dame was granted a United States postoffice.

First refused, the second application was made directly to
Henry Clay, who had been a friend of Father Gabriel Richard,
the Detroit priest-salesman, and through the neighboring Congressman Fitzgerald of Niles. Father Sorin became the first
postmaster and retained that income-producing post until his
death. The beacon and crossroads of the youthful University
had built a new bridge, between the campus and the federal
government in Washington, a bridge to be strengthened soon by
the contributions of Notre Dame and Saint Mary's to the
spiritual and nursing needs of the Union army.

There is a great reluctance as author to bring out now the
part of beacon, bridge and crossroad in the financial life of
Notre Dame. That part of its life is so inextricably interwoven
with alumni, such a constant factor, and such an area which
breathes the intercession of Heaven in the same breath as that
of the continuously laboring men who worked so unceasingly at
it, that it defies confinement by category or time.

But just for rich early roots, consider these.

The gift of the land by Bishop Hailandiere had been itself a
gift to him from Father Badin, whose mission it had been.

Then, a letter of credit was extended from Samuel Byerley, a
South Bend merchant, on the arrival of Father Sorin. Byerley, a
wealthy non-Catholic shipping merchant, had greeted Father
Sorin and his brothers on their arrival in New York from
France. With the development of the steamship, Byerley shortly
thereafter sold much of his sailing vessel property and moved
with his Catholic wife to the promising Indiana frontier. If that
is not a crossroad, building both bridge and beacon, and border-
ing again on the mysterious movements of God, there will be
more evidence ahead.

Then, a magnificent gift was received from Mr. and Mrs.
William T. Phelan, (Mr. Phelan was the stepfather of Father Neil
Gillespie and his sister, Mother M. Angela) of what was, in
effect, the Phelan estate subject to a modest existing mortgage
and a small annuity agreement.

The gift itself was extraordinary in its time. But the linking
of the factors of alumnus, priest, nun and benefactor formed a
pattern for many of the benefactions to come. It was also "la
vie intime" bearing one of its rich fruits.

It is in this already rich environment of Notre Dame that we
approach the silver jubilee and the organization of the first
Alumni Association.

This delay in mobilizing alumni strength on a formal basis is
easy to understand if we realize that the numbers remained

small. Forty graduates in course in the college division were listed in the jubilee alumni directory, extending from 1845 to 1869. Twelve honorary and elected alumni, most of them former students who had distinguished themselves after leaving Notre Dame, were added to this group.

Probably the most obvious factor which held back formal organization was that the alumni of Notre Dame, in a marked degree, were never removed from "la vie intime." They remained a part of the University as much as the present students, faculty and administration. A number of laymen remained to teach, yet in addition, even from that small number, the fabric of American life was being enriched by lawyers, doctors, journalists, educators and secular clergy, all attesting to the quality of their preparation by the budding success of their vocations.

It seems unnecessary but it brings truer appreciation if we remember that we are not comparing the Notre Dame of its first quarter century with the world in which we now live.

We see it taking root and expanding in an era that saw rubber first vulcanized (1844), the sulphite process for making paper from pulp (1844), the first cylinder printing press (1845), the first sewing machine (1846), the first practicable typewriter (1868) and the Bessemer process for steel (1855).

It was the world in which Roger Taney (1836-64) and Salmon Chase (1864-1873) were Chief Justices of the Supreme Court. The great potato famine in Ireland occurred in 1847 with the historic migration of the Irish to the U.S.

And the Civil War (1861-65) brings to mind a significant statement made by Father Hugh O'Donnell as World War II began on the eve of Notre Dame's Centennial Year. "The peaks of Notre Dame history are shrouded in the mists of war." This was true of the silver jubilee as it was to be true of the diamond jubilee and the centenary.

The disasters of the first quarter century were not unique, but a reflection of the epidemics and fires which plagued other areas of the country. Inflammable building materials and the absence of fire fighting equipment contributed to the fires. New York City and Pittsburgh had diastrous fires in 1845, Philadelphia in 1850, while St. Louis and San Francisco suffered from the same element in 1851. These cities were possible sources of more affluent students under ordinary circumstances.

Notre Dame took heart from the manner in which America rallied after such diasters and itself became an example for others.

The community of administration, faculty, students and

alumni was dedicated to the University, itself dedicated to Our Lady. Laymen and religious worked side by side and tirelessly, as I have noted.

I use alumni in an integral sense because the Notre Dame President, in 1866 and through the jubilee, was an alumnus, the illustrious Father William Corby, who had been recently released from the Union Army after his distinguished services as chaplain to the "Fighting Irish" Brigade, notably at Gettysburg. Father Neil Gillespie, the first college graduate in course, was professor of English literature. Professor Timothy Howard taught literature and astronomy. Professor Joseph Lyons taught Latin and English. Professor Arthur Stace taught mathematics. Professor Michael Corby taught vocal music. Brother Philip taught bookkeeping and English. Brother Francis de Sales taught geography and history. Brother Claud taught Hebrew. Brother Simeon taught Gaelic.

In addition to the Hebrew and Gaelic classes just mentioned, there were classes in Latin and Greek, and in French and German. Father Carrier, the librarian, had built up libraries for the departments of some 10,000 volumes, many from Europe where he traveled repeatedly.

Student organizations supplemented every avenue of intellectual and cultural interest, with faculty and administrative talents joined to those of students to produce the highest quality of programs.

The superstructure of religion and education proved already ample. Within it, "la vie intime" created the fraternity of Notre Dame men which was to remain a great common denominator of future alumni. As a pioneer Catholic university, on a frontier still marked by wilderness and hazards, Notre Dame was at its silver jubilee already a beacon, a bridge and a crossroad.

Its financial structure, fragile from the beginning, was held together by hard work, dedicated service, the cultivation of friends and by a timing of crisis and benefaction which makes the "importance of timing" far more than a memory of the Rockne shift or the modern quarterback.

The difficult thing to comprehend is how the small initial clearing, the limited missionary acquisitions to its religious staff, the necessary low level of its remuneration for lay teachers, the diversity of its educational divisions which covered elementary, secondary and college teaching, and the limited number of students who could be interested even in this wide range of schooling, can be reconciled with the unwavering concept of quality.

Yet here was a university, motivated by old-world persecution and operated in poverty, which never sacrificed its principle of quality and which from the beginning conveyed this commitment to excellence to those whose help was essential.

The early alumni and parents and frontier Catholics were obviously unequal to the challenge. But it is a never-ending surprise to find that Father Sorin, who made some fifty trips across the Atlantic to enlist support in Europe, was a friend and advisor to Popes Pius IX and Leo XIII. Father Joseph Carrier, founder of the first scientific department at Notre Dame, also procured much advanced equipment by his own trips to Europe. Napoleon III was one of the benefactors he interested. Both Father Sorin and Father Carrier were effective in securing funds for Notre Dame repeatedly from the Society for the Propagation of the Faith in their Vatican visits. Father Carrier's influence lived long after him, not only in the interest in science and his development of its facilities, but in the students he inspired, including the distinguished John A. Zahm, later a member of the Congregation and a world figure of international accomplishments.

The University of Notre Dame du Lac, which would have celebrated its calendar silver jubilee in 1867, was fresh from the Civil War years and involved in the exigencies which took the young President, Father Dillon, from his office on the campus to the Congregation's mother house in France. It was decided to set the jubilee date in 1869, the 25th anniversary of the official charter. The new President, Father William Corby, launched the preparations.

Among these was the first organization of an Alumni Association.

V

Organized Alumni–
A New Dimension

The alumni association as we know it, is an American concept. When Notre Dame alumni organized, there were few such groups in a country which was yet to see the foundation of many now familiar colleges and universities.

On Thursday, June 23, 1868, alumni attending the commencement gathered in the President's parlor for the purpose of forming an organization to be known as the "Associated Alumni of Notre Dame University." Father William Corby, C.S.C. was made secretary pro tem. Elections were the first order of business. The first officers of the Alumni Association were: Father Gillespie '49 president; Francis Bigelow '62 a young Dayton attorney, vice president; James B. Runnion '60 associate editor of the *Chicago Times*, second vice president; Prof. Joseph A. Lyons '62, treasurer and Prof. Michael Corby '65 secretary. In line with the custom of the era, and looking ahead to the silver jubilee meeting of the new association, Father E. B. Kilroy '52, a priest in the Sarnia, Ont., diocese, was chosen as orator, with James O'Brien '59, a Lansing, Iowa, attorney, as alternate.

This seems an appropriate time to comment on the participation of young men in early alumni activity. In this first instance, it was partly because there were no older alumni since the "oldest graduate," Father Gillespie, was graduated only 20 years before. But it also stemmed from the youth of the administration and faculty in general. Perhaps the factor of early deaths, with a much lower life expectancy than we now have, urged the prompt use of talents.

The last selection for the 1869 session was Professor Timothy

Howard '62, as official poet, with his alternate the able and entertaining Professor Arthur Stace '64.

The inclusion of the campus-based alumni in the direction of the association was a natural and very practicable one in this early stage. And the annual meetings of the Alumni Association as a part of the commencement programs were equally logical and practicable. It was an extension of "la vie intime." Both customs contributed to the activity of the association in years that it might not have stood alone. But it is also evident that this dependence on the direction and resources of the University accounted in large part for the very late establishment of the Alumni Association office and magazine, more than half a century later, and even then in a modified independence. The modifications have been no obstacle to the progress of either the University or the association because the long years of integral activity and the continued direction of the University itself by largely alumni-oriented administrators have more than offset any imbalance in the delicate area of autonomy. The relationships will recur in the pages ahead as factors in programs but are of enough importance to be considered and understood from the start.

The 1868 organizing committee submitted a constitution which it had discussed and amended prior to its presentation. It was simple in the light of its time and its significance.

The name of the association shall be the Associated Alumni of the University of Notre Dame.

The object of the association is defined to be: To preserve and strengthen the common tie that binds us to each other and alma mater, by means of yearly reunions and by literary correspondence.

The regular yearly meeting to take place on that Tuesday in the month of June next preceding the annual commencement of the University, when the order of business will be as follows:

Calling the roll.

Elections. First, of members, according to the considerations of eligibility specified below. (Members thus elected will be invited to attend the same meeting.) Second, of the officers of the society, to consist of a president, two vice presidents, treasurer, secretary, orator and poet, with their alternates for the coming year. The first five of these officers to be chosen from among the regular graduates; the last four, namely the orator and poet, with alternates from among the members in general.

The meeting to conclude with a sumptuous banquet, with commemorations of absent and departed friends.

The orator and poet to exercise their talents, in the departments assigned them respectively, at the annual commencement exercises one year from the time of their election, and their effusions to be published, with the general statistics of the association, in an annual report.

Membership. 1st. All regular graduates in the classical and scientific courses of Notre Dame University, and all who have received honorary degrees, are members *ipso facto.*

2nd. All those who have ever held offices of president, vice president, or prefect of studies in the University are members *ipso facto.*

3rd. All who have been actively connected with the University as professors or students are eligible as members. The election to be by a three-fourths ballot of those voting.

The members present at the regular meeting shall be the voters for officers and members.

The annual fee shall consist of 10 dollars.

The members of the association resident at the University of Notre Dame shall constitute a standing committee to receive communications, transact the general business of the association, and hand in its report at the yearly meeting.

The members are requested to attend a Mass on the day of meeting, celebrated in behalf of all the members, living and dead, of the association.

The President of the University shall be the chairman of the standing committee.

Resolved, that the list of graduates be prepared and published in the catalogue, together with the report of the meeting. Rev. Neil Gillespie, Professor Howard, and Rev. T. L. Vagnier were appointed a committee to select an appropriate badge and motto.

Rev. J. C. Carrier was then elected a member of the association; and on motion, the meeting adjourned. (Sig.) *M. T. Corby, Sec'y. of the Associated Alumni.*

This was the document which brought forth our Alumni Association.

Hidden within its simple structure are many of the principles which have governed our progress, and guided our programs.

For example, the association priority as a binding force was first "to each other," second to alma mater. This dual goal has provided the philosophy of much of the mutual respect and essential autonomy of the association. And "by literary correspondence" denotes a goal far beyond beer and reminiscences.

The conjunction with commencement provided returning alumni with the excellent intellectual, cultural, social and athletic events which, with the visiting parents and friends, they had long accepted as proper balance.

The provisions for election of members opened the association to many outstanding members from administration, faculty, parents, benefactors and others, who in effect were part of "la vie intime" but otherwise outside the technicalities of *ex officio* membership. This has been a persisting provision, of great value to both Notre Dame and the Alumni Association.

The "sumptuous banquet" was in the tradition of campus feast days but it also indicated a commitment to quality in the relations of the University and its former students which gave a tangible dignity and depth to traditional hospitality.

The orator and poet were the forerunners of the concept of continuing education. They were to remind the campus of the continuing quality and intellectual development of alumni.

The annual fee of 10 dollars was, in the light of the times and of the youth, economic limitations and clerical identity of many alumni a commitment to a generous relationship in the area of financial support, although it took many years for this seed to bear its envisioned and hoped-for fruits.

On May 25, 1869, in the *Scholastic Year* — the publication had not yet dropped the "Year" from its title, and Father Gillespie was directing its editorial destiny — Professor M. T. Corby, for the standing committee provided in the constitution, announced the first official alumni banquet, to be held on Tuesday, June 22, immediately preceding the silver jubilee commencement. The alumni day would open with Mass at six o'clock in the morning. An alumni reception would be held at 9:30 a.m. in the parlor, and at 10 o'clock the business meeting would be called. The banquet would be at 1 o'clock. Dramatic performances in the evening would close this historic first day. The advance notice was to inform and invite all alumni.

That the preparations succeeded is attested in a long account of the jubilee ceremonies contained in the *Chicago Tribune* of June 24, 1869.

> The second regular meeting of the Alumni Association (the first under the new constitution) was held in the spacious parlors of the College, Rev. Father Gillespie, the president, in the chair. . . . the association proceeded to the election of officers for the ensuing year, with the following result: president, Rev. N. H. Gillespie; first vice-president, Prof. T. E. Howard; second vice president, Dr. John Cassidy; treasurer, Professor Joseph A. Lyons; secretary, Professor Michael Corby; orator, Professor Paul Broder, alternate J. B. Runnion; poet, Professor Arthur Stace, alternate Rev. M. B.

Brown. The association then elected the following as members: Professor Max Girac, C. A. B. von Weller, and Rev. T. O'Sullivan. The meeting then adjourned.

The alumni banquet was considerably more than the "sumptuous banquet" of the constitution. Bishop Luers of Fort Wayne and Father Sorin were honored guests. Rev. Dom Paul Jaussion of France, Very Rev. Kundig, vicar general of the Milwaukee diocese, Father Boyle of Washington, and Father Hallinan of Lafayette, gave the guest table a national and international identity.

Father Gillespie presided. Letters were read from absent alumni. Toasts followed, and it is worth recording these initial toasts, familiar to the banquet-goers of that era, but in this instance containing the significant scope of interests of the new association.

The first toast was to "Our country — unrivalled in energy, blessed in its institutions. May it hold its place as the greatest republic the world ever saw, until all nations be blotted from the earth." Bishop Luers responded to this toast.

Second was "The hierarchy and clergy of the United States — pastors of the flock, promoters of education, guardians of virtue, protectors of true liberty. May they continue zealous for the real interests of mankind and be rewarded eternally for the good they have done, do, and will do." Professor Paul Broder responded to this toast, saying "everything truly great and good is in some way connected with the Christian religion."

The third toast was "The press — mighty in its influence for good or evil; the grand conductor of useful knowledge or startling ideas of man. May its energy be ever found on the side of justice, honor, and virtue." The response to this toast was from Elias Colbert of the Chicago Tribune.

Fourth toast was "The bar — the safeguard of our rights. May it ever be found true to its calling." Peter Dechant, a Dayton attorney of the Class of 1867, gave the response.

Fifth toast was "The medical profession — grand is their vocation; to give health to the sick, hope to the despairing. May they be prompt to attend every call, successful in every operation, honored among men, smiled upon by a beneficent Providence." Dr. John Cassidy, a South Bend physician of the Class of 1866 and an alumnus of Rush Medical School, responded.

Sixth toast was, "The professoriate — the fountainhead of all professions; their calling is divine." Father Hallinan of Lafayette responded.

Seventh toast was "The University of Notre Dame — may its past typify its future." James McBride, Class of 1868, a Toledo attorney, responded.

The eighth toast was "The alumni. May their deeds continually intertwine the brow of their alma mater with a bright halo." Professor Arthur Stace responded "in a humorous speech, which brought down roars of laughter."

The last toast was "The silver jubilee. May the pleasant recollections thereof be fresh in our memories when we meet to celebrate the golden jubilee."

E. S. Pillars, a bachelor of science graduate of 1868, who was entering upon a legal career, responded.

Father Sorin was also called upon to speak to the jubilee toast. He gave credit for the progress of Notre Dame to God, and expressed the hope that future alumni gatherings would find more numerous attendance. Certainly in the toasts, light as we are tempted to consider them in retrospect, there were the seeds of the many directions the young University had already taken, and an intimation of many more to branch from these.

Following the banquet, alumni dispersed, many of them back for the first time since graduation, to see the new buildings, including the growing library of Father Carrier's efforts. In the evening, the entertainment in Washington Hall provided what would seem to be the equivalent today of a major program of continuing education. The brass band and the orchestra furnished music, including a Haydn Symphony. There were vocal solos and "piano for eight hands." But the gem of the first half of the evening was a cantata prepared and composed for the silver jubilee by Professor Girac and Father M. B. Brown '62, involving 40 members of the University musical societies.

The second half of the evening was devoted to a four-act play, directed by Professor Michael Corby '65, called "Richelieu or The Conspiracy." This was enacted by members of the Thespian Society. It is significant of the diverse cultural content of the occasion and its volume that I neglected to mention that the evening in Washington Hall also gave to its audience addresses in Latin and in Greek.

In this first recorded official involvement of the Alumni Association in the programs of the University of Notre Dame we find the intangibles of the spiritual, the academic, the cultural, the sentimental and the fraternal — far ahead of the new dimension of organization. It is inevitable that we speculate somewhat regretfully on the long delay in tangible support that followed these impressive beginnings.

This observation having been made reminds me of a major fallacy too often found in looking at history — what is loosely defined as "comparing oranges with apples." They are different fruits entirely.

And so it was, for many years, perhaps not the handicap — this absence of alumni financial support — that it would be in this era when it is a major and essential source.

There were offsetting resources then. Most of the administrative work, most of the teaching, most of the supplementary efforts — farm, lumber, brick, laundry, kitchen, carpentry and masonry — were performed by priests, brothers and sisters, whose unremunerated services were given fully and intensively to the progress of the University. This was the "living endowment," the intangible wealth, that accounts for so much of Catholic education in our history—and for so much of its crisis as its ratio to lay staff has been reduced in Catholic schools.

In addition, at Notre Dame, the laymen who "remained to pray," and to teach, were dedicated to a degree of great personal sacrifice.

Also, in return for the interest, distinction and friendship which Father Sorin and his group brought to the entire area, with an ecumenism far ahead of its time and a broad cultural attraction amazing in the nature of the young University, neighbors of all persuasions — non-Catholics and Jews as well as Catholics — soon lost the suspicions aroused by false rumors in the beginning and became friends and frequent benefactors in the growing but still small needs of Notre Dame.

After all, the demands of higher education in those years were neither so specialized, so diversified nor so expensive. In 1870, for example, the total expense reported for the public colleges and universities in the United States was only $5,000.000. This figure is just a little less than 10 per cent of Notre Dame's budget reported for 1972.

It was less than the gifts from Notre Dame alumni alone in the final three years of the recent Summa program. An admonition repeated by Father John J. Cavanaugh, C.S.C. '23, applies. "A man's wealth is not so much what he has, as what he needs." Notre Dame's needs were very modest in that first quarter century.

VI

Instant Alumni

Alumni, individually, were a 20-year phenomenon from the first degree in course in 1849 until 1868 when the Alumni Association of the University of Notre Dame du Lac was launched.

As a result, there was an immediate source of competent and accessible leadership personally aware of the growth of Notre Dame and the pressures which accompanied it.

This obvious leadership simply took the familiar circumstances of the campus from its physical boundaries and, by the commencement program, the contacts through the *Scholastic* student press, and by the specified "literary correspondence" of the constitution, established the new campus boundaries wherever alumni might be. This was "la vie intime," enriched with new geographical dimension without losing any of its own distinctive unity or on-campus administration-faculty-student identity.

This worldwide campus concept, this universality of "la vie intime" has been in my opinion, the key to the distinctive nature of Notre Dame alumni and their association in the century which has followed.

This narrative of the progress of Notre Dame alumni through the years will reflect this continuity of unity, rather than the customary segments of time or administrations. These have been well covered and need little repetition except as they may lend force to the alumni thesis.

And I note here my unwillingness to make comparisons between the Presidents of the University with whose administrations I was officially connected:

Father James Burns, when I was a student; Father Matthew

Walsh, who hired me in 1925 and approved my Alumni Associa-
tion selection in January, 1926; Father Charles O'Donnell, who
preserved the association in the midst of the great depression;
Father John H. O'Hara, who knew most alumni personally;
Father J. Hugh O'Donnell, a strong advocate and friend of the
Alumni Association programs; Father John J. Cavanaugh, who
saw in the success of the Alumni Fund the needs of the Notre
Dame Foundation and aided in its birth; and Father Theodore
M. Hesburgh, whose presidency is (as this is written) approach-
ing the 23-year previous record direction of Notre Dame under
Father Sorin, who has kept a continuous challenge before the
entire Notre Dame family and who has given full modern
dimension to the "beacon, bridge and crossroad" concept of the
University.

All of these men, united by the common dedication of the
Priests of Holy Cross, made major contributions to the great
progress of Notre Dame. Talents differed, times differed, resources differed. The fact that the challenge was constant, and
the responses adequate, each in its time, is the primary perti-
nent and valid satisfaction of the alumni story.

It is probably appropriate enough to add here the corrollary
of Notre Dame coaches, the other group whose tenures have
been exhaustively explored, but who remain a persistent target
for comparisons. I hold the same personal thesis — each met the
challenges of his era to the best of his abilities. The total record
of football in the United States, which finds Notre Dame
consistently at its peak; the poll which showed that a Notre
Dame game was popularly considered the most exciting game of
the century (the Ohio State game of 1935); the presence of
Notre Dame alumni in the top ranks of collegiate coaching from
the Rockne era on; the records in the All-American selections
and the Heisman trophies add distinction — together they point
up the fact which alumni have known from the first games in
the apple orchard, that Notre Dame football is the sport which
captured the imagination of the campus from its intercollegiate
birth at Notre Dame in 1887, and subsequently, through many
factors, captured the American public's interest and enthusiasm.

There are many myths attached to football at Notre Dame. It
is more than a sport. It is a symbol of many deeper values the
campus has long taught. It was not a profitable enterprise for
the first 35 years of its existence. But when it became profitable, it continued to contribute in a tangible way what it had
long contributed in intangibles to the general good of the

campus, it did not stifle other sports. Rather, through its popularity, publicity and eventual profits, it accelerated the whole gamut of modern intercollegiate sports, and increased their campus resources. The collection of materials on world sports and games, now housed in the Memorial Library, is a logical outgrowth on a campus that started out with the *la crosse* tradition of the neighboring Indians, grew into one of the major centers of baseball in the first two decades of this century, and met the public football focus, which followed World War I, with the coincident genius of Knute Kenneth Rockne '13, the most outstanding coach in the history of the game.

Frank Hering '98, who came to Notre Dame as a playing football coach from his association with Amos Alonzo Stagg at the University of Chicago, probably brought to the sport at Notre Dame the conviction that there is no essential conflict between football and intellectual pursuits. Frank Hering was exceptional in both.

Knute Rockne established the later and more constructive thesis, that there must be a combination of the physical and the intellectual to achieve consistent success. This was a principle which extended far beyond the sport, as did the world stature of the man who expounded and exemplified it.

Here we are, seemingly far out of time in our approach to alumni history. But between the root and the branch, the seeds and the fruits, there is a life stream that cannot be cut, and a flow which is so basic and continuous that one forever involves the other.

During this period the University, taking heart from the status it had achieved by the time of its 25th anniversary, and from the wider dimension it now possessed in the body of organized alumni, had launched the Notre Dame Law School. Law classes opened on Feb. 1, 1869. A lay professor, M. T. Colovin, brother of the president of the University of a later date, Father Patrick Colovin, was its first director. Professor Peter Foote, a Chicago attorney; Francis Bigelow, an alumnus attorney from Dayton who later became a priest, and Hon, Lucius Tong, who had aided in the establishment of the commercial department, assisted in the faculty of the new school.

The real growth began in 1883 when Professor William B. Hoynes, an attorney from Chicago, a veteran of the Civil War, and a recognized orator, was made dean.

Commenting many years later, Col. Hoynes made this memorable analysis:

It was my intention on coming to Notre Dame to return and resume the practice of law in Chicago after four or five years, or after I had succeeded in putting the law department in running order. In fact, I resigned yearly for a time in order that (Father Thomas E.) President Walsh might not be embarrassed in the event of his wishing to make a change. Yet here I am (1919), still at Notre Dame, placidly participating in this complimentary celebration, thirty-six years after my coming to Notre Dame as a professor. I have remained here contentedly and happily. I have found here the most kindly, unselfish, devoted, humane, religious and altruistic of living men — upright in thought, beneficent in act, philanthropic in purpose and personally unblemished by contact with the world. It is an inestimable pleasure and blessing to live among and be associated with them. Here I have met men as undefiled and clean of soul as ever walked in God's favor or breathed in the genial sunshine the pure air of serene peace and happiness. My years here have passed more swiftly and conformably to cherished ideals of progressive usefulness than could reasonably be expected anywhere else in the world.

This is an eloquent expression of a part of the secret and the strength of the persisting "vie intime."

In the midst of this thriving academic community, the Alumni Association assembled in June of 1870. After a solemn high Mass, breakfast and reception, the alumni held their official meeting. Father Gillespie was reelected president; Professor Arthur Stace, first vice president; Orville T. Chamberlain, second vice president; Professor Joseph Lyons, treasurer; Professor Corby, secretary; O. T. Chamberlain, orator, with T. A. Corcoran as alternate; Father M. B. Brown, poet, with Francis Bigelow as alternate.

Professor Stace's humor found him predictably in the toastmaster's chair. Traditional toasts, at this second banquet, were raised to the Pope, hierarchy, laborers in the field of education, our country, our alma mater and the press.

But brace yourselves for a new and surprising toast, "The ladies." It seems unlikely that coeducation was yet envisioned. But the University from its start had extended its hospitality to the mothers, wives and sisters of students, and now of alumni.

An interesting and notable item accompanies the account of the 1870 commencement exercises. "Excepting the State University of Michigan, the University of Notre Dame has a larger number of scholars in attendance than any other university or college in the Northwest, a fact which speaks well for its superior merit, and evinces the confidence of those patronizing it."

There was another modern and innovative example in this year of 1870. The President and faculty of the University published an official protest against the invasion of Rome and the seizure of the Papal States. They said, in defense of Pius IX, one of the University's staunch friends and benefactors,

> ... we protest against the cowardly treason which has deprived Our Holy Father Pius IX of his temporal power. We hold it to be the duty of every Catholic to protest against the invasion of the Holy City by Victor Emanuel, instigated and inspired by the devil in the commission of this most iniquitous and foul crime, and in the completion of which he has been the instrument and tool of secret societies whose lives and aspirations have ever been devoted to the dishonor of our holy religion, and to the destruction of social order, genuine liberty and true government ... We protest against this invasion, because it is an insult to all Catholics, and because it is the momentary triumph of anarchy over order; wrong over right; vice over virtue; falsehood over truth; of the goddess of Reason over the Religion of Christ, and of usurping despotism over legitimate authority. ..."

Students and alumni shared these sentiments and there was talk of forming a military unit to send to the beleaguered Pope, until a letter from him, addressed to the University and its students, expressed his appreciation but asked instead for prayers and other forms of support necessary in readjustment to the loss of temporal power, which had not been an unmixed blessing to the Holy See.

The Pope's gracious reply was probably a relief to the University, however genuine its sentiments and fervent its expressions. Its actual resources were largely confined to its land and buildings, to the relatively rich endowment of its contributed services, to the modest gifts of friends, and to the very limited income from its student enrollment. It is true that this latter body represented progress and success in numbers. But the provision for orphans, the presence of the Manual Labor school for poor boys, the students who came from ambitious but poor families, the encouragement of talent at the expense of more rigorous bookkeeping and the necessity for paying the lay faculty and workers, no matter how small and sacrificial those demands may have been, all combined to preclude such generous initiation of outside programs.

The 1867 *Catalogue* listed the cost to a student paying his

full way as $5 for matriculation; board, bed, and medical
expenses for 5 months, $150; French, German, Italian, Spanish
or Hebrew $10 each, extra; instrumental music $12.50 and use
of piano or violin $2.50. The graduation fee was $10 and a
student remaining on the campus during the summer vacation
was charged an additional $35.

Of course there is no valid reason for comparing the costs of
this era with the charges in others. But it is another common
denominator in one of the impressive aspects of education at
Notre Dame which alumni and their families felt keenly.

In the 1892 *Catalogue*, approaching the golden jubilee, matriculation had become $10. The charge for board, room, tui-
tion, washing and mending is listed at $300, but for ten
months—in effect no increase at all from 25 years before. A
slight relief was indicated in a $45 fee for piano, $30 for violin,
flute, clarinet, saxaphone or guitar, $2 for a library fee and $2
for a lecture and concert series.

In the 1917 *Catalogue* for the diamond jubilee year of the
University, matriculation remained $10 while semester charges
were: tuition $60, board $175, library and lectures $10, athletic
fees $10, and laundry $12.50. Private rooms were listed upward
from $55 with Brownson Hall $30 and Walsh Hall $110 and up.

The centenary *Bulletin* in 1942 listed a comprehensive semester fee of $349.50 after a $10 matriculation fee. Room selection could increase this total to $394.50.

The 1972 register of expenses in comprehensive figures for
one semester, reads from $1,610 to $1,690.

Back now to the third meeting of the Alumni Association, at
the commencement of 1871, facing the challenges of that era.

Alumni voted Father William Corby, C.S.C., into the association's presidency. Professor Timothy Howard was made first vice
president; Professor Paul Broder, second vice president; Professor Joseph Lyons, treasurer; Professor W. J. Ivers, secretary;
Father E. B. Kilroy, orator with Professor Howard as alternate;
and Father Eugene O'Callahan, poet with Professor Broder as
alternate.

The amended constitution was presented to the membership
and a resolution passed for its publication in the *Scholastic*. The
only visible change is significant, reflecting as it does early
resistance of alumni to payment of dues. The amendment
states: "The initiation fee shall be ten dollars, the annual fee
thereafter, by those in attendance at the regular meetings, five
dollars."

You may recall that originally annual dues were set at $10.

Alumni returned and commencement exercises were in diversified depth. The banquet was the "feast of reason and flow of soul." The elections had installed a brilliant and mostly resident administration. All was well in the new world of alumni.

All seemed well with the University for the *Scholastic*, writing of 1870, says,

> Father Sorin had congregated around him a number of young men, Americans, Irishmen and Germans — some, as priests, helped him in campus and mission work, others as lay brothers enabled him to open the immense field of parochial schools . . . these schools increased in numbers and importance — the only limit to them was the supply of brothers. . . . Simultaneously Saint Mary's, removed from Bertrand in 1855, began to give evidence of the thorough training it was its destiny go give to the young ladies of the West.
>
> It was decided that the best table should be set for students, and that the opprobrium which the tradition of the ages has cast upon "college commons" should be cast off, or rather should never be attached to the dining rooms of Notre Dame and Saint Mary's. Judicious management of the commissiariat has enabled both institutions to set a table abundantly supplied with wholesome, appetizing food.
>
> . . . If so much attention is paid to the material well being of students, it may easily be inferred that great care has been given to every possible advantage to the students in the study halls to the classrooms by the professor who goes in person to the study hall door, and in a clear, audible voice, names the class that he requires for recitation . . . The students go in double file, and in perfect order and silence, to and from the classrooms, the professor accompanying them. Notes are given for recitation, and those are announced to all the students once a week by the director of studies who is vice president of the College. This is the modus operandi at the College. The same is practiced at Saint Mary's. . . .
>
> "For the discipline of the two institutions, little need be said; everybody who knows Notre Dame and Saint Mary's knows all about that — that it is not severe, but just so strict as to make honest and honorable men of young lads, some of whom may be first be inclined to be unruly, and to return accomplished young ladies to the homes of those parents who entrust their children to the admirable rule of the Sisters of Holy Cross."

Against this expanding and flourishing academic background, the fourth meeting of the Alumni Association was held in June, 1872. Bishop Dwenger celebrated the Pontifical High Mass at 6 a.m. The President of the University and of the association, Father Corby, preached the sermon. Professor Ivers presided at

the annual banquet. Toasts were given to alma mater, our
country, religion and education, and "Our society, the alumni
of the University of Notre Dame, the hope and pride of their
alma mater." With the treasurer reporting a satisfactory balance
in the treasury, Father Gillespie moved that for the future all
fees, except the $10 initiation fees, should be abolished. The
motion was passed. Elections resulted thus: Father E. B. Kilroy,
president; Professor Paul Broder, first vice president; Professor
D. A. Clarke, second vice president; Professor T. E. Howard,
treasurer; J. J. Fitzgibbon, orator, with Father J. A. O'Connell
as alternate; Father M. B. Brown, poet, with Rev. T. O. Sullivan
as alternate. The secretary seems modestly to have omitted his
election.

The reason for abolition to dues certainly could not have
been a lack of need for support of the University. It could well
have stemmed from the lack of response from a young alumni
group not yet endowed for this extra expense. It is most
probable that Father Gillespie, a statesman of the congregation,
saw in this temporary removal of an embarrassment the seeds of
good will that would in the future more than repay the very few
dollars represented by the suspension.

In 1873, the account of the annual meeting carried this note:

"One of the most pleasing features of commencement day
was the presence of the great numbers of old students, who
graced the festive occasion with their handsome, fresh looking countenances. We do not mean those of many years back,
who have settled down in life and become staid men of
business, but those of last year and the year before. At all
corners of the Old College we met them, but principally on
the porch in front of the College did they congregate. All of
them young, some had not yet ventured to try the effects of
hirsute adornment; others had promising moustaches, and
one—perhaps more, but one only of those we had the pleasure of accosting—came out in full beard. May they often
return to Notre Dame."

The eternal verity of whiskers!

Officers for the coming year were: Father D. J. Spillard,
C.S.C., president; Professor W. Ivers, first vice president; Father T.
O'Sullivan, LaPorte, Ind., second vice president; Denis A.
Clarke, Columbus, O., secretary; Professor T. E. Howard, trea-
surer; Father E. M. O'Callaghan, Fremont, O., orator with Gen.
William Lynch as alternate; Father Neil Gillespie, poet with T.
F. O'Mahony, Lake Forest, Ill., as alternate.

The *Scholastic* reported a more lively interest by alumni in the affairs of the association. Banquet toasts were raised to Pius IX and the Church; to the C.S.Cs.; to old times and old friends; to our flag, Army and Navy; and to American colleges. The reporter did express a dislike for the custom of toasts.

VII

"What Though the Odds"

It would be quite a few years before Father Michael Shea '04, and his brother, John '06, would write the "Victory March" but the spirit which inspired the lyrics was already writing history on the Notre Dame campus.

The world around Notre Dame was troubled. Economic America, barely away from the disastrous and draining Civil War, was dealt a blow by the gold speculations of Jay Gould and Jim Risk, culminating in the Black Friday of 1869. In the South the 15th Amendment of the Constitution, granting voting rights to Negroes, had stirred up new violence. In 1871 the Chicago fire killed 200 persons and did estimated damage of $290,000,000. This was to a neighbor and patron of the University, the home of many of its alumni and students.

The sorrow at Notre Dame was great. The celebration of Founder's Day on the Feast of St. Edward, Oct. 13, was already an annual tradition. But in 1871 it was postponed at the request of Father Sorin. When it was held on Nov. 4, the public was invited to the programs and proceeds were sent to help the stricken people of Chicago.

In that same year, 1871, a holocaust in Wisconsin took the lives of 1,500 persons, but that tragedy was obscured by the nature and scope of the Chicago fire, since Chicago was already a hub of travel and communication in the Midwest.

Generally speaking, the presidency of Father William Corby, who was to serve a second term later, ended on a happier note on the campus. The cornerstone of Sacred Heart Church was laid in 1871 by Archbishop Purcell of Cincinnati assisted by five other bishops. It was originally designed by Patrick Keely, a Chicago architect, but Father Sorin rejected Keely's plans as too

46

ornate and expensive. Brother Charles, who has definite credit later for the design of the steeple, may well deserve credit for the entire church, a Gothic delight throughout its lifetime.

In the summer of 1872, the end of Father Corby's term, Father Sorin convened a General Chapter of the Congregation of Holy Cross at Notre Dame. It was the first time a general chapter of a religious order had been convened in the new world, more than 350 years after its discovery by Christopher Columbus.

The students of Notre Dame at that period were for the most part American-born. In 1872 they were listed as Irish, 183; Americans 155; German 75; French 21; Spanish 3; Scotch 2; and English and Italian one each.

Father Sorin's activities, on the other hand, as Superior General, were of increasing world stature. Delegates to the Notre Dame meeting came from France, from Algiers, from Rome and from the East Indies. They came from Canada and from the various areas of the United States. There is an interesting volume yet to be written (of too little known history) concerning the schools and missionary enterprises which Father Sorin established away from Notre Dame. His devotion to the University seemed only to intensify the strength and the success with which he brought religion and education into new areas of America. Not all of the enterprises flourished, but all of them provide pages in the history of the progress of Catholic faith and education in the world.

Father Augustine Lemonnier, a nephew of Father Sorin, who completed his theology at Notre Dame in 1863, succeeded Father Corby as President of Notre Dame in 1872. Professor Howard, writing of Father Lemonnier says,

"It would seem that the presidency of Father Lemonnier came to add grace and beauty to what was already so laboriously and substantially constructed. There is hardly a science or an art in which he was not well versed; and, as Johnson said of Goldsmith, there was nothing which he touched that he did not beautify . . ."

Father Sorin was very proud of his nephew. Another nephew had not been so favored. Showing reluctance to adapt to American ways, he was shipped back to France by his patriotic uncle. Father Lemonnier's contributions were significant, but short-lived. He died in October, 1874, at the age of 34, followed in death, only a few days later, by Father Neil Gillespie, the first alumnus. The deaths were a great blow to the Notre Dame community, and to all the growing family which had shared "la vie intime."

Writing of Father Lemonnier, Father Sorin told his Congregation: "With my habitual fears of the dangers of nepotism, I never left him a chance to benefit by our relationship; it ever stood against him in my mind, and often proved to him a loss—and even now, when he is gone, I prefer abstaining from further remarks concerning him, save to thank, from my heart, the faithful souls who attended him through his long illness."

Father Patrick Colovin, "a ripe scholar, and a man of fine presence," succeeded Father Lemonnier, having been vice president during Lemonnier's illness. He held office until 1877. He was Canadian born and of strong Irish persuasions. He was an excellent theologian and a polished orator. In spite of these many virtues, Father Sorin did not enjoy a rapport with him. They maintained a surface community but with detectable undertones of opposition.

Father Colovin was not as indulgent of the students and the enrollment began to drop. According to rather obscure references of the period, Father Colovin resigned in 1877, assuming a pastorate at Watertown, Wis., while its former pastor, Rev. William Corby, returned to Notre Dame to begin an unusual second term as President.

Meanwhile, the *Scholastic* of July 1874 reports: "Not the least of the interesting features connected with the annual commencement exercises of Notre Dame University is the reunion of her alumni." The commentator, undoubtedly a campus alumnus himself, added, "Many others, too, sent in their regrets at not being able to attend the reunion; but a goodly number we are pained to say, slighted the invitation extended them and did not deem it worthy of the requested reply. . . ." Truth in journalism was thus enlisted to advance the association interest, but the occasion is also an early reminder of the failure of many alumni to respond to organized efforts which has plagued not only Notre Dame but all other alumni organizations throughout their history.

The annual meeting in 1874 remained undaunted. It elected Father M. B. Brown, C.S.C., president; Professor Howard, first vice president; N. S. Mitchell, Davenport, Iowa, second vice president; Professor Stace, secretary; Professor Lyons, treasurer; T. F. O.Mahony, orator with J. F. McHugh as alternate and M. H. Keeley, poet with M. S. Foote as alternate.

The business of the 1874 association meeting dealt, in part, with the republication of Professor Lyons *Silver Jubilee* book, evidently popular beyond the expectations of the limited first edition. The plates for the book were destroyed in the Chicago fire. Professor Howard was appointed a committee of one to notify the members that the book would be re-issued despite of this. He was to determine by individual solicitation how much each alumnus would contribute to the venture, and how many volumes they would purchase.

Guests at the annual banquet included the city comptroller of Chicago, the mayor of Burlington, Iowa, and the first graduating class in law. Professor Stace served as toastmaster. General Lynch, the official orator for the occasion, begged off, but addressed the group informally, as did the mayor of Burlington. Father Carrier, on behalf of the Notre Dame trustees "expressed his sincere desire that every alumnus may continue in the future, as he has done in the past, to reflect honor and glory on his alma mater." Father Lemonnier, though ill at the time, gave a brief welcome, urging continued alumni meetings and strengthening of their ties to Notre Dame.

In 1875 the annual alumni reunion was begun with a solemn high Mass. It is noted that the usual music for such a mass during the school year combined Gregorian chant, Cecilian music, and the regular music of the church. On this occasion, at the request of the alumni, Gounod's *Messe Solennelle* was sung by the Gillespie Choral Union, drawing special praise from the reporter.

Officers for the ensueing year were named: Father Sorin, president; Father P. J. Colovin, first vice president; Father W. F. O'Rourke, second vice president; T. A. Dailey, secretary; Professor J. A. Lyons, treasurer; John M. Gearin, orator with C. B. Berdel as alternate and J. D. McCormick, poet with D. E. Maloney as alternate.

Years later, when Professor Lyons' monument was unveiled in the Community Cemetery in 1892, William P. Breen, distinguished Fort Wayne alumnus, revealed one of the secrets of Professor Lyons's frequent election as association treasurer.

> Who could forget him as a unique and indispensable figure at the meetings of the alumni, as he sat in our midst, the favorite personage. Every lineament of his countenance bespeaking his pride in growing Notre Dame; every movement redolent with his anxiety for the perpetuity of our association, and his every glance an earnest of his devotion to his calling and his love for his college friends. Will you ever

forget the picture of him, with book in hand, as he arises to make his report as an officer of that Association, and then the earnest, dignified tones, with which we could not accord, as he unfolded the never-varying financial condition of the association which always disclosed a deficit which he has made good?''

In the election of Father Sorin and Father Colovin that year, there is also evidence of an effort by the alumni to express their admiration for both priests, and to soothe the friction of which alumni undoubtedly were aware.

The United States celebrated the centennial year of its existence in 1876. At Notre Dame, alumni attendance at the June reunion brought back more alumni than in any previous year.

Officers elected at this meeting were: Professor J. A. Lyons, president; M. A. Baasen, first vice president; H. D. McCormick, second vice president; Father J. A. O'Connell, secretary; Professor Howard, treasurer; Father Corby, orator with W. J. Clarke, alternate and T. A. Dailey, poet with N. S. Mitchell as alternate. The new elective office of historian introduced at this meeting was filled by Professor Stace.

Toasts were offered appropriately to Pope Pius IX, to the President of the United States, to the President of the University, to our fellow members, and to our departed fellow members. Death had taken a number of young and devoted alumni in the preceding several years.

In 1877, Bishop Dwenger celebrated the alumni Mass and delivered the sermon, with confirmation ceremonies for a number of young men added to the usual solemn occasion.

The business meeting elected new officers: Professor Howard, president; T. A. Dailey, first vice president; T. H. O'Mahony, second vice president; Father John A. Zahm, secretary; Professor Lyons, treasurer; W. J. Ivers, historian; C. J. Dodge, orator with A. W. Arrington as alternate and H. V. Hayes, poet with T. F. Gallagher as alternate.

This early affiliation of Father Zahm with the Alumni Association began a long series of great contributions which he made to the University, its students and its alumni, as well as to his congregation, and to the Church and science.

Professor Ivers officiated at the banquet, where toasts were raised to Pius IX, to President Grant of the United States, our alma mater, our deceased members and the press. The latter gentlemen paid for the recognition, through a resolution marking the deaths of Gen. William Lynch and Peter Dechant, mourning their loss as distinguished alumni, and promising imitation of their virtues. The resolution added that copies of it were to be sent for publication to *"The Scholastic, The Chicago Tribune, The Chicago Times, Catholic Columbian, Boston Pilot,* and *South Bend Herald, Register and Tribune."*

The report of the 1878 alumni reunion is brief, but very significant. Father Corby celebrated the solemn high Mass. A new name, Father Andrew Morrissey, appears in the proceedings as master of ceremonies at that alumni Mass—still held at 6 a.m.

New officers elected were: Professor Howard, president; Professor Corby, first vice president; Professor Stace, second vice president; R. W. Staley, secretary; Professor Lyons, treasurer; William W. Dodge, historian; D. E. Maloney, orator with W. J. Clarke as alternate and W. T. Ball, poet with David J. Wile as alternate.

The presence of the slate of officers of six young men from classes of the last five years again underlines the early Association's encouragement of young leadership. And the presence of David J. Wile is an early example of alumni ecumenism. The Wiles were a prominent Jewish family in Laporte, Ind. who had befriended Father Sorin and the University from its beginning, and who later sent their sons to it. A still later son, Frederick William Wile, became a distinguished alumnus in the corps of Washington journalists.

The alumni banquet, presided over by Professor Stace, presented a toast to the new Pontiff, Leo XIII, and a toast to the United States of America. And what could well have been the first case history of major alumni support, certainly a major item in its annals, was a telegram from Father E. B. Kilroy '52, a long active alumnus in the secular priesthood in Ontario, Canada: "Sorry cannot attend the banquet. Should the Alumni Association see fit to open an endowment subscription for the University, put my name down for $1,000."

It was apparent that the previous year's efforts to reconcile Father Colovin and Father Sorin had failed. It was Father Corby who greeted the alumni as the new President of Notre Dame.

Father Thomas E. Walsh became the new vice president. Among the first things done, probably to win back student good will after Father Colovin's lack of enthusiasm for student activity, was the expansion of facilities for student recreations and exercises. The Seniors, those over 16; the Juniors, between

12 and 16; and the Minims, those under 12, were branching into many games and sports requiring space. Some 30 acres were set aside for the purpose, with ample provision for baseball—the major sport of that era—and football. One account of those days contains a listed sport unlikely to be familiar to many alumni, since its devotees, the Minims, are long gone. This was identified as "velocipedestrianism." Father Sorin is reported on one of his many visits to Europe to have been entranced at the sight of Parisian children on velocipedes, and to have ordered some sent back to the campus for "his little princes."

In any event, sports were as indigenous to "la vie intime" as the pursuits of the spirit or the mind. It should be added that the acquisition of much of the present campus of the University—and the amazing availability of land for the physical plant expansion in the long story of progress—can be attributed to the growing and constant need for more play fields on the peripheral campus. *Mens sana in corpore sano* provided a cross fire of expansion pressures.

The relatively new Main Building housed most of the progress of the thriving University. Father Corby and Father Thomas Walsh worked diligently on the physical and academic developments. Father John Zahm was inspiring new effort and achievement in the science department.

Into this climate of constructive growth came another disaster, the fire of 1879. It has tremendous meaning for alumni, because from this catastrophe came one of the great and early examples of what may never be totally defined, but is undeniably a constant factor of power, the Notre Dame spirit.

VIII

A Most Successful Fire

It is only in retrospect that this title can be used.

The tragic impact of April 23, 1879 can still chill hearts on the campus. Then it struck administrators, faculty and students with horror. And as the news spread, alumni, parents, the church and friends everywhere—in the whole United States and in distant countries—shared the inestimable sense of loss.

The University was already known and esteemed for its insitutional accomplishments. On this historic date, 37 years after he had founded Notre Dame du Lac in a 10-acre clearing in Northern Indiana, Father Edward Sorin was known as a priest of great ecclesiastic stature, a missionary of outstanding zeal and widespread accomplishment and an American educator of great influence and vision.

Notre Dame had become in truth a beacon, a bridge and a crossroad for all of these many identities.

Then came a fire, which in the words of the *Scholastic* immediately thereafter, seemed to shatter the total dream, the accepted destiny, of this shrine of Our Lady, already favored with miracles of her patronage.

On fire, in flames, in ashes! Such is the history of Our Lady's College for a few short hours, beginning at about eleven o'clock on Wednesday morning. The tale of alarm, of hurried help, of almost superhuman but vain labor in extinguishing the raging flames, and finally saving whatever of value could be snatched from the fire, has all been graphically told in the daily press . . . but our friends have a right to hear from us through our own little paper and so they shall, for, thank God, our printing office is one of the precious things spared . . ."

No one knows exactly how the fire started. The little water that might have nipped it early, was too long in coming. The South Bend volunteer fire department was summoned. But South Bend—alumni will believe this—had not had a fire in two years, and both equipment and volunteers were less than prompt in functioning. Many citizens were in fact well ahead of the department, and joined the campus family in heroic, if sometimes bizarre and often fruitless, efforts to salvage the many priceless things which Sorin, Carrier, Lemonnier, Zahm, Lyons, Edwards and others had brought to enrich the spartan environment of the young institution.

Many evidences of minor miracles in the face of seeming disaster were reported. Little wind existed. The day was warm so that the dispossessed suffered no ills of exposure. Worker after worker in the feverish tangle of effort was literally saved by inches from flames or falling walls.

The great new college building was totally destroyed. The infirmary, which also housed the general office and the students office, was entirely burned out. The music hall was consumed. The students' trunks kept in it, however, were saved by the many helping hands. The minims hall was "utterly gone."

> "The church, the presbytery, science hall (the rear of the old church, then used by Father Zahm for that purpose), the kitchen, the steam house, and the printing office are left, as is also Washington Hall.
> "This destruction was accomplished in about three hours."

Father Corby called his council together in mid afternoon. We have grown and thrived on the legend of Father Sorin's heroic reaction when he viewed the ruins. But it should be recorded in justice that Father Corby was equally inspired. It had been decided that there was no other course but to close down the entire University. A meeting of all students was called and they were so notified. Many South Bend and area neighbors had offered accommodations, but the burden was too great and the functioning of the school too formidable to attempt to complete the scholastic year. The *Scholastic* says of Father Corby's address to the students, " . . . He promised them that a new college, more excellent than the one burned down that day, would be ready to receive them on the first Tuesday of the following September . . ."

Father Sorin, then 65 years old, his attentions directed to

many of the growing challenges of the Congregation, was in Montreal, beginning another of the 50 trips he made to Europe during his lifetime. Father Corby and his associates feared the effect of the tragic news on Sorin. So they selected Professor James Edwards, 29 years old, director of the Lemonnier Library, already deep in his work of assembling valuable records of the Church from the bishops of America, to go by train to Montreal and notify the founder in person. Edwards, who had come to Notre Dame when he was 10 years old, and who had been a friend and associate of Father Lemonnier, was a logical choice for this sad personal mission. Father Sorin immediately returned to Notre Dame with Edwards.

It is not difficult to envision the sadness with which he looked upon the ruins of the flourishing campus he had so recently left.

Professor Howard says in his *Golden Jubilee History,*

Those who listened to him on his return, when he spoke to the assembled community from the altar of the Church of the Sacred Heart, will never forget the holy heroism of his words and appearance. Far from yielding to the pressure of the calamity, his soul seemed to rise superior to all the affliction that had fallen upon him and upon the community. It was as if an inspired prophet of old stood before us; and every priest and brother went out of the sacred edifice strengthened as if with the absolute assurance of help from Heaven. In God and His Blessed Mother he had trusted from the beginning, and they would not fail him and his stricken community in their hour of need. If it were all gone, Sorin added, I would not give up.

Father Sorin for the time seemed to have recovered his youth again. Uninterrupted activity, and a vigilance that seized upon every source of aid, returned to him as they had been with him when he laid the foundations . . . He had, besides his own community, so conducted the University as to win the love and good will of the American people, regardless of religious belief. . .

The loyalty of the community, religious, lay, faculty and students, was tempered to a new strength by the disaster. Any vestiges of prejudice in the immediate area vanished in the generous response of South Bend, and all the other neighbors in the broad mission area, to whatever needs they could fill. Many of the merchants gave materials and credits, recognizing the value of the University to the community. Many citizens who could not give materially, gave labor, joining in the work of clearing and rebuilding. The first pupil at Notre Dame, Alexis Coquillard, launched financial aid with a personal contribution of $500.

The girls of Saint Mary's, mindful of the zeal of Father Sorin for their education, offered all their pocket money to Notre Dame. Chicago, remembering Notre Dame's helping hand in 1871, organized committees and held public meetings to secure aid for Notre Dame.

Father Sorin made one valuable discovery in the immediate wake of the fire, which will explain to alumni the sometimes seemingly rigid policy of the University in collecting student fees. In an effort to secure immediate aid—$200,000 was the conservative damage estimate; only $45,000 the insurance in force—Father Sorin wrote a letter to some 200 families of students and former students still indebted to the University. He hoped to receive a substantial sum from the estimated $75,000 outstanding. In an understandable disappointment, he let it be known that of this amount his letter brought in response the incredible total of $22.

Plans for a new college submitted by W. J. Edbrooke, a Chicago architect, were accepted and the new building was staked out on May 17. Its construction, largely of brick from kilns in South Bend and Bertrand, and employing 300 workmen, is one of the achievements in University history which some writers may accept as a natural phenomenon. I extend it into my own category of supernatural manifestations.

The girls of Saint Mary's chose the replacement of the giant statue of Our Lady, which had crashed with the fire from the top of the old college, as their contribution to the new Main Building. Provision had already been made for the huge dome to support such a statue. The girls selected the statue of Mary in the Piazza di Spagna in Rome, erected there by Pius IX to commemorate the Immaculate Conception, as the model from which the Notre Dame replica would be made.

The fire caused a disruption in what seems to have been the first major appeal to the Alumni Association. Plans to dedicate Sacred Heart Church in 1879 had been postponed a year earlier, in the planning stages, by a decision that the church could not accommodate the expected participants. Instead it was decided to proceed with the construction of a proposed Sacred Heart Chapel, this to be a beautiful addition to the rear of the already constructed section. The *Scholastic* says,

. . . in the minds of the originators, as in the mind of the
Church, the Chapel of the Sacred Heart must be the richest,
finest and noblest part of the whole edifice . . . hence the
thought of offering the honor of its erection to those best
loved here, to the noble band of students who since 1844 had
the best chance of knowing Notre Dame, and who . . feel as
justly proud of their alma mater as she herself does of the
brilliant army she has sent forth through our happy land,
which, we trust, they will continue long to adorn and enrich
from the priceless store of sound knowledge and virtue acquired here under the eyes of the Heavenly Queen to whom
every soul is consecrated on these lovely premises . . .

Father Sorin wrote,

We would have deemed it an offense in the building of what
the public voice already calls a monumental church, to ignore
and pass by our students, that is to say, the very first element
for which Notre Dame exists in this land. We make no appeal,
but simply deem it an act of justice to offer them the honor
of erecting themselves the crowning part of this glorious
monument of faith and piety, the Chapel of the Sacred
Heart. To this honor we feel confident they will respond with
an exceptional zeal . . . The cost is estimated at $12,000. But
what is that, where so many generous hearts will exert
themselves to excel each other in liberality. Each name, and
we know them already, will be inscribed with its donation in
a manner that will perpetuate the memory of the glorious
deed. . . . Alas, many of Notre Dame's best students have
already enetered into eternity. Here is an opportunity for
parents and friends of extending to them the benefit of a
daily Mass, the most efficient means to help the dear departed ones. As we intend going to work at once, we will
consider a prompt reply a favor: for we must know before
beginning what we may depend upon. Should any one want a
little time we could wait six months from this date. The
names of the donors will appear, as they come every week, in
our (Scholastic) columns.

Father Sorin thus inaugurated a major alumni campaign, at
the same time identifying the now familiar custom of memorial
gifts, the practice of deferred giving, and the incentive of a
donor's roster—first on a current basis of receipt, and then in
some permanent accessible form attached to the chapel itself.

This was indeed a founding father of foresight and talent,
familiar with the essential unity of faith and works.

The chapel appeal to alumni obviously gave way to the
greater and more urgent needs of rebuilding the total University.

The preparation for the alumni appeal, however, and the continuous experience of seeking every source of support during those turbulent 37 years from foundation to fire, stood Notre Dame in good stead.

The familiar and friendly sources of support in Europe were contacted. The Propagation of the Faith, the Vatican, the generous benefactors in France were drawn upon anew.

The toasts at the alumni banquets of the 10 years of the young association took on new significance, as the American hierarchy, clergy, civic leaders, educators and press, made significant contributions to the reconstruction of the popular University in the burgeoning Indiana countryside.

From the *Fort Wayne Sentinel* of May 12, 1879, we find evidence of the prompt action which followed Father Sorin's decision to rebuilt.

Rev. J. A. Zahm, C.S.C., professor of physical science at Notre Dame, Ind., is now in the city soliciting aid for the rebuilding of the University, destroyed by fire on the 23rd ult. He will call upon the old students and friends of the institution during the week, and hopes to find all prepared to do something toward repairing the great loss that has been incurred.

The *Western Home Journal* on May 8 reported:

We direct attention to the appeal of Very Rev. Edward Sorin, C.S.C., which we publish elsewhere. Rev. Father L'Eterneau, C.S.C., is in the city soliciting aid for the institution.

The *Western Watchman* of St. Louis, on May 10, said,

Rev. James Gleeson of the University of Notre Dame, near South Bend, Indiana, lately burned to the ground, is in town, a guest of Father Henry, of St. Lawrence O'Toole's Church. The archbishop has permitted the Rev. Father to solicit subscriptions in the diocese to aid in the building of the new institution. He will, as far as possible, visit the charitable in person, but if any who wish to contribute should fail to see him, donations left with Father Henry, or with Mr. Fox, the bookseller, on Fifth Street, will be most gratefully acknowledged.

Father Gleeson arrived here Saturday of last week. Many of our readers may be acquainted with him, as some years ago he was connected with the Cathedral in this city. His stay in St. Louis will be prolonged two weeks, and from this city he will go to Southern points. The Rev. Father has paid our sanctum a visit this week, and expresses himself very well satisfied with the way he has been received this far. He is most confident that the College will again be under headway by September.

Thus was born the extension of the boundaries of the campus through the involvement of administrators, faculty, alumni and students, so that "la vie intime" reached far from the University which was its radiating center. And the precedent of the broad base of financial support was firmly and effectively established some 40 years before the pressures of expansion brought Notre Dame to its first endowment campaign.

The influence of Father Sorin's faith, the example of his activity, and the inspiration of his vision, which had achieved so much and which now refused to be buried in the ahes of even so great a fire, won immediate and general sharing.

The *Scholastic* of May 10, 1879, 17 days after the holocaust, said:

> The excitement is all over, and Notre Dame in sad and sober earnest is beginning to realize the heavy losses she has suffered . . . Colleges, like everything else, have felt the strain of the financial crisis through which the country has been passing during the past few years. Notre Dame had weathered the storm, and was just beginning to congratulate herself that a new era of prosperity was about to dawn, when the fire came . . . However, relying on the blessing of Heaven, which has never been refused her in the past—on the energetic efforts of a devoted community and faculty, and on the assistance of innumerable friends—foremost amongst whom she counts her students, past and present, whose sympathies have gone out towards her stronger than ever in her trial, she has bravely set to work to repair her immense loss. 'Heaven helps those who help themselves,' is a familiar proverb, and to this assistance Notre Dame is determined that she shall be entitled. And if the hundreds who in past years have learned to know and love the University take this opportunity of lending it a helping hand, what fear can there be that Notre Dame's mission of good is destined to be long interrupted?"

Father Sorin has been quoted as saying he believed the great fire was a chastisement by Our Lady because he had not dreamed boldly enough for the institution bearing Her name. Certainly he set out to remedy this alleged "contentment with too little." The University of Notre Dame has never since rested on its laurels.

The fruits of Sorin's new goals were almost instant. The giant new Administration Building—as we know it now, and as it has served as the hub of the expanding University for the ensuing 92 years—was ready for the students in September of 1880. Through some inexplicable reasoning, a cut in tuition for the new year had been announced before the fire in the preceding spring. But in spite of the change and urgent circumstances, it was decided to abide by the cut as promised, and this was one of the pleasant greetings for the new students.

There were surprises of lasting significance. Gas illumination offered much improved study lighting. Steam heat, and hot and cold water were modern conveniences associated with the most advanced colleges and universities. Jacob Ackerman uncle of later and long time professor, F. X. Ackerman, had already begun the artistic series of frescoes of world famous Cathedrals on the walls of the new refectories on the ground floor of the new structure. What they lacked in pure art, they compensated for in the use of familiar campus figures as models for the scenes of life around the cathedral squares.

With all this, enrollment dropped to a total of 324 students in all three divisions. The Law School, by contrast, showed an encouraging increase.

At this milestone in Notre Dame history, a survey of the still young and still small Alumni Association was made. Who and where now were the graduates, from 1849, when Father Gillespie received the first degree, to the class of 1879, which had received its diplomas in emergency Commencement exercises, the day after the fire, April 24, 1879?

> Of the young men who have graduated in the classical and scientific courses at Notre Dame, about 18 percent are priests, 27 percent are lawyers, 8 percent are educators, 6 percent are physicians 3 percent are editors, 7 percent are engineers, 4 percent are farmers, 10 percent are business men. Of the others, some are dead, several are now studying law, medicine, theology, etc. Two or three are doing nothing. When graduated, four-fifths of the whole number were Catholics, two or three Israelites and about one-fifth Protestants.

An impressive, frank, and typical account of an alumni association.

IX

The Straightaway

It was as if the devastating fire of 1879 had been the last hurdle of a long race. Now the straightaway opened toward the goals the University set.

Many things had evidenced great progress before the fire. The University's identity as a "mediator" in large social areas of progress was reflected in recommendations made on the campus that diocesan school boards could be very important in the growth of parochial schools. Notre Dame recommended to the Catholic press that it increase its payments to writers to insure quality. The *Scholastic* carried a criticism of "hazing" on any campus, citing the Princeton scandals and rowdyism publicized in connection with that practice in 1878.

A significant concurrent development of promise was the organization at Saint Mary's in June of 1879 of the Association of Post-Graduates of the Academy. Miss Rose Devoto was elected president, Miss Helen Foote, vice president, Miss Katherine Joyce, secretary and Sister Rosa, treasurer. The names of Devoto and Foote were familiar on the Notre Dame side of the coin, reflecting the integration of families in the enrollments of the two schools which has never been lost. The first project was the procuring "for Notre Dame a magnificent statue of the Blessed Virgin for the dome of the college."

The American scene, in which Notre Dame was meeting its challenges, was itself in a period of great ferment and progress. The echoes of Indian wars and a vast frontier still reverberated from the Custer massacre in 1876. The arc and incandescent lights were products of the year that saw Notre Dame destroyed by fire. Malaria was just being identified and fought successfully and diptheria was still 10 years away in its cure. Pasteur did not solve the problem of hydrophobia until 1885. Chicago's first "skyscraper" was not built until that same year. Tubercle and typhoid bacilli were contemporary discoveries, one—typhoid—in 1880, and the other in 1882. The states of our great Northwest, with the exception of Oregon (1859), were a decade or two away from admission to the Union. Illinois and Indiana did not yet have compulsory school attendance laws.

But challenge, progress and opportunity were dominant. And nowhere were they more zealously met than in the burgeoning University of Notre Dame du Lac.

It is of course obvious that no alumni banquet was held in 1879, in the bustling reconstruction of its traditional setting.

But the promises of Fathers Sorin and Corby having been magnificently met, the banquet and meeting were resumed in 1880. Attendance was unusually large, a facet of the faith and hope attending the whole Notre Dame family. Father Corby celebrated the 6 o'clock morning Mass and, appropriately as President on this historic renewal, preached the sermon.

At the business meeting and elections, Father E. B. Kilroy, whose generous endowment offer had been so stimulating to Notre Dame, was elected president. Professor Ivers, first vice president; Rev. D. A. Clarke, second vice president; Florian Devoto, secretary; Professor Lyons, treasurer; John J. Coleman, historian; Father E. J. McLaughlin, orator with John P. McHugh as alternate; Timothy E. Howard, poet with Father Thomas E. Walsh as alternate. The account says that "after the election of officers some very sensible remarks were made." The toasts were raised to the new Holy Father, Leo XIII, to the President of the United States, to Notre Dame, to religious education, to the press and to our absent members.

The *Scholastic* in December of 1880 carries a comment of great interest in this first post-fire year affirming the continuation of "la vie intime," evidently not a common denominator of American campuses.

> It is a matter of surprise to many beyond our college halls, who are aware of the difficulties and ill-feeling existing between the faculties and students of many of our American colleges, that such amity exists at Notre Dame. Not that there are not misunderstandings, and differences too, at times, but as a rule these do not culminate in that open defiance of authority that exists in many places elsewhere. Many outsiders cannot understand this, and in consequence attribute it to oppressively coercive measures on the part of the faculty and a want of spirit in the students. Nothing

could be farther from the truth. . . . The personal sacrifices continually made by members of the faculties in the Catholic teaching orders are well known to all who have attended their institutions, and must call forth the admiration of all who witness them. Without these, such institutions could not exist in the absence of the liberal public patronage now in great measure or altogether withheld. Here we behold men devoting their lives to the education of youth, without salary or pension; for all that comes in over and above the actual necessaries of life is devoted to the support and extension of the college and comfort of the students. The general action of the faculty towards the students, too, must, in order to accommodate itself to the circumstances, be the very reverse of what was above supposed. The greater good of the governed is, plainly, the object, as far as possible, of the governing power; hence to a certain degree a family feeling is created, and with the great sacrifices made by the faculty before his eyes the student will not readily find fault even when there is reason for it. This is not so much reasoned out as instinctively felt . . . These thoughts have been suggested by an editorial in the recent number of the Harvard Echo bearing upon the relations of faculty and students at that college.

In 1881, Father Kilroy, president of the association, celebrated the alumni Mass, assisted by Father D. A. Tighe and by Father D. A. Clarke, editor of the *Catholic Columbian*. Father Kilroy later presided at the annual meeting, with 60 members present. Professor Howard read the poem. Father Clarke was the historian. Father Sorin was guest of honor at the annual banquet and was elected honorary president of the Alumni Association. Father Kilroy was reelected president; Father Clarke, first vice president; Dr. John Cassidy, South Bend, second vice president; ex-mayor Lucius Tong, South Bend, secretary; Professor Lyons, treasurer; Professor T. O'Mahony, orator; W. T. Ball, Chicago, poet and Professor Stace, historian.

It was also in 1881 that the Congregation of Holy Cross, or Father Sorin—the distinction was sometimes difficult of definition—decided that Father William Corby should not be burdened with his dual jobs of Provincial and President. Father Corby, zealous for Notre Dame, would have chosen the University, but Father Sorin decided upon the appointment of Father Thomas E. Walsh, who had shown great promise as student and administrator, serving as vice president during the trying period of the fire. Father Walsh was only 28 years of age when he became President.

In 1881, student enrollment increased to 351. The commencement found only seven degrees conferred in the arts, science and law, whereas Commercial Diplomas were given to 31. On occasion, this seeming imbalance has been charged to small academic stature of the University on the college level. It seems much more likely, as we meet the brilliant men, and observe the advanced equipment of the departments and the library of Notre Dame, that the condition reflects the circumstances of the era. Few men attended college. Fewer still were graduated. The preparation for college was rare, indeed, which offered the backgrounds in science, languages, and literature which were required by the collegiate degrees. Some of the professions still did not demand degrees. And the economics of family life, together with the limited educational backgrounds of most families, argued still further against the attainment of degrees. But the small number of students completing the collegiate courses offered the best men of the faculty a compensating opportunity for self-development, which provided continuing and profitable strengthening of the total competence of the University.

An interesting note of the period regarding a seemingly nonacademic activity, points up the unity of programs and purpose that motivated the campus.

> Once again military training on a limited scale became part of student life . . . Through the good offices of Sen. D. R. Leeper (South Bend), the government contributed one hundred Sharpe's breech-loaders of the latest pattern. Father Corby was, naturally, partial to the military. He noted, too, that in nearly every educational institution in the country there was a group of military cadets. He favored this revival because, as he said, it was a great source of recreational and physical culture. Nor did he forget the disciplinary angle.

In 1880, the *Scholastic* began the custom of printing *Alumni Class Notes*, not only serving the interest of the young Alumni Association, but maintaining the close ties between administration, faculty, students and alumni so firmly a part of the distinctive spirit and tradition of the University.

The young President Walsh who took office in 1881 had been ordained at Notre Dame in 1877. He had reorganized classes in the fall of 1879, calling upon an excellent memory in the absence of all records, which had been destroyed by the fire. He had originally been at St. Laurent in Canada. Father Sorin recognized the promise of the young man and sent him to study in France. Even before the completion of his theological studies

there, Father Sorin called him back, not to Canada but to Notre
Dame, to bolster the somewhat turbulent presidency of Father
Colovin. His handling of this assignment, without question
undoubtedly resulted in his ordination and immediate high post
of responsibility under Father Corby, with his selection as
President coming shortly, and almost before the young priest
could possibly have grasped its full demands. But he entered his
new duties with faith and ability. And his term of office, from
1881 to 1893 was one of uninterrupted progress, in spite of the
limited resources available for the burgeoning programs of a
growing University.

In 1882, it was Father Walsh who greeted returning alumni as
President of their alma mater, but already a friend and active
participant in association programs. One of Father Walsh's innovations was celebrating the alumni Mass at 8 a.m. instead of 6,
lending gusto to the Te Deum if the report is accurate. Bishop
John Watterson of Columbus, a relative of Henry Watterson,
Louisville editor, and himself an outstanding member of the
American hierarchy, preached the sermon. Attendance was recorded as a new high.

The association honored the new Notre Dame head by elect-
ing him its president. Father Clarke of Columbus, and Dennis
Hogan of Chicago, were elected vice presidents; Father N. J.
Stoffel was named secretary, and the perennial Professor
Lyons, treasurer. W. J. Clarke was chosen orator with John
Ewing as alternate while Father M. B. Brown was selected poet
with Professor Stace as alternate and also as historian. Toasts
were reported only as the customary "grave and gay."

Some of the promise of Notre Dame, and the immediate
evidence of Father Walsh's academic interests, appeared during
1882. A decision was made to build a new Science Hall. Father
John Zahm and his brother, Albert, still a student, were already
making significant contributions in science with the limited
facilities occupied behind the church still in the building stage.
Father Alexander Kirsch had just joined the science faculty,
returning from studies at Louvain. Edbrooke, architect of the
majestic Main Building, and later of the U.S. Treasury, was
chosen to design the new hall. Another decision of that year,
implemented the following January, was to bring an alumnus
and member of the Chicago bar, William J. Hoynes, back to
head a strengthened Law School, in which the legendary "colonel" had taught earlier. John Ewing and Lucius Hubbard also
joined the law faculty.

In June, 1882, Washington Hall was opened. It was, for its time, a major auditorium and general facility for music, theatre, and exhibitions. Its acoustics were excellent. It was electrically lighed, as was the exterior campus at this date. Washington Hall utilized the recent invention (1879) of Thomas A. Edison, and outdoors, Father Zahm had installed the arc light, also a product of 1879. This may be a proper time, in indicating the essentially modern mind of the University, to report that the great administration building was thought to be the first major building in the U.S. to have built-in duct facilities for removing used air and maintaining a freshness of breathing for its occupants.

The *Scholastic* of October, 1882 carries a story from the *Cincinnatti Gazette*, of lasting impact for all who have ever visited the campus.

> In the year 1874, the Very Rev. Father General Sorin was in Rome and was introduced to artist Luigi Gregori by Cardinal Franchi, who had then been his patron for many years. The Father General was in search of a real Roman artist, who would accompany him to America, and take charge of the Art Department . . . Signor Gregori was strongly recommended for this position by the reigning Pope, who knew him personally, and by Cardinal Franchi, Cardinal Barnabo and Msgr. De Merode who had patronized him liberally during his long stay at the Vatican. Gregori consented to the proposal and eight years ago came to this country with Father Sorin. He immediately commenced to decorate the church at Notre Dame and continued until three years ago, when the University buildings were burned down; but his work was fortunately not destroyed. During the rebuilding of the University he lived in Chicago, but returned to his college home two years ago. Since that time he has been engaged upon a series of historical paintings, frescoed on the walls of the corridors of the Main Building. Scenes from the life of Christopher Columbus will occupy ten pictures, each twenty feet long by ten feet in height, and Gregori is to fresco the inner surface of the lofty dome with allegorical representations of the sciences, of colossal size. It may be noted here that Mrs. Gregori and a daughter, Fanny, lived during this time at Saint Mary's College, where Mrs. Gregori later died (1892). Signor Gregori and his daughter than returned to Italy.

Another area of interest, barely intimated by quiet studies already underway, is reflected in a letter from Albert F. Zahm, of the Class of 1883, dealing with the pursuit of man's efforts at air travel. This was printed in December, 1882, while Zahm was still a senior.

Let me remark, in concluding, that although the prospects are good, there is still a vast amount of work to be done. A great deal has been written, it is true, on the theory of flight; many delicate experiments have been made in the analysis of the movement of birds, and a few profitable attempts at flying have been made, but we still have to answer these three important questions: What will the air support? What is the most efficient motor? and what is the most favorable form? On the other hand, we may encourage ourselves with the fact that experiments and inventors of the present day can do more practical work in a year than the people of other centuries could accomplish in a whole lifetime. With the present means, a few men could perform all the mechanical work of Watt in one or two years. The construction of an electric generator and lamp is by no means an easy task; yet see how many have already come before the public. When men of so much ability, energy and capital shall come into competition in the manufacture of artificial eagles, dragonflies, carrier pigeons, etc., we shall see the periods of speculation, invention, adoption and refinement passed through in one decade.

It was in fact only two decades after this youthful projection that Orville and Wilbur Wright, applying some of Albert Zahm's subsequent theories of flight, successfully launched their historic plane at Kitty Hawk.

Apparently at Saint Mary's the first urge for alumnae organization, based on the sole purpose of securing a new statue for Notre Dame, had faded with the prompt success of that project. In any case, in 1883, the graduates were back petitioning for an organization "in hope of effecting a bond of sympathy and affection that may exist among the members of the classes of each succeeding year." (The actual terms "alumni" and "alumnae" seldom appeared in the earlier records unless in Latin. The concept of such organizations was an American development which grew slowly, Notre Dame being one of its earliest manifestations.)

The campus which Father Walsh now directed was the frequent beneficiary of the scientific genius of Father John A. Zahm. He was already utilizing the principle of audio-visual education, sprinkling public lectures with exciting experiments, to attract Catholic interest in science.

After the disastrous fire, Father Zahm was appointed campus fire chief. He installed a pump and strategic tanks of water around the campus. He also purchased a pump which could draw water from the lakes and fill the campus tanks within an hour.

Father Zahm purchased a dynamo-electric machine which powered a lamp of 2,500 candle power, permitting the Sorin Cadets to drill at night, and the Minims to play what may have well been a first—a night football game. A newspaper, commenting on an electric plant which would permit outdoor lighting on the campus, was quoted: "It seems to us that the learned gentlemen of Notre Dame are making scientific advancement pretty rapidly for people who are supposed to live mainly in the mists of the middle ages." It was only 1884 when the Statue of Our Lady, now atop the golden dome, received an electrically lighted crown.

Another of Father Zahm's enterprises combined scientific materials research with student recruitment. His practical talents soon discovered lower railroad rates for groups, and the appeal to families of having a priest-supervised train bringing their sons to Notre Dame. He established the tuition discount for more than one student from a family, and included the Saint Mary's girls in his shepherded excursions which extended to Mexico, New Mexico, Colorado, Wyoming, Arizona and intervening States. In 1882, he brought back 25 students from the Denver area in a special "palace car."

A *Scholastic* reporter, accompanying one of the Zahm homeward excursions, is high in his praise of the arrangements, of its benefits to students and parents. The trips prolonged the "vie intime" of the campus.

> At LaPorte, the Southern students changed cars, and at Chicago we parted those from Old and New Mexico, after hand-shakings and adieus, with hopes expressed of a general meeting at the University in September. We found a number of old students and other friends awaiting our arrival in Chicago. Father Zahm is planning a similar arrangement for his return.

Father Walsh organized a program to bring distinguished speakers to the campus who would inspire the students, widen the scope of their knowledge, and add distinction to the University by their involvement.

From the beginning, Notre Dame enjoyed phenomenal public relations, as we now call the program, without any of the now familiar mechanisms to create them. As far as I can determine from the records, I was the first person directly hired by the University administration to organize and disseminate academic publicity. That was in 1925. Even then, it was considered a nebulous if not dubious job, which is why I was happy to move to the Alumni Association in January of 1926.

Father Thomas Walsh implemented another great public relations program in 1883 for Notre Dame that has flourished through all the years since. Those who had been in Rome were familiar with the Papal award on each Laetare Sunday of a Golden Rose to some Catholic whose work for the Church has been outstanding. Professor Edwards, in a faculty discussion, proposed that Catholic laymen in the United States were not involved enough, or recognized enough, to evoke their best efforts for the Church in America. The two unrelated items, one a Vatican practice, the other a Notre Dame theory, were combined to create at Notre Dame the Laetare Medal, an award on the Laetare Sunday of each year to an American Catholic layman or -woman whose contribution to the advancement of Catholicism had been outstanding.

John Gilmary Shea, historian, was the first recipient in 1883. Patrick Keely, architect, was the 1884 medalist. In 1885 the medal was awarded to Eliza Allen Starr, poet and writer on religious art, a lecturer at Notre Dame, and the first woman so recognized. In 1886 the medal went to Gen. John Newton, soldier, scientist and engineer. Only in later years was the 1887 recipient publicly identified—Edward Preuss, who like St. Paul had at one time bitterly attacked the Church, to be converted later to an outstanding apostolate in it. In 1888, Patrick Hickey, distinguished editor, was the recipient. Thus, on the occasion of Sorin's jubilee, Notre Dame was well established as the crossroads of the Church in this recognition of the part American Catholic laymen were playing in it. The variety of distinction represented in the first six medalists already reflected its broad goal.

In June of 1883, Father Walsh celebrated the alumni Mass. Following the Mass, Bishop Watterson of Columbus laid the cornerstone of the new Science Hall. Confidence was expressed that it might further the work of the students who would soon enjoy its modern facilities.

The annual meeting elected Father General Sorin as honorary president of the Alumni Association; Father Dennis A. Clarke, president; Father J. Dinnen '65, Crawfordsville, Ind., first vice president; John G. Ewing, M. S. '77, Lancaster, O., second vice president; Timothy Howard '62, secretary; Joseph Lyons '62, treasurer; William Hoynes '69, orator, with George Sugg

'81, Chicago, as alternate; E. McNally, A. M. '64, Huntington, Indiana, poet, with Eugene Arnold '83, Washington, D.C., as alternate; and James Edwards '72, historian.

Father Sorin presided at the banquet, flanked by Father Walsh and by Msgr. Benoit, vicar-general of the Ft. Wayne diocese. Professor McNally acted as toastmaster, initiating toasts to Our Holy Father, Leo XIII, The President of the United States (Chester A. Arthur); the Press; the University of Notre Dame, and absent friends.

The *Scholastic*, in its Founder's Day issue of Oct. 13, 1883, reports an event of great moment even then, but of far greater and continuing importance throughout the subsequent life of Notre Dame:

> The great event of the past week was the placing of the colossal statue of the Blessed Virgin on the dome of the University. As is well known, since it was first brought to Notre Dame in the summer of 1880, the statue has been adorning the front porch of the main building, and awaiting the time when its pedestal—the dome—would be completed . . . Everything was ready by Wednesday afternoon, and slowly but surely the grand figure ascended to the roof of the College. On Thursday work was resumed, and at length, at five p.m., amid the ringing of bells, the statue was seen to rest firmly and securely on its grand pedestal. The statue is the work of the late Giovanni Meli of Chicago, and is the largest of its kind in the U.S. It stands 16 feet in height and weighs over 4,000 pounds. The work of raising it to its present position was skilfully accomplished under the direction of Alexander Staples of South Bend.
>
> 'The statue is on the dome!' was the general exclamation on Thursday night. Few and simple were the words, yet they contained a wealth of meaning. They announced the accomplishment of long-cherished desires of the heart, the filling up of a void too long open at Notre Dame, the crowning act in the public expression of honor to Her under whose patronage this home of religion and science is placed. Notre Dame—Our Lady. These two short words speak volumes in explanation and praise of the motive which has led to the erection of this glorious monument to the Mother of God. On the very first day—almost half a century ago—that Father Sorin and his little band took possession of this little spot of earth, it was called by Her name, consecrated to Her honor, and placed under Her protection. Through the long years that have followed, this confidence in Her watchful care has been signally rewarded, and most fittingly to find suitable manifestation of gratitude has ever been the desire of the venerable Founder and his spiritual children. Amid all the changes

wrought during the 37 years that preceded the great fire of 1879—while old buildings were torn down and new ones erected—while additions and enlargements were made, the statue of Our Lady has ever stood surmounting the main structure, and typifying the maternal care exercised over its inmates . . . Today this grand statue, so familiar to the visitor and student at Notre Dame, stands upon Her magnificent throne and, with extended arms, gives assurance of the continued protection of Her whom it presents.

The above inspiring sight greeted returning alumni in 1884. The annual meeting elected Father John Dinnen as president; Col. Hoynes first vice president; Florian Devoto, second vice president; Father Stoffel, secretary; Professor Lyons, treasurer; John Gibbons, orator; Father Alexander Kirsch, poet with George Sugg alternate and Professor Edwards, historian. The climate of progress on the campus seeped into the business meeting.

Among the important business transacted, a resolution expressive of the sense of the association touching the alumni scholarship, was introduced and unanimously adopted. In pursuance of it, a committee consisting of Father Stoffel, Col. Hoynes, and Professor Devoto, was appointed to notify the alumni of the action taken, and request responses in reference to same. The hope was expressed that scholarships, open to general competition, will hereafter be founded from time to time, and that the alumni may improve this opportunity to take the initial steps in the matter and found the first of them. Animated by a desire to further this laudable undertaking, Father T. E. Walsh, President of the University, expressed his willingness to contribute $100 toward it on behalf of the institution, and promised to give a like amount from year to year. This leaves but $200 to be raised annually by contributions from the alumni. It was the sense of the meeting that the matter ought to receive immediate attention and that the scholarship should be made available for a competitive examination before the commencement of the September term.

"A banquet followed, with Father Sorin flanked by Rt. Rev. Montes de Oca y Obregon and Father Dinnen. Toasts honored Leo XIII, President Arthur, and Associated Alumni, (evidently recognizing pride of accomplishment), and the press.

Father Walsh celebrated the alumni Mass at the 1885 commencement reunion. Father Daniel Spillard preached the sermon. Emphasis was on the magnificent decoration of the church by Luigi Gregori. Alumni were high in their praise that

weekend of both the church art and that found in the Main
Building, and of stained glass windows, by the Carmelites of Le
Mans, enhancing the Gregori works in the church.

New officers elected were Father Dinnen, president; Professor Hoynes, first vice president; Professor Devoto, second vice
president; Father Stoffel, secretary; Professor Lyons, treasurer;
Orville Chamberlain, orator; Maurice Francis Egan (a new and
distinguished name in Notre Dame faculty history), poet and
Professor Edwards, historian. Egan had written a volume of
poems in 1879 and offered the proceeds from this volume to
the rebuilding of Notre Dame after the fire. When Charles
Warren Stoddard, the distinguished author and professor, a bit
of an early liberal, found Indiana climate, and possibly Father
Walsh's enthusiasm for temperance, too much for him, Egan
was persuaded to take his place. He was a recognized man of
letters, later U.S. Ambassador to Denmark, and a distinctive and
cultured personality who exerted influence on the entire Notre
Dame community. His home, the legendary "Lilacs," was built
for him and so christened by him. It was a radiation center of
fine arts for both the University and South Bend.

The months between the annual alumni functions were not
barren. The "vie intime" was reflected in many ways. Students
were still few in numbers, as were alumni, and the contacts
between the two in their home areas were frequent. Similarly,
the mission activities of Notre Dame brought many religious
into alumni communities and homes. And always there was the
"literary correspondence" of the first constitution which provided a personal tie between alumni and faculty, updating their
knowledge of the campus and preserving the family spirit.

In June of 1886, a significant discussion at the annual alumni
meeting probably reflected the consciousness of the graduates
of the rich and changing patterns of the campus. It was proposed that the annual meeting be scheduled during the scholastic year, rather than at its close. New officers elected were:
Father E. J. McLaughlin '75, Clinton, Iowa, president; Father
Luke Evers '79, New York, first vice president; William P. Breen
'79, Ft. Wayne, second vice president; Father Stoffel, secretary;
Professor Lyons, treasurer; John Ewing '77, Lancaster, O., historian; William H. Johnston '85, East Townsend, O., poet and
Rev. T. O'Sullivan '59, Chicago, orator.

The suggestion of the preceding year to advance the annual
meeting date apparently died in discussion. The annual meeting
in the *Scholastic* of June 29, 1887, seemed to follow the older

pattern. New officers elected were: Father McLaughlin again, president; Father Evers and William Breen, vice presidents; Father Stoffel and Professor Lyons as secretary and treasurer; Hon. M. H. Keeley '72, Faribault, Minn., orator with Samuel T. Murdock '86, Michigan City, as alternate; William Johnston, poet with Dennis J. Hogan '74 as alternate.

These several years marked continuous progress, and the happy absence of any disaster. Presumably, alumni exerted effort toward the sopted scholarship program, but the economic and age factors of the membership undoubtedly modified their success in this early philanthropy. This ability of Notre Dame to create an air of prosperity, in the complete absence of it remained one of its major handicaps until the realistic Father A. Burns '88, launched the first major endowment campaign many years later (1921). But the mid-eighties were a constructive lull before the pleasant storm that marked Father Sorin's golden jubilee as a priest in 1888.

X

"Golden Is Thy Fame"

These words from a later talent, Father Charles L. O'Donnell, which are at present part of the alma mater song of Notre Dame, were never more meaningful than in 1888. This year marked the world celebration of the golden jubilee of the priesthood of Leo XIII, distinguished reigning Pontiff.

But at Notre Dame, inevitably, the focus was on the similar marking of the 50th year of the priesthood of Notre Dame's founder, Edward Frederick Sorin. Father Sorin did not hold the world allegiance of the Universal Church as did Leo, but he had far surpassed in stature, in high regard, and in recognition at home and abroad, the boundaries of the University which was his first and enduring love.

He was Superior General of the Congregation of Holy Cross. In 1882, his high place in the Church in America found him an invited guest at the Provincial Council in Cincinnati, and in 1884 he was invited to attend the Plenary Council of Baltimore, the largest assembly of Catholic bishops since the Council of Trent (1545-1563).

Great plans attended the efforts of his Notre Dame to express its deep regard. The first campus observance was for the family of Notre Dame closest to Sorin's heart—the students and faculty. On May 26, in the appropriate beauty of Washington Hall, a reception featured programs, prepared long and arduously, by the musical, oratorical and theatrical groups. Representatives of the senior, junior and minim divisions extended congratulatory messages to their patron.

On the same evening, after a band concert and artillery salutes on the campus,

74

...a handsome open barouche drawn by two coal black steeds emerged from the shady avenue leading to the University. Surrounded by the students, Professor John G. Ewing made a presentation speech in behalf of the students, as well as the alumni and the faculty who had contributed. After several trials had been made, and it was proved to the satisfaction of all that docility as well as fleetness was a quality of the horses, Fathers Sorin, Zahm and Corby, and Professor Edwards climbed into the carriage and drove off amidst student cheers.

In the light of the concentration of Notre Dame history and genius which the carriage then contained, the cheers could hardly have been more appropriate. If you note the absence of Father Walsh in this group, it was simply because he was in Europe at the time. Evident in the programs was Father Zahm's gifted direction, as acting President. Darkness revealed to the crowds the still thrilling sight of the incandescent lights shining "out of every window."

Father Sorin himself, patriarchal but vigorous and sonorous, celebrated the Mass on Trinity Sunday in the magnificent Church of the Sacred Heart. Father Corby, a happy and appropriate choice for the honor, preached on the life and works of Father Sorin.

Following this Mass, the jubilarian laid the cornerstone of the new and exciting student residence hall which was to bear his name. Indiana entered this ceremony by shortening it with the familiar phenomenon of rain.

A "copious French dinner" in tribute to the background of the guest of honor followed. One of the toasts was delivered by a student, James A. Burns. The thread of destiny did not then identify him as a successor to Sorin in both the presidency of Notre Dame and the provincialship of the Congregation of Holy Cross.

In June of the jubilee year, alumni, undoubtedly enjoying attendance at the preceding May celebration, and anticipating the great August observance proposed, held a modest reunion and business meeting. The softening process of a more affluent alumni society appeared in the alumni Mass: a half-hour later, schedule of the Father Walsh, back from Europe, was its celebrant. Father J. Fitzharris '68, New York City, preached a sermon described as "of a most eloquent and impressive character." New officers elected were: Rev. Andrew Morrissey '78, president; Rev. Luke Evers '79, first vice president; Ferd Kuhn

'83, Nashville, Tenn., second vice president; Father Stoffel, secretary; Professor Lyons, treasurer; John G. Ewing, historian; William P. Breen '77, orator with George Clarke '86 as alternate; and Harold Hayes '74, Chicago, poet with Denis J. Hogan '73 as alternate.

The school year ended, and the campus began preparations for August. The United States, too, was observing an historical year. President Grover Cleveland was opposing proposals of extravagance in government caused by a surplus in the national treasury!

At the ceremonies of the campus family observance in May, Father Sorin had said to the audience in Washington Hall:

> . . . . what intensifies still more my gratitude to God for my elevation to the sacred priesthood is the selection by God Himself of the rich field where I was to labor; oh, how often it has filled my heart with joy! It is not for me to state here the unspeakable consolations which awaited me in this new world, which I loved so dearly long before I landed upon its happy shores; and above all, on this glorious domain of the Queen of Heaven . . . Allow me then to declare here honestly that I claim but a very small fraction of the merits you assign me, but justly return it all to the Blessed Virgin herself, and to the devotedness of my modest and faithful colaborers in the field, already promising such an abundant harvest for the advance of science and the salvation of immortal souls.

Few who knew Notre Dame allowed this virtue of the founder's humility to deter their recognition of his accomplishments.

The attitude of the press generally was reflected in the *Baltimore Catholic Mirror*, commenting on the announced hiring of Maurice Francis Egan for a course in belles lettres at Notre Dame:

> The University of Notre Dame is one of the most, if not indeed the most, progressive Catholic educational institutions in America. Its growth within this past decade has been marvelous. Not only in respect to the number of scholars upon its rolls in this true, but chiefly in the means adopted to meet the requirements arising from this increase. The high standard of studies in each department of the University has been steadfastly maintained, and the tendency is to raise it still higher by the introduction of the newest features of the best educational systems of the world. . . .

The eloquent tributes at the August ceremonies of the jubilee contain volumes of appreciation for the stature already attained by the University and its founder. It is undoubtedly in the personages involved on that occasion that the conviction of these tributes to Sorin's labors and their fruits, and of the great future then unfolding, is best conveyed in these long years after.

Through Professor Howard's history at the time of Notre Dame's golden jubilee, and Father Hope's enlightening reasearch in his centennial history, the grandeur and significance of Father Sorin's own golden jubilee remains a vivid page in the annals of the University.

The visitors, including many alumni, were greeted by a Notre Dame Avenue decorated with arches flying the papal and American colors. At the campus entrance a log cabin was built to remind everyone of the only building that greeted the founder on Nov. 26, 1842. The facade of the Main Building was draped with bunting and hundreds of American flags fluttered from its windows and those of the surrounding buildings. The church entrance was decorated with a double arch, featuring the papal colors and golden roses.

Highest ranking of the visitors was James Cardinal Gibbons, Archbishop of Baltimore. (I was privileged to see the same venerable Cardinal again on the campus of Notre Dame, when he attended the ceremonies of the diamond jubilee of the University in the war-torn year of 1917.)

The arrival of Cardinal Gibbons on his first visit was delayed several hours because of his earlier participation in the funeral of General Phil Sheridan, of Civil War fame. Finally, at dusk, a large escort accompanied by the band announced the cardinal's approach. He occupied Father Sorin's carriage, with Father William Corby. The Ancient Order of Hibernians were a part of the honor escort, as were the colorful Polish Lancers.

Assembled to greet him were leaders of the American hierarchy long familiar to him—Archbishop John Ireland, newly appointed to the See of St. Paul; Archbishop Elder, of Cincinnati; Bishop Dwenger of the host Diocese of Fort Wayne; Bishop Burke, of the frontier See of Cheyenne; the eloquent Bishop Spalding of Peoria; the Bishops Ryan, one of Buffalo and the other of Alton; Bishop Jansen of Belleville; Bishop Watterson of Columbus; Bishop Gilmour of Cleveland; Bishop Phelan of Pittsburgh; Bishop Richter of Grand Rapids; and Bishop Keane of Richmond, who had been appointed rector of the new Catholic University of America. The new university, to be established in the nation's capital, was in large measure the result of the zeal and effort of Archbishop Ireland. But it is a tribute to Notre Dame, and to its esteem among the American bishops, that Bishop Keane remained at Notre Dame for a

month after the jubilee, composing the original Statutes of
Catholic University. This document now forms a part of Notre
Dame's Archives. Another significant development of the jubilee was the announcement that Father Sorin and Father Walsh
had expressed the desire to make Notre Dame auxiliary of the
new University and to send their best students to it for graduate
studies.

Holy Cross College, the graduate school of theology of the
Congregation of Holy Cross on the Catholic University campus,
was the product of this cooperation. The future of Catholic
University, at the time of its inception, was to be a center for
the best in Catholic graduate studies. The young Catholic colleges, like Notre Dame, were still struggling to develop adequate
undergraduate facilities and faculties, and welcomed this effort
toward acceleration of an outstanding graduate school within
the Church. Notre Dame more than kept its bargain. It was in
1893 that one of the great young faculty members and alumni
left the Notre Dame faculty to join the faculty of the promising
Catholic University. Albert Zahm, an 1893 graduate and a
significant leader in the field of aeronautical science, had, with
Octave Chanute organized the first Congress of Aeronautical
Science in the United States in conjunction with the Columbian
Exposition in 1893 in Chicago. Albert Zahm's work at Notre
Dame, and his subsequent accomplishments at Catholic University are a vital part of the early development of successful
aeronautical science in America.

Upon the cardinal's arrival, Father Walsh read an address of
welcome in Latin. Weary from duties and traveling, the cardinal
retired early to rest for the extensive program of the following
day, appropriately the Feast of the Assumption of the Blessed
Virgin Mary.

The program began at 6 a.m. with the consecration of the
Church of the Sacred Heart by Bishop Dwenger. This ceremony
continued until 9 a.m., when Bishop Burke of Cheyenne blessed
the bell in the steeple, naming it St. Anthony of Padua.

The public was admitted to the church at 9:30. A procession
of uniformed Catholic societies proceded the general crowd into
the church—the Hibernians, the St. Hedwige Society, and the
Knights of St. Casimir. Father Sorin, the patriarchal focus of
the occasion, celebrated a Low Mass, to which Leo XIII had
attached a plenary indulgence.

Shortly after this first Mass, the Solemn Mass of the Jubilee
was begun in the splendor of the newly consecrated church. A

long line of clergy and acolytes had escorted Cardinal Gibbons, who pontificated, to the church from the Main Building. The sanctuary was filled with the members of the hierarchy. The music was Haydn's Third Mass. The majestic organ was assisted by the choir from the Jesuit Church in Chicago.

Archbishop Ireland delivered a memorable sermon in commemoration of the founder, appropriately based on St. Matthew's text of the increase of talents by the good and faithful servant of the Lord. Commenting on the outpouring of friends, Ireland said,

> A prince of the Church .. is enthroned in the sanctuary, and around him are grouped archbishops, bishops, and priests from all parts of the United States and from Canada. Here, too, are laymen, distinguished in all walks of life, non-Catholics as eager as Catholics to give evidence of extreme veneration. From distant lands come messages as warm and as sincere as devoted hearts can make them. The Eternal City is not silent. Congratulatory letters have come from the Cardinal Prefect of the Propaganda; and he who rules the Universal Church, the vice regent of the Master Himself, pours, for this occasion, upon Notre Dame special and unusual blessings. These facts have a significance, and it is this: Father Sorin has fulfilled the mission confided to him by Providence, and he stands before us today, the great priest who in his day pleased God, and was found just, full and complete in his works . . . The prime purpose to which Father Sorin directed those who placed themselves under his guidance was the education of youth. He understood the power belonging to the intellect, and he resolved he would do his utmost to wield that power for the triumph of virtue and religion. Notre Dame and Saint Mary's are monuments of his zeal. These monuments will endure and will make his memory immortal . . .

Inevitably, a French dinner was served to the guests. One signal departure from the French tradition, however, was the drinking of the toast in water. The Catholic Total Abstinence Society was one of the great movements being encouraged by the hierarchy. It had received great attention and impetus at Notre Dame, where Father Walsh, the President, was himself an ardent and total abstainer. It is probable that he welcomed the opportunity of a French feast to emphasize this cause.

Following the dinner, several University buildings were blessed by Bishop Watterson and placed under the special protection of Our Lady. Archbishop Ireland from the steps of the Main Building delivered a more generally oriented address on the subject of Christian education. Cardinal Gibbons then spoke briefly, paying tribute to the work of Father Sorin.

A supper followed the afternoon exercises. One of the features of this event was the presentation of the pallium, a symbol of the archepiscopacy, which had been brought from Rome, to Archbishop Ireland. Cardinal Gibbons made the presentation, which made the previously announced appointment official in the Church.

Fireworks and music closed this greatest celebration day in the history of the University. There was hope that the venerable Founder would be a part of the 50th anniversary of the University itself. But this magnificent personal tribute turned out to be the final major recognition of his long career. The scope of this jubilee had already caused the decision of the University to defer its own 50-year observance to the anniversary of the Charter, 1894. Father Sorin died in 1893.

In a letter in the *Scholastic* of August, 1888, to thank those who had joined in his jubilee, Father Sorin wrote,

> Never in my life did I feel so completely at a loss to know how to thank properly the numerous and beloved friends whose delightful presence and beautiful offerings, or kind expressions of regard by letters or telegrams, have most joyfully surprised me during the past week. May God reward them for their generous and spontaneous feelings. He alone can repay them as they deserve; and as long as I live I will continue to pray for them, to the best of my ability. Indeed, I have no words to express the feelings of my heart . . . Fortunately, I find relief in the well-known fact that my sacerdotal golden jubilee, on the Feast of the Assumption, was only the occasion, not the cause, of the great manifestations we all admired so much, directed as they were exclusively to the honor and glory of the Blessed Mother of God, reigning here supreme with universal love on the little domain now and forever consecrated to her glorious name.

The tribute to Father Sorin was merited. As founder, he had from the beginning of Notre Dame been its leader, in ever sense of the word. By the time of his death, the University had been for so long the synonym of its head that the tradition never completely died. The President has continued to share the identiy of Notre Dame as it has progressed under his patricular direction.

The sunsets of the campus continued to be followed by the sunrises. Even as the shadows of Sorin's years deepened, the sun was already rising on the increasing numbers of outstanding men who were dedicated to his mission, to his institution, and to Our Lady. There were sorrows. The cholera epidemic had taken some of his beloved young priests and brothers. The brilliant Dillons, Patrick and James, were lost in comparative youth. Father Lemonnier's death at the age of 35 was a deep disappointment. And now, only a week after the jubilee, as though with his customary courtesy he had not wished to cast any shadow on it, Professor Joseph A. Lyons died. He had, as I have noted, received his entire enducation at Notre Dame. His rich reciprocal devotion to the University was already a legend. The *Scholastic*, reporting his joining the faculty, said,

> He then entered upon the duties of his chosen profession, and became one of the most efficient and popular professors Notre Dame ever had. For 26 years he has been the soul and leading member of the faculty. Professor Lyons seems to have been born to govern students. He had a perfect control over every class he ever taught, and his success as a teacher was commensurate with his power of government, especially in the classics and elocution which had a special attraction for him. He was the very life of the student societies, both religious and literary. In giving the students the necessary preparation for our public exhibitions, Professor Lyons seemed to be indispensable.

Four years later, dedicating a monument which his former students had erected in his memory, in the Community Cemetery which contained so many friends and colleagues of his years at Notre Dame, his confrère, Colonel Hoynes, said of Lyons:

> We have come here to pay our last solemn tribute to the memory of one whom many of you knew and loved; a man who for 40 years was associated with the University of Notre Dame; a man whose life was interwoven with its history. For all that period it could not be said that the memory of Professor Joseph A. Lyons and his work and his labor could be dissociated from the progress and building up of this great University. Hence you and I, and all of us, feel a certain sense of sorrowful pleasure in meeting here under these circumstances ... This noble shaft fittingly symbolizes and illustrates the affection for him of the old students of Notre Dame. There it stands, modest and plain, like the man whose character it typifies.

It is one of the unfortunate conditions of the careers of men in institutions like the Church, and Notre Dame, where humility is a virtue, that the first realization of their greatness often comes with their obituaries. The compensation seems to be that the realization frequently creates a richness of memory and a strength of desire to make up in emulation what was missed in their lifetime, which in fact continues the reality of their contribution beyond these graves.

Father Sorin, accompanied by Father Zahm, a cherished companion on such trips, made his last trip to Europe in May, 1891. He returned to Notre Dame, in impaired health, but in 1892 he visited the Atlantic seaborad to rest. The trip was short, and he presided at the General Chapter of the Congregation, at Notre Dame, which opened on the Feast of the Assumption.

A modest observance, on Nov. 27 of 1892, marked the 50th anniversary of the arrival at Notre Dame of Father Sorin and the brothers. Solemn High Mass was celebrated by Archbishop Riordan of San Francisco, who had himself been a student in the early years of the University. An address from the students of Father Sorin was delivered by Michael A. Quinlan, later a priest of Holy Cross and a vital force in the growth of the Alumni Association. Father Sorin, far from well, still spoke feelingly to his beloved community. Father Sorin was 80 years old on February 6, 1893. In June he was far from good health, but received the apostolic delegate, Archbishop Satolli, returning from a visit to the great Columbia Exposition in Chicago.

Father Sorin's condition was aggravated by two deaths of priests who had been close to him. Father Alexis Granger, a lifelong companion of Father Sorin, his first vice president, and for all his life the prefect of religion of the University, died on July 26. But on July 17, Notre Dame had lost its President, Father Thomas E. Walsh, a man and a priest greatly admired by Father Sorin, whom he had recognized in his seminary years and quickly elevated to responsibilities which Walsh had discharged with great competence. The illness had been visible for several years, and Father Walsh told friends at the 1893 commencement that it was his last.

He was in his 12th year as President, but was only 40 when he died. Father Sorin himself weakened, and on Oct. 31, the month of the traditional and memorable founder's day, he died.

Bishop Rademacher of Fort Wayne celebrated the Requiem Mass. The sermon was preached by the distinguished American churchman, Archbishop Elder of Cincinnati. Rome, the spiritual home of Father Sorin, and France, the home of his family and his Congregation, sent condolences, as did all of America.

The year was one which added lustre indeed to the growing number of graves, so eloquent in their reflection of the faith, and courage, the hard work, the unselfish devotion to students so far beyond the call of ordinary duty, the great range of origin, the reminiscences of differences resolved in charity, of the fraternity of priests, the fraternity of brother, the fraternity of the dedicated laymen constantly sharing the challenges of Notre Dame—merging in this cemetery into the last brotherly round-table of a greater King.

For here was no guilty Guinevere or flawed Lancelot, but a joyous knighthood in the service of an eternal Queen, Notre Dame.

XI

"Gladiators of God"

I use this strong figure from Chesterton's poem written for Notre Dame, because it contains in essence the playing-field spirit of Notre Dame.

The subject comes up here because, in a sense, this is the point in Notre Dame history and alumni involvement where the myth and the truth of its dependence on athletics should be identified as such.

The magnificient and prestigious sacerdotal golden jubilee of the founder occurred at a time when the only venturing of Notre Dame into the new intercollegiate game of football had been three unofficial instructional games with an older University of Michigan team, arranged by two Notre Dame alumni, George DeHaven and W. Harless, who were then playing on the Michigan team. Harvard and Yale had adopted the rules of English rugby football in the '70s, to throw the American balance away from soccer and toward football.

Notre Dame students, in the nature of the all-male, isolated, and spacious campus, had always been urged to exercise. In describing the time given to exercise, the *Silver Jubilee History* states, "This protracted attention to books thus alternating with recreation is not found to have any bad effect on the health. On the contrary, the regularity of life, the simplicity of diet, the removal of too engrossing or otherwise noxious forms of excitement is found eminently adapted to conduce to the formation of the *mens sana in corpore sano.*"

Rugby was played. Baseball was even more popular. Boat races were highly developed competitive events. Student participation was almost total. According to a report 120 students participated in one rugby game. Brother Paul, patron of sports,

84

who arranged the first games with Michigan, fostered the strong campus sports spirit. Prizes of barrels of cider or of apples, would spur on the final competitions.

Certainly victories and gate receipts did not motivate the departure into intercollegiate competition. Michigan, gracious tutor, won five games from Notre Dame before losing twenty-one years later to the 1909 team, heralded thereafter as the new "Champions of the West." It would be the era of the "Four Horsemen" (1921-1925) when a post-World War I American public, clamoring for the peaceful excitement of the playing fields, found its greatest response in the genius and showmanship of Knute Rockne.

In 1914 Rockne was graduated from Notre Dame in science, an outstanding student of chemistry, the product of another great alumnus, Father Julius Nieuwland '99. Father Nieuwland was himself an earlier student under Father John A. Zahm. He had won a prize in his own graduation year with an essay "Keats As a Poet," which may explain his enthusiasm for the sharp mind of Rockne, and which indicates the depth and breadth of the interests and education of both men. Rockne was offered a teaching post at Notre Dame in chemistry, but, based on his experience as player and postgraduate coach under Jesse Harper, he elected the coaching career, assuming the head coach spot in 1917, to the ultimate lasting good of Notre Dame and football. The point to remember is simply that Rockne found a strong University, with a rich tradition and a wholesome respect for both classroom and sports, when he entered in 1909 as a track athlete. He nurtured and expanded these strengths.

Father Nieuwland was urged to join the Catholic University faculty but he, too, chose to remain on the Notre Dame campus, working his far-reaching experiments—notably those which produced the basic formula of Dupont's neoprene—in the limited facilities of increasingly cramped quarters in Science Hall, teaching classes and for a time administering the College of Science as its dean.

These were truly great alumni.

The *Scholastic*, in 1887, commenting on the first game with Michigan, says, " . . . This occasion has started an enthusiastic football boom, and it is hoped the coming years will witness a series of these contests . . . Father Walsh thanked the Ann Arbor team for their visit, and assured them of the cordial reception that would always await them at Notre Dame."

The Notre Dame men who played on that first team became outstanding alumni, a number of them attending in 1924 a campus celebration in their honor, linking that pioneer effort with the national championship stature of the Four Horsemen, then on their way to repeating that achievement. Jewett, Cusack, Luhn, Cartier, Houck, Fehr, Nelson, Melady, Sawkins, Hepburn, Springer, Prudhomme, O'Regan and Maloney were hardy pioneers!

I am not underestimating the history, the tradition, or the stature of athletics at Notre Dame. Certainly the tremendous leadership which the Alumni Association has received from former athletes during its long history has been a constant tribute to the constructive quality of sports, the validity of the sports tradition and an eloquent testimonial to the coaches, most of them alumni as well. If the overall space for sports is limited, as this story must be in all its facets, it will be primarily because this exciting and glamorous field of University sports effort, involving the public and the press, has been so covered in song and story as to need little more for its understanding.

One more thing does need comment, strictly as a part of alumni history: The appearances of Notre Dame teams in all sports, in all parts of the United States, meeting increasingly the best teams of other colleges and universities, presenting young men of outstanding character in Notre Dame uniforms, receiving warm treatment from the press and from the communities involved, especially the Catholic. This has been a great force in preserving the widespread alumni of Notre Dame in a closeknit family. The program has been a public relations factor for the University beyond purchase price. No system of new student recruitment, nonathletic as well as athletic, can equal the impact of the teams. It has been so constructively conducted that it has been, within the campus system, a career training for the many alumni who later have coached college and secondary teams around the United States. The decision to send campus teams to the four corners of America has been nothing other than to recognize the alumni who come from, and go back to, those same four corners, and the national character of the University, which from its origins was heralded far beyond its borders.

That the ultimate profit from football became in later years a substantial contribution to the general progress of the University, which had fostered it during its deficit decades, is a fact of mutual satisfaction. These profits, receding in ratio in the late surge of total University costs, continue to make possible the scope and diversity of all intercollegiate and intramural sports, which are continuing the long tradition of *mens sana in corpore sano.*

The first baseball game on record was also played against the University of Michigan on April 21,1892. Unlike football, and reflecting perhaps the priority of enthusiasm on the campus at that time for the popular American pastime, Notre Dame won that historic game 6 to 4. It was also apparently easier to come by collegiate competition as the early limited scheduels reveal. Purdue and Minnesota played in 1894, both winning. Michigan beat Notre Dame in 1895 but Notre Dame defeated Illinois, Wisconsin and Purdue.

Baseball thrived. From 1906 to 1908 Notre Dame reached its peak, winning 60 games and losing only 9. Winning 20 games each season, Notre Dame lost only 5 in 1906, 3 in 1907, and 1 in 1908. The latter was the best season in Notre Dame history. The team made a swing through the East and won over such teams as Williams, Darmouth, Boston, Fordham, Syracuse and Georgetown. Vermont was the one opposing team that won.

That was the year the Alumni Association permanently re-organized. In "la vie intime" the strengthening of one member strengthens all.

The record of Notre Dame in the big leagues is long and distinguished, from Adrian "Cap" Anson to Carl Yastrzemski. Those records are available. But for a sample glimpse into this rich vein of sports history consider: Roger Bresnahan, George Cutshaw, Bert Daniels, Ed Reulbach, John Dubuc, Bill Lathrop, Mike Powers, Frank Shaughnessy or Cy Williams. The teams had no coaches, or only unpaid player coaches, in those early years.

Baseball offers, still, a major case history in our thesis that alumni have woven an integral part in Notre Dame history. Clarence J. Kline, who won monograms in baseball in 1915-16-17, returned to coach at Notre Dame in 1933 and has continued in that capacity through 1972. "Jake" was also a popular teacher of mathematics.

Basketball did not attain the overall popularity of baseball or football, in spite of what was to become its later designation in high school circles as "Hoosier Hysteria." Five games were played in 1898 and 1899, against Rush Medical and several non-college fives. It was 1908 when a full schedule of games (29 of them) appeared. This was still against an odd assortment of opponents, only Wabash, Michigan Agricultural (now State), Indiana, Lewis and Armour Institutes and Lake Forest having a collegiate ring of identity.

Track achieved a stronger start because of the emergence of outstanding track men from the natural training ground of the Notre Dame campus. Hal Jewett, later an automobile manufacturer in Detroit, was the first name to flash, scoring 15 points for the only Notre Dame representation in an invitational meet at the University of Michigan on May 24, 1890. Jewett achieved the outstanding marks, for that era, of 10 seconds for the 100-yard; 21.4 for the 220; 49.8 for the 440; 4:58 for the mile; 5 ft. 10½ in. for the high jump; 21 ft. 8½ in. for the broad jump; and 39 ft. 10 in. for the shot put. Marks long surpassed, but amazing then. Small wonder that Jewett's feats comprised the whole track record until 1898, when Notre Dame was invited to a meet with Chicago, Wisconsin, Northwestern, Illinois and Minnesota. Notre Dame scored fourth with 12 points, but the occasion reflects a foundation for Notre Dame's later expectations of membership in the Midwest group that eventually became the "Big Ten."

Among names that jump from the monogram lists of those late '90s are several of multiple later significance: M.A. Quinlan, later M.A. Quinlan, C.S.C., officer and ardent alumnus in the Alumni Association; T.A. Steiner, basketball, later to come back from an engineering career to become a member of the Congregation of Holy Cross, Dean of the College of Engineering, and Provincial of the Indiana Province; and Father John F. Farley, football, basketball and track, one of the great hall rectors of all time, known variously as "King" and "Pop," a patron saint of interhall athletics particularly.

On the playing fields of Notre Dame were won some of its great alumni administrative and prestige battles, if we may borrow a thought.

Frank Hering was the first football coach of record consequence. He was later editor of the magazine of the Fraternal Order of Eagles, and nationally acknowledged "Father of Mother's Day." He was non-Catholic, but an active and ardent alumnus, one of the major Presidents of the Alumni Association.

Louis J. Salmon, Notre Dame's first "All-American" and a legend, was both player and coach, followed in the ensuing years by hit-and-miss coaches until 1909 when Frank Longman came from Michigan and coached the team as the first of its professional coaches. He was aided by an alumnus, Edwin Lynch, and succeeded by L.H. Marks and the young alumnus quarterback, Don Hamilton, the latter another of the non-Catholic alumni to become president of the Alumni Association.

Jesse Harper assumed the reins in 1913. He was assisted by a great alumnus athlete, Howard "Cap" Edwards, in his first year, and for the rest of his five years as football coach by Knute Rockne, who succeeded him in 1917. It was during this time, through the able coaching and through the aggressiveness of two later Alumni Association presidents, John P. Murphy '12, and William E. Cotter Sr. '13, that Notre Dame, escaping a restrictive scheduling policy of its neighbors, and meeting alumni welcome from its scattered family, became a nation-wide competitor.

South Dakota, Army, Penn State, Texas, Yale, Syracuse, Nebraska, Rice Institute and the Haskell Indians appeared on the football schedules from 1913 to 1917.

Rockne, Anderson, Chevigny, Layden, Leahy, McKeever, Devore, Brennan, Kuharich—all but McKeever alumni—took their turns for varying tenures as head coach or acting head coach. They compiled a total record that brought Notre Dame to the top of the won-lost achievements of American college teams.

In 1964, Notre Dame again turned to a non-alumnus, Ara Parseghian. Parseghian seems, like Rockne, to have found at Notre Dame the ingredients from which his particular talents can fashion consistently good teams, sometimes champions.

In baseball Frank Hering was also the first coach of record. Other alumni, Robert Lynch, Harry Curtis, Fred Williams among them, appear between Hering and Jesse Harper. Charles E. "Gus" Dorais succeeded Harper. In 1920, Walter Halas was brought from Illinois. In 1923 Rockne, as director of athletics, brought in George Keogan from Valparaiso. With an interim two years under Tommy Mills from Beloit, Keogan coached baseball until 1933 when the long tenure of alumnus "Jake" Kline began.

Alumni, Frank Hering and Fred Powers, are the first basketball coaches of record, in 1897-1898 and 1898-1899. Non-alumni, Bert Maris and Jesse Harper, appear from 1907 through 1917, when Charles E. Dorais took over. Walter Halas coached basketball for three years, 1920-1923, and George Keogan, 1923 until his death in 1943. Alumni Edward "Moose" Krause, John Jordan, and John Dee are among the successors in the interim since Keogan's death. At this writing, Notre Dame has turned again to a non-alumnus, Richard F. "Digger" Phelps, of Yale and Fordham, to direct the basketball destiny of the University.

In track, the talented and versatile Frank Hering was the first coach of record. A South Bend resident of track prestige, John "Banty" Engledrum, succeeded Hering. Following a coachless season, 1904-1905, and defeats by Indiana and Purdue in those years, William A. Draper, one of the all-time track greats of Notre Dame, coached the team, to be succeeded by the athletic regimes of Bert Maris, Jesse Harper for a single year, and Knute Rockne. Track had been Rockne's major interest when he came to Notre Dame and, even at the height of his football fame, he never lost his interest in its advancement. Rockne coached track from 1914 to 1927, with the exception of one year when he turned the job over to one of his outstanding cross-country stars, John Wendland who was succeded by John Nicholson. During that period, the teams did not set the track world on fire, but Notre Dame stars kept the University in the track headlines, from dual meets to Olympic games. Bill Hayes, Gus Desch, Tom Lieb, Ed Meehan, Earl Gilfillan, John Montague, Tom "Cy" Kasper, Gene Oberst, Paul Kennedy, Paul Harrington, Bud Barr, Jim Stack, Jimmy Murphy, Jack Elder, Greg Rice and Bernie Coughlin, were among names that added to the rich traditions of such earlier men as Jewett, Corcoran, Eggeman, Steers and Wasson.

The active era of intercollegiate sports that began in the years under Father Thomas Walsh had not been held up by an opposition of those who preceded him at Notre Dame. This was simply the dawning of the age of intercollegiate athletics on the national scene. This was not without opposition, as the *Scholastic* of February 1898 indicates:

> The following statistics, taken from the Literary Digest, give the ratio of deaths resulting from the various sports: swimming, 1350, boating 986, hunting 654, bicycling 264, horseback riding 333, ice boating 22, football 11. If these figures mean anything, it is the prohibition of all athletic sports. There is not justice in suppressing football and allowing the other more dangerous sports to continue. Without football the physical side of college life would be paralyzed.

The *Scholastic* of that same date adds a note that reflects an old criticism and a consistent answer, from that day to this:

As a rule, people are of the opinion that football players are poor students. It is not so at Notre Dame. The average standing of the varsity football player in 1897 was nine per cent higher than the general student average. The inference drawn from this must be that students had better spend their recreation at playing football instead of lounging around the smoking room.

The century ended on a happy athletic note for football, as expressed in the letter from the University of Notre Dame to Warren A. Cartier '87, Ludington, Mich.: "Grateful for the generosity which prompted you to bestow on your alma mater an enclosed field to be used in perpetuity for the athletic games and contests of the students, the University of Notre Dame offers you this assurance of thankfulness. The gift will be forever known as the Cartier Athletic Field, and your name will be inscribed on the list of eminent benefactors of Notre Dame. By your generous gift you have earned the gratitude of the University, and of the students, present and future, to whom you have set a wholesome and conspicuous example by your loyalty to your Alma Mater and your solicitude for her welfare."

This was the long-time loyal alumnus, for years successor to Prof. Lyons as treasurer of the Alumni Association, and for a term its president. The words "perpetuity" and "forever" were often recorded by emotions of genuine appreciation that occasionally overlooked the contingencies of future changes. Like Knute Rockne after him, Warren Cartier would prefer to have the Notre Dame Stadium called just that. But the University has kept its basic covenant, continuing the Cartier Field designation for those playing fields East of the original location, which is now occupied by the Memorial Library.

In 83 seasons, Notre Dame football teams have won 534 games, lost 145, and tied 38. This is a .786 winning percentage. Rockne's percentage was .898; Frank Leahy's .888; Ed McKeever achieved .800 in the war year of 1944; and Elmer Layden produced .783.

The multiple and glorious records of sports are available in other publications. But the alumni of football, which is the sport in which public acclaim and awards have been most evident, who have brought publicity and prestige to Notre Dame, and whose exploits have contributed to the enjoyment and prestige of all alumni, ought not to be dismissed without at

least a mention of such signal and competitive bonus awards as
Angelo Bertelli, John Lujack, Leon Hart, John Lattner, Paul
Hornung and John Huarte received in the Heisman Trophy:
Leon Hart and John Lattner twice, and Jim Lynch, in the
Maxwell Trophy; George Connor and Bill Fischer in the Out-
land Trophy and Walt Patulski in the recently established Vince
Lombardi Trophy. Even dearer to the academic heart of the
University are the Notre Dame Academic All-Americans: Joe
Heap, three years; Don Schaefer, Bob Wetoska, Bob Lehmann,
Tom Regner, Jim Lynch, Jim Smithberger, George Kunz, Jim
Reilly and Tom Gatewood, two years, and Larry Di Nardo, Joe
Theisman and Greg Marx, one year.

I like a general observation made by D.C. "Chet" Grant,
alumnus, monogram man, in his interesting book, *Before
Rockne at Notre Dame:*

> I doubt that Notre Dame's greatest football stars have
> identified themselves with the Round Table knights, or cru-
> saders like Richard the Lionhearted, and Raymond or God-
> frey the Protector; or Cuchulain of the Red Branch Knights
> of ancient Eire. Allow for poetic fervor and hyperbole. But
> there's no secret that Notre Dame's teams have been ac-
> claimed by two generations of Americans for their distinctive
> spirit: that incorporeal stuff lighter than gossamer, stronger
> and more resilient than the toughest coiled spring; that con-
> tagious exuberance of disciplined and schooled *esprit de
> corps* without which no group enterprise of consequence can
> succeed in fair competition—as in football, war, or a market-
> ing campaign . . .

Our Lady, Father Sorin and football are not the University.
In fact, they have suffered identity crises in these recent years.
But to those who enjoyed the logic of Father Thomas Crumley,
or should have, it is only necessary to try to imagine the
University of Notre Dame without them. "All for one and one
for all."

There is so much unsaid in this high spot approach that I
shrink from the consequences. On the other hand, justice has
been done, will be done over and over again and can be achieved
individually, by those of more detailed sports persuasion. The
task for me is to get on with the story of the development of
the Alumni Association of this University.

XII

Who Was
Rev. Andrew Morrissey?

Father Andrew Morrissey, first of all, was the seventh priest of the Congregation of Holy Cross to become President of the University of Notre Dame. He assumed that office in 1893, at the age of 33, allegedly at the death-bed request of his predecessor, Father Thomas Walsh, whose vice president he had been. Father Morrissey, in one of the more apparent patterns of the weave of destiny, came to Notre Dame from Ireland at the age of 12 because of the stories he had heard from his cousin, Brother Bernard, CSC, back from Notre Dame in 1870 for a visit.

Father Morrissey was a brilliant student, said to have taught some of his younger Minim compatriots alebra when he was only 12. He was professed in 1880 and ordained in 1884. He received his A.B. from Notre Dame in 1878 and his A.M. in 1880. He was President of Notre Dame from 1893 to 1905.

The question in the title stems from my inability to reconcile the analysis of Father Morrissey as a man with little more than prep school aspirations for Notre Dame, with little encouragement for scholars and with a fear of debt which opposed the expansion which was already a hallmark of Notre Dame when he took over its direction—and the expanding story of Notre Dame during his presidency.

I have become convinced that the answer lies in the part of the description which says that Father Morrissey was easy to get along with, and was in effect adept in the desirable arts of politics. There are other factors which may have obscured some of his accomplishments. He began office in the deep shadows of the deaths of Father Thomas Walsh, Father Alexis Granger and

Father Sorin. Since Father Sorin had been regarded, if benevolently, as the real director of University destinies, no matter who might be President, it would stand to reason that a kindly and competent heir to this first adminstation freed from the real or implied domination, would not use his authority flagrantly. And, if he were a financial realist, he might pursue a moderate course in faculty development understably chafing to the idealism and the convictions of a direct scholar like Father John A. Zahm. The selection of Father Zahm as provincial, on the death of Father William Corby, may have spotlighted the disagreement, if any, with Morrissey's slower pace—in which case academic history has usually been unkind to the conservative.

Some evidence had already been building that helps explain the absence of some of the older forms without seeming loss of the substance of progress.

For example, in 1889, the alumni reunion report, in addition to listing Father Morrissey, then vice president of Notre Dame, as the newly elected president of the Alumni Association, spotlighted the increasing strength of the Chicago alumni.

> One hundred fifty 'old boys' constituted the delegation from Chicago that arrived Tuesday evening. Accompanied by friends, they made up a special train. It was intended that they should march in procession, headed by a brass band, from the city to the College, but the terrible rainstorm (frequently falling on reunion alumni heads) interfered with the programme ... All wore appropriate badges, and the train upon which they came was handsomely decorated. We hope the example given by the Chicago boys will be followed by others, and thus strengthen the bonds of union between alma mater and old-time students.

In 1908, the *Dome*, The Notre Dame yearbook, was to say "Although the old students and graduates of Notre Dame have been representative men in every phase of human activity and although they have done much for their alma mater, they have not for many years had an organized Alumni Association. . . ." and "The total number of living graduates is between six and seven hundred," it is clear, therefore, that the alumni spotlight was about to turn from the single commencement reunion meeting of a family reunion style, to a more serious development of the concept of an Alumni Association, while still enjoying the traditional mingling of the commencement weekend, but with the added off-campus functions which would ultimately grow in scope and diversity. Several communities were even then organizing alumni clubs. But the predominance of Chicago was manifest.

Father Morrissey's fellow officers in 1889 were William T. Ball '77, first vice president; George Sugg '81, second vice president; Father Stoffel '76, secretary; Professor William Hoynes '72, treasurer; George Clark '87, orator with Albert Brown '86 as alternate; John G. Ewing '77, historian and Mark Foote '74, poet with Dennis Hogan '73 as alternate.

Maurice Francis Egan, writing in the *Scholastic* of January, 1890, made some interesting comments on Sorin Hall, a phenomenon in Catholic higher education, which had intrigued him in his first year as a memeber of the Notre Dame faculty:

> Catholic colleges in the United States find themselves confronted by conditions which seem to require adjustment of time honored methods of discipline. The Declaration of Independence, as interpreted in our country, has come to mean that a son is equal to his father, and entitled to a voice in the manner and matter of his instruction and education. Whether this be right or wrong, it is de facto, and it must be considered by the heads of educational institutions . . . It is certain that boys from the age of 17 to 21 need restraint—or rather, restrictive influence; for at that time there seems to be a special league of the world, the flesh and the devil against them. The world of the college town is too prone to look indulgently on the sins of the students and perhaps to play the part of Falstaff, not without a thought of profit, to their Prince Hal. If everybody concerned would be entirely frank, there is no doubt that residence of students outside college bounds would be condemned . . .
>
> Notre Dame has shown how to draw older students to its lecture rooms; it has made an audacious experiment which, now that it is so thoroughly successful, seems to have been the only thing that could have been done. All of us who are interested in Catholic education desire, above all things, to see our colleges well filled with those older students who drift to what are called nonsectarian schools but which are more dangerous to religion and morals than the professedly sectarian schools. In the latter, belief in God and respect for the Commandments are at least a part of public teaching. I confess that no question, social or political, seems to me more important than this: How shall we keep our own?. . . . As an anxious observer of the progress of Catholic higher education—as a student of the method of the Catholic colleges—as a man too well experienced in the objections which are made against them—as a teacher who puts a quiet environment above all things, except morality, in a student's life, I beg leave to call attention to this new departure in discipline at Notre Dame. The success of Sorin Hall marks an epoch and the beginning of a synthesis between traditions and the demands of the present time.

The "beacon and bridge" concept scores again.

In 1890, the Associated Alumni elected Father Nathan J. Mooney '77, of the Cathedral of the Holy Name, Chicago, as president; Mark Foote '73, first vice president; John Ewing '77, second vice president; Col. Hoynes '77, treasurer; Father Stoffel '76, secretary; William Ball '77, historian; George Clarke '83, orator with Professor J.P. Lauth '68 as alternate and Louis Hayes '74, poet with Father T.O'Sullivan '58 as alternate.

The success of the fund for Professor Lyons' monument was announced. Col. Hoynes was appointed to arrange for the monument and its unveiling.

Significant in our alumni history is this report, "It was resolved that the Associated Alumni have a mid-winter banquet at Chicago, the time and other arrangements to be determined upon by a committee consisting of Father N.J. Mooney, W.T. Ball, Louis Hayes, Rev. T. O'Sullivan and Mark M. Foote, all national officers of the Association, all of Chicago.

This is not the place for a fuller treatment of the theater on the campus, but it is significant that in June, 1891, the *Scholastic* carried a story from the Chicago Herald which reveals the quality of events which were becoming increasingly frequent in the life of the University:

> Students of the University of Notre Dame honored Augustin Daly in a manner which college boys usually reserve for the boss football player of the season. And Mr. Daly returned the compliment with a distinction which he has sparingly granted to Shakespeare's birthplace and other historic spots that can be counted on one's fingers. He took Ada Rehan and the rest of his company of players down to Notre Dame, and there they gave an afternoon entertainment just for the boys and the friends of the boys. When he went away he was followed by the rousing college cheer, and Miss Rehan, looking back from her carriage, saw big fellows in mortar boards and gowns scrambling for the roses which she had tossed into the road. Mr. Daly is an LL.D. of the University, and it was partly out of affection for the instiution, and partly because of his friendship for Maurice Francis Egan, the poet-professor, that the manager planned the visit. As an additional compliment to Professor Egan, the company performed Francois Coppee's "The Prayer" which has been exquisitely turned into English by the professor. Mr. Daly and his company went to the University Sunday night in a special train. There were twelve of the players in the delegation besides the manager and the musical director . . . Their coming had been a mighty social event for the country around the college. Everybody in society wanted to see the

performance, but the students asked only a few. It was a big privilege to be bidden to this feast.

When the curtain went up there was a marked eagerness among the students to see how a woman would look on their little stage. There are no women in the College plays. The boys have done "Hamlet" without Ophelia or the queen mother, "The Merchant of Venice" without Portia. Then they came to "Uncle Tom's Cabin," were stuck, and asked Prof. James Edwards to help them out . . . "Why a Little Eva . . . why not Little Edgar?" So Little Edgar it was, and one of the Minims was wafted away to the angels, while a corked-up Uncle Tom sang "Way Down Upon the Shawnee River," and the real bloodhound tried to get some of Mr. Mark's leg in the wings. The professor's expedient will seem hollow henceforth. The boys have seen how a woman looks on their stage, and they are convinced that she is an ornament. In Miss Rehan's years of success she has seldom had a more enthusiastic welcome than the one that came from the Notre Dame collegians when, as Mlle. Rose Morel in "The Prayer," she stepped upon the stage.

Here was the "crossroads," bringing the best of one segment of the world outside to the informed and receptive minds of the University.

At Father Sorin's sacerdotal jubilee Archbishop Ireland had publicly acclaimed the diverse and innovative programs of Notre Dame.

The safe conservatism which never moves lest it fail, I adhor; it is the dry rot in the Church and my heart goes out to the man who never tolerated it in his calculations. Safe conservatism would have left the Apostles in Palestine . . . Do all you can, and then your prayers for divine blessing will be heard. The divine is needed; and the priest or the Christian who will succeed must love God and seek His aid. I will mention but one fact—a striking one in Father Sorin's life, with regard to its supernatural element. It is his tender devotion to the Mother of God. He loved her with childlike simplicity and ardor; all his projects were brought by him to her altar to be blessed by her, before he sought to put them into execution . . .

The heritage of Father Morrissey was not conservative. Nor had he learned it under the guidance of Sorin and Walsh.

In spite of the deaths of its great pioneer leaders, Notre Dame was almost by logic, and certainly by interest, involved in the 400th commemoration of the discovery of America by Christopher Columbus, focused in the Columbian Exposition in Chicago, in 1893. The world of the time was aware of the honor paid to Columbus by Notre Dame in the magnificent frescoes of

Luigi Gregori. In addition, the University had exhibits in four booths in the Liberal Arts building of the fair. One was the life-size portrait of Father Sorin by Gregori, accompanied by examples of art work done by students of Gregori and Professor Ackerman, who had done the cathedral frescoes in the new dining halls. There were also photographs taken by Father Kirsch's class, a new field of study at the time. In the second booth was a small but rich collection from the already impressive Bishops Memorial Hall. A third booth held autographed letters and other documents from the Catholic American Archives developed by Professor James Edwards. Similarly, in a fourth booth, were numerous precious articles, mementos of early bishops and other historical persons, including precious books, intended to represent the libraries and museums of the University.

It is inevitable that the great majority of Notre Dame alumni, residing primarily in the Midwest states, had the opportunity to see this prestigious display of their alma mater. Hospitality on the campus continued to welcome any alumnus visiting there. Commencement found facilities always open to returning alumni. And the "literary correspondence" between alumni, religious and lay faculty, together with the personal ties with students, preserved the family spirit even as formal organization seemed to give way to trends not quite yet grasped. The *Golden Jubilee History* had no doubts. In its closing message, as it summarized accomplishments of 50 years, it said, "We go forward in joy then, and in thanksgiving . . . trusting that those who come after us, in 1942, will find that we, too, have done our work well; that we have not buried the five talents given us, but have carried on with still increasing success the work of Christian education begun a hundred years before by Father Sorin and his brethren of the Holy Cross."

One of the faculty members exerting scholarly influence under Father Morrissey was Dr. Austin O'Malley. It was Father Morrissey who hired Professor Jerome Green in 1894. Professor Green built the equipment for his pioneer successful experiments in American wireless in the machine shops of the University. Professor Green was also the first one in Northern Indiana to experiment with X-rays. He constructed the first such equipment in this part of the country, and taught its uses to the doctors of the Medical Society. Many patients of the area were brought to the campus to use the new device.

Father John Zahm was enjoying great influence through his

scholarly achievement and his inspiration to young scholars, especially the young priests of the Congregation. The Vatican recognized him in 1894 with a doctorate in philosophy.

In the library of Notre Dame, which had been located in the third floor of the new Main Building, Professor James Edwards was dedicating his life and his great talents to the expansion of the library itself, and to the Catholic Archives of America, and the Bishops Memorial Hall, an almost integral development though not as directly related to academic use as the library itself.

The *Scholastic* of June, 1894, reports:

> The *Scholastic* reporter had observed, from time to time, in the express office boxes marked 'valuable documents.' Rumors had reached him of the great numbers that were gradually and quietly being brought together in the Catholic Archives of America. . . .
>
> If Cardinal Gibbons, Archbishop Elder, Archbishop Janssens, Monsignor Seton or Bishop Spalding were accosted with regard to the Catholic Archives, any one of these worthy prelates would inform us that these could be found in a remarkable collection of manuscripts, letters and other documents at Notre Dame, Indiana, and the bringing together and forming a collection of these priceless papers was due to the untiring zeal and labor of a layman—Professor James F. Edwards. . . .
>
> The *Scholastic* reporter called on Professor Edwards quite recently for the purpose of gaining some idea of the nature, present condition and future outlook of the Catholic Archives. An interview was kindly granted. The reporter was soon ushered before shelves upon shelves of documents neatly filed for reference, secretaries filled with letters, walnut cases gorged with manuscripts and baskets heaped with papers and historical references, but untouched and not arranged. Picture the astonishment of the reporter, who expected to see some few hundreds of these valuable papers, when he gazed on thousands before him. Professor Edwards said, "You see, I have undertaken a laborious task. The collection before you represents the work of a quarter of a century . . .
>
> Ensconcing himself in a large arm chair, the reporter felt that he was ready for a surprise; but when letters written by saintly clergy, who were the pioneers of the Church in America, and documents written in French, German, English and Spanish, colored with age, were laid before him, his amazement knew no bounds. Here were letters of Archbishops Carroll and Hughes; Bishops Bruté, Flaget, Dubois and hosts of other prelates; manuscripts by Badin, Gallitzin, Nerynx and DeSmet.

Professor Edwards explained further,

When I was a young boy, I was one day in a room where
much rubbish had accumulated, which was about to be
removed. Amongst the heaps of papers I discovered several
documents in Father Badin's handwriting, also letters of
Bishop Cretin, Father DeSeille and several other missionaries.
I preserved these letters, and from time to time chanced upon
other documents which I added to the collection. I decided
that such papers could be collected centrally, and access be
more insured than if they were scattered about the country
in different dioceses. The bishops find it difficult to supply
their churches with priests and can ill afford to designate
special men for this work. My plan to locate the Catholic
Archives at Notre Dame—a place centrally located, and away
from the dust and smoke of a large city—was heartily approved by all the clergy who were informed of it . . .

Professor Edwards was to go on for another 15 years of this
immeasurable devotion. It is almost with disappointment that
his deliberate approach to the creation of the Archives, and the
practical assent of the clergy and hierarchy to it, destroys the
rather romantic legend of deception and piracy which tradition
often attached to 'Jimmy' Edwards and to the incredible significance of the University collection.

The Notre Dame theater, already an old tradition was spurred
on to new achievement by the excellent facilities provided by
the new Washington Hall stage. It was undoubtedly true, too,
that such highlights as the visit of the Daly company with Ada
Rehan would have repercussions of enthusiasm. Add to that the
alert spirit that was always anxious to introduce innovations to
the campus, and a part of the early scope and success emerges.

In March, 1895, the *Scholastic* announced the formation of a
Notre Dame Stock Company.

There can be no doubt that the Stock Company, if conducted on right lines, will prove a welcome addition to the
many attractions of our University. The success of the enterprise rests then with the company itself; for there is every
reason to believe that the college public will heartily welcome
and support an effort which is capable of giving it productions of merit, both from the artistic point of view and that
of entertainment . . . A stock company should first of all
possess as perfect a balance as it is possible to attain. There
are, of course, no stars. Each man should, as far as possible,
be given a certain line of work to do, and his duty then is to
make the most of it. The most insignificant role may be lifted
into prominence by the right person.

After the company, the selection of a play is of the utmost
importance. The aim will be to secure a repertoire which will

embrace as great a variety as possible. Much attention will
likely be paid to works in one act . . . The manager is always
on the alert for something new and good, and would be glad
to secure any work which may be done by a writer at Notre
Dame.

Thus was the glamorous rabbit placed in front of the academic greyhound. That success attended the effort appears
from a June article in the *Scholastic:*

> This year's productions on the stage of Notre Dame have
> been happier than usual. The Cecilians led off with a wonder-
> fully successful play; the Thespians excelled all their previous
> efforts; the Columbians, despite adverse circumstances, ad-
> hered to their ordinarily high standards; the Philopatrians,
> too, joined the progressive throng; but to place the palm
> where it belongs, it must go to the University Stock Com-
> pany. The *Scholastic* policy has alwasy been one of encour-
> agement, and we may have been, at times, too kind to our
> players; but now, at least, let the praise of our Booths, and
> Barretts, and Jeffersons, be as extravagant as it may, and it
> would still be but justice. The secret of the Stock Company's
> success is hard work. They have been rehearsing their parts
> for weeks, and under the able management of Father
> Moloney and Mr. Marmon, who organized the company, they
> have more than realized our most sanguine expectations.
> They have made a new departure in Notre Dame theatricals
> by the introduction of the one-act 'curtain raiser' and the
> two-act play. Many have expressed the hope that this prec-
> edent will be well seconded in the future, and that the
> sentimental trash, of which we are all weary, will vanish.

We have already seen that the early '90s were marked by the
emergence of intercollegiate competition in baseball and football, largely with the state universities we now identify as the
Big Ten, but themselves then in their early years.

The decision at Notre Dame was to observe the golden jubilee
in 1895, after the sadness of Sorin's death, and the excitement
of the Columbian Exposition had softened.

One of the outstanding events of the jubilee was the week-
long celebration in conjunction with the June commencement.
The *Centennial History* says,

> For a full week in mid-June, old Notre Dame students
> came to the campus and relived their college days. They came
> from every section of the country and every walk of life,
> bishops and barristers, bankers and bookkeepers, priests and
> soldiers of Blue and Gray. It was a holiday crowd. They sat
> about the lawn or, in the evening, they walked about St.
> Joseph's Lake, which had been illuminated for the occasion.
> The thrills and heartbreaks of school days, the escapades and

pranks, the old classes and the ancient discipline, these were the things they talked of, and which grew in the telling. Far into the night, as is the habit of alumni everywhere, they passed in review, stimulated by the bracing night air, all the incidents that had made Notre Dame an unforgettable phase of their youth. And in the morning, when the great Bourdon echoed from building to building, they roused themselves and went to church. Then, too, that big bell meant dinner, a series of dinners, which took them back to a childhood when they were hungrier . . . 'Sure it's an army' exclaimed the sisters in the kitchen.

Not even the latest of Notre Dame's graduates—the Class of 1895—were bored with the reminiscences of Father Edmund Kilroy, who came to Notre Dame as a boy in the forties. When Father Tim O'Sullivan, whimsical and erudite, went from group to group, there was a whisper, "That's the one that blew St. Patrick's Day In the Morning from the dome," and there was a cluck of admiration as he passed. As Father Morrissey and the governor of Indiana reached the stage, enthusiasm reached a high pitch . . . There was a sobering moment, too, when the old students gathered in Sacred Heart Church to pray the requiem for Notre Dame boys who were celebrating the jubilee, it was hoped, in Heaven. All in all, it was a grand celebration in which bodies and souls were well fed.

In shorter and modified form, this golden jubilee weekend with its historical, spirtual, cultural, academic, fraternal, recreational, and up-dating programs, remained the pattern of alumni reunions for many years to come. For a number of those years, some times with little plan, they remained a part of the commencement weekend, whose ceremonies, numbers, and formalities eventually began to overshadow the camaraderie of the alumni, and to lessen the contacts of the occasion with the administration, faculty and strdents. It was in recognition of this, and its inevitability in the path of progress, that the alumni reunions were moved to the weekend following commencement. The move was fortuitous. Its own numbers have increased year by year. Its programs have been alumni-oriented but in the same broad patterns; and the contacts, except for the departed Seniors, are less interrupted with the priests and faculty members on the campus. And a fee has for many years relieved the University of the rising cost of hospitality it never itself questioned.

The jubilee alumni reunion found a new residence hall on the campus, Corby Hall, built to be a "professed house" for the priests. It was in this building that many of the returning alumni were housed. Four years later, student enrollment caused Corby to be turned over to the students. Like Sorin, its popularity stemmed from the private rooms for senior students, "in accordance with the more liberal view that had come to be held at Notre Dame."

The golden jubilee found Father Morrissey the popular and gifted host, on a campus that seemed to alumni to be carrying on in the fullest traditions of Father Sorin. The question of Father Morrissey's real merits was not part of that group.

XIII

Harvest and Planting

These may seem quaint terms. But they were still symbolic in the Indiana countryside.

Of much greater significance is their application to the University. In the '90s, the seeds that had been sown by Sorin, Dillon, Corby, Lemonnier, Colovin and Walsh, at Notre Dame in the spiritual and historical ground of the St. Joseph Valley, were producing a rich harvest. The plowing, the cultivation and the other burdens of preparing the harvest had been expertly and lovingly attended to by the priests and brothers, the sisters and the laymen who made up the family that lived on these acres.

Faith and prayer had been no small contributions to success.

Equally symbolic of the achievement then and of the years that have followed, is the custom of accompanying the harvest with the sowing of new seed, so that the storehouses of learning are never without the challenge of expansion and the assurance of replenishment and Father Morrissey's administration was true to both traditions.

Tuesday of the 1895 jubilee week had been designated alumni day. Some thousand guests were estimated to have attended. In the course of the day, the crowd was swelled to an estimated seven thousand, with four bands brought from the surrounding area. The ceremonies in Washington Hall in the evening were based on the theme "Notre Dame of the Past." The University orchestra played an arrangement from Rossini's "Semiramis." Three orations marked the occasion, one by the alumnus-priest Father Kilroy, a second by Father E.J. McLaughlin '75, and a third by William P. Breen '77. T.E. Howard '68, now a distinguished jurist, read a poem prepared by him for the occasion.

Those who were back for the jubilee, and most alumni were, had only to look about them and to talk with their fellow alumni, to appreciate the magnitude of the harvest. This experience in itself was perhaps the first and best seed of future harvests.

Father Thomas Carroll, a student at Notre Dame in 1855, a priest of Holy Cross for a while, and then priest in the Diocese of Erie, Pa., on a visit to the campus, proposed to Father Corby the gift of a reproduction of the Grotto of Lourdes, an appropriate shrine on the campus of Notre Dame. They decided on the site back of the Presbytery. In 1896 this Grotto became a reality. From a niche in the great boulders from which it was built, a statue of Our Lady looks down on a replica of Bernadette, and the Grotto has seldom since been without a rich glow of candlelight, and a kneeling contingent of students, asking favors for the faithful.

In 1897, with the new Corby Hall, a priest's house not yet given over to student residence, Father Morrissey had two wings added to the popular Sorin Hall, thereby adding room for another hundred senior students.

Another good seed was planted in 1896—the establishment of the first scholarship by a layman at Notre Dame. The effort of the University, faculty and Alumni Association to found a scholarship under Father Walsh had not succeeded in the face of adverse circumstances. But in June of 1896 it was announced that a scholarship had been given to the University by Col. John R. Fellows, then district attorney of New York City. The gift opened definite new doors. Non-Catholics had long befriended Father Sorin in his early days, and the University in its many crises. But here was a voluntary contribution to progress. It may well have been unsolicited but somewhere a seed was sown that bore this fruit. A dramatic gift of millions from an unknown woman benefactor in New York State in the 1960s is an eloquent modern corrollary.

The present annual University scholarship aid to students, including loans, approximates $4,000,000. You share with me, I am sure, the feeling that somewhere between such a seed and such a harvest the patronage of Our Lady must play some part.

In 1897, St. Joseph's Hall, the Manual Labor School, was already a rich tradition. It was also a badly deteriorating building. The *Scholastic* said of it:

> When this building, which we now look upon more as a disfigurement of the campus than anything else, was completed in 1851, it was one of the largest and most attractive

buildings in Northern Indiana. We consider it a very small affair indeed; but in those days visitors from the surrounding country looked upon it as something massive and entirely too large for the purpose for which it was built. At that time the school contained not only the students' study hall and dormitory, but the workshops as well. There the apprentices were taught several trades, with the exception of blacksmithing, carpentry and printing, which were taught in separate buildings. The manual labor lasted a certain number of hours and the remainder of the day was given over to study. It was here the boy, Joseph Lyons, made the wonderful pair of boots that won the prize at the county fair, and it was here also that he laid the foundation of an education that later on made him one of the most scholarly and valuable teachers that Notre Dame has ever had. He is but one of the many clever men who look back with pride and pleasure to the days when they were students at St. Joseph's Hall.... The new hall was formally opened in November of 1897. The structure is as homelike and comfortable within as its exterior is attractive. All the rooms are bright and well ventilated. Brother Boniface, the esteemed prefect of the hall, has labored hard to procure for his students the conveniences that are now theirs, and he has been assisted by Brother Celsus and Brother Hilary. The men of St. Joseph's Hall have him to thank almost entirely for their new home; for it was he that practically planned and made a reality this new ornament to Notre Dame. The only drawback to the building is the lack of steam heat, but this will be remedied as soon as the contemplated steam plant is completed. In the meantime, the building will be heated with large stoves.

This building, with a few revisions through the years, is Badin Hall of today, where the newly arrived coeds of Notre Dame—new seed—are perhaps unware of their rich heritage, as they look out on the other and more palatial coed Walsh Hall.

It becomes evident that the Alumni Association in June of 1897 has lost the chain of commencement-reunions that preceded the deaths of Sorin and Walsh. Perhaps the unleashed initiatives of administration and faculty were being turned to the attractive challenges of campus development. And it is more than probable that the popular Father Morrissey and the many alumni surrounding him in the University's offices and classrooms, were still steeped in "la vie intime" sufficiently to assume a continued alumni involvement and interest, without the ceremonies of the annual meeting and banquet. It is certain that hospitality was continued and that the prominent and loyal alumni continued to bask in the reflected glories of the commencements.

But the large alumni group in Chicago was not content with a seeming relapse into congeniality. They had already seen the opportunities of alumni influence. Perhaps they had in mind the implicit autonomy of separation from the congenial, constructive, but nevertheless authoritative, predominance of the University which had marked the campus meetings.

In any event, on May 24, 1897 a committee of 12 was appointed by the Notre Dame University Association of Chicago, to draw up a set of rules for the organization. The rules provide that "no religious or political discussions are allowed; that four meetings be held every year in Chicago and one meeting and annual reunion at the University of Notre Dame; that there be no fees or dues, but only an annual assessment of $2 to cover incidental expenses; that the aim of the organization be to inculcate the spirit of fraternity among Notre Dame men all over the United States and promote the welfare of the University."

Officers of this newly formed association were elected: Judge John Gibbons '77, president; George Crilly, first vice president; Davie Wile, second vice president; Mark Foote, secretary and Harold Hayes, treasurer. A board of directors was introduced in the new organization, the first being made up of Hugh O'Neill, P.T. Barry, Dr. J.A. Hemsteger, Kickham Scanlon and Charles T. Cavanagh. That the new association was not in opposition to its predecessor, or to the wishes of the University, is implicit in the former national officers who instigated the Chicago move. To confirm this thesis, the organization's first major meeting featured the reading of greetings from Father Morrissey, from William P. Breen and from "forty distinguished alumni" in different parts of the country.

Committees were appointed on entertainment, admission, organization and promotion. Notre Dame men in any part of the country were declared eligible for the Chicago Association if passed upon by the committee on membership. Headquarters were 323 Reaper Block, Chicago. Eminent men were to be invited to take part, and several of the "most prominent men in public life have signified their intention to deliver addresses under the auspices of the new association."

From the above it seems clear that the new association proposed not only to revivify the benefits of the earlier Associated Alumni, but to bring to Notre Dame men the continuing stimulus of closer ties with alma mater and with men in the mainstream of American life whose addresses would constitute continuous education.

True to their purposes, a special train took the Chicago

group to the June commencement at Notre Dame where they
were met by students and the band, in spite of inclement
weather. A comment, "The rain ceased and umbrellas gave way
to gaudy parasols," indicates that the visiting alumni had, as in
older days, brought mothers, wives and girl friends with them.

The new association presented Father Morrissey with an
illuminated scroll listing its charter members, designated a
"Guard of Honor." Judge Gibbons introduced Hugh O'Neill to
the meeting, held in the parlor of the Main Building. O'Neill,
orator for the occasion, said:

> As the children of the same family are linked together by
> bonds of love, so the scattered sons of a great University are
> bround together by mystic ties more strong than chains of
> adamant. For over half a century this University has sent men
> out into the learned professions and into the different avoca-
> tions of life where they have acquitted themselves with credit
> and reflected honor on their alma mater. Today, this Univer-
> sity can point with pride to men eminent in every walk of
> life. In the arts and sciences, at the bar and on the bench, in
> the counting house and in the senate hall, in the pulpit, on
> the rostrum, in the sanctum of the writer, Notre Dame men
> are preeminent. In the development of the great West, in the
> intellectual growth of the whole country, they have left their
> imprint. In political life have they not always been the
> advocates of law and order? Have they not always conserved
> the people's rights when placed in public office? Have they
> not when our country's flag was in danger, rushed to death
> and the cannon's mouth in defense of our country's liberties?
> And have they not shown by their bravery on many a
> well-fought field that this is the most thoroughly American
> institution I know. It bars no man on account of his religion,
> race or condition in life; it honors no man except for his
> intellectual attainments. . . . For years there has been a grow-
> ing sentiment among Notre Dame men in favor of an organi-
> zation which should cultivate the spirit of fraternal union,
> promote the welfare of its members and draw together at
> stated intervals the men who have helped to make this
> institution famous. Such an association has at last been
> organized in Chicago, the center of America's activity . . . It
> is founded upon the broad principles of the University. Its
> president is distinguished as an economist, a writer, a thinker,
> a lawyer, a jurist—one of Notre Dame's illustrious sons, Judge
> John Gibbons. . . .

Father Morrissey was visibly affected by this token of the
love of the old students for their college and in eloquent and
forceful words he thanked the members for the interest they
take in Notre Dame. He promised them in return that Notre

Dame will continue to progress as it has progressed in the past, and that the efforts of the faculty will be to further the cause of education, to erect a standard of scholarship at Notre Dame that will be the pride of her sons and the envy of the country. He dedicated Founder's Day, Oct. 13, the Feast of St. Edward, to the Alumni Association, as an annual day of meeting on the campus for alumni from the entire country.

In September, the Chicago Association held a meeting, which set Oct. 13 for the annual meeting on the campus. The commencement excursion had netted $225 for the organization. The secretary was empowered to hire a stenographer and pay incidental expenses. Col. Hoynes and Dr. O'Malley of the faculty were added to the committee for the October meeting arrangements. Tentative plans for fall and winter lectures were announced.

In June,1898, the *Scholastic* reported that "The regular monthly meeting of the Notre Dame University Association of Chicago was held at the Tremont House, the close of the first year of the association." Membership had trebled during the year, and the treasurer's report indicated a balance directed toward a scholarship. John Hummer was elected president; George Crilly reelected as vice president; Professor Ewing was made second vice president; Mark Foote and Harold Hayes were reelected secretary and treasurer. The president announced that the association had been granted a corporate charter by the State of Illinois. The group was sponsoring another special train to the commencement. Parents of students, who wished to attend the commencement weekend, were invited to be a part of the special train group.

In 1898 Father Morrissey announced the construction of a new gymnasium. It was a large building, with a dirt floor, and a second-floor room across its front which was used for modern gymnasium apparatus. This layout was smilar to its unexpected successor, built in 1901, for so long familiar to all students.

The new gymnasium was dedicated in March of 1899. On November 9, 1900, Father Morrissey was introduced to one of the vicissitudes of his predecessors when fire completely destroyed the new structure. Showing that he also enjoyed some of the fortitude of his predecessors, Father Morrissey immediated ordered the building of a new and better gymnasium, this time fire-proofed. The testimony to its efficient construction rests with its continued presence, no longer a gymnasium, true, but a spacious, if somewhat primitive, center for some of the

University's arts programs. The aesthetic axe of the administration has been hovering over it in recent months and may fall even before the final chapter of this story.

Father Morrissey, aided by Father Zahm, continued to make major improvements. The scattered and expensive heating plants were replaced by a central heating plant, completed in 1900. A model of the new plant was sent to the Paris Exposition of that year.

Meanwhile, the first annual banquet of the Chicago Alumni Association was held at the Tremont House on Dec. 6, 1898. Many of the alumni and friends present had not seen the campus since 1879, others had lost contact with faculty and administration, but the report remarked on the continued fraternal spirit. Carter Harrison, then mayor of Chicago, was a distinguished guest and extended greetings to alumni from beyond the Chicago boundaries. Father Morrissey made an eloquent address. Judge Gibbons talked on practical education, saying, " . . . the best education to give a man is moral training." William P. Breen, Fort Wayne, spoke on campus life and the men on its faculty and in its administrative office, who had made memorable contributions to the development of alumni. Col. Hoynes waxed eloquent on the place of education in the professions, whose entrance standards were rapidly rising. Hon. Marcus Cavanaugh spoke on the college man as a soldier. He said many of the Civil War soldiers had college degrees. "The higher a man's ideals, the better his patriotism." Hugh O'Neill reminded the guests that "the educated men had built Greece and Rome; they wrung the Magna Charta from King John; they drafted the American Constitution. America needs learned and great men and she must look to her universities and colleges for the highest and noblest types of citizens."

In June 1899, the *Scholastic* welcomed the Chicago Association to the commencement weekend.

> In you we find many of our old confreres at the editors' table; many a favored athlete, and many that will always wear the gold and blue with honor. Notre Dame is proud of you, and is most happy to show the present student body that when they leave, they may join with alumni that were Notre Dame students once, that are Notre Dame people now, and that always will be Notre Dame people. Once a Notre Dame man, and the gold and blue will be your colors for life.

The dubious issues of the Spanish-American War did not win substantial campus enthusiasm. John Shilington, a boy who had been dismissed for disciplinary infraction in 1897, was a sailor on the ill-fated battleship Maine, apparently Notre Dame's only fatality. A shell from the Maine forms part of a marker on the campus in his memory. A number of Notre Dame men did see action in that short struggle. C.C. Fitzgerald, long a distinguished engineer in Cuba in later years, had, as a student, been given a rosary by Father Alexis Granger. In a letter in later life he wrote that he had carried the rosary through the Spanish-American War, in Cuba, and in World War I in France. He had had it for 50 years at that time and prayed daily for the great priest who gave it to him.

It is this unity of kindness, friendship, spirituality and memories which pours into the mold of Notre Dame man a significance beyond academic content and professional competence.

The year 1899 marked another achievement, of heroic proportions then, in the academic world of the present.

In 1879, Notre Dame was assembling its scholarly dramatic talent to produce the Greek tragedy "Oedipus Tyrannus" in Greek. The great fire of that year caused postponement of the project. Harvard produced a Greek play a year or two later, to score the historic first in America. In 1883, the year of the founding of the Laetare Medal, Father Nicholas Stoffel, Greek scholar of extraordinary merit, who had planned the original effort, produced "Oedipus Tyrannus" in Greek as the commencement play. Students had produced the libretto, in type set by them and their teacher, Father Stoffel. Now, in 1899, Father Stoffel was pastor of St. Joseph's Church in South Bend. But he wished to repeat the success of "Oedipus." Interest in the theater was greater. Facilities were improved. So each morning he drove to the campus in his buggy. There were many rehearsals. In May the play, completely in Greek, the audience furnished with the Greek text and corresponding English translation— all prepared by the students—was presented. The audienced included Greek scholars. Friends from all over the country came for the occasion. Archbishop Martinelli, the apostolic delegate, later to become a cardinal, was in attendance. The director of music, Professor McLaughlin, had composed the music of the choruses. Costumes and stage settings were designed for historical conformity. A brilliant student, later to become a noted priest and administrator, Father Mattew Schumacher, was given special mention as Jocasta.

Father Morrissey, like his earlier predecessors, found it

necessary to maintain the ties with Europe. When he returned from such a trip in 1899, he brought with him ideas on curricular revision. Economics was among the new courses suggested. A school of journalism was proposed, in which the use of the English language was to be paramount, and graduate students in economics and history recommended. Father Morrissey urged a moderate course in economics, but nevertheless one which taught adjustment of private interests to the public welfare. A master of letters in journalism was to be given at the end of a fifth year of advanced studies. I mention this first adventure in journalism because when I entered the journalism department in 1921 under Dr. John M. Cooney, it was this program of broad based education for the more specific task of the journalist that guided the studies.

The art department, long and widely known for the outstanding talents of Signor Gregori and Professor Ackerman, had declined in prestige. Father Morrissey brought in Jobson Emilien Paradis, who had studied in the schools of Rome and Paris. Paradis later returned to Paris and made a name for himself in that most competitive of art capitals.

During these years of development, Notre Dame was conscious of the values inherent in distinguished lecturers from outside the campus. The result was that during the years of Father Morrissey's presidency, William Jennnings Bryan twice visited Notre Dame; F. Marion Crawford delivered a lecture; Prof. Van Dyke of Princeton University, author of "The Other Wise Man," lecturered on Tennyson; the great Irish dramatist, William Butler Yeats, came for three days and discoursed on Irish literature and the Irish stage. William Howard Taft, then Secretary of War and former governor of the Philippines, lectured on the Church in those islands. Henry James spoke to the students on "Balzac" and Dom Francis Aidan Gasquet, O.S.B., lectured on "France and the Vatican."

If these do not indicate a cultural program comparable to the campuses anywhere, in that era, and an effort over and above the resources of the University, with the value of Catholic higher education still suspect in its own milieu, then I will sing you a chorus of doubt about God making little green apples, or rain in Indianapolis.

The burning of the gymnasium revealed that Father Morrissey was also willing to follow earlier example and appeal for outside aid. A committee for the lay faculty, headed by such familiar names as Austin O'Malley, John Ewing, William Hoynes and Martin McCue (the latter to become a dean of engineering), was joined by a committee for the students, headed by such outstanding athletes as John Eggeman, Fred Powers, Pat O'Dea and Patrick Corcoran, in issuing an appeal to Notre Dame alumni:

> Letters and checks already sent in were one of the prime motives in inducing us to make this appeal, which the President and trustees were diffident in entertaining lest it might be misunderstood, although they were urged by members of the lay faculty to take this step.
>
> Through the burning of the gymnasium the University has suffered a severe inconvenience not only from the pecuniary loss, since the building with its equipment cost $40,000, but because the loss came at the beginning of the winter season when a gymnasium is absolutely necessary as a place of recreation for students and for other reasons. Moreover, college men fully understand how important athletic standing is in American college life, and we cannot hold our reputation without a gymnasium. We have a track team that should win the Western Intercollegiate Championship but it will not do so unless we have a gymnasium.
>
> We shall have a gymnasium. The contract is already signed. But the University must go into debt to build it at a time when building materials are unusually dear. It should be distinctly understood that the University authorities are not a money-making body. They are religious, who give their learning and work to educate boys intellectually and morally, and for their pay they receive only board, clothing and criticism. Within the past four years Notre Dame has spent $298,616 on buildings and improvements and every cent of that money is literally devoted to the students. The fees alone coming from the boys do not reach within $10,000 of paying the annual expense for the education and boarding of these students. The older an alumnus grows the more he appreciates what Notre Dame has done for him, and the bills his father pays for him while he is here do not settle this account. We therefore, alumni and students of Notre Dame, appeal to you to help pay for the new building for the sake of old times.

The response was encouraging.

A friend whose modesty keeps his identity hidden, sent in a thousand dollars after the fire; another friend gave "a hundred dollars to buy a few baseball uniforms to replace those burned up; another gentleman, who is not an alumnus, sending money, writes to the President, 'The destruction of the gymnasium is certainly a double loss to the University, occurring just at this time on the threshold of a new scholastic year. But I notice that with your usual progressive spirit,

you had commenced arrangements for the erection of a new
building before the fire burned itself out.'

A prominent lawyer of Indiana, whose son is at the University, sent a check the day after the fire, and he said, 'I enclose
you a small remittance toward the building fund. It is small,
but if every father who has a son with you does as well, the
loss will not be nearly so hard to bear.' Again, an alumnus,
sending a check, added, "If the enclosed check will be of any
help to you, you will do me a favor by accepting it. I trust
alumni better able than I will not overlook this occasion for
remembering the benefits conferred by Notre Dame University."

The enrollment in 1900 was seven hundred students, still
divided into Seniors, Juniors, and Minims.

An interesting story in the *Scholastic* of Feb. 2, 1901, reports
the organization of the new Western Track and Field Association. Nine universities took part in this organization, stating
that other colleges would be admitted later as they showed
merit. The organization committee consisted of representatives
from the nine faculty and student bodies, and the students were
reported in disagreement with the restriction of membership to
the "Big Nine,"—Chicago, Michigan, Wisconsin, Minnesota, Illinois, Iowa, Northwestern, Purdue and Ohio State. The report
comments, "We infer from the article that all Notre Dame will
be asked to do to gain admission into the new association will
be to make a good showing. Well, we still do that with a
vengeance. We learn from another source that Notre Dame is to
be admitted anyhow before any of the other colleges that are
not now included in the big nine."

The commencement *Scholastic* of 1901 says,

The University, as is the hospitable custom of the members
of the Holy Cross, was placed at the visitors' disposal. A
delegation, 75 strong, came on an excursion from Chicago.
This excursion had been planned and carried out by the
Notre Dame Alumni Association of Chicago. The president of
the society, Daniel P. Murphy, was most instrumental in
making the affair a success. When President Morrissey cordially shook hands with the Chicago visitors he noted many of
his former graduates among them.

The *Scholastic* for the Commencement of 1902 spotlights
another of the customs about to become a major factor in
Notre Dame progress, the cultivation of individuals of wealth,
not alumni, who might be expected to make major contributions to the University.

Large delegations of distinguished visitors, including many eminent clergymen from Chicago, kept coming in. A large crowd filled the shores of the Lake for the regatta, and among them was Charles Schwab, president of the United States Steel Co., who had come with his party on a special train from Cresson, Pa., to be present at the graduation of his cousin, Francis C. Schwab. The evening exercises in Washington Hall found the hall filled. When the large audience was seated, President Morrissey and Bishop Alerding, followed by Dr. John B. Murphy of Chicago, who was the Laetare Medalist, Hon. William P. Breen, Charles Schwab, Father Zahm, the provincial, and a number of distinguished Chicagoans, came to the stage.

The cultivation of Charles Schwab, with its great expectations, bore little fruit. The contributions of United States Steel in recent years have very improbable roots in those early symptoms of fund-raising diplomacy.

The June, 1903, commencement and reunion brought familiar activity.

Every train brought its contingent of visitors, all of whom are welcome guests at Notre Dame. As in past years they were provided with rooms in the College buildings. The priests were assigned to Corby Hall, the layment to Sorin, and the ladies were cared for by the Sisters of Holy Cross in the comfortable apartments of the Infirmary. This generous arrangement on the part of the University is much appreciated by the students and their visiting friends. It places relatives or members of the same family within easy reach of one another and not infrequently enables them to eat together at the same tables in the College refectories. It also affords visitors a much better opportunity of inspecting the many halls, other buildings, interesting landmarks, and surroundings that may be seen at Notre Dame.

Among these was the grave of the great Catholic philosopher, Orestes Brownson, in the basement chapel of Sacred Heart Church. Brownson had been invited to join the Notre Dame faculty, but the details for this cherished mutual hope were not completed before his death. Brownson Hall for many years perpetuated the memory of the great and admired scholar. His body had been brought to Notre Dame in 1886. He had written on the Blessed Virgin, for the *Ave Maria* magazine and had won a prize for an essay concerning her, offered by Father Sorin to commemorate the new Main Building and her statue on its top. His grave almost beneath her outstretched arms is not inappropriate.

The 1903 commencement marked the announcement that the University of Michigan had conferred a doctorate of laws on Father Morrissey, only the 32nd such honor bestowed by that school in its history, and at this time already one of the largest schools in the United States.

There is not much detail on the program of the 1904 commencement, but its list of guests was prestigious.

The most distinguished guest was Cardinal Satolli, who, in company with Monsignor O'Connell, the rector of Catholic University, the Very Rev. Provincial Zahm, Father Luke Evers, alumnus-priest from New York, and a group of clergy from Rome, arrived early in the week. Other Church dignitaries who followed them included Archbishop Quigley of Chicago, Archbishop Ireland of St. Paul and Archbishop Glennon of St. Louis. The Catholic societies of South Bend, distinguished alumni of the community and civic officials, joined Father Morrissey, his vice president, Father French, and many others in a procession which formed at the South Bend depot and escorted the cardinal to the campus.

Father Andrew Morrissey, as each President before him, had met the many challenges of the dynamic University of Notre Dame, from 1893 to 1905, and had left Our Lady's school a bigger and better place for his efforts. That these efforts enjoyed the support, abilities, work, and dedication of faculty, students, and alumni, does not diminish their significance.

XIV

The Power
of the Spoken Word

Father John W. Cavanaugh, C.S.C., stands in Notre Dame history as its most eloquent President. Many were fine orators. Many spoke with force and persuasion. But throughout the presidency of Father Cavanaugh, from 1905 to 1919, he spoke on many occasions, of great diversity in goals and audiences. The collection of these addresses indicates the range of his mind, the mastery of his words and the lasting effect upon his hearers. He became one of the nation's great orators. The printed word cannot convey the music of his voice, or the aura of culture and confidence that were there even before the first word was spoken. I knew Father Cavanaugh, not as president, but in the golden years after his retirement. Ex-presidents at Notre Dame tend to follow the path of humility, rather than the corporate path of chairmanship of the board. And because he overshadowed anyone on a platform where he spoke, it was not good public relations for the University to find its new "establishment" overshadowed. In spite of this, he won ardent disciples in the classes he taught. He held faculty members spellbound in the mellow discourses he enjoyed in the library, amid the Dante collection which was his nominal responsibility. And I persuaded him to continue to enrich the cultural lives of alumni by contributing articles on books to the *Alumnus* magazine. Seldom did he confine his writing in our pages to books in a review sense. But his writing continued always to be an inspiration.

Father Andrew Morrissey resigned in 1905, and the Provincial Council accepted his resignation. As his successor they chose the golden voice of the young priest, 35 at the time, who

had been superior of the Holy Cross Seminary from 1898 to
1905, and who had been a member of the *Ave Maria* editorial
family of the scholarly and saintly Father Daniel E. Hudson,
from 1892 until 1905. Father Cavanaugh had come to Notre
Dame from Leetonia, O., at the age of 16. He received a Litt.B.
in 1890. His parents were born in Ireland, and he formed a high
regard for Father Morrissey.

In 1905, possibly to keep the increasing Irish influence in
perspective, Father John Zahm, the Provincial, had sent a letter
to alumni and friends of Notre Dame:

> Those who achieve greatness need no monument, it is true,
> for the deeds that entitle them to place are inseparable from
> their names. Still, as time dims the past that deserves to live
> as well as the past that ought to perish, and this simply due
> to the excitement and endeavors of the present, the fitness of
> a memorial of some kind for a worthy end is evident. A
> sensible sign, of whatever character, has an undoubted effect
> on all who see it; of these some are bound by the glad fetters
> of gratitude and the remainder are constrained by the ever-
> present desire of the ideal. The alumni of Notre Dame belong
> to the first class; the friends of the institution and those
> interested in things of value comprise the second. To both it
> will be a pleasure to know that a statue is to be erected at
> Notre Dame to the memory of the pioneer, missioner, schol-
> ar, educator, saint — Father Edward Sorin.
>
> It is to be the work of one of the most noted sculptors of
> Italy, and will be a work of art, as well as a speaking likeness.
> The monument will stand at the main entrance of the Univer-
> sity grounds . . . The statue will face outwards, and the majes-
> tic form and features of the venerable founder will thus be
> the first to meet and welcome students and alumni returning
> to their alma mater, and all who visit Notre Dame.
>
> The cost of the monument which has been planned will be
> approximately $25,000. The work will be completed this
> coming fall.
>
> As an old student or friend of Father Sorin, it is believed
> that this attempt to raise a befitting monument to the mem-
> ory of Father Sorin will appeal to you as an undertaking
> worthy of your active cooperation. You are, therefore, ear-
> nestly invited to contribute to it.

So it was, that on May 3, 1906, the first year of Father
Cavanaugh's administration, Bishop Alerding celebrated a Mass
and Archbishop Keane of Dubuque preached the sermon to
open the day of dedication of the monument. It was a sign of
the rich years ahead when, undaunted by the hierarchy or other
dignitaries, Father Cavanaugh, speaking at the unveiling, gave in
part this memorable comment:

... Therefore, in the name of the sainted apostles who carried the Roman cross into countries over which the Roman eagle never passed; in the name of the holy missionaries of every age, the evangelizers of every land, who have ventured for God where the merchant would not venture for gold nor the soldier for glory; in the name of those Christian educators who believe, as he believed, that the heart of culture is the culture of the heart, and that the soul of improvement is improvement of the soul; in the name of humanity whom he loved and served without distinction of race or creed; in the name of America, the scene of his labors and the land of his predilection; in the name of generations of young men whose lives have been touched and sanctified by his consecrated hands; in the name of alma mater whose foundation stones were cemented with his sweat and blood; in the name of the noble army of priests, brothers, and sisters of Holy Cross who with him bore the burden of a long day and are now trembling in the everlasting ecstasy; in the name of venerable religious here present into whose souls come rushing back so many holy memories today; in the name of the Holy Catholic Church whose loyal and faithful priest he was; in the name of St. Joseph and the Blessed Virgin whose names he magnified; in the name of Him, the Savior of us all, whom he served and loved with almost perfect love and service — I say, unveil the statue of Sorin.

In the glow from our television screens this may sound flamboyant. It was simple eloquence of that day. Even then some suggested he was broader than deep. But when the national stature of his oratory was combined with an Irish temper of almost equal stature, if less known, it is not difficult to understand that as his position and power as President of Notre Dame grew, few indeed questioned his decisions or debated his pronouncements. If retrospect wishes to cavil at all — and it shouldn't — it might be the seeming "one-man rule" sometimes attached to his administration—an almost equally valid label, in fact, for most of the University's presidents, insofar as the public identification is involved. My own objection in looking back to the administration of Father Cavanaugh was that, by his magnificent presence and by the implication of power and wealth contained in his pose and confidence, it was inconceivable for the strangers he met, and indeed many alumni and friends of the University, to believe that Notre Dame could possibly be in need of outside aid.

On the same day that Sorin's statue was unveiled, in a not unrelated ceremony, the remains of Father Stephen Theodore Badin, brought from the Archdiocese of Cincinnati after long

negotiation, were interred in the Log Chapel, on the shores of
St. Mary's lake. In his last years, he had asked Father Sorin to
build a log cabin for him on these shores, where he might end
his life in the peace of the mission he had restored to the
Potawatomis, and in the shadow of the growing University his
hopes had helped to make a reality. It was impossible then to
provide the care the elderly missionary needed, and he went to
Cincinnati, where he died and was buried in the cathedral. The
calm which emanates from the statue of Father Sorin may stem
from the carrying out of this wish of Father Badin, to whom
the University has always felt a close tie.

Father L'Etourneau, who had served Mass for Father Badin
in the early years of the University, was present at this inter-
ment. There have been no years at Notre Dame when there have
not been people on the campus whose years of service over-
lapped, so that the purpose of the founder seems always to have
been handed from generation to generation with friendship, as
well as with understanding and dedication.

There is another member of the Notre Dame family, mentioned at this time. I include him here because he symbolizes so
many of these men—not students, not religious, poor in material
goods and uneducated in a formal sense—whose lives were as
dedicated to the development of the University as the religious,
lay faculty, alumni or students. In June, 1906, Michael
Hastings, such a man, died, and was buried in Cedar Grove
Cemetery on Notre Dame Avenue. The *Scholastic* said of him:

> Mr. Michael Hastings, known to all as 'Mike,' was one of
> those lovable characters who grew old with Notre Dame, and
> there are few old students who will not recall some pleasant
> meeting with the gardener of St. Edward's Park. For forty
> years Mike has labored at Notre Dame and has brought
> sunshine to all who met him. Who does not remember that
> cheerful 'good morning' or the pleasant Irish ditty which he
> was wont to sing as he trained the plants and vines of St.
> Edward's Park. Mike loved Notre Dame, and he was ever
> ready to lend a hand when he could be of any service. In
> 1879, when the Main Building of the University was de-
> stroyed by fire, Mike Hastings took fifty dollars from his
> small savings to contribute to the relief fund. A few years ago
> the University Gymnasium was totally destroyed by fire . . .
> Mike came again with his spirit of loyalty and contributed
> twenty-five dollars. Only this year his name appeared on the
> list of contributors to the Sorin statue fund, for twenty-five
> dollars. It was this spirit of loyalty that made Mike loved and
> admired by those at Notre Dame and will make him long
> remembered in their prayers.

On June 6, his funeral services were held in St. Joseph's Church, South Bend. Notre Dame President Father Cavanaugh preached a beautiful, touching sermon. He dwelt on those beautiful qualities that made Mike so well loved by all who met him, and held him up as an example of devotedness and loyalty worthy of imitation. After the funeral services in the church, the procession went to Cedar Grove cemetery where Father Cavanaugh blessed the grave and recited the final prayers. Many of the brothers and priests of Holy Cross, and a number of sisters from St. Edward's Hall, were present at the funeral.

Father Cavanaugh relished tradition as he loved the intangibles that create characters like Mike Hastings. He knew the significance of such men in the growth of an institution whose direction was under a dedication to poverty, chastity and obedience. The financial donations Mike Hastings made were, in the light of his compensation, princely gifts. But the 40 years of service and friendship were the endowment which for so long substituted at Notre Dame for the finances of its academic compatriots as they rapidly rose. Alumni were not only aware of this same heritage, but deeply appreciative of it in the lives of religious and lay people on the campus.

Father Cavanaugh was not blind to tangible needs. He wanted two badly needed residence halls. In addition he stated, "We need a great fire-proof library, we need a great school of technology and new laboratories, professorships and scholarships. This glorious old college, with its 60 years of sincere and laborious effort for the best in education and the best in human life is as worthy of the love and loyalty of her children as any in the land."

But somehow, when he spoke, the aura of distinction far outshone his aura of poverty. I did not intend to single out classes or clubs. But I must mention here the Class of 1906. This was Father Cavanaugh's first graduating class as President. It was the class which in his first year as President had instituted the first yearbook, the Dome. And it was a class which, in proportion to its numbers, reflects amazing alumni glory.

John F. Shea was coauthor of the "Victory March." Father Charles L. O'Donnell was a distinguished member of the Holy Cross order, a professor, a priest and a poet, a chaplain in World War I, a President of Notre Dame and the Provincial of the Indiana Province of his Congregation. He was also one of the great builders of the University. Father John C. McGinn became a C.S.C., one of the early priests to venture into the growing

problems of sociology. He was the gadfly of the first endowment campaign, and served for a short while as secretary of the
Alumni Association. Father Eugene P. Burke was a writer, an
editor, a teacher and one of the most delightful minstrel priests
of Holy Cross to mingle with Notre Dame men. John F. Cushing
became the head of the Great Lakes Dredge & Dock Co.,
associated many alumni in his company, and was the donor of
the Cushing Engineering Building to the college from which he
was graduated. Father Charles Doremus became a Holy Cross
priest, keeping alive until this writing the rich and appropriate
accent of the founding fathers of Notre Dame which he brought
from Brittany, along with an interest in Catholic education and
faith which enriched both classroom and confessional under
many administrations, and brought him many visits from his
former students. Father Edward Finnigan was another of the
World War I chaplains, retaining traces of wounds in action
throughout the subsequent years as rector and pastor on the
campus. Father James H. Gallagan remained at Notre Dame to
become the popular and influential "Diamond Jim" of classroom and legendary disciplinary contributions. The eloquent
logic of Father Cornelius Hagerty, C.S.C., continues to remind
us, even now, of his popularity and excellence as a teacher and
friend. His prowess in piloting a cross-country canoe or in a
debate were both formidable. Father John M. Ryan was another
class contribution to the Congregation, whose memory is
stronger on the disciplinary side, where he relished the nickname "Toughy," than on the side of history, his academic field.
Father Henry M. Kemper became a diocesan priest, settling in
the Southwest in the face of major health problems. But there,
for miraculous years, he developed an institution named Notre
Dame to aid boys, reminiscent of the history of early Notre
Dame. Terence Cosgrove became one of the great attorneys of
California, specializing in water rights so vital to that state, and
became a lay trustee of Notre Dame. Frank "Shag" Shaughnessy was a star athlete, and for many years achieved international prominence as head of the International Baseball
League, headquartered in Canada, extending throughout the
United States and Cuba. Another distinguished member of the
class was Ernest M. Morris, Ernie Morris, a non-Catholic founder
of the Associates Investment Company, member and chairman
of Notre Dame's Lay Trustees before his death, is known to
most Americans as the farm boy who came to Notre Dame's law
school because Father Cavanaugh let him stable his horse and

buggy on the campus while he attended class each day, and who repaid this kindness to a poor boy by giving his alma mater the Morris Inn in 1951. Morris gifts have been given on many other occasions, and the family has continued in the tradition since the death of Ernest M. Morris. Actually, it seems that the really great Morris contribution was in his persuasion of the University Lay Trustees to a change in investment policy, which has permitted significant growth in endowment, even though contemporary expansion and rising costs have fought annually with total income. Conservative traditional policy had prevailed, in spite of change in trustee administration elsewhere and burgeoning endowment funds in other colleges. Morris' leadership swung the majority to the more liberal approach, with outstanding gains for Notre Dame.

There were a corps of lawyers and engineers from 1906 also, who are not here mentioned singly, but who competed very successfully in their professions throughout the country. The whole class was reflective of academic astronauts, launched from a most successful pad.

That first *Dome*, along with other media, contained the needs of Notre Dame, so headlined. The pioneering page in the *Dome* pointed out

A duty of loyalty incumbent on every student and alumnus is to dissipate the curious superstition that our alma mater is wealthy enough to develop unassisted, and that endowments are not urgently needed. The fact, as we are authoritatively assured, is that when current expenses are paid at the end of the year there remain only a few thousand dollars for repairs and expansion. The cost of maintaining the University amounts to almost $800 a day, and to meet these expenses there are no resources except the students fees. There exist four endowed scholarships and, with the income derived from these, four students are educated. The University holds title to much unproductive land, but that is an encumbrance rather than an asset. Here are a few of the things that Notre Dame needs urgently and immediately:

A library building to cost $150,000. Two new dormitory buildings at a cost of $60,000 each. A fund for the purchase of books for the library. A fund for the endowment of athletics. A fund for the better equipment of the laboratories in all the courses. A fund for the education of clever and deserving boys who cannot afford a higher education. A fund to provide special lectures by men distinguished in all walks of life. These are a few of the immediate needs of the University; expansion will multiply these needs in proportion.

Let the alumni start the ball rolling. Make up your mind just which of these needs you would best like to supply. If you can not give $100,000 give $1,000. If not so much as that, send $250 for the purchase of equipment in the laboratory in which you are most interested. A plan is now under advisement for the creation of a special board composed of laymen to administer all monies contributed to the University.

You can reread the preceding quotes to advantage. The rather startling figures for the buildings are really not too significant, because they are relative to the economy of the era. But the concept of Living Endowment in the fiscal life of Notre Dame—giving what you can each year $100,000 to $250—was one which it took until 1941 to establish. And the board of laymen to invest University funds, possibly even then reflecting the thinking of father Burns as well as Father Cavanaugh, did not come into reality until 1920. Rome was not built in a day, and some of its outposts have shown the need for time to develop even sound ideas.

It is a paradox that the President who so early seemed to see the needs of the University was the distinguished and eloquent spokesman who made the urgency of those needs disappear in the glow of his charm.

Father Cavanaugh was conscious of the growing numbers of students, and thereby of alumni. And he was conscious of their widely scattered locations. In 1903 the Cuban students had held a celebration at Notre Dame on the first anniversary of Cuban independence. One of the students, Eugenio Rayneri, was to become a prominent Havana architect, designer of the Cuban capitol building. In that same year the New York State students held an organizational banquet.

The *Scholastic* of January 21, 1905, reports a meeting of the Notre Dame Club in New York.

We are not satisfied with the making of friends, we yearn to have them before us, at least in thought, to 'grapple them to our soul with hoops of steel' and to have the assurance that they in turn are not unmindful of us. This assurance of continued friendship Notre Dame is proud to possess in her numerous alumni, in their associations, and last but not least in the so-called 'State Clubs' of recent organization. Of the last named societies, the New York Club was the originator, and has ever since remained an exemplary model . . . We learn that our Alumni Society in the Empire State had its annual dinner and reunion on the seventeenth of December.

The hall was decorated in gold and blue, the table was "richly spread in regal mode" and Doretti's Royal Italian Orchestra supplied the music. The names of those present remained for many years thereafter on the rolls of the cumulative programs of the New York Club. On Jan. 19, the club held a smoker, and announced its annual dinner meeting in April, when elections would be held. *The Brooklyn Daily Standard* reports that the April election chose Father Luke Evers as president of the club. Father Evers had won fame in the city by the establishment of an early morning Mass for printers, newspaper men and other late Saturday night laborers. Father William A. Olmstead, former Brig. Gen. U.S.A. Ret., was elected a vice president as was Frank P. Dwyer. Father John McGrath was chosen third vice president; Thomas Murray, treasurer; Charles Gorman, recording secretary and Peter McElligott, recording secretary. William Gerdiner was elected historian. An executive committee was elected to aid the officers.

In May of 1907, the Boston alumni and those from surrounding areas met at Young's Hotel to honor Father John W. Cavanaugh, the visiting President. In the afternoon Father Cavanaugh was shown around Harvard by distinguished alumni, by Congressman O'Connell, by ex-president Richards of Georgetown University, and Dr. John P. Fennessey. The party was entertained at luncheon by the Notre Dame men at Harvard. Byron V. Kanaley, a Chicago alumnus of '04, then at Harvard, was toastmaster of the banquet. His name was synonymous with Notre Dame Alumni Association progress from his graduation until his death. Father Cavanaugh delivered one of his outstanding addresses. Following this, alumni were called upon, and expressed their varying ideas on the University and its future, subject matter ranging from technological experiments in science to the great common denominator topic of athletics. A discussion period was devoted to the organization of alumni on a national basis. The approval of the idea was evident in the immediate organization of a Massachusetts Alumni Association, with headquarters in Boston. Dr. Francis Carroll '78, was elected its president; William P. Higgins '03, then a Massachusetts legislator, was chosen vice president and Dr. Fennessey was made secretary-treasurer.

On May 8, at the Astor Hotel, the New York Club held its annual banquet and featured Father Andrew Morrissey, Provincial and former President, as their speaker. Toasts at this banquet, in the old campus tradition, were: Prosit, alma mater, the graduate, chance and achievement, character, professional success, and fraternity, the latter responded to by Father Morrissey.

Father Cavanaugh was never accused of being athletic-oriented. Yet in 1907 the Notre Dame baseball team played 23 games, lost only to Illinois, Purdue and Minnesota. In 1908 the basketball team played its first major schedule, 19 games. And in 1908, Michigan, absent from the football schedule since 1902, returned for a game at Notre Dame which it won 12 to 6. In these several years, Harry "Red" Miller and Don Hamilton, future presidents of the Alumni Association, Howard "Cap" Edwards, George Philbrook, Robert "Pete" Vaughan, Bill Schmitt and others among the growing ranks of football heroes, swung the weight of Notre Dame athletics away from Dubuc, Waldorf, Cutshaw, Daniels, Ruell and the Scanlans who with their predecessors had loomed large in college and big-league baseball.

It was in 1908 that the enrollment passed 1,000—for the first time.

The Chicago Alumni Association had heroically tried to fill the role of an association for its own alumni and for alumni at large. But in the face of the expanding opportunities of the University, and its rapidly increasing needs for resources beyond the old dependence upon student fees and unremunerated services for religious (and the minimum salaries of a dedicated lay faculty), Father Cavanaugh was convinced that a strong, permanent Alumni Association would be an essential factor in progress. To this end he addressed a letter to all living graduates of the University, on Feb. 10, 1908:

> Dear Friend: In reponse to a general demand for the organization of the alumni of the University of Notre Dame, I have decided to summon all the living graduates to assemble at Notre Dame on June 17, 1908, for the purpose of drafting a constitution and perfecting an organization.
>
> The need of such an association is as keenly felt by the University as it is by the alumni; and the educational work to which alma mater stands dedicated is sure to receive great impetus from it.
>
> This invitation will be restricted to graduates of those courses which at the present time demand the high school diploma or its equivalent as an entrance requirement. Under this ruling graduates of any course leading to the degree of bachelor or engineer are entitled to a seat in this first convention.

The commencement exercises are fixed for the evening of Wednesday, June 17, and the morning of Thursday, June 18. For the benefit of those who may not be able to tarry long at the University, the organization of the Alumni Association will take place on Wednesday morning at 10 o'clock. The alumni dinner will follow.

This movement means much to alma mater as well as to all her loyal sons. It is hoped that every alumnus of the University will be present, no matter what the inconvenience. So far as possible the former officers, teachers and prefects of the University will be in attendance.

I enclose a postal card for your reply. Be sure and add your present address. Very cordially yours, (sig.) John W. Cavanaugh, C.S.C.

Like Noah on Arrarat, like Columbus on the shores of America, like the first astronaut on the moon—the solid footing was imminent which had been planned for many years and earned through many ordeals.

XV

Volunteer Army

The important period of history in the life of the Alumni Association which began with that call to organization from Father John W. Cavanaugh and which extended from 1908 to 1923 owes its achievements to the volunteer alumni—on and off the campus—who envisioned the growth of the University and its alumni and who could understand then the importance of an organized alumni constituency. Like the arguments for other volunteer armies, they were involved because they believed in the program. They enlisted willingly. They served faithfully. They worked hard. They asked no pay other than the prestige which their collective effort brought to Notre Dame and the greater stature which accrued to alumni as the University grew. The pleasant leaven of fraternal association was a rewarding by-product of the larger and more serious goals. This atmosphere of relaxed enjoyment is one which can solve many of the problems that attend volunteer participation anywhere.

The race between William Howard Taft and the still eloquent William Jennings Bryan for the presidency of the United States stimulated the year 1908. A conference of state governors called by the White House to discuss conservation indicates that many problems of early origin have not enjoyed early solution. The total gifts to American higher education in 1908 from all sources were $19,763,421, less than half the present annual budget of Notre Dame.

And as any history unfolds, it is important to keep in mind the relation of its goals and accomplishments to the concepts of its own era rather than to the much larger concepts time has created. Alumni programs in 1908 were isolated. It was 1913 before alumni secretaries discovered the joys and profits of comparing notes between their respective institutions. The national pattern was primarily volunteer. Yale had begun an annual giving program among its alumni in 1892 but the concept of alumni giving to their alma mater after graduation was in its infancy and its results so unimpressive as to remain for many years unrecorded in the arenas of intercollegiate competition.

In South Bend, in 1908, Studebaker's were still advertising "Wagons, Carriages, Harness and Automobiles." An insight into the discipline of the University could be found in Louis Nickel's saloon. Each fall, Louis would present a fresh table top to the senior class, and by the end of their last year, their names would be carved into the table's top, with clarity, and often with flourish. A prefect of discipline could have decimated a class with those carvings—had he wished. Such was the understanding of "la vie intime" that none so wished.

In the 1908 Easter *Scholastic* satisfactory progress was reported in the preparation for the alumni reunion and reorganization in June. The clerical work was considerable, as any alumni office will attest. "An effort has been made to have each graduate of the University report personally his present whereabouts, and to state whether or not he will attend the meeting."

In May, 1908, the Notre Dame Club of Portland, Ore., was formed at a meeting of 23 alumni at the Commercial Club. Hon. John M. Gearin was elected its first president, John F. Daly, vice president and the secretary-treasurer was Frank J. Lonergan, later in life to become grand exalted ruler of the Elks of the United States. Before its organizational meeting adjourned, the club voted the establishment of a day scholarship at Columbia University, the Holy Cross school which became the present University of Portland. Father Joseph Gallagher, C.S.C., was then its president and extended the hospitality of the College to the club for one of its proposed semi-annual dinners.

The beacon in the original Notre Dame clearing was becoming brighter. And the roads which crossed it were extending to the far corners of Ameria.

In May of 1908, as a great prelude and stimulus to the alumni reunion, Notre Dame celebrated the silver jubilee of the Laetare Medal. Katherine Conway, Dr. Francis Quinlan, the Hon. Timothy Howard, Hon. William Onahan, Dr. John Murphy and James Monaghan were among the medalists present for the occasion. Timothy Howard's inclusion highlights the ultimate presence of

a goodly number of alumni among these honored outstanding
Catholic laymen in America. Father Cavanaugh was the celebrant of the jubilee Mass, assisted by Fathers Thomas Crumley
and Matthews Schumacher. I am sorry that no picture is extant
to show those three magnificent priests in the vestments of the
Church they served so brilliantly. Dr. John Talbot Smith, one of
the great Catholic orators, preached the sermon. The faculty
and senior class hosted the guests at a reception. They were
taken on a tour of Saint Mary's. In the evening both the band
and the orchestra added to the program. Dr. Quinlan delivered
the jubilee address. The Laetare Medal had come of age as a
major Catholic institution in this country, a record and a
prestige attaching to it which have grown in the subsequent
years.

The *Dome* of 1908 heralded the alumni organization:

Although the old students and graduates of Notre Dame
have been representative in every phase of human activity
and although they have done much for their alma mater, they
have not for many years had an organized alumni association.
As a result of a wide-spread demand among members of the
alumni for such an organization, on Feb. 10, 1908, the
President issued a call to all the graduates of Notre Dame.

The total number of living graduates is between six and
seven hundred. More than half of these have declared their
intention to be present at the University on the date set for
organization. Among the more venerable guests of honor who
will be present are the two oldest graduates of this institution, Major General Robert W. Healy, retired, of Chattanooga, Tenn., and Hon. James O'Brien of Caledonia, Minn. Both
these men were of the Class of 1859.

In addition to this projects, the President is exhorting the
old students of the University to organize Notre Dame Clubs
in all towns or cities where the number of Notre Dame
students warrant such an organization. To the membership of
such clubs not only alumni but all former students who care
enough for their school to wish to be identified with her
would be eligible.

Considerable work has been done in this direction already.
Several of our large cities have such clubs—Chicago, New York,
Boston, Philadelphia, Pittsburgh, Portland, Ore., and Dayton,
O., are among them. It is desired that, in response to this
exhortation from the President, many more clubs will spring
into existence in the near future; that, in connection with the
Alumni Association, these clubs may preserve among the old
students those friendly ties which were formed in their college days; and that they may also keep the affection between
the students and the University ever warm and unimpaired.

The commencement number of the *Scholastic* in 1908 carried a comment with portent for the years ahead:

At 10:30 on Wednesday morning a meeting of the alumni was called in Brownson Hall for the purpose of organizing an alumni association. The movement is one that will bear much desirable fruit, for the permanent organization of all the sons of Notre Dame will keep alive in their hearts a warm love for their alma mater and a lively interest in her success and development. Moreover, it will work much good for themselves, for as a band of Catholic laymen united by a common tie and directed in their movements by the greatest exponent of enlightened education and sterling virtue, the University of Notre Dame, the effectiveness of their efforts for the advancement of Catholicity and the acceptance of Catholic ideals will be multiplied.

Admirable spirit was manifest at this meeting and great success waited upon the work of organization. So great was the zeal of those present for securing the best constitution and the best officers for carrying out the constitution that two additional meetings were necessary for the satisfactory conclusion of the business. The alumni banquet was announced for 1 o'clock, and Brownson refectory was gay with music and flowers . . . A feast was there in very truth, feast for the eye and the ear as well as for the inner man. But the best part of the banquet came after the last dish had been removed, when the toastmaster, William P. Breen '77, called on different members of the alumni body for an expression of their sentiment regarding the heroic past, the glowing present, and the all-promising future of their alma mater. Limited space does not permit us to speak in detail, but full treatment will be given the subject in the next issue of the *Scholastic* which will be the alumni number.

The *Scholastic* announced also the publication of the first *Alumni Directory*. All the graduates, honorary and in course, from the foundation of the institution to 1908 were included. Also listed were their year of graduation, the degree or degrees received and the present address of each living graduate. A chronological list of the degrees awarded by the University was added. The compilation, which had entailed a great amount of labor and correspondence, was the work of Father Michael A. Quinlan, C.S.C. '93.

The official minutes of that first meeting in 1908 were significant.

In accordance with a call issued by Very Rev. John Cavanaugh, C.S.C. '90, the President of the University, the alumni of Notre Dame met at 10:30 a.m. on Wednesday, June 17, for the formation of an association. President Cavanaugh in happy and well-chosen words bade the gentlemen assembled welcome. Hon. Timothy E. Howard '62, was chosen temporary chairman and Daniel P. Murphy '95, temporary secretary. On motion, made and carried, the chair appointed Hugh A. O'Donnell '94, Thomas A Daily '74, and Rev. Thomas A. Crumley, C.S.C. '96, as a committeee of three to report a Constitution for the association. The Constitution as reported was discussed and the same after amendments made was duly adopted. The text of the Constitution is as follows:

Art. I.—This organization shall be known as the Alumni Association of the University of Notre Dame.

Art. II.—The officers shall consist of an honorary president, a president, six vice presidents, secretary, treasurer and a board of eight trustees. All the officers shall be elected annually except the members of the board. The President of the University and the president of the associa ion shall be exofficio members of the board. The remaining six members shall be chosen, three for a term of one year, their successors to be chosen for a term of two years.

Art. III.—The association shall meet annually in connection with the commencement exercises of the University.

Art. IV.—The object of the association shall be to promote friendly relations among the alumni of the University and to further the interests of alma mater in such ways as may be considered best.

Art. V.—The members of the association shall be active or honorary. The active members shall be: first, all graduates of Notre Dame University in those courses which demand the high school diploma, or its equivalent for admission: second, masters in course of the University and doctors of philosophy; and third, present and past presidents, vice presidents and directors of studies of the University.

The honorary members of the Association shall be: first, all who receive from the University degrees *in honorem*, and second, anyone who has ever been actively connected with the University as professor or student and who on application is elected a member at a regular annual meeting.

Art. VI.—The members of this association shall pay an annual fee of five dollars to defray the expenses of the yearly reunion.

Art. VII.—This constitution may be changed at any annual meeting by a vote of two-thirds of the members present at such a meeting, provided the proposed change be published in the *Scholastic* at least three months in advance.

The following officers of the association were then chosen:

Father A. Morrissey, C.S.C. '78, Notre Dame, Ind., honorary president;

William P. Breen, '77, Fort Wayne, Ind., president;

Hon. James B. O'Brien '59 of Caledonia, Minn., Gen. R.W. Healy '59 of Chattanooga, Tenn., Father Timothy D.

O'Sullivan '88 of Chicago, Ill.; Hon. Timothy E. Howard '62 of South Bend, Ind.; Father Denis A. Clarke '70 of Columbus, Ohio, and John B. Ewing '77 of Chicago, Ill. vice presidents;

Father Michael A. Quinlan, C.S.C. '93, Notre Dame, Ind., secretary;

Warren A. Cartier '87, Ludington, Mich., treasurer;

Ex-officio trustees: Father John W. Cavanaugh, C.S.C., Notre Dame, Ind., and William P. Breen '77, Fort Wayne, Ind.; for one year, Hon. John M. Gearin '71 of Portland, Ore., Gustavo L. Trevino '08 of Monterey, Mexico and William Dechant '78 of Middletown, O.; for two years, Samuel T. Murdock '86 of LaFayette, Ind., Byron V. Kanaley '04 of Chicago, Ill., and Hon. Charles P. Neill of Washington, D.C. The elected members of the former Society of the Associated Alumni were declared elected members of this association.

Membership was voted to the following, once students of Notre Dame—Most Rev. Patrick W. Riordan, D.D. Archbishop of San Francisco, Calif.; Rev. Patrick Crawley, Marion, Ind., and Augustus F. Meehan, Chattanooga, Tenn.

It was voted that on the day of the annual reunion a requiem Mass be offered for the deceased members, the Mass next year to be sung by honorary president of the association. It was voted that the dues of the association shall be payable by Jan. 1 each year. On motion the meeting adjourned.

> Rev. M.A. Quinlan, C.S.C., Secretary.
> William P. Breen, President.

The general story in the *Scholastic* contained some important additions to the minutes themselves:

Nothing of the recent years has given greater satisfaction to the Faculty of the University and all the well-wishers of Notre Dame than the reunion of the alumni, held on Wednesday, June 17. The President of the University had during the course of the past winter taken up and discussed with many of the old students the advisability of the formation of an alumni association which should meet at Notre Dame. His aim was practically to revive the old Society of the Associated Alumni, since the new association was to have like purpose and aims.

The Society of the Associated Alumni, formed in 1868, had for certain reasons ceased to exist during the course of the 80's. The last meeting was held June 24, 1890.

The response to the call was most satisfactory both in the number and the representation of the alumni who were present. Practically every class that the University has sent forth was represented by at least one member. In fact, with the exception of the classes whose members are all dead, only seven classes, those of '64, '69, '71, '73, '76 and '82 failed to

be represented. The gathering gave ample promise that the
succeeding years would see the alumni in greater numbers
returning to the annual commencements. The gathering was a
source of intense pleasure to the old boys, from the representatives of '59, who for the first time since that year met face
to face, down to the boys of '07. Old ties were renewed and
the memories of the past days revived. The bonds of attach-
ment to Notre Dame were strengthened for all by the meeting among the old scenes of those who had gone forth and
become engrossed in the cares of daily life. The enthusiasm
and devotion of her sons for Notre Dame was greatly increased.

The informal talks of those who were called on during the
business meeting and the remarks of those who responded to
the formal toasts at the dinner were a source of great pleasure
to all. The members were expecially delighted with the remarks of Healy and O'Brien, the men of '59, redolent of the
olden days and full of fund recollections, and the eloquent
words of Kanaley '04, the representative of the younger men,
who told of Notre Dame's future.

The meeting itself was harmonious. The only topic that
aroused debate was the determining of the membership of
the association. None but graduates of the academic courses
of the University had been invited to the meeting. The
committee appointed by the chairman to draft a constitution
and submit it, reported an article on membership which
enlarged the body. In addition to graduates in course and in
honorem they proposed to admit all at any time professors in
the university, and all students of the University who subsequently received Holy Orders. The meeting rejected the article and framed one of its own. Membership is to be active or
honorary. The active members can be the Presidents, vice
presidents and directors of studies of Notre Dame; graduates
in those courses requiring for their admission high school
requirements, masters in course and doctors of philosophy of
the University. The honorary members are to be those receiving honorary degrees from the University, and anyone who at
any time was connected with the University as professor or
student and who upon application has been elected a member
at a regular annual meeting. There was no disposition to keep
out those once connected with Notre Dame, but who had not
received her degrees; but there was decided opinion that they
should not become the governing element in the association,
and that they should be submitted in each case to a vote of
the members. With these restrictions, their admission will, in
a desired case, be but a matter of form.

The early impetus of the new alumni spirit was evident in
September of 1908 when 20 alumni met at the Fort Pitt hotel
in Pittsburgh for the purpose of organizing a club. D.C. Dillion
'04, gave the opening address, and appointed T.P. Butler as

temporary secretary. A constitution which had been previously drafted was presented, amended after spirited discussion, and adopted.

"Then followed the election of officers. By a unanimous vote, Father Cavanaugh, President of the University, was elected honorary president. R.J. Daschbach was elected president. Raymond Burns '05, was named vice president; T.P. Butler '05, secretary and Howard Diebold '05, treasurer. A committee was appointed by the chair to act in conjunction with the officers. It was moved and carried that the Pennsylvania (campus) Club of Notre Dame should act in union with the Notre Dame Club in holding the annual ball at Christmas time, and that the duly elected president of the Pennsylvania Club should be a vice president of the Notre Dame Club. Father Michael A. Quinlan, C.S.C., representing the University, gave the address of the evening."

In December, another manisfestation of the new alumni spirit was reported:

"Notre Dame may well be proud of her alumni. That the alumni are proud of Notre Dame is evident. This fact was demonstrated to a nicety last week at Milwaukee, when the Alumni Association of Wisconsin turned out to welcome the football team . . . At the game (Notre Dame defeated Marquette 6-0) the Notre Dame bleachers were turned into a reception room. Here alumnus and student met as brothers. The mere fact that a man was rooting for Notre Dame was sufficient introduction to any other man of similar qualification. At the banquet the same spirit prevailed.

An interesting paragraph appears in Father Hope's *Notre Dame - 100 Years.*

> During the school year of 1908-09 the faculty had been strengthened, particularly in the Law School. Many newly ordained priests gave added vitality to the teaching force. Notre Dame received public commendation for its care of the moral life of its students. In Houston, Tex., an article appeared urging the country to turn its eyes on this school which fostered "the moral training of the student with equal tenacity to that shown for his intellectual and physical uplift." To be sure, Notre Dame had her share of undesirable boys, but once they were discovered Father Cavanaugh would not tolerate their presence . . .

The second annual reunion of the newly organized Alumni Association was held in June, 1909. A solemn High Mass at 8 o'clock opened the program. The morning was spent in visiting

the buildings, and in the relaxation of reminiscence. The alumni
banquet was held at noon in the decorated Brownson refectory.
The familiar Brownson study hall, with its desks and "throne"
was the scene of the business meeting. William P. Breen '77.
president, chaired the meeting. The minutes of that second
meeting follow:

At half past one o'clock on June 16, 1909, the members of
the Alumni Association of the University of Notre Dame met
at the University for the election of officers for the ensuing
year and for the transaction of the ordinary business of the
organization. The treasurer's report was read and accepted. It
showed that dues had been received from 196 members and
that the cash balance on hand was $856.75.

The attention of the association was called to the illness of
George Clarke '81 and the secretary was instructed to extend to
him a message of sympathy, regretting Mr. Clarke's inability
to be present at the meeting and hoping for his early recovery. Attention was also called to the fact that five of the
members of the association had died since last June, and a
committee of three, J.F. Shea, B.V. Kanaley and J.J. Sullivan, was named to draft suitable resolutions for publication
in the *Scholastic* . . .

A change in the constitution was adopted to the effect
that Article VI is to read, The members of the association
shall pay an annual fee of five dollars to be disposed of by
the association on the recommendation of the board of
trustees, members of the Congregation of the Holy Cross to
be exempt from this fee. This change is to be retroactive after
being approved at the next annual meeting.

A report was received stating that Gen. St. Clair Mulholland desired that the alumni be invited to contribute to the
memorial that is to be erected on the field of Gettysburg in
memory of Father Corby. Acting on this report, the association invited Father Cavanaugh to send out an appeal at the
expense of the association.

A letter expressing his regret at being unable to attend the
meeting was sent to the association by Hugh O'Connell '04,
and was read for the members. A souvenir menu card of the
Notre Dame Club of New York was presented to the association with the greetings of the club. A communication was
also received from C.S. Mitchell '94, in regard to an endowment plan. The secretary of the association was notified to
inform Mr. Mitchell that the matter would be taken under
advisement.

The election of officers resulted as follows: Father A. Morrissey, C.S.C., Notre Dame, Ind., honorary president; Hon. Warren
A. Cartier '87, Ludington, Mich., president; Hon. William P.

Breen '77, Fort Wayne, Ind., treasurer and Father William Maloney, C.S.C. '90, Notre Dame, Ind., secretary.

Trustees 1908-1910: Byron V. Kanaley '04, Chicago, Ill. and Hon. Charles P. Neill '93, Washington, D.C.

Trustrees 1908-1911: Hon. John M. Gearin '71, Portland, Ore.; Gustavo L. Trevino '08, Notre Dame, In., and Hon. William Dechant '78, Middletown, Ohio.

Ex-officio trustees: Father John Cavanaugh, C.S.C. '90, President University of Notre Dame.

Vice Presidents: John J. Kennedy '09 of Scottdale, Pa., Father Timothy D. O'Sullivan '88 of Chicago, Ill., Hon. Timothy E. Howard '62 of South Bend, Ind., John G. Ewing '77 of San Juan, Porto Rico, Daniel P. Murphy '95 of Chicago, Ill., and Daniel V. Casey '95 of Chicago, Ill.

The Alumni Association of the University of Notre Dame was now firmly rooted in the University, where its center properly must be. But it took its new direction as an association from its officers, as it properly must do.

The good fortune of Notre Dame and the association was in the dedicated strength of those officers.

William P. Breen '77, president the first year and treasurer the second, remained active and a pillar of the volunteer years. He is only partly commemorated on the campus by Breen-Phillips Hall-named for himself and a brother-in-law, Frank Phillips, whose benefactions permitted the Hall to be built—and in several scholarships in the Law School, so dear to Breen's heart.

Warren A. Cartier '87, Ludington, Mich., donor of Cartier Field, was the treasurer of the association in its first year and its president in its second. He resumed the treasurer's post later and retained it throughout the volunteer years, during which time the association pursued a program to raise enough money to build an Old Students Hall. We will say more of the success of that project later, but Cartier was invaluable. Father William A. Moloney, C.S.C. '90, became the secretary, a post which he also held effectively during the years of volunteer activity, without help from an office or magazine. This association office is one who then, as now, belongs on the campus.

Trustees and vice presidents comprised a formidable group, with seven states and Puerto Rico represented in the group.

From this newly organized association, enjoying the full cooperation of Father John W. Cavanaugh and his faculty, the unwavering course of the Alumni Association was charted. The alumni response to the plea of Gen. Mulholland for funds for the Corby statue was only one of the many responses alumni were to make to Notre Dame or the illustrious causes which traced their purpose or their personnel to the spreading clearing in the St. Joseph Valley. The bridge and the beacon based at Notre Dame now had microcosms of the campus on most of the main highways of America, and the crossroads became busy.

XVI

Peace, Progress and Polish

Being familiar with South Bend you may mistake this title as partly ethnic. It isn't. It simply brings us to an era of peace and progress, marked by a polish reflecting the maturity of the University and the glow which surrounded its President, on and off the campus. In part, too, it reflected an aura of growth and maturity in the United States, although both were as far removed nationally as they were on the campus, in what was yet to come.

The year 1910 was a census year. In 1840, the year before Father Sorin arrived in America, the total population of the United States was 17,000,000. In 1910 the population reached 92,000,000. Notre Dame was growing in a national climate of growth. The per capita wealth in the United States in 1850, the first year it is listed in census figures, was $307. In 1910 it had increased to $1,965. America was still a land of opportunity, rather than a land of plenty—especially for the Catholic families who provided the majority of students for Notre Dame.

In January, 1910, the Notre Dame men in New York City and vicinity congregated in the King Edward Hotel on 47th Street. This meeting was a forerunner of a great gathering to take place in the spring, which the group announced would make all other Notre Dame societies and all other college societies in the land "sit up and take notice." A group of young alumni including Frank Ward O'Malley, Peter McElligott, Anthony Brogan, Thomas Reilly and Ambrose O'Connell were at work. Father Luke Evers read the meeting a letter from Father Cavanaugh which inspired them to cheers, and a pledge that they would never permit an opportunity to pass to advance the best interests of their alma mater. The promise has been consistently exceeded by the performance of the club throughout the years.

The alumni reunion in June was successful. The alumni banquet, in the Brownson dining room, which was decorated, found 200 alumni listening to the music of Professor Peterson's University orchestra. Toasts reflected the maturing confidence of the Alumni Association. "First impressions," "Rec days in the '60's," "How to bring up a prefect of discipline," "The Jubilee Class," "How times change" and "Notre Dame orators" brought informative, nostalgic and humorous responses.

The third annual meeting was called to order by President Warren Cartier. After minutes and the admission of the Class of 1910, the president recommended several changes in the constitution, which were referred to a committee—Rev. William A. Moloney, C.S.C., Samuel Murdock and Byron Kanaley. Resolutions for members who died during the year were passed. It was announced that extension of the *Alumni Directory* would include residential as well as alphabetical and chronological data. And a biographical directory was in the making.

The 1910 meeting heard a letter read from C. Stockdale Mitchell, who urged that the members take definite steps towards the erection of an alumni memorial hall. The President of the University reported that his letter to alumni had brought $1,500 towards the Corby monument at Gettysburg. The meeting was apprised of the fine athletic records compiled during the year, which had included the victory over Michigan in football and the title "Champions of the West."

The election of officers brought Father John Dinnen '65, Lafayette, Ind., to the post of honorary president and Frank O.Shaughnessy '00, Chicago to president. The vice presidents were William Hoynes '77, Rev. M.J. Regan '85, William A. McInerny '01, Anton C. Stephan '04 and Harold M. "Red" Miller '10—the latter honor expressing the enthusiasm of the association for the Michigan defeat.

The treasurer, William P. Breen, who had been delayed by a train wreck, read his report at the banquet, revealing a balance of $1,494. The constitutional committee reported its endorsement of the recommendation that no fees be collected from members who have been given honorary degrees by the University, and that an amendment to Article VI read, "The members of the association shall pay an annual fee of five dollars to be disposed of by the association on recommendation of the board of trustees." The committee believed that no change should be made in the time appointed for meetings, "unless the faculty deem that the interest of the Univeristy will be better served by biennial meetings. Moreover, as to the sentiment of the association in regard to officers holding their positions for more than one year, your committee recommends that election of officers be held annually." History produced another rich overlap when Father Provincial Morrissey said the alumni Mass, assisted by Father Dinnen '65, and Father Matthew Walsh, C.S.C., '03.

The *Dome* of 1910 was warm in its praise of the association support of the Gettysburg monument to Father William Corby, C.S.C., the chaplain who had mounted a boulder on the battlefield in those deadly July days to give general absolution to the Irish Brigade about to go into battle. On Oct. 19, on the battlefield, this bronze monument was placed on a rock from which he had given the absolution, and a bronze plate has identified his heroism and spirtuality for millions of visitors to the historic site. Notre Dame men remember him best as priest, prefect of discipline, director of the manual labor school, President of Notre Dame, founder of Sacred Heart College in Watertown and provincial of his Congregation.

Another event of increasing significance through the years was the formation in 1910 of the Notre Dame Council of the Knights of Columbus, the first council to be established on a college campus. John C. Tully '10, LaGrange, Ill., later a lay trustee of the University, was the first grand knight. John F. O'Hara '10, was a member of this first group—yet to add C.S.C., prefect of religion, dean of commerce; bishop in the military ordinariate of World War II; bishop of Buffalo, and ultimately John Cardinal O'Hara, C.S.C., archbishop of Philadelphia. It has taken a large and fine book to unfold the biography of Cardinal O'Hara, authored magnificently by the late Father Thomas McAvoy, C.S.C. '25.

Notre Dame Council 1477 has through the years sent men back to most of the Knights of Columbus councils in America. A number of alumni retain their campus membership. Alumni of the council have risen to the supreme council of the order. Faculty and students before 1910 had been active and interested in the South Bend council, but the University was reluctant to create a student group not wholly directed by Notre Dame. The question of the autonomy of the partly campus and partly national council has always been a delicate, but happily resolved area. The move brought to the national Knights of Columbus an interested and informed contact with the Univer-

sity, a tie reflected in the presence of many sons of knights in
the student body. And the campus grand knights, being a
minority of student leadership responsible to outside mature
superiors, developed a maturity and a capacity for program
organization reflected in their many subsequent careers of distinction.

In March of 1911, the students of Corby Hall, in a meeting
attended by Father Cavanaugh, and addressed by Father
Thomas Irving, agreed to underwrite a replica of the statue of
Father Corby at Gettysburg, to be placed on the Notre Dame campus in front of Corby Hall. They opened the contributions to any
other students on the campus, and immediately sent a letter to all
former students who had lived in Corby Hall. The statue was
the work of a Philadelphia sculptor, Samuel Murray, who probably had no idea that the gesture of blessing would be translated
into "Fair Catch," the more frequent designation of Father
Corby's statue by succeeding generations. There is general agreement that the good Father Corby would have been the first to
enjoy this by-product. In any event, the statue was indeed
delivered and dedicated on Memorial Day of 1911. "Religion,
eloquence, music, military display, a large audience and a perfect summer day added each a glory to the solemn event." The
students and the military companies, numerous visitors, and the
seniors from Saint Mary's were in attendance. Col. William
Hoynes presided. Father John Chidwick, who had been chaplain
on the Battleship Maine and was now president of Dunwoodie
Seminary, delivered an appropriate address.

There is a misunderstanding among alumni, which I had
shared until I looked at the record, that even during these years
from 1908 to 1923, the Alumni Association functioned only at
the commencement week reunion. There was actually much
during each of those years that supplemented alumni interest
and involvement. "La vie intime" was augmented by the
Alumni Association and its progress, but it was not displaced by
them.

For example, Professor James Farnham Edwards died in
January of 1911. The *Scholastic* wrote of him: "From his
earliest years Professor Edwards had consecrated himself at the
shrine of Christian education and labored within its sanctuary
for nearly half a century with unswerving fidelity. Few members of the faculty were as well known to the outside world."
He had inherited from Father Lemonnier the task of building
the library. He had expanded that task into the Catholic Ar-

chives and the Bishops Memorial Hall. He was one of the founders of the Laetare Medal. He had been a friend and confidant of Sorin, and continued much of Sorin's dedicated fervor. Professor Edwards, as a mark of community appreciation, was buried in the Community Cemetery where Sorin and his many other priest and brother friends had preceded him, as well as close to colleagues of his early days, Professor Joseph Lyons and Professor Michael Corby.

In April the New York Club held its announced spring meeting at the Waldorf-Astoria Hotel, then at the pinnacle of American hostelries. Guests from the clubs in Boston, Philadelphia and Washington were on hand. Father Luke Evers, a pioneer in the New York organization, presided. Daniel P. Murphy acted as toastmaster. At the speakers table were Father Provincial Morrissey, Father President Cavanaugh, Sen. Benjamin Shively of Indiana, Laetare Medalist Dr. Thomas Emmet, U.S. Commissioner of Labor Charles P. Neill, Laetare Medalist and former Professor James Monaghan, Dr. James J. Walsh, Dr. Austin O'Malley, Dr. John Talbot Smith, Father James A. Burns, Msgr. Lavelle, Laetare Medalist Dr. Francis Quinlan, Joseph M. Byrne Sr., and Frank P. Smith. Father Cavanaugh delivered one of his outstanding addresses, which was nationally quoted. Scenes of buildings and faculty were flashed on a screen. Programs were printed in gold and blue. Notre Dame was "playing the Palace."

May of 1911 marked the death of Father Martin Regan, C.S.C. Although only 59 at the time of his death, he had long been a dynamic part of the life of the Notre Dame campus. For 23 years he was prefect of discipline. He had served as a teacher in the Congregation's schools in Watertown and Cincinnati, but it was Notre Dame and its students that he loved. The *Scholastic* said, "His enthusiasm for the advancement of the University and the welfare of all connected with it was a striking characteristic; but perhaps the most remarkable feature of his work was the fact that, compelled every moment of every day to restrain here and check there, to refuse requests and administer admonitions and penalties, he enjoyed a remarkable degree of respect and admiration in the affection of the students, past and present. In the hearts of the thousands of young men throughout the country, the influence of Father Regan is cherished and his memory revered." The nickname "Daddy" indicates his appeal. One of the apocryphal legends of his disciplinary regime was that he possessed an uncanny instinct for those who

were smuggling forbidden spirits into the halls, and while few
were punished for the offense, confiscastion of the smuggled
goods was an inescapable penalty.

And thus the passing of the baton of the family that was
Notre Dame continued. Father Charles L. O'Donnell, C.S.C., a
brilliant young priest, joined the Notre Dame faculty as Prof.
"Jimmy" Edwards and "Daddy" Regan were taken from the
campus. He was never to bring the personal warmth of those
two men to his career, but he brought a new stature to the
University and to the Church by his intellectual and cultural
achievements, and by his somewhat paradoxical administrative
abilities as University President during the disastrous years of
the Depression.

Alumni had made an impression on the editors of the 1911
Dome.

> Alumni day is always a day of great rejoicing at the Univer-
> sity, for it is a day when men become boys again, and
> forgetting the cares of the business world revisit familiar
> places and recall forgotten scenes. Perhaps it is their wont to
> comment a little sadly on the changes that have taken place
> since their time, or to chide us, their successors, with light-
> ness or ill regard for tradition . . . To the alumni our best
> wishes go out. Their prosperity and success mean the success
> of the University, and we rejoice with them in it. The
> measure of their success must be their loyalty to Notre Dame
> and its principles of honesty and integrity.

My early reminder to you that "success" of alumni means
something other than, and more than, material success, had
early and deep roots. So did the observation that at the reunions, men became boys again. This wholesome rejuvenation
was the reason later for the separate reunion weekend and for
the long years of discouragement of the bringing of wives or
children.

One of the outstanding alumni, who enjoyed to the full these
gatherings of alumni and was always present, provided the
policy with a strong case history. Byron V. Kanaley '04, was
fond of telling how he finally yielded to the persuasions of his
wife, Kate, to bring her to the campus for such an event. He
said that at the conclusion of the festivities, he boarded the
train for Chicago, as he had so many times before. But as he
neared Chicago, he felt a nagging memory overtaking him,
which it did. He had forgotten to bring Kate home with him. In
his later years as trustee, both he and Kate enjoyed the visits to
the slightly more formal weekends of that dedicated group.

In 1912, the University received an unexpected benefaction, a gift of $15,000 from Max Pam, a Chicago non-Catholic, to be used for a chair of journalism. Pam felt that at Notre Dame much could be achieved toward his hopes that journalism could be bettered by the injection of religion and morality into the vital means of communication. He felt that the immoral and unjust practices in newspapers at the time were attributable largely to editors and reporters without religious or moral education. He believed that "the man who makes public opinion should, by education, by conviction, and by habit in all he does be led by conscience and truth, courage and honesty born of conscience."

Father Cavanaugh, unsuccessful in his effort to bring Dr. John Talbot Smith to Notre Dame to head the journalism department, appointed Professor John M. Cooney to the new post. But having reservations about Cooney's stature nationally, he prevailed upon James Keeley, nationally known general manager of the *Chicago Tribune*, to become the dean of journalism. Keeley was swayed in his acceptance by a letter from a Chicago newsman who said, "I would like to add that Notre Dame for some reason I never quite understood has furnished us a higher percentage of repertorial successes than any other school from which we draw applicants. I think you have the best body of men in the West to work on."

There is also the theory that Notre Dame already considered as basic in its education for all students the principles which Mr. Pam hoped to see in journalism. It remained the policy of the department of journalism throughout its lifetime.

In January, 1912, the Notre Dame Club of Chicago sponsored a dinner at the Great Northern followed by a theatre party. Monthly dinners were being held. And the club had reserved a section of seats in the First Regiment Armory for that organization's track meet. (Notre Dame scored 25 points.) On the Notre Dame team at the time were two men to be active in Chicago and alumni activities for many years, Fred Steers and Knute Rockne.

On February 29, 1912-Leap Year-one of Notre Dame's great bachelors, Col. William Hoynes, was honored by the Notre Dame Club of New York at a banquet in the Manhattan Hotel. The colonel had just returned from Rome where he had been granted papal knighthood by the Holy Father. He was accompanied by Father Morrissey. The two arrived at the White Star docks in New York and were met by a committee from the club, which escorted them to the banquet. Father Morrissey

talked on the nature of the honor conferred on the colonel, the
Knighthood of St. Gregory. James P. Fogerty '00, Philadelphia,
spoke on the personality and scholarship of the guest of honor.
Dr. James J. Walsh, long a figure on the lecture platform at
Notre Dame, as eloquent and distinguished as the colonel him-
self, rounded out the program.

In May, the Notre Dame Club of Chicago similarly honored
the newly knighted Colonel Hoynes at a banquet which filled
the University Club auditorium. The honor was relatively new
to American Catholics and the "best elements" of business and
professional life in Chicago were on hand.

For the modern club, and for the few who remain skeptical
about the academic stature of Notre Dame—possibly, even, for
those who enjoyed some of the eloquent sessions of the colonel
in his Sorin Hall offices—it must be noted that speeches were
delivered in German, Spanish, Scandinavian, Polish and Gaelic.

In May, also, the Minnesota Notre Dame Club was rechris-
tened to mark its expansion beyond the Twin Cities boundaries.
It now numbered 75 members, which the report stated, made it
one of the largest of the Notre Dame Clubs. Louis P. Chute '90,
was elected president.

In May, too, Archbishop Riordan of San Francisco, an old
student of the University, now 70 years old, visited the campus
and spoke to the students. "His was a message from the past;
the men he knew and loved—Sorin, Granger, Shortis, Corby,
L'Eterneau—his voice grew husky with feeling when he expressed his large love for his alma mater, which neither miles
nor years have ever been able to make less warm or less
bright . . . "

The Notre Dame baseball trip East marked the organization
of a permanent club in Washington, D.C., following a banquet
tendered the team by area alumni at Maison Raucher. Seventy
persons were present. Elmer J. Murphy '97, presided at the
banquet. Father Edward Pace, of Catholic U.; Dr. Hannis Taylor, former Minister to Spain; Father James A. Burns, C.S.C.,
rector of Holy Cross College; Hon. Henry Barnhart and Hon.
Charles Rarbely, congressmen from Indiana, were among the
guests. Both congressmen spoke on the values of education and
athletics, and the need of men of character in public life.

Dr. Charles P. Neil. '93, U.S. Commissioner of Labor, was
elected president of the new club. A constitutional committee
was appointed.

The baseball team, winners over Mt. St. Mary's, were apparently moved by their welcome, and lost to Catholic University 8-2.

After a win over Seton Hall, 4-3, on the same Eastern trip, the team was banqueted by the New York Club. Joseph M. Byrne, Sr., a former Notre Dame pitcher, and a prominent alumnus in the metropolitan area, gave the principle talk. The *Scholastic* reported that "the boys were royally entertained." This phrase became almost synonymous with the names of Joseph M. Byrne Sr., and Joseph M. Byrne Jr. '15 who carried on his father's tradition throughout the regime of Knute Rockne.

The alumni in Boston and a Catholic Club in Burlington provided hospitality for the baseball visitors. Notre Dame defeated Tufts 3-2 and the University of Vermont 4-1. There is no record of a Rhode Island celebration since Brown University defeated Notre Dame 13-0.

But all this was the changing concept of a campus, moving its parts to new frontiers, and bringing formerly distant alumni and friends into its family circle.

The fifth annual meeting of the Alumni Association reflected this new spirit and closer tie. Daniel F. Murphy, president, called the meeting to order. The Class of 1912 was admitted to membership, and with all alumni present, took part in a pledge of fidelity to the Constitution of the United States and the principles of the Alumni Association. After resolutions of condolences and congratulations had been provided for the deceased and the living, new officers were elected: Father Denis A. Clarke, '80, Columbus, O., was made honorary president; Hon. William P. Higgins '03, Boston, Mass., was elected president; vice presidents were Joseph J. Sullivan '01 of Chicago, Clement C. Mitchell '02 of Chicago, Louis J. Salmon '05 of Syracuse; John F. Shea '06 of Holyoke, Mass., John C. Tully '11 of Chicago and Russell G. Finn '12 of Detroit. Father William A. Moloney, C.S.C., was reelected secretary; Warren A. Cartier, Ludington, Mich., was made treasurer. Trustees for two years were—Thomas A. Dailey '74, Adrian, Mich.; Thomas Medley '98, Owensboro, Ky.; and Harry G. Hogan '04, Fort Wayne, Ind. That last name was to recur often and in the brightest pages of Notre Dame history.

The meeting moved that an issue of the *Scholastic* in April be designated the Alumni issue, to contain articles by alumni, and to contain news of alumni. Father Charles L. O'Donnell, C.S.C., was selected to edit this special issue. The meeting was told that the accumulating funds of the association were not earning as much as they might. The treasurer was advised to confer with the University trustees on the investment of such funds.

The annual banquet followed the meeting. Daniel F. Murphy was toastmaster. Judge Howard recalled early days and showed the guests a copy of *Progress,* the students' first attempt at a paper. Dudley Shively talked on the training of a lawyer. Col. Hoynes gave a review of the Presidents from Sorin to Cavanaugh. Thomas Hoban amused the group with an address on the art of "skiving" - which is A.W.O.L., for the benefit of the unenlightened.

Father T. O'Connell '06, Toledo, spoke of the increasing sphere of influence of the Notre Dame man. And for the first time on record, the group sang *The Notre Dame Victory March,* led by the new vice president and author of the lyrics of this budding classic, John F. Shea '06.

The alumni Mass was celebrated by Father O'Connell. An alumnus, Robert E. Lynch '03, sang the offertory solo. Father Paul Foik C.S.C. remembered as librarian and historian, and Father William A. Bolger C.S.C., one of the great teachers of economics and coach of debate, assisted.

The Notre Dame Club was flourishing in Chicago in the fall of 1912. Theater parties remained popular. One, planned for the Notre Dame football team, was changed from "Ben Hur" to "Fine Feathers" indicating that the scope of education was beginning to broaden in the minds of alumni. Weekly meetings were decided upon, and drew in this particular period what was described as "the best attended meeting the club has ever held." Father J. Keogh of the South Side was present at the invitation of Frank McKeever. He praised the loyalty and spirit of Notre Dame men, and said that "it was too bad that more of the Catholic Clubs did not show their loyalty and fidelity to their alma mater."

The club was planning the big football weekend when Notre Dame played Marquette in Chicago. The 1912 team was undefeated coming into the Marquette game from a short schedule of seven games. It had defeated St. Viator's 116-7, but had barely won over Pittsburgh, 3-0. The team consisted of Knute Rockne, Keith Jones, Freeman Fitzgerald, Al Feeney, Walter Yund, Paul Harvat, Charlie Crowley, Capt. Charles E. "Gus" Dorais, Alvin Berger, Joe Pliska, and Ray Eichenlaub as its starter. Ray Miller, another of the famous family of the Five Millers, later Mayor of Cleveland, O., was an end behind Rockne.

The Notre Dame eleven repaid their Chicago hosts handsomely, by defeating the Marquette team 69-0.

The *Dome* of 1913 contained an article on the "Genius of Notre Dame" which does much to explain the unity of alumni and the intangible Notre Dame spirit:

> It is but natural that Notre Dame, as the great exemplification of the Catholic ideal in higher education, should be a college democracy; for the genius of Notre Dame is religion. The Church recognizes no barriers of caste. The first vicar of Christ was a poor Galilean fisherman, and an Italian peasant sits today on the throne of Peter. It is the strong tie of a common religion that at Notre Dame binds together students and professors in love and sympathy, making the University a true college home. That there is no closer bond than this of religion was recognized by the old Greeks and Romans, who numbered as of their family those who worshipped with a common rite; and Cicero's *De Officiis* was inspiration for the remark that "Friendship founded on worldly principles is natural, and therefore mutable and frail, for it belongs only to a unity founded on religion to continue through an endless duration.". . . .
>
> Religion is a genius that draws the hearts of men together, inspiring them with love of a common ideal. At Notre Dame that ideal is the ideal of Catholic Christianity, Christ, and the beauty of that ideal is shown the student by reflection in the lives of the men who are his guides and teachers.
>
> Education is something more than a mere exercising and development of the mind and body; it is an inspiration and strengthening of the heart and soul, of character. Physical and mental power acquired without corresponding development of the heart is inimical to the symmetry and stability of individual and society, and leads both to lose their balance on the edge of the abyss of materialism. The head of the modern social order is heavy with knowledge, but its heart is atrophied; and the unhappy effects of that disproportionate development are evident on every side. It is the equipment of well-balanced men that Notre Dame is dedicated and it is to such men that society must look for its regeneration.
>
> The Notre Dame man has had an opportunity that is afforded to few of his fellows: Intimate association for four years with men of noble ideals, exemplifying in their lives the efficacy of Christian virtues in the transfiguration of human nature into sanctity; the fast friendship of ambitious men of his own age, with whom he has lived and whose hopes and ideals he has shared as a brother; initation by instruction and daily devotions into the beauties of his Church and habits of devotion;—all these advantages have been his in addition to the usual services of a university. May he prove true to the ideals he has shared as a brother; initiation by instruction and ever his guide.

Small wonder the Alumni Association was enjoying great fraternal strength.

The Notre Dame Club of Chicago announced its annual banquet on May 3, with Gov. Dunn of Illinois as its invited principal speaker. From the *Scholastic* of April 19, "Not a month passes but what this energetic and enthusiastic crowd of alumni does something excellent in the cause of good fellowship or in loyalty and support for alma mater."

The sixth annual meeting of the association was called to order in Brownson Study Hall on June 16, 1913. Lt. Gov. William P. O'Neill '06, of Indiana, administered a broadened pledge to the Class, including not only fidelity to the constitution and the Alumni Association, but also regularity in payment of dues and attendance at annual meetings. The treasurer's report showed that a majority of the association's funds were now invested in real estate mortgages. It was resolved that printed copies of the treasurer's report be sent to all members annually.

Officers elected for the following year were: Father John J. Burke '83, Peoria, Ill., honorary president; Hon. Charles M. Bryan '97, president; Hon. J. Joseph Cooke '94, of Beardstown, Ill., Hon. John Eggeman '00 of Fort Wayne, Ind., William McInerny '01 of South Bend, Ind., Hon. Peter P. McElligott '02 of New York City and William E. Cotter '13 of Chicago, Ill., vice presidents; Father William A. Maloney, C.S.C. '90, Notre Dame, Ind., secretary and Hon. Warren A. Cartier '87, Ludington, Mich., treasurer.

Trustees to serve two years were Thomas Hoban '09 of South Bend, Ind., Clement O. Mitchell '02 of Chicago, Ill., and Father Michael Shea '04 of Rome, Italy.

The greater part of the remainder of the meeting was consumed in discussing the advisability of joining with the local council of the Knights of Columbus, who have in view the erection of a building on the University campus. The sentiment of the members present seemed to be against affiliation with any exclusive society or organization in any project whatever. The erection of a building in which members might stay when they visit the University was then discussed and a resolution was adopted declaring that it seemed to be the sentiment of the meeting that the association should use its funds, and that the members should otherwise contribute to the erection of a hall or building to be known as the Old Students Hall or Alumni Hall or be designated by some other appropriate name. It was further moved that notice of the feeling of the members present at the meeting be sent to all the members of the association for expression of opinion. The treasurer was instructed to send out copies of the resolution with his annual report.

Complimentary references to the alumni number of the Notre Dame *Scholastic* were then made and the Father Charles L. O'Donnell was again selected as editor of the alumni number for the coming year.

Immediately after the adjournment of the buisness meeting at seven o'clock came the annual alumni banquet. Judge Francis J. Vurpillat of Winamac, Ind., graduate in the class of 1891, reviewed some of the incidents and characters that made life interesting at Notre Dame a score of years ago. The newly elected president of the association, Charles M. Bryan '97, now city attorney of Memphis, Tenn., spoke most entertainingly in his warm southern manner of the difficulties and achievements in the varsity athletics of his day. All the alumni are rejoicing that "Bryan Boru", as he is known by his class, is now their leader and that he, as toastmaster, is to supply the inspiration at the banquet next year. Henry Wurzer '98, spoke of the tie which binds the Notre Dame man to his alma mater, citing his own inability to get any farther away from her than South Bend. Then following was the lt. governor of Indiana, William P. O'Neill on the achievements of Notre Dame men in public service. The University's work in debate in the past and at present was the topic of enthusiastic speech by Congressman George Sands '11. The concluding address was by the newest member of the association, Paul R. Martin '13, who urged the duty of practical loyalty on the part of all the alumni in promoting the interests of the old school by making her merits known.

The alumni clubs were beginning a practice which has remained a constant challenge to the national Alumni Association. As the Notre Dame microcosm in its own community, the clubs tried to create programs of outstanding merit. Often their success would have done credit to the annual reunion or banquet.

The Washington, D.C., club had just come up with another great program to mark the 1913 visit of the baseball team. Dr. James A. Flynn had arranged for the team to meet President Woodrow Wilson, the popular Hoosier vice president, Thomas Marshall, and Secretary of State William Jennings Bryan.

In the afternoon, the Notre Dame nine had defeated Catholic University 9-5. At the banquet in the evening, Father Elliott of the Paulist Fathers, Msgr. Shahan of Catholic University, Dr.

Kerby, also of Catholic University, and Father Matthew Walsh, vice president of Notre Dame, were speakers. Father Walsh had been in New York for the presentation of the Laetare Medal a few days earlier to Charles Herberman, editor of the first edition of the *Catholic Encyclopedia.* The team left at midnight for New York where the Washington charisma carried Notre Dame on to a victory over the formidable Fordham team 6-3.

This was Notre Dame in 1913. Its alumni were individual agents charged with representing the University to their friends and associates. Growing clubs were making an impact on communities. Teams were winning acquaintanceship in ever widening circles. The President of the University was a national figure of top ranking among a large number of great orators. Need for a public relations department had not even become a gleam in the administrative eye.

In the fall of 1913, the *Scholastic* printed an article on "Notre Dame's Greatest Football Player." It praised Harry Miller, John Farley, John Eggeman, Don Hamilton, George Philbrook, Ralph Dimmick, Ray Eichenlaub, Pete Vaughan and Sam Dolan but it held up as the all-time player the legendary Lou Salmon '05.

In the same summer of 1913, a group of Notre Dame students were working at a Lake Erie summer resort, Cedar Point, at Sandusky, a custom of long standing. In the off hours, two members of the football team would take to the sandy beach, where Gus Dorais would throw forward passes, still little used in American football, to Knute Rockne.

It is from such lulls in time that history so often springs almost full-blown.

On Nov. 1, 1913, before a small crowd on the plains of West Point, Notre Dame's football team— which had played Ohio Northern, South Dakota and Alma at that point, and was far from favored against the glamorous Army Eleven—brought into the public eye the "Dorais to Rockne" forward pass, defeating the favorites 35-13.

Jesse Hayer, Notre Dame's first paid full-time football coach, the summer dedication of two intelligent and competent athletes, and the surpassing genius of Knute Kenneth Rockne, came together at this unheralded moment in destiny, when Notre Dame moved into the "big time" of athletics.

The University moved into the national limelight through what continues to be one of the great common denominators of the American public—athletics.

And the world of football was never the same again.

XVII

History Can Come Quietly

Across the pages of the contemporary records of the University there began to pass items that presaged the multiple interests of the future. It seems unlikely that their significance escaped the keen and practical minds of the time. It is more likely that new ideas were beginning to occur faster than the manpower and financial resources of Notre Dame could absorb them. The only idea that seems possibly to have escaped was the one that perhaps a direct appeal for outside help could provide opportunities that the most valiant internal consideration had to forego.

For example, in the *Scholastic* of June, 1913, the President of the University published the contents of three appeals he had received for qualified alumni—one to serve as a lawyer, one as a school principal and one as a college teacher. The status of the college professor is indicated in the statement regarding the college post, "It is a good position and will pay about a thousand dollars to the right man."

It would be in the mid-thirties before the Alumni Association finally set up a placement service for alumni within the alumni office and under William R. Dooley '26, then assistant to the alumni secretary. It was even some years later before the University recognized placement as a full-time University program of which Bill Dooley became the first full-time director.

The Chicago Club was functioning well. Its opening meeting in the Sherman Hotel was excited about the prospect of a post season football game with Nebraska. It was 1915 before a Nebraska game materialized. John B. Kanaley was the new president of the club; Thomas Sexton, vice president; John Tully, secretary and Rupert Donovan, treasurer. Fred Steers, Mark Foote, John O'Connell, William Devine, Daniel Madden and Judge Michael Girten provided a broad spectrum of campus backgrounds as the executive committee.

Another death occurred in November, reminding alumni of the great faculty members, lay as well as religious, who gave so unselfishly to the development of Notre Dame. Professor Charles "Pete" Peterson, who had made the "Lilacs" a memorable residence at the campus perimeter, came to Notre Dame in 1890 as a professor of French and German. His buoyant personality and social disposition made him a favorite. His qualifications as a musician were discovered and he was made head of the music department. As such, he had the direction of the University band and orchestra, whose concerts became increasingly popular with students, alumni and all who attended Notre Dame functions. He was born in Germany and educated at Frederick Wilhelm's Academy and the University of Bonn. He had also studied in Paris and London.

I am not dwelling on the details of the historic 1913 athletic triumph over Army. Those can be found in multiple sources, well and excitingly recounted. I mention this because there is no desire to "play down" athletics. I doubt whether any person really knowing the University—administrator, teacher, student, or alumnus—has "put down" the part of athletics in its development. On the other hand, I am sure that many of us share a zeal for "playing up" the many qualities of greatness, the many significant programs and the many great men of the University outside the sphere of athletics. The two attitudes are entirely different and ought not to be confused. The compatibility of the athletic and the academic has been convincingly advanced by Notre Dame leaders. One of the finest expressions, in response to uninformed criticism in the golden era of the championship Rockne teams of the '29-'30 years, was by Father Charles L. O'Donnell, C.S.C. '06, outstanding then as a scholarly President, a spiritual priest, and a nationally acclaimed poet.

College, Father O'Donnell said in part, is more than a school. It is a life:

> . . . It is a school life, of course, and the major emphasis is, as it ought to be, on study. But even if it were not, even if football ran away with one quarter of the year, there are so many worse things that could happen to a school if that healthy outlet of young energy and enthusiasm were closed. . . . Man is not all mind; he is a creature of flesh and blood; he has a heart, and the heart, too, must be schooled in a curriculum which life itself supplies in those four years

crowded with wonder that make up the college career of the student today . . . Two and two make four, and the college student will learn the lesson through whatever complexities the formula may be extended. But there is another mathematics, a madder, wilder learning, more divine and nearer the source of the truth . . . It is the lesson which the heart learns of life itself .,.,. it is dedication and consecration of self to an ideal and a cause, even though in the particular premises that cause is only the elementary one of winning a football game for the sake of the school.

In the Spring of 1914 the University was disturbed by a press story that described Notre Dame students as having thrown some Mexican students into the St. Joseph River to observe the sending of the U.S. Fleet to Vera Cruz. The *Scholastic* vigorously denied that any grain of truth existed. The Mexican boys, it pointed out, lived with and played on teams with American fellow students. It was reminiscent of the sensational press that fanned the Spanish-American War. But the campus was too familiar with the rich tradition of Father Zahm's visits to Mexico and the boys from the finest families in that country whom he brought back on his famous special trains.

The baseball team visited Washington, one of the favorite centers of hospitality. The club entertained the team after its defeat by Georgetown 4-1. On this trip the team went on to beat Army and Navy, to lose to Princeton, but to defeat Catholic University. Speakers at the Washington event for the team included Sen. Benjamin Shively of South Bend and Sen. Joseph Ransdell, the prominent Louisiana member of Congress, who was later to give the Commencement Address at the 1914 graduation at Notre Dame.

Few Presidents of Notre Dame had escaped major fires. On May 31, 1914, St. Joseph's Novitiate was burned, the fire occurring at supper time. Disciplinary authorities sought to hold the students of the University in their dining rooms, but that effort was replaced by a call for help. The *Scholastic* reports,

> When we finished our half-mile dash around the lake, the roof of the Novitiate was a mass of flames. There being no fire plugs in the vicinity, the fire departments were of little good, but "the entire student body" was on the job and made heroic rescue of sundry old hymn books and Pluto water. Brother Mathias was the individual hero of the evening, saving great quantities of coal by shoveling it from the cellar. Col. Hoynes saved a dish of pudding from the kitchen.

The tenor of the report seems to offer an undertone of

doubtful sympathy for the novices. But true to the better traditions, Bro. Columbkill, C.S.C., immediately designed a new bigger and better Novitiate, which was quickly built under his supervision.

The Alumni Association meeting in June of 1914 proved to be one of great historic consequence. The minutes were read, the Class of 1914 was admitted and the treasurer showed a balance of $1,553 in the bank, plus $2,000 invested in mortgages. Condolences were resolved for the deceased.

A tradition was born when the secretary reported that he had made special efforts to bring to the commencement and reunion the classes five years apart, in the 4- and 9- years, beginning with the Class of 1864.

The treasurer then reported that as a result of his letter sent to all members of the association calling for expression of opinion regarding the erection of an alumni hall, he had received replies from a small number, but of those the majority favored the erection of the hall. The plan in general way was submitted for discussion. It contemplated a residence hall to accomodate about 150 students, to be erected by the alumni on the grounds of the University; the cost of the buildings and furnishings to approximate $125,000; one-tenth of the number of rooms to be kept free for occupancy by the alumni on their visits to the University; the remainder of the rooms to be rented by the University to students and the income from such rental to be devoted to scholarships for the education of worthy students. . . . A building committee was then named to take up the details of the building and to push it to completion. The members of this committee were: Patrick O'Sullivan '74, Warren A. Cartier '87, John W. Eggeman '00, William McInerney '91, William Higgins '03, Byron Kanaley '04, William P. O'Neill '06 and John O'Connel '13.

Officers for the new year were: Rev. D. J. Spillard '64, honorary president; Byron Kanaley, president and John McIntyre '84, Maurice Neville '99, John Neeson '03, Robert Milroy '12 and John O'Connel '13, vice presidents. Father Moloney was retained as secretary and Warren Cartier as treasurer. Francis J. Vurpillat '91, John M. Flannigan '94 and Ed. O'Flynn '07 were the trustees.

Conscious effort was made throughout the Cavanaugh administration to turn the spotlight of both internal and external attention toward events and persons of academic luster, so that the rising tide of intercollegiate athletics and social life would not obscure the primary purpose of the University.

Speakers were outstanding men from abroad as well as from the American forums. Charles W. Fairbanks, vice president of the United States under Theodore Roosevelt, was a prominent early attraction. That prominence was not always overpowering to the intelligent community was reflected in the reaction of Col. Hoynes to Fairbanks, ". . . .he succeeded in further obscuring the already existing opacity of our national problems."

Father John Talbot Smith, head of the Catholic Actors Guild, was a sophisticated visitor, popular for his speaking ability and the colorful implications of his acquaintanceship with the stage stars of the era. He also had a sense of humor. He was asked, and actually began, to write the *Diamond Jubilee History* of the University. Regrettably, it was never completed.

William Jennings Bryan, often hailed as the foremost orator of his time, was asked to the campus, perhaps with the underlying thought of challenging his title with Notre Dame's own candidate for that title, Father Cavanaugh, who spared nothing in introducing Bryan.

England was rich at the time in intellectual Catholics, many of them converts, whose work had great impact on the Church in America. Father Cavanaugh was instrumental in bringing to Notre Dame Wilfred Ward, Msgr. Robert Hugh Benson, and Cecil Chesterton, brother of a later visiting celebrity, Gilbert K. Chesterton. Ward and his father had worked with Cardinal Newman in the Oxford movement. Science brought Edward Lee Greene, a friend of Father Nieuwland, whose *Midland Naturalist* magazine attracted leading American botanists. Greene, from the Smithsonian Institute, eventually gave his magnificent herbarium to Notre Dame.

Dr. James J. Walsh, New York, and Hon. Joseph Scott, a Los Angeles attorney and outstanding Catholic layman, were frequent and inspiring lecturers on the Washington Hall stage. Senator Thomas Walsh of Montana, Senator Albert Beveridge of Indiana, both orators of note in the competitive halls of Congress, and Indiana Governors Thomas Marshall and Ralston, were frequent visitors under the Cavanaugh spell.

With all this focusing of national interest, it was inevitable that publicity and public relations should at last become a conscious area in the Univeristy mind. In April of 1915, the *Scholastic* records what seems to be the first initiative on the campus. Under the guidance of Professor John M. Cooney, we know it launched the careers of several outstanding alumni in journalism.

Whether the average student knows it or not, Notre Dame has added to its equipment a live publicity bureau, through whose efforts the University is receiving as much newspaper mention as any institution of its size in the United States. To believe this assertion one need only visit the Journalism room on the third floor of the Main Building. Here is the *sanctum sanctorum* of the budding editors who are helping to put Notre Dame before the eyes of the public all the way from Boston to the Pacific Coast. But the correspondence carried on with the Catholic weeklies throughout the country should not be overlooked. This part of the work is done by the freshman journalists, each member being assigned to a different paper, from a chain extending from Denver, Colo., to Hartford, Conn. Each week the student prepares a newsletter and mails it to his weekly.

In the spring of 1915, Father John Cavanaugh wrote a significant and historical letter to his friend, F. Henry Wurzer. It reflected a realization of increasing needs on the campus and an appreciation of the early club experience:

... A Notre Dame Club is absolutely and inevitably the fruit of sentiment. It cannot be reasoned into existence or scourged into existence any more than a man can be reasoned or scourged into loving his mother or his country. Sentiment is the fragrance of life which exhales from human relations as perfume exhales from the flower. This is precisely why sentiment or feeling is distinct from reason. Hence I suggest that you make no attempt whatever to persuade unwilling men to join the club. Let it be a club of six glowing enthusiasts at first if it cannot be more than six. But let every man be there because his heart persuades him there ...

... No student ever paid, in money, for the work his alma mater did for him. Whoever feels that he owes no debt of loyalty and love to his old school was never capable of education from the beginning.

A Notre Dame Club is therefore the crystallization of the love of Notre Dame men for the old school. Let all the men of Notre Dam know of the existence of the club but beyond that make no special effort to bring them in. Make the obligations imposed by the club as few and as light as possible. The world will be exacting enough, and the Notre Dame Club should mean rest and good-fellowship and kindliness for its members. Finally, let Notre Dame men feel that it is the duty not only to speak a good word for the University but to live noble lives to exemplify our teachings. As a good son is the best praise of his mother, so a noble Christian gentleman is the highest eulogy of his school.

Small wonder that under this philosophy of club organization, the alumni of Notre Dame had created a federation of excellent small associations of alumni long before the central office and the the *Alumnus* were founded. The principles were basic and have persisted. The grass roots experience was invaluable in the establishment of the national association programs. The significance of this primary pronouncement is now reflected in the recently created and prestigious alumni senate, consisting of the presidents of the Notre Dame Clubs, which are approaching the 200 mark in number and are international in scope.

The eighth regular meeting of the association in 1915 was presided over by Byron Kanaley. Minutes were dispatched and the Class of 1915 was admitted. Clement C. Mitchell, '02, in the name of Rt. Rev. Monsignor F. O'Brien, honorary alumnus and donor, then presented a portrait of Father Andrew Morrissey, seventh President of Notre Dame, which had just arrived from Italy in time for the presentation. Mitchell gave an eloquent eulogy of Father Morrissey and his influence on the students, and thanked the Kalamazoo monsignor, long a friend and a doctor of laws of the University. Father Morrissey responded briefly, noting the great loyalty of alumni. On this occasion also, Byron Kanaley, in the name of the Alumni Association, presented to Notre Dame a portrait of Father Cavanaugh.

Both of these portraits were among the group that for so long graced the walls of the President's parlor in the Main Building, now the office of the provost. Father Cavanaugh responded, saying that the devotedness of the alumni to alma mater had been an inspiration to him as it had always been to his predecessors.

The treasurer's report showed $2,790 in mortgages and $1,408 in the bank. Resolutions of condolences for deceased members were drawn.

The building committee of alumni hall reported after careful consideration of the depression in business and the uncertainty of the war in Europe—Archduke Ferdinand had been assassinated in Sarajevo in June of 1914—that it was thought advisable, before proceeding to make an active canvass for funds, to await further expression of opinion from the association in the annual meeting. In the discussion that followed the report, it was the unanimous opinion that activity in collecting money be begun at once. The only variance in opinion regarded the extension of time over which installment payment should be spread. The method of rasing the necessary amount to begin the building operations was left to the building committee. A subscription list was then opened and in a short time $10,000 was pledged. It was decided to call the building Old Students Hall or some other appropriate name which would embrace all those who had been students at Notre Dame. A discussion arose over a motion to send copies of the *Scholastic* to each member of the association. A committee of Harry Hogan, Joseph Lantry and Robert Sweeney, appointed to study the resolution, reported favorably.

New officers elected were: Very Rev. Edw. McLaughlin '75, of Clinton, Iowa, honorary president; Angus McDonald '00, New York City, later to become president of Southern Pacific Railroad, was elected president; John McIntyre of Milwaukee, Maurice Neville of Indianapolis, John Neeson of Philadelphia, Robert Milroy of Aurora, John O'Connell of Chicago and Harry Newning of Houston, Tex., vice presidents; Father Moloney, re-elected secretary; Warren Cartier, treasurer and Thomas Hoban of South Bend, Clement Mitchell of Chicago and Father Michael Shea of New York, were elected trustees.

The reports show the many changes, within and without, which were always swirling about the University. But there were unchanging factors which helped to adjust to desirable change, and to reject the undesirable. Among these were the veneration of the older alumni, and the active involvement of the young.

It was also evident that the dominance of the Chicago alumni, a natural result of numbers, proximity and initiative, was beginning to be challenged by the growing number of alumni from other clubs and areas.

Former coaches at Notre Dame had been either students or alumni, or had been brought to Notre Dame to coach while continuing their own studies. Coach Barry from Brown, Coach Place from Dartmouth and Coach Longman from Michigan were among these. Now Jesse Harper, brought from Wabash as a full-time coach of football, and for several years of his tenure coach of baseball and basketball as well with a year as track coach thrown in to test his versatility and stamina, was bringing Notre Dame athletics to their full potential. His assistant football coach, Knute Rockne, a track athlete of some prowess, relieved him of the track responsibility in 1914. The year 1913 marks the first time that Notre Dame reported a sport making a small profit. It took another decade to bring prosperity. The Big Nine, reorganized from a broader and heterogeneous group of colleges and universities, would not admit Notre Dame. Father Cavanaugh was indifferent. But Father Thomas Crumley, chairman of the athletic board at the time, was adamant in defense of Notre Dame standards. He lost the battle, but announced that it had been "fought on theological rather than athletic grounds."

Harper continued to widen the scope of the football schedule, which was promising to produce needed income. He strengthened the caliber of the opposition. And his season records in football were - 1913, 7-0-0; 1914, 6-2-0; 1915, 7-1-0; 1916, 8-1-0 and 1917, 6-1-1, for a total of 34-5-1, against teams which included Army, Penn State, Texas, Yale, Syracuse, Nebraska, Rice, Michigan State (then Michigan Agricultural College) and Wisconsin. Notre Dame was not hurting from its conference rejection.

In February of 1916, students culminated a long growing feud with the street car company by "burning the street car" at the Notre Dame end of the line. The incident was provoked by company strong-arm men beating two students. Whatever the justification for the company's attitude, the method was guaranteed to produce retaliation. The following evening, Father Cavanaugh and two priests of the Community were returning to the campus when their car was stopped by a large group of students. When the students recognized the occupants, they waved them on. Father Cavanaugh was recounting his easy conquest of the boys whom he had ordered back to their rooms, when he looked out a window and saw the street car burning. Chet Grant told me just recently that one of the priests with Father Cavanaugh, who had stayed to see what the trouble was about, was so stimulated by the student spirit that he became one of the active torch-bearers.

One result of the incident was the introduction of movies to the campus. The protest from South Bend theaters prevented full-scale scheduling but Washington Hall became a center of Saturday night entertainment, especially attractive to those who could not afford a trip to town—and they were legion. "Quo Vadis" was an early attraction.

Life on the campus had also gleaned more comfort. From the relative austerity of life in Sorin and Corby Halls, the student standard of living had risen sharply with the erection of Walsh Hall, well designed and constructed with unheard-of suites available. It was early dubbed the "Gold Coast" and retained that title for many years, becoming valiant in its defenses against its

162   *Onward to Victory*

Spartan neighbors. Problems of the transition can be detected in
a story concerning a doting mother who was entrusting her heir
to Walsh's facilities and who arrived with chauffeur and lim-
ousine along with materials to hang proper drapes in the boy's
room. One of the more seasoned veterans of campus life,
relegated to a modest corner of Walsh, greeted the heir on his
arrival and offered to show him to his room. He graciously
yielded his corner to the somewhat bewildered newcomer and
promptly occupied the luxurious quarters himself. For how
long, I can't say.

Walsh Hall was the first of the two dormitory halls for which
Father Cavanaugh had asked in his early administrative outline
of needs. The *Scholastic*, swayed by the campaign among
alumni for funds for Old Students Hall, made a premature
announcement that it would be built in the summer of 1916. It
would have been the second of the hoped for residences.

One of the historic performances in Washington Hall under
the new policy of on-campus movies, was the showing of D.W.
Griffith's "Birth Of A Nation" accompanied by an orchestra.
The effect of this spectacular on the campus can be easily
imagined. A letter to Father Cavanaugh, soon thereafter, from
David Wark Griffith, should be noted:

"I feel the sincerity of your fine expression of appreciation
of what I attempted to do in the work which you refer to.
Likewise believe me when I say that your praise holds for me
a peculiar gratification. I have long since known Notre Dame
as one of the peaks that stand out across our country for real
culture, learning, and, perhaps what is more, breadth of
thought and heart. I have always considered your publication, *The Ave Maria*, one of the best examples of English, as
it should be written, current in our country today . . . I shall
treasure the token from your University. Somehow the things
that come from the hands of the young bring to us something
of the freshness and goodness of their days. Sincerely, (sig)
D.W. Griffith."

In March, 1916, the Notre Dame Club of Detroit was organized in the Hotel Pontchartrain. Forty-five alumni were present. Father Moloney and Father Foik represented the University. Henry Wurzer '96, became the first president. Father
Moloney spoke on the University and on Old Students Hall. The
club appointed a committee of three to make a subsequent
canvass for subscriptions to the effort.

President Angus McDonald called the ninth annual meeting
of the association to order on June 11, 1916. The regular

business of the agenda was carried out. The treasurer reported $2,461 in the bank, and $2,405 in mortgages. Dues receipts for the year had totalled $715. The treasurer asked to be bonded, and declined to serve longer unless he were bonded and audited. A motion was passed approving his past record, but acceding to his requests. Charles Girsch, Chicago, himself an old student, was named auditor. Checks of more than $150 were also to be countersigned by the association president.

The building committee reported that three letters had been sent to all alumni, two from the committee and one from Father Maloney. Between five and six thousand letters were sent out in the first appeal and three thousand five hundred in the second. Results were considered slow. Subscriptions totalled $24,750. Of this, $6,167 was in the bank, the remaining amount in pledges of varying times. The association recognized the burdens attached to the campaign, and requested the University to appoint Father William Maloney to devote full time to the program. Subscriptions were then opened to the alumni present, and $7,250 additional was pledged.

It was decided that in the future names of former students proposed for membership should be in writing, along with their qualifications and the endorsement of two members of the association.

New officers were elected: Father Luke Evers, New York, honorary president; William A. McInerney, South Bend, president; M.F. Healy of Fort Dodge, Iowa; James J. Conway of Ottawa, Ill.; William D. Jamieson of St. Paul; John W. Costelle of Chicago; William Corcoran of Portland, Ore. and Eugene McBride, Pittsburgh, vice presidents; Warren Cartier retained as treasurer and Father Maloney as secretary. Trustees to serve two years were Peter McElligott of New York, Henry Wurzer of Detroit and Michael Fansler of Logansport.

Angus McDonald acted as toastmaster for the alumni banquet, where a parade of familiar dignitaries spoke, largely on the Old Students Hall campaign and its significance to the University and the association.

The *Dome* of 1916 contained an interesting article updating the "Needs of Notre Dame:"

That so much that is magnificent has been achieved at Notre Dame without endowment is a source of constant wonderment to visitors. They little know how each building has its own particular history of toil and self-sacrifice written into every brick and beam. They little realize that the smooth

lawns where the sun filters through the mighty maples in
golden patterns, have been brought to their present splendor
through long hours of dedicated labor anointed by high
purpose and sanctified by exalted ideals. The new library, to
be erected at the cost of a quarter of a million dollars, will
inaugurate a finer order of architecture at Notre Dame.
Limestone seems more fitting, somehow, more consonant
with the school's permanence of purpose, than mere quick-
crumbling brick. The campus, one of the very finest in the
United States, is well worthy of it. The prestige of the school
and its tremendous growth well warrant it. Rapidly increasing
attendance has made at least one more residence hall imperatively necessary. The Old Students Hall, to be erected at a
cost of approximately $125,000, will require your assistance,
if it is to be completed by 1917, the school's 75th brithday,
and the occassion of the diamond jubilee.

The rapidly growing law school, one of the best in the
west, is in urgent need of a separate law building. It should be
the ambition of every alumnus and student of the College of
Law to help put it up, in its chosen place beside the splendid
new library. The new quadrangle is to be a thing of beauty.
With its completion Notre Dame will have one of the largest
and finest of campuses in the country. The proposed new
Law Building should be up and occupied by 1918. What are
you going to do to help? Think it over! Don't let your
loyalty be of the pitifully useless "lip" variety! Every dollar
the school can spare is being expended in a superbly cou-
rageous campaign of improvement. But their funds—earned
to the last penny—are not sufficient to effect all the urgently
needed improvements. If the spirit of the old school is not all
a myth, its thousands of former students and graduates all
over the country will assist their alma mater substantially.

The veracity of the need for another student residence hall
was evident in the growth of the Day Students Association. This
group, at this time, were largely the envied students whose
homes were in South Bend, who lived with their families, and
who, in the eyes of the more cabined and confined on-campus
confreres, escaped much of the supervision of the prefect of
discipline. The organization was said to have done much in its
first year of existence to unify and cement Notre Dame and
South Bend.

In a sense, this was the end of an era, a statement that seems
to recur again and again in Notre Dame's story. It is attributable
to the willingness of the campus to adjust to change, in fact to
seek and welcome change. The older veterans of the University
family have had little sympathy for the shibboleth of the young
moderns that they alone champion change and that the "establishment" is always adamant against it.

XVIII

Base Camp

On a mountain climb, the base camp is where you breathe a little, and regroup for the climb ahead.

We are at that point in the Notre Dame story.

In 1917, the University celebrated its diamond jubilee; in the same year, the United States entered World War I, its first great international conflict, from which it emerged a dominant world power.

In 1917, the growth of Notre Dame, its increasing enrollment, its expanding physical plant and the explosion of knowledge already on the world horizon, were vivid reminders that the 75-year tradition of self-sustaining sacrifice could no longer keep pace with the 75-year tradition of quality education and environment offered to its students. The war provided in one sense a break in which the future could be studied and it created a disruption that made some of the essential changes to come seem much less disruptive.

For the first 25 years of alumni history, there were only individual alumni, a small and intimate group who retained close ties with the campus.

For the next 50 years, until this time, the opportunities of formal alumni organization were recognized in principle. The need for alumni help was implicit if not urgent. But so close were the members of "la vie intime" and so constant the role of the individual alumni in publicizing the merits of Notre Dame and in sending students to the University, that the pressure for rigid organization remained low. The 1868 association bogged down later in the failure to find adequate function to give it a stimulating identity.

Alumni clubs, notably that of Chicago, where separation

from the campus underlined some of the potential of alumni organization, developed fine programs in the club communities and—Chicago again—even tried to rally the national strength.

There were no factors of disinterest or opposition among alumni. The annual meetings were often informal but rich in enthusiasm. The role of the individual alumnus has stood out in our story along with the administrators and faculty members— of whom the majority were themselves alumni.

I have mentioned the early clubs and the pioneer alumni because they achieved so much with so few resources, with such little formal recognition. The one thing they had in common with those who followed them was the inspiration of a University dedicated not just to higher education, but to Our Lady and to the Church which her Son founded.

Like the history of the young republic in which it was growing and flourishing, the history of Notre Dame alumni is not an association springing full-armed from the brow of a founder. It is more like the first little clearings which dotted the countryside, as individuals of hope and faith and initiative saw the opportunities for, and of, a new freedom. They became villages and then a nation.

Now, in 1917, the Alumni Association of the University of Notre Dame, as an integral part of the diamond jubilee, had called its individuals and its increasing number of villages—the clubs—to look toward the opportunity and the strength which it could contribute to the unversity from which it derived.

This has been a constructive story. You have found little report of factionalism. There has been little of the protest and violence reflected in so much current literature. There have been no quotations offensive to common decency or good taste. There have been no revelations of idols with feet of clay.

Obviously, I do not claim that here was Eden, without temptation or sin. I can only assure you that here were men of religion, men of education, men of culture and refinement, passing along all these qualities by teaching and by example to the young men entrusted to their care. Together, these formed the climate of Notre Dame. In my opinion, as I warned you earlier I would express it, the educational institution that grew at Notre Dame brought honor and distinction to the Church and glory to God and the Mother of God. They in turn rewarded the University with strength and grace beyond natural explanation.

As we move into the maturing and more crowded years, with

two major World Wars and a great Depression, we cannot cover, as we have to this point, so much of the detailed activity, or so many of the individuals.

I do go forward with the sincere hope that you know now the rich roots of our alumni heritage; that you know the story is not one of isolated items in simple sequence, not even one of just overlap of persons or of time—but the glowing flow of a story in which people and events blend in a sparkling tributary moving toward a great sea in an ever-widening stream.

If I am so completely polarized from the dubious content of the "best sellers" I presume I should apologize for the lack of sensuous appeal but I offer no apology for the hopeful appeal to your good sense.

If I am painting the Notre Dame man as a good man from a good University—missing an occasional flaw, as I must miss an occasional genius or saint—I am only doing it this way because, by God, that is what he is, always was, and can continue to be.

XIX

Diamond Jubilee

In the 4th century St. John Chrysostom asked, "What greater work is there than training the mind and forming the habits of the young?" Fifteen centuries later the University of Notre Dame was thriving evidence that the Church had never found a substitute answer to St. John—and had not yet approached the problem of the separation of the training of the mind from the forming of the habits.

In this 75th year of 1917 Notre Dame had passed through great growth and revolutionary changes without the loss of fundamental principles, or the gain of outside financial support. Now another peak in University history was moving toward the shrouding mists of another war.

The *Dome*, in the spring of 1917, outlined "Some Needs of Notre Dame," indicating that the administration was not unmindful of the handwriting on the academic wall:

> Notre Dame, like many other Catholic colleges, has a precious endowment in the genius and devotedness of the religious men who make up the Congregation of Holy Cross, and who devote their lives, their education and their energies, without money and without price, to the work of the University. Like the devotedness of mothers, this heroic sacrifice of the priests and brothers is rarely appreciated, but it is safe to say that without it such a University as Notre Dame would be impossible.
>
> The progress of Notre Dame, therefore, is assured whether wealthy and generous patrons come to her assistance or not. But the progress will be slow if the University is obliged to creep upwards without the assistance that wealth can give. We mention a few of the opportunities now lying open to men of means who love Notre Dame, or who sympathize with her aspirations and her efforts, and desire to assist her.

There is need for more scholarships. There are only five at the present time and there ought to be two or three hundred. The President of the University assures us that the saddest aspect of his work is the multitude of deserving and promising young men stretching out appealing arms from farm and factory, beseeching an education which neither their means nor the resources of the University can supply without the aid of scholarships. Much attention is bestowed upon the conservation of the natural material resources of America. But are we—especially we Catholics,—doing all that we ought, and could do to conserve the moral and intellectual resources of the country? A scholarship endowment costs $8,000, but any sum of money is accepted as a part scholarship, the income of which will help some needy student to meet his college expenses.

Salary Endowment. Notre Dame has been happy in her lay professors from the beginning. Many of them have manifested a devotedness and unselfishness as heroic as that of priests and brothers. But it is fair to say that laymen, not having the convenience of the vow of poverty, but having a responsibility like other gentlemen of the world, must derive from their labors a competency to meet their daily needs. In order to associate the best lay talent with the University, therefore, it is necessary to pay good salaries. With the meager resources obtainable only from the fees of students, this is hardly possible. No need of the University is more urgent at the present time than gifts of money to constitute an endowment fund for salaries of laymen. There is simply no limit to the development of the University if this great and eminent need is met.

School of Engineering. At the present time, we have a great School of Engineering. It is manned by competent and experienced professors and the quality of the work compares well with that done in the best engineering schools elsewhere. But it is not worthily housed, and the equipment, while sufficient for actual needs, is far from what the University desires. A generous gift for this purpose would be a notable help.

School of Law. This school has grown so rapidly as to promise to overshadow all of the departments of the University. Within the last decade it has increased four hundred per cent. Naturally, it has outgrown its old home and the need of a larger and fuller Law Library is urgent. Friends of the Law School are invited to send contributions for this purpose.

School of Dentistry. There is need of establishing a medical school covering the first two years of the work in medicine. It would not be difficult with the equipment already at hand, to organize a School of Dentistry. This will not be done, however, without practical encouragement from friends.

Agriculture. A modern and thorough course in agriculture has been added to the curriculum. Provisions for the actual

needs in the way of laboratories and other equipment have
already been made, but a considerable sum of money will be
necessary to house the new department fittingly and to
supply buildings, etc., for what is sure to be a rapidly growing
school.

There is always need of more dormitory buildings. It is a
felicitous form of embarrassment but it is an embarrassment
nevertheless. It is contrary to the policy of the University and
the wish of the alumni to have Notre Dame men boarding in
town.

Preparatory School. It is the hope that the Congregation of
Holy Cross will soon be in a position to separate the Preparatory School from the University proper. Not only as at
present, in work, but also in association and geographical
neighborhood as well. This is a matter which old Notre Dame
men ought to understand thoroughly. The separation will be
made as soon as the necessary funds are had.

Benevolent spirits need not be deterred from making contributions by the thought that they can not take care of even
one of these needs completely. Donations in any amount will
be gladly accepted in the hope that others may follow the
good example, once it has been set."

The logic of a program for financial aid was established. But
Father Cavanaugh's nature tended to shrink from the task—
already commonplace among American college presidents—of
implementing the reasoning with a direct solicitation that Catholic administrators on most Catholic campuses were to consider
for many more years of academic poverty as begging.

The tragedy of the Notre Dame picture was that Father
Cavanaugh's personal appeal could well have given him a pre-
eminent place in the field of fund-raising. As it was, this appeal
of personality worked against Notre Dame, by the implication
that such a commanding presence, representing such a flourishing institution, must easily acquire any necessary support.

Despite this difficulty in asking for support, Father Cavanaugh was for 14 years one of the greatest public relations
factors the university enjoyed. A small instance is his comment
on Professor Timothy Howard, recently deceased, at a meeting
of the South Bend Round Table, a top citizen organization. "He
was a profoundly spiritual man, beautifully tolerant of the inner
life of other men, his own radiant mind lit up with the light of
faith, his own generous heart warmed by the fires of hope, his
noble spirit mellowed with the rich liquor of charity. He was a
reverent man with an enlightened sense of the presence, and the
power, and the beauty of God; he was a lovable Christian

brother, with a fine appreciation of the confidence and friendship of men. His word was wisdom, his spirit joy, his friendship almost a sacrament."

So his eloquence was heard, on the nation's platforms, in the halls of the neighboring community and on the many occasions of the Unversity year when faculty, students and alumni were informed and inspired by his faith and pride in the accomplishments, the ideals and the men of Notre Dame.

In the spring of 1917, the United States declared war, revealing a rather poor preparation for the national challenge ahead. Even the traditional military training at Notre Dame proved to have suffered from the feeling of the era before the war, that such training was more a disciplinary scheme of colleges than an essential contribution to national defense. Notre Dame was not even selected as a training school for recruits. But Capt. Stogsdall, a retired West Point man, and Sgt. Campbell, U.S.A. retired, who had been in charge at Notre Dame, urged all the students to begin military training. Father Matthew Walsh added a personal appeal which moved many students. Within a week, 600 young men were training, with new units including a hospital corps, an engineers corps, a company composed of athletes, a company composed of upper classmen and a company made up from the day students.

The University, in spite of its projected diamond jubilee celebration in June, decided to end the semester early, to confer degrees on those who enlisted before the commencement and to hold undergraduate examinations before the commencement. It was this adjustment of the academic procedures which created the later classic of the awarding of a Notre Dame degree to Dan McGlynn, '17, on the battlefield in France, by Chaplain Matthew Walsh, vice president of the University on leave, so that McGlynn might be eligible for a commission and an intelligence mission of significance.

Father Walsh, Father Charles O'Donnell—both to become Presidents of Notre Dame—Father George Finnigan, to become bishop of Helena, Mont.; Father Edward Finnegan, who had been a prefect of discipline; Father John McGinn, sociologist, endowment fund staff member and alumni secretary in the years just ahead, and Father Ernest Davis, chemistry professor, were the first six chaplains sent from Notre Dame, in an act of loyalty rivalling that of Sorin half a century earlier.

Four days in June were set apart for the jubilee ceremonies, despite the World War I programs dominating the country. Father Morrissey and Father Cavanaugh headed a procession of campus and civic dignitaries and societies to meet the train in South Bend which brought the venerable Cardinal Gibbons, who had been the chief ecclesiastic in 1888 at the golden jubilee of Father Sorin's priesthood.

Alumni were entertained in Washington Hall by a stereopticon slide show of older men and scenes on the campus, narrated by Father Michael Quinlan. An address dealing with the early years of the campus, and the memorable lay and religious figures who populated it, was given by Father Walter Elliott, nationally acclaimed Paulist preacher, who had been a student at Notre Dame during the Civil War period.

The Apostolic Delegate, Most Rev. John Bonzano, came the following day, accompanied by Admiral William Shepherd Benson, U.S. Chief of Naval Operations, who was the 1917 Laetare medalist. Admiral Benson received the medal in special ceremonies, including the reading of congratulations from President Wilson and Josephus Daniels, Secretary of the Navy.

The Solemn Pontifical Mass of the Jubilee, presided over by Cardinal Gibbons, was given an embellishment when the ushers, under the charge of Father William A. Moloney, long-time Alumni Association secretary, appeared in formal morning clothes. The famous Paulist Choir supplied the music of the mass. Archbishop (later Cardinal) Mundelein of Chicago extended the apostolic blessing of Pope Benedict XV, and then delivered the sermon for the occasion. He spoke feelingly of Father Sorin and his dedication to the mission of the University. "Today, I know of no other institution which, while it is so thoroughly Roman in its doctrine, is so completely American in its spirit."

The dedication of the beautiful new Indiana limestone library, a dream of Father Cavanaugh's come true, was a highlight of the jubilee. Bishop Shahan, rector of Catholic University, was the minister for the blessing of the library. Bourke Cockran, "the last of the great Irish orators," delivered the dedicatory address—one of the longest on record. An auspicious omen for the future was the presentation of two checks for $1,000 each, to the University, by the Ancient Order of Hibernians and by the Catholic Order of Foresters, "to further its great work."

Of particular interest to alumni was the comment in the *Scholastic*, made concerning the days of the jubilee by Seumas Macmanus, who received an LL.D. on the occasion:

Were the wish not too extravagant, I would that most of my days winged pleasantly as the couple of happy days I spent at Notre Dame's diamond jubilee.

Though all the time there I treaded my way through throngs, I was filled with quiet happiness—that balmy heart happiness which comes from observing the happiness around one and being subtly infected by it.

And the crowd at Notre Dame was not a crowd as usually understood—had none of the fret, fatigue and restlessness of a crowd. It was a concourse of joyous people possessed by a peaceful gladness and a glad restfulness. That is how my subconscious self sensed my surroundings. To everybody, everything seemed good and pleasant.

It was good to see the evidences of striking progress furnished by the finished new library and the started new Science Hall. It was good to see there pillars of Church and state (six feet four inches of Governor Goodrich, stands out among the pillars) gracing the occasion by their presence. It was good to see poet from the Atlantic meet novelist from the Pacific. And it was good to sit spell-bound under some of America's first orators.

All this was good. But to me it was still more pleasant to observe the meeting, from their far-scattered abiding places and widely divergent walks of life, of the many who in years gone past, had trod these paths as high-hearted boys, had underneath these trees bound their friendships, dreamt their dreams, and builded their castles—and, above all, had grown in their soul's rich soil the beautiful love which time's tempests never could uproot, of their thrice-endeared alma mater. Now they had forsaken the world's frets, shaken off the world's worries and returned to renew their youth, sweet, glad and carefree, underneath the welcoming elms and in the holy halls of Notre Dame.

Father Cavanaugh's anger over Notre Dame's rejection for a recruit training program was better understood when an interview in the South Bend Tribune with Secretary of the Navy Josephus Daniels in 1915 was recalled. Daniels, who had visited Notre Dame at Father Cavanaugh's invitation and who had taken part in a ceremony marking the placing of the Maine monument in memory of John Shillington, said afterward: " . . . The training of the young men at Notre Dame in military instruction gave evidence of the highest order of capability and the very efficient man who has charge of that instruction has just cause for pride in the results achieved. The evolutions all showed a high order of skill and the effect of good training . . ."

But the University continued to gird for the imminent hardships of a war which would obviously remove most of its senior students.

The 10th annual meeting of the Alumni Association was held on June 10. The exercises of the jubilee had occupied all the time up to the hour of the meeting. William McInerney '01, called the meeting to order. Regular business, of new members and condolences proceeded, underlined by the death of the venerable and distinguished Timothy E. Howard during the year. The treasurer's report showed receipts of dues totaling $725. Paid-in subscriptions to the Old Students Hall fund now were $19,518 and the unpaid subscriptions represented $37,330. A resolution was passed that the association be authorized to accept U.S. Liberty Bonds in payment of subscriptions to the fund. The treasurer was also authorized to invest the hall funds on hand in Liberty Bonds.

The secretary of the association was instructed to send a message of fealty and devotion to the President of the United States, assuring him that the Alumni Association upholds his hands in the present dreadful war and informing him of the intent of the association to invest the funds in Liberty Bonds.

A resolution was passed that the officers be appointed a committee of the whole to consider the advisability of issuing a monthly *Alumni Bulletin* and that they be empowered to take appropriate action.

Officers for the ensuing year were elected: Father John Burke '83, Peoria, honorary president; Clement C. Mitchell '02 Chicago, president; Henry Wurzer '98 of Detroit, Paul Martin '13 of Indianapolis, Col. Joseph Cusack '89 of Toledo, Judge Kickham Scanlan '14 of Chicago and Judge John Eggeman '00 of Ft. Wayne; vice presidents; Father William A. Moloney C.S.C. '90, reelected secretary and Warren Cartier '87 of Ludington, reelected treasurer. Trustees for two-year terms were M.F. Healy '83 of Ft. Dodge, James Murphy '99 of Rock Island and Father Michael Moriarty '10 of Cleveland, Ohio.

After the 1917 football season, marred by war, by a tie with Wisconsin and a 7-0 defeat by Nebraska, Jesse Harper, who had brought Notre Dame into national prominence and intersectional scheduling, resigned. In his five seasons he had won 35 games, lost 5 and tied 1. Harper was to return as athletic director after Rockne's death in 1931, in a much less effective administration of the difficult transition period in Notre Dame football. But his earlier role was a major contribution.

The career of Knute Rockne is as well known to Notre Dame men as the Gospels and under less attack. But it is interesting, and a little enlightening, to read what the *Scholastic* said of his selection as Harper's successor in the spring of 1918:

The announcement that Coach Knute K. Rockne is to succeed Athletic Director Jesse C. Harper when the resignation of the latter becomes effective in June, gives assurance that the high standards of Notre Dame Athletics will not be lowered by the change of directors. Rockne, as no other man, seems ideally fitted for the directorship of athletics at his alma mater. He was a brilliant football and track athlete during his days of competition and he has proved to be an exceedingly good assistant under Coach Harper.

Rockne first came to Notre Dame in the fall of 1910, reaching the heights of his football prominence in the seasons of 1912, and 1913. He captained the eleven in his last year, the team that some critics are inclined to believe was the best that ever represented Notre Dame. As an end Rockne had few equals. He was a sure tackler and one of the best handlers of the forward pass in the history of the modernized game. While he was captain Notre Dame defeated the Army, Pittsburgh and Texas.

In 1914, Coach Harper finding the work of coaching different Notre Dame teams unaided too arduous a task, employed Rockne to assist him. Rockne since then has been invaluable as an assistant football coach and a track instructor. The linemen of the Notre Dame football teams the last four years have been the equal of any in the country. Rockne seems to have the ability to impart his knowledge of the game in such a way that the man he is instructing immediately grasps what he is being told. With the track teams Rockne has been no less successful. He has developed a number of men who have had no previous track experience. Notre Dame has fared well in dual meets during Rockne's regime, while his relay teams of the last two years have been most noteworthy.

Rockne has been an unprecedented success thus far because he has been an insidious student of human nature. He tries to understand thoroughly each man whom he is instructing. He counts each athlete as his personal friend, and his assistance does not stop when the athlete gets into civilian attire. He has been paid back a thousand times in increased effort for all the pains he has taken with his men. There is every reason to believe that Rockne will be quite as successful at the head of the athletic department as he has been as an assistant. He has the will to succeed, and his energy and enthusiasm are common knowledge.

The wartime campus was of course in turmoil. Alumni visitors in uniform became an almost daily occurrence. Unprecedented incidents enlivened the student life, such as the brush which a later prominent Chicago judge had with the military. He had been equal to the disciplinary regimes of the mellower C.S.Cs. But in the new rigidity he found himself being accompanied to his classes by two armed guards. The glamor of this distinction appealed more, he admits, to his fellow students than it did to his teachers, notably the articulate Father Crumley.

News of casualties began to reach the campus. The *Scholastic* carried in the June, 1918, issue, a story of the serious wounding of Lt. Harry F. Kelly, a graduate of the diamond jubilee class of the previous year. He survived formidable odds and his letters were reassuring, despite the word that he had lost one leg. This incident is selected, not entirely at random, but to illustrate that the first World War was indeed serious, that it affected Notre Dame and alumni seriously, but that it also brought out the great strength and spirit of the University's teaching. Harry Kelly returned to the United States, practiced law, was a most effective President of the Alumni Association in the critical years of World War II, was elected Governor of Michigan, and later became a member of the Supreme Court of that State.

The June, 1918, commencement, was opened in Washington Hall, by a special program featuring Mrs. Ellen Ryan Jolly. Mrs. Jolly was chairman of a committee to erect in Washington, D.C., a statue to the nuns of the Civil War battlefield, among whom were the Sisters from St. Mary's led by Mother Angela. Mrs. Jolly was also a former president of the Ladies Auxiliary of the Hibernians. She presented to Notre Dame the pen with which President Woodrow Wilson had signed the long-sought bill for the Sisters monument, in the name of her deceased son, James, who had been a student at Notre Dame.

It is sometimes difficult in reviewing a decision to know whether it involved expediency or inspiration. The war years did not give Father Cavanaugh the luxury of either consideration or delay.

We have just commented on the appointment of Knute Rockne.

We now face the great decision to introduce a Summer School at Notre Dame, which would feature three desirable goals—it would offer undergraduates an opportunity to make up lost credits; it would be open to women, especially nuns and lay teachers in need of additional training and credits; and it would encourage graduate studies by bringing in the teacher group, particularly, in need of acquiring graduate degrees.

It could well have been that 600 students in service provided enough reason for the decision. But the development of the Graduate School through this demanding Summer channel was to accelerate its development. And the presence on the campus during these Summer School programs of nuns from all orders and all geographical areas, created a student recruiting program and a public relations result which delayed any other need for these factors until World War II altered the whole Summer School program. A Brown County Ursuline nun, whose community was enthusiastic in its patronage of the Summer School, wrote of the first session in 1918:

> Fine old Notre Dame University has opened its doors to summer students and more than 200 enrolled are now looking with real regret to the closing of the first term.
> Of teaching sisters, to whom Walsh Hall has been assigned as theirs in fee simple, there are Franciscans, Dominicans, Visitandines, Ursulines, Sisters of Mercy, of Immaculate Heart, of St. Joseph, of Nazareth, of St. Agnes, of St. Mary's of Charity, of St. Augustine and of the Holy Cross. For sisters, Notre Dame is unique in this country as a place for summer study; away from the bustle and stir of town, its broad stage of 1600 acres is aloof and cloistral, yet delightfully resourceful.
> At Badin Hall are gathered clerical students, Benedictines from several different communities, besides representatives of the secular clery and the Christian Brothers.
> With these are lay students, young men from Peru, Bolivia, Guatemala, Hong Kong, Greece and the Philippines. A number of young woman, mostly teachers and some of them Protestants, are assembled from various vicinities, and the usual quota of Notre Dame's own boys doing special work, come hurrying along, books under their arms, when the chimes from the church tower ring out over the campus. Each coterie seems to find its own proper environment in a happy way, and like some rare old picture, all are blended in the wholesome atmosphere of earnest purpose that is Notre Dame's own.
> Big:—that is the word for Notre Dame! Big in its traditions, its spirit, its purpose!

In September, the government may have put together the conflicting parts of the absence of military training at so logical a spot as Notre Dame. In any event, in September Capt. William Murray arrived to establish a unit of the Students Army Training Corps. It was a mixed blessing. The presence of an outside authority was compensated by the assurance of enrollment, government payment of the annual tuition ($120) for each trainee and $30 a month for their subsistence. The S.A.T.C. began functioning on Oct. 1, 1918. Ensign Moeller was sent by the Navy to induct 100 students into the Navy branch of the Corps. Father Cavanaugh gave the new program the blessing and the hallmark of his genius in an address which praised the

S.A.T.C. and its officers, and which emphasized the love of God and country which had existed at Notre Dame from the day of its founding, the "twin passions of religion and patriotism." And he added words that were reminiscent of Sorin when the Civil War called for the University's action, and which were to be echoed again by Father J. Hugh O'Donnell, when World War II thrust itself upon the campus of 1941. "Notre Dame belongs to God and America. And as her perfect consecration to religion demands that she place her resources generously and unreservedly at the service of religion, so does her sense of patriotism make her feel that every energy, every power and every force within her control must be magnanimously placed at the service of America."

"God, Country, Notre Dame"—the words inscribed later over the Memorial Door of Sacred Heart Church designed by Vincent Fagan '20, to commemorate the 46 Notre Dame men who died in World War I, were three vital factors in the growth of Notre Dame, three real goals in its education.

To the men of those first 75 years, there was dedication to each, and to their unity, which gave the University added strength. In our later days, we have been exposed to the thought that all three of those basic forces may have deteriorated—God and His church; America and its fundamental political principles; and Notre Dame in its religious and academic duality.

It seems, in the light of this diamond jubilee, and as we contemplate the ensuing years, that deterioration, if any, is not so much in the goals as in the seekers after them.

The 11th annual meeting of the Alumni Association was held on June 9, 1918, with all its war limitations. President Clement Mitchell was among those absent, and Warren Cartier opened the meeting. The regular business was transacted, the Class of 1918 admitted and a committee of Father John F. O'Hara, C.S.C. '11, Knute Rockne '14, and Edward Cleary '09 drew up the condolences for the deceased, including one of the first war casualties, Arthur Hayes '15 who died at Camp Grant.

The treasurer's report showed bank deposits and other assets of $4,662. The Old Students Hall Fund totaled $803 on deposit, $300 in Liberty Bonds, $25,000 loaned to the University on notes and $40,665 in unpaid subscriptions. The meeting ratified the University loan, and the treasurer was instructed to turn over to the University any amount which exceeded $1,000 as they were received, in exchange for notes. Interest was fixed at 4 per cent and the association decided to proceed with the fund raising if it did not conflict with government war funding efforts. The treasurer was instructed not to send bills for dues to members of the Association in service.

Officers elected were: Very Rev. Peter Blessing LL.D. '18, Providence, R.I., honorary president; Harry G. Hogan '04, Fort Wayne, president; J. J. Conway '85 of Ottawa, Ill., Joseph Haley '99 of Fort Wayne, Col. William Hoynes '88 of Notre Dame, William Jamieson '05 of St. Paul, Max St. George '12 of Chicago and John B. Kanaley '09 of Chicago, vice presidents. Father William A. Moloney, C.S.C. was reelected secretary and Warren Cartier, treasurer. Two-year trustees were Clement Mitchell '02 of Chicago, Robert Proctor '04 of Elkhart and William McInerney '01 of South Bend.

This is one of the "miracles" to which I have alluded. The new 1918-19 president of the association, Harry Hogan, served a traditional but unexceptional term. It might well have consigned him to the limbo that is all too often the address of ex-presidents. But this was the same Harry Hogan who returned to serve additional terms as president of the association after World War II, revitalizing the Alumni Association, and brining to the University both the concept and the historic reality of the Notre Dame Foundation.

The Armistice ending World War I was signed in November. Notre Dame had accumulated many casualties. Its chaplains, now numbering eight with the additions of Father James O'Brien and Frederick McKeon, were sorely missed on the campus. Its transformed campus life had preserved numbers, but the identity of the University was another question. The *Scholastic* heralded the end of the S.A.T.C., when the government ordered its demobilization in December, after its two short months at Notre Dame. The University was reassured by government provision to reimburse colleges seriously affected by the sudden cessation of the program.

Father Hope includes a letter from Father Cavanaugh to Father John Talbot Smith which contains an eloquent analysis, "The soldiers are gone with only slight damage to Brother Philip's campus. Mentally, morally and socially, the University was never so well conditioned before. The old spirit has come back with a rush, and Notre Dame is perfectly herself again. It is the sweetest miracle of my life."

In April, 1919, Father Cavanaugh celebrated the silver jubilee of his ordination. The students evidenced great admiration and affection for him at this time. This tribute proved to be a farewell, as Canon Law now required the succession of another President, who would be limited in his terms to one or at most two three-year terms.

Father John W. Cavanaugh was not yet 50 and he went to Washington to reside at Holy Cross College in the Catholic University, to write and to lecture, as his prestige and friendships expanded.

It was suggested to him, Father Hope adds, that he write a history of the University. And Father Cavanaugh himself had started acquiring information for a book which he tentatively titled, *The Story of the Little Graveyard*.

There is indeed a rich history in the Community Cemetery, where Father Cavanaugh, an illustrious alumnus, now lies. I hope some future author will approach the never-ending wonder of Notre Dame by way of this holy Lyonesse, whose heroes died for Our Lady under the legendary banners of poverty, chastity and obedience.

XX

Maturity Comes
to the Campus

Notre Dame was never immature. Notre Dame was always young. But there is a time when growth and pressures insist that the exuberances of youth be placed in the mold of responsibility. The result can be a loss of vitality, and a weakening of function. This was not the case at Notre Dame. On any campus, the forever young student body tends to create a forever young administration and faculty. Where the family spirit is close, the goals are good, the principles are sound, and the whole institution is dedicated to Our Lady, the emergence of a mature University, retaining all the vision and vitality of its heritage, is not surprising.

It was an era, around 1919, when World War I had seen the collapse of the historic houses of Hapsburg, Hohenzollern and Romanov. Revolution was in the world air. The League of Nations was created at the close of the War, to channel the revolutionary forces into a world of peace. It was typical of America that revolution here took the shape of rejecting proposed membership in the League of Nations, which was in large part a product of President Wilson's negotiations with our allies.

But the United States shared the optimism of the times which said that the world had been saved for democracy. We saw a world becoming "more like us." And the United States turned the full powers it had revealed in the War to pursuing the divergent paths of peace. Education was one of the major challenges. We were still largely a people of recent immigration. The college population was still small. In 1920 only 38,000 bachelor's degrees and 4,800 graduate degrees were conferred in all the colleges and universities on record.

At the end of Father Cavanaugh's administration, the 1919
enrollment at Notre Dame was almost half preparatory and
Minim. These and the college students were becoming mutually
crowded, with the age of the college students arguing for their
unpopular relegation to off-campus residence when the campus
overflowed.

Meantime, constructive revolution was taking place in the
Congregation. Father Corby and Morrissey had tended to preserve the total campus of the Sorin tradition. Father Zahm had
argued for more higher education of religious, and college
emphasis.

Fathers John Cavanaugh and James Burns, together in the
seminary days, had been taught and influenced by these men.
Father Cavanaugh's disposition inclined him toward the older
tradition. Father Burns, a serious student of Catholic education,
believed in the higher education of priests and in emphasis on
the quality of the college training at Notre Dame.

It seems probable that the forces supporting the development
of the University prevailed in 1919 in the selection of Father
Burns as successor to Father Cavanaugh. Father Burns had
taught chemistry at Notre Dame from his ordination in 1893 until
1900, when he was made superior of Holy Cross College in
Washington, D.C. He remained in this post until called back to
Notre Dame as President. And while the genial Cavanaugh won
the hearts of Notre Dame by his talents and by his love of its
traditions, Father Burns was winning the minds of the generations of young priests of the Congregation who took their
theology under his supervision. In Washington, he studied the
broad field of Catholic education in the United States and was a
pioneer in the formation of the Catholic Education Association.
He published books on education and received his doctorate in
that field. When he became President of Notre Dame he brought
to the campus a maturity and a professional approach to the
academic community above that of any previous administration.

Father Burns was 52 at the time he became President. In the
three short years of his administration, he initiated or realized
many of the projects which were to play prominent parts in the
growth and the stature of Notre Dame from then on. Among
alumni, among adminstrators, among priests of the Congregation, he was one of the greatest and most respected. Few traces
remained in 1919 of the young man from Michigan City who

enrolled in the Manual Training School, then in the college, where one of his least suspected accomplishments was his position as catcher on the varsity baseball team in the era when catchers wore no glove.

Sparks flew from the time he took office. The campus was ready. The nation was attuned. The alumni, many of them back from service, were plunging into their own careers, but deeply interested in the progress of Notre Dame.

An editorial in the Fort Wayne *Journal Gazette* in April, 1919, reflects the prestige of the University, its great World War I record, but more importantly a program which reveals that the growth of Notre Dame had not lost the "vie intime" which marked the small families of its pioneer years:

> . . . Never in history has she responded better than in the war just now coming to a close. It is said that the upper classes were almost wiped out. The memorial tablet to be erected will set forth that counting students, professors, and former graduates there were 2,093 Notre Dame men with the colors. . . . Not least among the qualities of service which distinguished the University was its systematic plans to keep in touch with the boys. Through a letter-writing bureau the "spirit of Notre Dame" was at all times in touch with the men who had passed from its classic halls to the battlefield.

In June, 250 alumni attended the annual Alumni Association meeting. The meeting was preceded by the dedication of the William Hoynes College of Law, understandably a popular event with his fellow alumni. Harry Hogan opened the business meeting, welcoming the large group, some just back from overseas. The Class of 1919, one of the smallest classes because of the war, was admitted to membership and promptly exhibited its spirit by making the largest subscription per man to the Old Students Hall fund of any graduating class. Efforts in increasing the fund had been suspended because of the war effort but were now renewed. The treasurer reported that $8,500 had been subscribed without effort, that $75,000 was now in the fund, with $5,000 in the general funds of the association.

The meeting appointed a committee to request from the Congregation and the University a permanent secretary for the association, and to make plans for the building and financing of Old Students Hall as previously intended. Warren Cartier, Francis O. Shaughnessy, Joseph Sullivan, Clement Mitchell and Byron Kanaley composed the committee.

A resolution was passed endorsing the work to secure self government for Ireland, the endorsement to be in harmony with the stand taken by the United States Senate. Beacon, bridge and crossroad had not been forgotten in "la vie intime."

Officers elected were: Col. Hoynes, honorary president, a recognition by alumni of the new dignity of his College of Law; Patrick Malloy '07, Tulsa, president, marking the extending boundaries of alumni involvement. Vice presidents took on the War flavor. They were: Lt. Gerald Fitzgibbon '06, Chicago; Paul Martin '09, Indianapolis; Lt. Rupert Mills '15, Newark, N.J.; Lt. Joseph Pliska '15, Chicago; Lt. Harry Kelly '17, Ottawa, Ill., and Lt. Bernard Voll '17, Philadelphia. Father Moloney was retained as secretary and Warren Cartier as treasurer. Two-year trustees chosen were Joseph Haley '99, Ft. Wayne; T. Paul McGannon '07, Albany, N.Y., and Lt. Ray Miller '14, Cleveland.

The concentration on the war years had overshadowed the divergence of Notre Dame's development. The renewed vitality following the peace brought the spotlight back. Toward the close of the second Summer School, which had brought coeducation to the University, the campus was host to the silver jubilee convention of the Priests Eucharistic League, which had held its first meeting in the United States at Notre Dame 15 years before. Every section of the country was represented by the delegates. This further instance of the working bridge, beacon and crossroad begins to explain the distinctive hold which the University has had from its beginning on the Catholic population of the country.

On Oct. 4, 1919, the *Scholastic* reported "the most important vocal concert ever given here." Three thousand five hundred tickets had been sold for the decorated gymnasium setting. An unheard-of fee of $3,000 was being paid the singer. The event demonstrated the much underrated appreciation of the campus for varied and top quality experiences. The singer? Mlle. Amelita Galli-Curci, Italian-Spanish star coloratura/soprano of the Metropolitan Opera, who had sung with Caruso, Ruffo and other outstanding stars, and is rated the greatest of sopranos. Oddly, she was trained and graduated as a pianist, her vocal talents emerging almost without training. Speaking five languages and boasting a repertoire of the great feminine roles in Opera, the attraction was a highlight of the academic and civic community.

In another historic innovation, seemingly not in character

with the academic discipline of the new President, Father Burns appointed a Students Activities Committee, fountainhead of the varying forms of student government which have blessed and burned the pages of history thereafter. Three members of the faculty, the presidents of the several classes and seven additional students, were charged with giving the best expression to student opinion, and with unifying student activities, which, the *Scholastic* added, "heretofore have been haphazard and irresponsible."

Here comes a paragraph you will not believe—an appeal to students to interest alumni in coming to the football games on the campus. Low attendance had resulted in the better games being played away from Notre Dame. For example, the only 1918 game played at Notre Dame was the Great Lakes game, which found a number of Notre Dame alumni on the Great Lakes team. In 1919, Knute Rockne asked the people of South Bend to buy season tickets to encourage games at home and found a ready response. The students were asked to create a homecoming game to attract alumni, and the Purdue game of 1920 was advanced as the inauguration of the program.

As if to back both proposals, Rockne fielded his undefeated 1919 team against Michigan State before a crowd which overtaxed the capacity of Cartier Field, with automobiles parked around three sides of the field and overflow crowds on foot joining the students lining the field. Keeping the playing field clear was a problem. Michigan State had brought its band. Against the previous home games that year, with Kalamazoo, Morningside and Western State Normal, Michigan State seemed the big-time team it was to become so definitely. Notre Dame attendance figures stem from 1919, the total for that year being 56,500 for nine games. Five years later, brilliant teams and undefeated seasons, together with vastly improved schedules, had raised the total 1924 attendance to 265,000 for a nine-game schedule, and an additional 53,000 in the Rose Bowl on Jan. 1, 1925, the only bowl game that Notre Dame was to play until the Cotton Bowl game in Dallas in 1969.

It was inevitable, as it was just as surely in the astute mind of Coach Rockne, that the move for a stadium at Notre Dame should follow the 1919 season. The promise of better games and better crowds excited the campus and the civic neighbors.

Another factor—one which I believe is a distinctive contribution to the family spirit of Note Dame throughout the years, though difficult to weave into the academic story—was crystal-

lized in this first year of Father Burn's regime. It is humor, and
in the rich gamut between Galli-Curci and an undefeated football team, the Notre Dame *Juggler* was born. Sponsored by
three upper-classmen, it ended the *Scholastic* monopoly.

From its inception, the *Juggler* was bright and perceptive. It
was a clean publication, never quite censored, but never quite
free from academic suspicion. It was widely quoted among the
growing number of campus humor magazines that brought relief
from both the memories of war and the rigors of study. It
treated the foibles of the time, on and off the campus, with a
concise and stimulating analysis in cartoon or in quip, softening
many of their impacts that might have otherwise assumed
undeserved proportions. (A little chauvinism possibly, but I was
on its staff and knew its goals, only four years after this
founding. I deny prejudice, because I was also on the staffs of
the *Scholastic* and the *Dome*, when the publications were the
laboratories of the journalist.))

In November, 1919, the *Scholastic* came out with a premature, but enthusiastic report that Old Students Hall was an
imminent reality. The creation of a new residence hall, as part
of a new quadrangle of such halls, and the establishment of an
alumni headquarters on campus, were heralded by the students.

In the spring of 1920 Notre Dame spotlighted another academic first. It joined the general academic thrust, but it also
reflected the interest and patronage of a young priest interested
in Latin America, Father John F. O'Hara. The distinctive event
was the publication of *Nosotros*, a yearbook similar to the
Dome, but published entirely in Spanish. Alfonso Anaya was
the editor-in-chief, Enrique Rosselot the business manager and
Roman Restrepo the art editor. The *Dome* itself was high in
praise of its counterpart, expressing the belief that as it was sent
to the various schools and governmental agencies throughout
Latin America it would be a great advertising medium for Notre
Dame, as it was already a tribute to the Latin-American Association on the campus which sponsored it.

The 1920 annual meeting of the Alumni Association reflected the serious and extending considerations of the association, which were leading inevitably to the headquarters on
campus, the permanent secretary and the alumni bulletin which
were already requests of record.

> The 13th annual meeting of the Alumni Association of the
> University of Notre Dame was held in Brownson Study Hall,
> at five o'clock. In the absence of the president of the associa-

tion, Patrick M. Malloy '07 of Tulsa, Oklahoma, who was detained in New York City by an accident, the meeting was called to order by Warren A. Cartier '87, who appointed as chairman to preside at the meeting Byron V. Kanaley '04.

The general assets of the association amount to $6,235.20; Old Students Hall Building Fund, cash and Liberty Bonds to $85,981; unpaid subscriptions to Old Students Hall to $40,057. Byron V. Kanaley '04 as chairman of the building committee of Old Students Hall reported that the inability of contractors to forecast labor, transportation and building material conditions, and therefore, their inability to offer contract figures on anything except a cost plus basis, with no assurance of any approximate date for completing the building, had led the committee, after careful deliberation with the architect and contractors, to defer the beginning of building for a few months until the markets in labor and material have become more stabilized. The association was given the assurance that the committee is anxious to begin the building at the very first favorable opportunity and is watching conditions carefully.

The chairman then requested the Rev. Dr. James A. Burns, C.S.C. '88, President of the University, to address the meeting, and appointed Charles P. Neill '93, and William P. O'Neill '06, to escort the President to the chair. President Burns spoke with feeling concerning the loyalty of the alumni and the support he had received from them in the first year of his administration. He reviewed briefly the work of the association in relation to the University, laying special stress on the campaign for funds for Old Students Hall.

It was then proposed that members of the Alumni Association be named as members of the University Athletic Board of Control to act with the faculty members who at present compose the board in the administration of the athletic affairs of the University. On motion the chairman was requested and empowered to name the alumni members of the board after consultation with the University authorities.

The students followed the suggestion of the previous year that alumni be invited to a Homecoming Game. The Purdue weekend was chosen. A Friday night parade and rally in South Bend was to be followed by a smoker with boxing and wrestling, in the University Gymnasium. Alumni were asked to come for two days if possible. Five hundred good seats "in the middle of the new stands" were being held for alumni, and the alumni clubs were asked to decide on their quotas as soon as possible. Two high school teams would provide a curtain-opener on Saturday. Prices for general admission were $1, $1.50 and $2, with box seats $3—six seats in a box. Orders were to be addressed to K.K. Rockne, athletic director, Notre Dame, Ind.

Rockne achieved his second undefeated season in football in 1920. The men of those teams were to provide some of the nation's great coaches in the subsequent years—Lawrence "Buck" Shaw, Heartley "Hunk" Anderson, Edward "Slip" Madigan, Maurice "Clipper" Smith, Charlie Crowley, Eddie Anderson, Harry Mehre and Frank Thomas come easily to mind. The schedule was "beefed up" in 1920, including Nebraska, Army, Purdue, Indiana, Northwestern and Michigan State.

But all this was realized in retrospect, after the drama of George Gipp. I missed Gipp by one season as a Notre Dame student and never saw him play. But in an era when you had to do it all, he could do it all. His name still is prominent in the Notre Dame all-time records. He led his team in rushing in 1918 and 1919, in passing in 1918, 1919 and 1920, and in scoring in 1918, 1919 and 1920. He died from a strep infection on Dec. 14, 1920, at the age of 25, with the headlines featuring his Number One selection on Walter Camp's All-American team, and that of the INS.

The drama was not alone in the excellence of his performance. In fact, like the current Joe Namath, it stemmed in origin and in legend from the fact that Gipp achieved his distinction seemingly without effort—disturbingly in the face of those formulas for athletes that are dear to the hearts of coaches, teachers and parents. Gipp, who had come to Notre Dame as a baseball prospect from Laurium, Mich., was reputedly as much at home in pool or poker as he was in punting or passing. The legend is that he needed little scholarship aid as long as he could visit downtown South Bend. Even, a fellow student told me, in the light of his present effort, that he had found it a pleasure to lose consistently to the talented Gipp. It was an early mark of the virtuosity of Rockne as a coach that he understood Gipp, as he did all of his players, most of them happily less complicated than the versatile star.

And it was a mark of George Gipp's good mind that in the midst of a rich life, his religious heritage from a minister father combined with his years at Notre Dame to bring his request to die a Catholic. An admiring priest, Father Patrick Haggerty, C.S.C., baptized Gipp accordingly. Death seems to add a dimension even to the great. And Gipp lives, along with Rockne, whose conversion to Catholicism was after his success was eminent, in the continuous annals of Notre Dame.

Tributes poured in from everywhere on the death of Gipp.

Father Charles O'Donnell wrote a commemorative poem in the emotion of the occasion. I think he was not too happy with it professionally in retrospect, but I think that in one quatrain he gave a magnificent prayer to the Catholic world of Notre Dame:

O, Lady, you have taken of our best,
    To make a playmate for the Seraphim.
There, on the wide, sweet campus of the blest,
    Be good to him.

A tribute of great significance in many ways came in the following letter addressed to Father Burns.

"May I, just to show admiration and respect and friendliness, send $10 toward the memorial to be erected to Mr. Gipp. Last year I was traveling in Illinois and happened to meet the Notre Dame eleven, who were on their way to Nebraska. I did not speak to them, but I never saw a finer set of young men—they were splendid looking athletes and behaved in every way like gentlemen. You have every reason not only to be proud of your team's record, but of their appearance and character. I am always proud of our Yale teams, whether they win or lose, and it is a pleasure to send this tribute to your men. The death of Mr. Gipp is mourned everywhere.

Faithfully yours, Wm. Lyon Phelps
(Professor of English Literature at Yale)"

The 1920 annual meeting of the Alumni Association had appointed Father Matthew Walsh, C.S.C. '03, as resident chairman of the membership committee, to succeed Father Michael A. Quinlan, C.S.C. '93, who had held that arduous office and published an alumni list from time to time.

Officers for 1920-21 were Rt. Rev. Francis H. Gavisk '14, Indianapolis, honorary president; Joseph J. Sullivan '01, Chicago, president and John H. Neeson '03 of Philadelphia, Charles P. Neill '93 of Washington, F. Henry Wurzer '98 of Detroit, Robert E. Proctor '04 of Elkhart, Hugh J. Daly '12 of Chicago and Thomas J. Shaughnessy '16 of Winnipeg, vice presidents. Father Moloney and Warren Cartier were retained in their posts as secretary and treasurer. Trustees were Patrick T. Sullivan '72 of Chicago, Gallitzin A. Farabaugh '04 of South Bend and Daniel J. O'Connor '05 of Chicago. Frank E. Hering '98, announced his establishment of the Hering Awards for athletes having the highest academic standing. Warren Cartier announced an increase in his Old Students Hall gift from $500 to $5,000 and this touched off a number of major increases from other alumni present.

No new buildings appeared during the tenure of Father Burns. But the fires of progress never died down. Instead, they were turned to the academic progress of the University which Father Burns understood better than any of his colleagues. He knew that the private universities of America were already substantially endowed. He knew that these endowments, both in their sources and in their investment, were usually in the hands of trustees who were themselves wealthy and leaders in business and industry. His own experiences in seeking support for Notre Dame had found many men who should have been generous to Notre Dame completely uninformed of the financial needs of a University and somewhat less than inclined to give to a cause which they felt had been self-sustaining for 80 years.

This situation, and the plan already forming for a campaign to raise some needed endowment, resulted in the formation of the Associate Board of Lay Trustees in 1920. After a summer school at Harvard, during which he studied that University's financial structure, Father Burns proposed the board, to be composed of 12 elected members half of whom would be alumni of Notre Dame, the others prominent men chosen from the country at large and not members of the University's alumni.

A long-distinguished alumnus, William P. Breen, Fort Wayne '77 was elected the first president of the board. Ill health forced him to retire in 1921 and he was succeeded by a non-alumnus, Albert R. Erskine, president of the Studebaker Corporation, who retained the post until his death in 1933. The board members, alumni and non-alumni, were selected on the basis of their familiarity with the investment of money, their own substance and the contacts which they would normally enjoy with a much wider circle of men of wealth. On the basis of his study of other colleges, Father Burns must have held the hope that his trustees would not only hold and invest the endowment funds safely, once raised, but would frequently be benefactors themselves, and interest others in the development of the University. The fruition of that hope has been most rewarding.

The history of the lay trustees has been a bright chapter in Notre Dame history, and in the part Notre Dame alumni have played in the University's progress. After the first appointments, the trustees have elected their new members. For a number of years the alumni elected the alumni members. But the election process became cumbersome as numbers increased, and class and club pressures began to be felt in the elections. The result was a mutual agreement that the trustees would elect all new members, as vacancies occurred. The caliber of alumni representation has been as constant as it has been constructive. The alumni who became members of the first board of lay trustees were names long familiar with the growth of the Alumni Association: William P. Breen '77, Clement C. Mitchell '02, Joseph M. Byrne '79, James D. Callery '73, Warren Cartier '87 and Angus McDonald '00. It was not a "youth movement," but it brought men of proven ability to a responsibility in which Notre Dame could not afford risk. Non-alumni members of that first board were A.R. Erskine, Max Pam, Solon Richardson Jr., Miles W. O'Brien, Francis J. Reitz and Edward N. Hurley.

The spring of 1921 saw the death of the memorable Father Andrew Morrissey, former President and Provincial. At the time of his death in Paris on May 27, he was returning from Rome where he had represented the Congregation of Holy Cross as Coadjutor Superior General.

Six months later, Father John A. Zahm, internationally distinguished now as scientist and author, and greatly respected for his many and constructive contributions to the progress of Notre Dame, died in Munich, on Nov. 11, where he was a guest of the Benziger family. Father Zahm's most recent benefaction to Notre Dame had been his Dante collection, which was made a separate division of the new Library in 1917. The collection has been compared to the leading Dante collections in this country, at Harvard and Cornell. The number of different editions, in Italian and in translations, is said to be greatest at Notre Dame.

In the years after his Presidency, Father Cavanaugh, who had provided space in the library for this great gift, served as curator of this Dante collection, a tribute and an insurance which would have pleased the donor.

Another of Father Burns' strategic moves toward academic advancement was the closing of the Preparatory Carroll Hall.

George D. Haller, writing in the *Dome* of the demise of Carroll, said:

> Romance and Adventure were every boy's companions those mystic years from 13 to 15, when, grammar school behind with its troublesome female teachers, he stood upon the threshold of youth's estate, ... Not only physically

irrepressible, the loyalest, longest-hoping rooter Cartier Field
ever saw; the loudest, most restless, yet often the most
appreciative auditor Washington Hall ever housed; but also
the dauntless voyager of the infinite realms of imaginative
Mind and innocent Heart—every boy his first year in old
Carroll was sometimes the most refreshing student that poor
plagued professors ever kindled the lamp of knowledge in,
and very, very frequently the sincerest, happiest, most pleasing visitant to that shrine where waits the Holy Brother of all
the children of men.

Carroll Hall was for many years the mid-section and the heart
of "la vie intime." The continuation of unity can be said to
represent a pioneer heart transplant.

The *Dome* of 1921 reports that the Students Activities Committee is off to a strong start. Part of this is attributed to a
student-drawn plan, under the chairmanship of Thomas
Beacom, its first chairman, toward the close of the 1919-20
school year. Part is implied in the separate meetings of the
three-member faculty council of the S.A.C., and the 13-member
student group, including the four class presidents and nine
elected members—six Seniors, two Juniors, and one Sophomore.
The *Dome* states that the S.A.C. got off to a slow start initially
because of a lack of definition of purposes, a fault remedied by
the group in evolving a constitution.

The first balloon went up for the pioneer University fund-
raising campaign with the announcement in the March, 1921,
Scholastic of the grant of the General Education Board to the
University of $250,000, on the condition that Notre Dame raise
$750,000. The *Scholastic* reported mixed optimism and pessi-
mism. But it took the optimist viewpoint, and suggested that
the scattered alumni throughout 48 states, with fifty regional
cities of importance should insure success. The raising of
$10,000 by each of these cities would practically solve the
problem. If these fail, the *Scholastic* says—and in so saying it
points up one of the greatest assets of Notre Dame—there are
hundreds of small towns, with prominent Notre Dame alumni,
which might each raise $1,000. The *Scholastic* pulls out all the
stops of traditional fund-raising, from 'socials' to concerts,
recitals, even magazine subscriptions. The immaturity of Notre
Dame in fund-raising experience was reflected in the article.
And the campaign was to suffer in its pursuit of the seemingly
modest goal. But the student poet, Vincent Engels, who wrote
the article, was matched in his enthusiasm, or in substituted
determination, by Father Burns and his staff. Father Burns had

already raised the salaries of lay professors by 25 per cent, and of instructors by 10 per cent. His die was cast. He had crossed the Rubicon of the academic budget. Even the raised salaries could not hope to hold any but the deeply dedicated laymen, and the postwar enrollment was indicating enlargement of the lay faculty. The same student increase spotlighted the need for new buildings.

Notre Dame's first endowment campaign among alumni and friends outside the campus was inevitable.

XXI

Money in the Bank

The late arrival of a major campaign for outside financial support is not an indictment of the administrations of the earlier years of the University. No President, from Sorin on, was unaware of the financial struggle of the campus, or unwilling to take any necessary steps to overcome them.

Father Sorin, in one of the earliest crises of his seedling campus, sent Mrs. Alexis Coquillard and the wife of another South Bend merchant to Cincinnati, to seek funds from a friendly community there who knew Notre Dame and its goals.

You have read of crisis after crisis—fires, plague, wars, debts, aid given by Notre Dame to the Congregation of Holy Cross. But in each instance, the small and close-knit Notre Dame family, by the living endowment of its priests and brothers, by the low salaries of its dedicated lay professors and staff members, and by the important use of auxiliary enterprises, such as farms, missions, and astute real estate deals, was able to overcome these pressures. So common and frequent were they, however, that there was never an opportunity to put any money in the bank. This cushion is referred to in academic circles as endowment and was becoming a factor in American higher education, sometimes to the obsession of administrators. Notre Dame continued to invest completely in the education and in the life style of its students, with the religious and lay faculties and staffs filling in the gap that always existed between the cost of education and the charge to the student for it. This gap was beginning to widen.

The number of students was expanding, with a deficit attached to each. This expansion caused increase in faculty, a proportion of whom had to be laymen. It also caused new building needs—residence halls, classrooms and other facilities. Volume of consumption on the campus was rapidly approaching the stage where Notre Dame had to look to outside sources for goods and processing that had for so long been the role of the farm, the sisters and the brothers. The young Graduate School was projected as more costly than the traditional undergraduate, but essential to development. As the beacon drew more and more areas of the outside world to the campus and as the bridges and the crossroads became more jammed with the traffic the cost of these additional dimensions began to crop up in budget discussions. It was either keep them in the growing family or revert to a stunting status quo. No argument.

So it was that the following historic appeal from Father Burns appeared in the June 11, *Scholastic:*

> Colleges and Universities today are thronged with students as they have never been at any other period in their history. There is hardly a school of any importance in the United States which has not found itself all too straitened in resources to render towards its rapidly increasing student body the same measure of effective service that it gave in other times.
> What is true of colleges and universities generally is true in very special measure of Notre Dame. For several years young men have been turned away from Notre Dame by the hundreds, because of lack of adequate educational facilities such as teachers, classrooms, living quarters and equipment. These young men came seeking the training that is given at Notre Dame. They came because in thousands of American homes the training for Christian manhood and patriotic citizenship that is characteristic of Notre Dame is felt to be a vital need of the time. Proportionately, the increase at Notre Dame has been as great as that of any other college in the United States. This means, first of all, that no argument is needed as to the kind of service Notre Dame has been rendering in the past. If the work done by Notre Dame along whatever lines had not been of recognized merit, we should have no problems such as the one that we now face. But there is a problem and it is one which the University itself cannot cope unaided. The University would have been able today, as it was able in the past, to meet all normal and ordinary need of equipment and expansion but the present need is unprecedented. Buildings have been erected, extensive equipment installed, new departments have been organized, professors and instructors added to the faculty and yet the University is unable to meet the demands of its annually increasing student enrollment. It needs to grow 10 years almost over night.
> The University of Notre Dame exists for service. For upwards of 80 years it has struggled along without any

financial endowment. The phenomenal progress from its
humble origin in a frame building, 20 by 40 feet, to its
present expansion of 28 buildings, has been accomplished by
means of a living endowment, men whose consecrated lives
have been devoted to the service of education. These men
have served the youth of America without any recompense
other than the satisfaction of giving to their country an army
of young men well trained in sound economic, scientific and
philosophical principles. Associated with these men has been
a group of loyal lay professors and instructors without whose
faithful service the Notre Dame of today would have been
impossible. This living endowment still serves at Notre Dame
but it must be reinforced by a still larger corps of lay
professors and instructors and augmented by financial assistance on the part of the public if it is to realize all its
possibilities for service. Consequently, the University of
Notre Dame, for the first time in its history, is inviting the
public attention to its needs; for the first time in over
three-quarters of a century it is making a general appeal for
financial assistance.

In making this appeal our only hope and ambition is that
the University may be empowered to give today and in the
days to come, to an ever larger portion of the public, the
same kind of service which it has rendered for upwards of 80
years. We should have no warrant for making this appeal were
it based on any assumption for the future different from the
tested record of the past.

JAMES A. BURNS, C.S.C., President"

The broad tone of Father Burns' first appeal indicates the
reluctance which the University felt in this precedent-breaking
approach. You find no mention of the details, in this primary
opportunity, or even the total figure sought. Notre Dame did
not yet appreciate that this fund-raising principle was already
well under way in many of the universities it hoped to emu-
late—a disadvantage in chronology which was to be aggravated
by the subsequent modesty of achievement in goal, by satisfaction with a response that could have been much greater, and
which might have been transformed then into the continuous
machinery for supplementary support which in the years after
World War I became an integral reality in higher education.

The same issue of the *Scholastic* did, however, supply more
details.

Notre Dame has, in its 75 years of existence, attained or
perhaps surpassed the ideals of its valiant founders. Through
sleet and snow, Sorin and his zealous companions blazed a
path into the wilderness of Indiana and dreamed the dream
that is now Notre Dame. The tremendous upheaval in educa-

tion that the world is now experiencing has made it imperative that something be done to aid our school in the march of progress. Truly, we have, in the words of the reverend President "come to a crisis—and we must adopt a policy which will affect the future of the university for the next 50 years." The remedy for this situation is at hand—a situation which overcrowded classrooms, dormitories and inadequate laboratory facilities will partly explain. Notre Dame must and will put over that $2,000,000 endowment drive with the support of her student body which has never yet fallen down in a matter that called for a real exemplification of "Fighting Irish" spirit. We have been assured of the sincere cooperation of the citizens of South Bend and of loyal alumni throughout the country. In addition to this there is one more thing that must be evident in order that the enthusiasm be kept at fever-pitch and that is the unstinted support of every man who is proud of the fact that he is a Notre Dame man. Go into "the highways and the by-ways" this summer and sell the endowment proposition to your friends who, perhaps, know little more about the greatest school in the middle-west than the fact that you attend it. It's up to you, Mr. Notre Dame Man, to carry on with the plan that means more to this institution than any other task it has yet undertaken.

The extension program includes: An endowment of One Million Dollars to secure more lay professors and laboratory equipment; the erection of an engineering building, a commerce building, three residence halls and the making of needed improvements in the gymnasium. It will mean better facilities, better courses, and better service all the way.

Even this presentation contains more of the rah-rah approach to the campaign, an insecurity like that which gives a cheer after a fumble a sort of hollow hope. The cold targets of the campaign are added at the end, in the apparent hope that the "Fighting Irish spirit" will absorb them just as details in its continuing euphoria.

It was Harry Hogan—and I may repeat this several times, because it is truly significant in Notre Dame's history—who ultimately established at Notre Dame the fact that philanthrophy, no matter how we admire it as a virtue, consists of someone knocking on someone else's door and asking him for money. Many good causes have died of malnutrition because they were content with the "better mousetrap" theory and waited at their own doors.

The June, 1921, annual meeting of the Alumni Association, was called to order by president Joseph Sullivan. Father Moloney, so long secretary, was absent because of illness, and Father John C. McGinn, C.S.C., was named temporary secre-

tary. The class of 1921, swelled by postwar enrollment, and
including many members of the 1919 and 1920 football champion teams, was enthusiastically admitted.

In the details of the war years, I think I forgot, and should
now mention here, that the Class of 1917 was the first college
class to exceed 100 graduates. We are still dealing at this time in
campus history with small classes, and a small Alumni Association.

Father Burns addressed the annual meeting, praising the Class
of '21, the returning alumni and outlining in some detail the
new Board of Lay Trustees and its composition and duties. Here
is another point of importance, in connection with that distinguished group. It was founded, and continued, as the Associate
Board of Lay Trustees, the actual legal trustees of Notre Dame
being a group composed of priests of the Congregation of Holy
Cross.

The treasurer's report showed $5,155 in the bank, $49,000
loans to the University, $1,350 in Liberty Bonds, $45,589 in
unpaid pledges to Old Students Hall and $1,499 in the hands of
the University. All assets totaled $102,645.67.

The association, recognizing the increased activity of its program, suggested a new *Alumni Directory* as soon as possible.
Don Hamilton '12 praised the work of Rockne and the other
coaches and urged alumni to interest high school athletes in
visiting the campus.

A resolution was passed commending the citizens of South
Bend for their cooperation with the University in its proposed
endowment campaign.

Election of officers chose Rt. Rev. Peter Muldoon, LL.D. '16,
honorary president and Joseph M. Byrne, Sr. '79, president.
Vice presidents were Gerald Fitzgibbons '06, Ray T. Miller '14,
Alden Cusick '21 and Daniel Hilgartner '17.

Warren Cartier read a letter of resignation from Father
William A. Moloney, since 1908 the secretary of the association.
"I desire to present my resignation to the Alumni Association as
its secretary. Continued failing health and failing sight are my
plea for retiring from office."

Upon such pillars was the Alumni Association built. A slight
denture defect had brought to Father Moloney one of those
perceptive nicknames reserved at Notre Dame for the truly
loved and respected, "Whistling Bill." The alumni from 1908 to
1921 will be happy, though not surprised, to hear that familiar
whistle among the harmony of the harps, where at least Father
Moloney is sure to be.

Another forshadowing of new dimensions in alumni support was contained in the Unversity's thanks for the gifts of valuable books from T. Paul McGannon '07, J. Paul Fogarty '00 and Warren Cartier '07.

The *Scholastic* of Sept. 24, 1921, praised the alumni for the work they were doing through the alumni clubs and through individual effort in interesting boys in attending the University. The *Dome* stated that the University depended upon this representation almost entirely for its enrollment. In the light of Father Burns' report of overcrowded conditions, there was no need for a recruitment program. The nuns of the Summer School were already active boosters. The priests of Holy Cross, still doing mission work among the parishes of America, were the first contact many families had with the University. The *Ave Maria* magazine formed a tie with Catholic families, especially through the visits of brother solicitors which often resulted in boys coming to Notre Dame.

I am sensitive to this particular situation, because September, 1921, marked my own matriculation. Niles, Mich., though close in distance, was not particularly friendly to Notre Dame at the time. The Thursday afternoon invasion by Notre Dame students on thier "free day" disturbed the tranquility of that era. And the occasional Brownson Hall basketball team that played the Niles High team was usually overpowering and always suspect. I had been moved by missionary sermons in the parish, usually by Father James French for the fear of the Lord, and by Father Thomas Crumley for the beginning of wisdom. But the major influence was Professor John M. Cooney and his family, often visitors in our home. My aunt and I agreed that if I wanted journalism, and I did, there could be no finer teacher than Professor John M. Cooney—and there wasn't.

That same fall marked the registration of a group which ultimately took the spotlight away from Brother Hugh's horse, then a campus institution. The group were the Four Horsemen and the Seven Mules, who brought two more undefeated football teams to Notre Dame and Knute Rockne, and moved Notre Dame permanently and spectacularly into the big time of the growing American sport. The 1921 team remained awe-inspiring, except to Iowa, and contributed to the humility of the incoming freshmen, most of whom were dwarfed by the monogram men they met. In their heyday, Stuhldreher was listed at 151 pounds, Crowley at 162, Miller at 160 and Layden at 162. Small wonder Rockne's recruiting genius was doubted, but small wonders the quartet became.

In October, 1921, Rockne issued an invitation to all the "old boys" to come to the campus for the first appearance of the formidable Nebraska football team on the home schedule. Among other things, he said, " . . . Here is your chance to stroll down the quad again, past the Grotto and the Lake and over to St. Mary's—your chance to see the faces of that happy bunch of fellows you left on graduation day. Come down and swap experiences. You may not have made a million, and do you suppose we care for that? We want you and your spirit."

Therein was expressed another of the great secrets of the spirit of Notre Dame men and the success of the University—a true economic democracy. A Notre Dame man is what he is, not what he has. Rockne was still his own ticket manager, dispensing large numbers of tickets daily from his pockets. The Nebraska game drew 14,000 attendance, 2,000 more than the Purdue homecoming game on Cartier Field the previous year. The 7-0 win for Notre Dame clinched the enthusiasm of alumni for big-time schedules and for increased facilities for the home games. The game had been designated the homecoming. South Bend streets were decorated. The Oliver Hotel lobby—as it was to be for many years—was the focal point of the weekend alumni enthusiasm. Even the Nebraska squad praised the preparations of the campus for their visit. The Student Activities Committee had planned two dances for Saturday night. Old familiar haunts of alumni, in and out of bounds, reported crowds. One of the significant comments I was to hear from other campuses in the years ahead was intimated in the plans for the weekend. "Why is it that Notre Dame plans its celebrations for Friday nights? You must be awfully sure of winning." Well in most instances, the certainty was justified. But in the losing, there was the even greater spirit which praised effort in defeat as it did in success. With an all-time football record of 534 games won, 145 games lost and 38 tied, there has been cause for graciousness. In only 9 seasons have games won been equalled by or exceeded by ties or losses—1887, 0-1; 1888, 1-2; 1933, 3-5; 1950, 4-4; 1956, 2-8; 1959, 5-5; 1961 and 1962, 5-5 and 1963, 2-7.

I have often been asked about alumni pressure. With a record like the above, intelligent alumni could find little cause for pressure. In addition, the coach was in most years an alumnus and members of his staff were alumni. His bosses—the President and vice president (chairman of the athletic board) were alumni. This part of Notre Dame was never an alumni worry.

The drama during Father Burns' administration may seem to

have been in the meteoric rise of Rockne and football. Possibly the visit of DeValera, the new president of the long-awaited Irish Free State, attracted a widespread audience, too, with most alumni sharing their allegiances. But within the University deeply significant changes were being effected.

Until 1865, Notre Dame had been in effect a College of Arts and Letters. Courses in science were introduced in that year that marked the close of the Civil War and in 1869 a Department of Law was created. In 1873 came a Department of Civil Engineering, another pioneer contribution to Catholic higher education. Departments of Mechanical Engineering, Architecture, Pharmacy, Electrical Engineering and others were added before 1900. In 1897 the University was divided academically into four units—Arts and Letters, Science, Engineering, and Law. In 1905 these divisions were designated as Colleges. It was during Father Burns' administration 1920, that these colleges were given deans and Father John F. O'Hara, C.S.C. became dean of the newly formed College of Commerce, a project he had worked toward from 1913 when its first courses were established.

Father Julius Nieuwland, C.S.C. '99, dean of the College of Science, believed that the purpose of teaching science was to equip students for the discovery of new principles, compounds or species. "The contribution of a critical review of previous work," he wrote, "is only an expression of personal opinion and, as such, scarecely merits the appelation of research." He was already a distinguished chemist and botanist whose discoveries had enriched both fields. In 1921, Professor W. Lee Lewis, whose development of Lewisite gas had been credited with ending World War I, when news of the mass production of the new gas reached Berlin, revealed that his work was itself based on a discovery by Father Nieuwland in the laboratories of Catholic University. Father Nieuwland was never happy with this dubious distinction but it marked him as a major scientist. This terrifying first public distinction was overshadowed in later years when his basic research in acetylene chemistry produced a formula for synthetic rubber, which Du Pont refined into its present Neoprene process. Again, the ability of America to produce synthetic rubber was a major factor in the supply problems of World War II that alledgedly brought a less costly if not earlier end to that great conflict.

In the *Dome* of 1922 a feature outlines the growth of the Notre Dame Chamber of Commerce, an organization of students founded in 1916 by Father John O'Hara, and now num-

bering 500 students. Forty states and 10 foreign countries were
represented. The dual purposes of the group were to acquaint
students with business and industry and to give them a chance
to apply the classroom teaching of the broad field of commerce
to actual problems. Prof. James McCarthy was in charge of the
four sections the larger numbers now dictated. The South Bend
Chamber of Commerce was cooperating with the campus for
actual research benefits. Students were finding employment
through their contacts, the courses were receiving national acclaim, and outstanding business and industrial leaders were
coming to speak to this flourishing young college. One phenomenon was that in its first years as a full-fledged college of the
University, Commerce boasted half the total campus enrollment.

The *Dome* of 1922 also was high in its praise of the campaign
for endowment and building funds, especially of the efforts
being given full time to that project by Father Matthew Walsh,
C.S.C., vice president of Notre Dame and by Father John C.
McGinn who was also acting as alumni secretary.

The commencement *Scholastic* carried an official article on
the campaign, from the pen of the President, Father Burns:

> The scholastic year which is now closing has been a
> remarkable year at Notre Dame in several respects, but it will
> probably be especially memorable for the effort that has
> been made—for the first time in our history—to raise an
> endowment fund for the University. It is fitting that the
> graduates, the alumni and old students, and the friends of
> Notre Dame should now learn definitely of what has been
> accomplished in this way.
>
> It is scarcely necessary to remind you that, in thus seeking
> the means to enlarge and render more efficient our work, we
> have been doing only what almost every college and univer-
> sity in the land has been doing. The impetus towards expan-
> sion which has characterized American higher education dur-
> ing these last few years has no parallel in our history, or
> perhaps, in the history of civilization. This movement fol-
> lowed America's attainment of world leadership in the realm
> of international relations and sprang from a feeling that, in
> the new order of things, our colleges and universities were
> called upon to enlarge their service to society and civilization
> in accordance with their enlarged opportunities.
>
> Notre Dame fully shared in this feeling. The chief diffi-
> culty that confronted us lay in the circumstance that we had
> never before asked for such aid, and that the raising of
> money for endowment was something almost unprecedented
> in the field of Catholic higher education. Nevertheless, since
> we had neither teachers nor accommodations sufficient for

hundreds of young men who were applying here, we decided, about a year ago, to endeavor to raise two million dollars, one-half of which was to be devoted to endowment and the other half to the erection of the most urgently needed buildings. It was resolved to devote the present year to the raising of the endowment fund and next year to the raising of the building fund.

The generous interest shown in the University by the General Education Board and its gift of $250,000 has been of the very greatest help to us. The condition on which this gift was made, that we should secure the remainder of the million dollars in cash or pledges, by July 1 of the present year, has served as a lively stimulus to others to cooperate generously with our efforts. The example of the General Education Board was followed by the Carnegie Corporation, which also made a conditional gift to the University amounting to $75,000.

The work was begun in South Bend last June where a committee of citizens, of which Miles O'Brien was chairman, was busy with its task all through the torrid summer and during the early fall. In December a committee of the alumni was formed in New York City, and a little later in Boston, in order to reach our friends in New York City and in the New England states. Chicago was made headquarters for the states of Indiana, Illinois, Wisconsin and Iowa, and early in March the central executive committee in Chicago was formed, C.C. Mitchell and Thomas T. Cavanaugh being chosen chairmen. From what has been said, it will be seen that our systematic efforts were confined to less than a dozen states and that a very large proportion of our alumni and friends throughout the country have not as yet been reached. The student body of Notre Dame, under the guidance of Alfred Ryan, of the Class of 1920, have, during the past six weeks, been conducting a very vigorous campaign of their own, and in spite of certain handicaps they have been highly successful.

A big helping hand was extended to the University in its hour of need when the Knights of Columbus of Indiana, in their state convention at Terre Haute, on May 31, unanimously voted to raise $50,000 as the contribution of the Knights of Columbus of Indiana to our endowment fund.

The result of these efforts may be summarized as follows:

General Education Board	$ 250,000.00
Carnegie Corporation	75,000.00
South Bend	252,138.00
Chicago District	197,386.36
Metropolitan District	58,990.50
Alumni Association	60,000.00
Miscellaneous	77,583.02
Knights of Columbus of Ind.	50,000.00
Students Campaign	27,066.76
	$1,048,164.64

(The difficulties in making contacts and securing gifts can be easily found in the tabulation which Father Burns supplied of amounts and numbers of gifts—in spite of the total amount success.)

1	$60,000.00
2	50,000.00
1	35,000.00
1	30,000.00
1	25,000.00
1	15,000.00
1	10,500.00
2	10,000.00
13	5,000.00
4	3,000.00
1	2,750.00
5	2,500.00
9	2,000.00
2	1,500.00
1	1,200.00
129	1,000.00
1	800.00
1	700.00
86	500.00
1128 below	500.00
1387 Total	

From the bottom of my heart I wish to thank all those who have given so freely or labored so devotedly to make our endowment campaign a success. The time was unpropitious for such an effort, but we could not wait. If the effort has been successful, it has been so only because the friends of Notre Dame rallied in prompt and generous response to her call. To all of these—to our neighbors the people of South Bend and especially the members of the executive committee in South Bend; to our alumni and friends in New York and New England, in Chicago and Fort Wayne, and throughout Indiana, Illinois, Wisconsin and Iowa, to the Knights of Columbus of Indiana, to the Alumni Association, and to the students of Notre Dame, I express the University's profound acknowledgment of what they have done in her behalf with the assurance that she will never cherish a most grateful memory of it all.

During the coming year we hope to be able to raise an additional million dollars for new buildings. We imperatively need several new dormitory buildings, an engineering building, a commerce building, and an enlargement of the gymnasium. In view of what has been accomplished and in view of the large number of alumni and friends of Notre Dame throughout the country who have still to be called upon, it is not, it seems to me, too much to expect that the means to provide for the carrying out of this building program may be secured during the next 12 months.

The historic annual meeting of the Alumni Association in 1922 was called to order in Brownson Study Hall on June 11 by president Joseph M. Byrne, Sr. The Class of 1922 was admitted to membership. President Byrne paid a glowing tribute to Notre Dame men in all walks of life and urged alumni to cherish the traditions of Notre Dame. This was a sentiment held in later years by Joseph M. Byrne, Jr., and in even more recent years by Joseph M. Byrne, III. Notre Dame families—still rare in the alumni records—were beginning to join the very traditions which inspired and created them.

Condolence resolutions included the distinguished Father Zahm, Adrian "Pop" Anson, a member of the baseball team of 1867 and one of the nation's pioneers in the national game, and Stuart Carroll '17, brilliant young journalist.

In the absence of Warren A. Cartier, the secretary read the treasurer's report, showing receipts of $2,305. These included $85 in dues for the year. The low figure undoubtedly stemmed from the endowment campaign among alumni. Disbursements totalled only $2,058, which included a $2,000 architectural fee to the alumnus architect of the proposed Old Students Hall, W.G. Uffendell.

The election of non-graduate former students was a belated admission of missed opportunities by the University and Association in involving men whose interest in Notre Dame has always been as valuable as graduate interest in the many programs of the University and the Alumni Association. The South Bend campaign for the endowment fund undoubtedly had something to do with the 1922 inclusion of J. D. Oliver, Sr., J. D. Oliver, Jr., and James Oliver, founding family of the Oliver farm equipment business, and George O'Brien, head of the O'Brien Paint Co.

Father Burns gave a detailed account of the progress of the urgent campaign to raise the first million dollars. At the conclusion of his talk, Father McGinn read a letter addressed to the Alumni Association from Father Burns:

"The treasurer of the Alumni Association, Hon. Warren A. Cartier, in a letter just received by the secretary, Father John C. McGinn, C.S.C. states that the Alumni Association now has in its hands, in cash, the sum of approximately $60,000, and he recommends or suggests that the association contribute this money to the Endowment Fund of the Univer-

sity, in order to complete the fund of One Million Dollars
($1,000,000) which it has to have by July 1, in order to
secure the conditional gifts of the General Education Board
and the Carnegie Corporation.

As President of the University of Notre Dame, I hereby
state that, if the above suggestion is agreed to by the association, the University will erect Old Students Hall as soon as it
is able to collect sufficient money to do so and will observe
the arrangement made by the building committee of the
association as to architect to be selected and other such
details as will substantially carry out the original purpose of
the association. It is the intention of the University Administration to begin at once the work of raising one million
dollars for new buildings, including several dormitory buildings, and we would thus make Old Students Hall the first
dormitory building to be erected. (sig) James A. Burns,
C.S.C., President."

After a full discussion of the recommendation of the treasurer, the following resolution was made by William A. Mc-
Inerny '01, and unanimously approved:

Be it Resolved by the Notre Dame Alumni Association
that all moneys and securities in the Old Students Building
Fund as well as all unpaid pledges to the same be turned over
to the University of Notre Dame in use in its endowment or
building fund as suggested in the communication of Father
Burns, C.S.C., President of the University. It is understood
that by the terms of said letter, the first additional dormitory
to be constructed by the University will be known as Old
Students Hall, and shall answer the purpose of the building as
planned by this association, and be it further resolved that
the proper officers of the association be and they are hereby
authorized and directed to make the necessary payments and
transfer to the University of all such funds, securities and
pledges.

In the light of the reported receipts of the association outside
the Old Students fund, this was a generous gift indeed. It
fulfilled the University's obligations to qualify for the $325,000
conditional gifts. New Horizons and new scope were beginning
the undertone of big business into the relationships of alumni
and University. But there still existed the alumni identity of the
administration, the close-knit family of the alumni, and the
good faith and good will of common cause.

Election of officers followed. Father Moloney, the retired
secretary, was named honorary president in tribute to his dedicated service as secretary of the association from 1908 to 1922.
F. Henry Wurzer '98, was chosen president. Vice presidents

were Thomas T. Cavanaugh '97, G.A. Farabaugh '04, K.K. Rockne '14, William E. Cotter '13 and Joseph Rhomberg '22. Father McGinn was elected secretary and Warren Cartier re-elected treasurer. Trustees elected were Robert Proctor '04, Joseph Haley '99 and Daniel B. Hilgartner '17. These associa-tion trustees were empowered to present the names of alumni for membership on the University Board of Lay Trustees.

Joseph Rhomberg, speaking for the new Class of 1922, pledged their aid in the continuing building fund program. Byron Kanaley suggested that the annual meeting of the associa-tion be changed from commencement to homecoming weekend. Discussion but no action is reported.

The freshly impoverished association showed the continuing sparks of love and loyalty by appropriating $50 for Brother Phillip Neri, custodian of the campus, to mark the trees on the campus. The project of having planted every tree indigenous to the United States which could grow at Notre Dame, was well under way. The small metal tabs which give both the Latin and English names of the varied species have edified students, alumni and visitors in the years since this benefaction.

Father Burns had come to the end of his first three-year term, under the strictures of the new Canon Law on superiors. The success of the endowment campaign might easily have insured the second term he was permitted. He chose instead, because he had seen the uphill battle ahead in securing the important second million dollars for buildings, to leave the presidency to direct the continuing campaign. Father Matthew Walsh, C.S.C. '03, vice president, distinguished World War I chaplain, and popular history teacher, succeeded him. For three years Father Burns struggled untiringly to achieve the campaign goal. Its major achievement was the interesting of many people, whose response often came later and generously, and the con-viction on the campus that fund-raising was a work of many parts. Father Burns later returned to Holy Cross College in Washington for a year, and then became Provincial of the Congregation, where he again exerted his academic influence on the formation of priests and brothers. He was in ill health during two years as Assistant Superior General and died on Sept. 9, 1940.

It was my privilege to meet Father Burns a number of times during the years after his presidency and after his campaign direction. He retained a deep interest in the Alumni Associa-tion. I am sure he realized its importance to the University in the years ahead. He was distressed by the quick drop in alumni giving which followed the intensive campaign, and he would have liked to have seen some continuing organized effort toward a general University program of outside support, other than alumni, following the campaign itself.

He had, in three years as President, made a contribution which is still growing in its significance. The academic organization of the University proved vital to the needs of the post War years. The emphasis on the preparation of priests and brothers for teaching posts in higher education resulted in strong congregational involvement in the University and in the expansion of priests and brothers in areas beyond the Notre Dame campus.

He left Notre Dame a flourishing University with an informed thrust toward the future, and money—far from enough, it is true—but nevertheless its first money in the bank, a cushion of confidence which helped formulate the phenomenal growth which was to follow.

XXII

The Spirit Is Willing

No period, in my estimation, offered a greater challenge to the University and its traditions than these years after World War I. The essence of Notre Dame had been the close-knit community on the campus. Administrators, faculty, students and the frequent visitors from parent and alumni groups, were the community of scholars we now seek constantly to create. There was a fellowship which transcended the group identities, inspired by the dedication of the University to God, Country and Notre Dame, ahead of college, class or activities.

In the residence halls on the campus, which fostered this universal spirit, was found the major cause for the absence of fraternities. It is probable that Notre Dame would have opposed fraternities as they existed then in many other colleges and universities. But the great tradition of "la vie intime" made them so unnecessary that the question never seriously arose.

In the post-World War I years, the returning service men and the continuing enrollment pressures of the high school graduates, afforded the first example of an enrollment crisis that was to be repeated on a larger scale after World War III, when the G.I. bill found thousands of old and new students storming the campus. Notre Dame was not so well prepared for the first crisis.

When I entered in the fall of 1921, the freshman class was so large that it resulted, in 1925, in the largest graduating class in Notre Dame history, 315. Half of the total student body were forced to live off-campus, in hastily recruited rooms in private homes of citizens who were friendly, but not sure that the removal of this barrier between campus and community would avoid the pitfalls of the "college town" and its headaches.

Worse yet, only the Freshman could be fed in the traditional Brownson and Carroll dining halls. The common meal hours had been one of the greatest contributors to the family spirit, with administration, faculty and students eating in the same rooms. Now O. A. Clark had taken over a cafeteria in the basement of Badin Hall (after a student revolt had driven out "the Greeks" who had operated it for its first several years). Campus students and off-campus students were filling downtown South Bend restaurants and creating boarding house groups. It was this type of student life which had led to fraternities elsewhere.

Another imminent casualty of the off-campus population was the traditional involvement of students in campus activity. Students were not allowed to have cars. And it was not easy to reconcile sports, publications, band or glee club, dramatics and the professional clubs, with class schedules and the street car line, particularly when the lack of food facilities on the campus added a major hurdle.

The inevitable sprinkling of graduate students and returned and older veterans in this off-campus group bolstered the growing number of "day dogs," who had formerly been residents of the area commuting to the campus from their homes, as I did from Niles via an electric line which dropped me off on the St. Mary's campus.

Father Matthew Walsh was confronted with this challenge, when at the age of 40 he was named President. He had served as vice president under both Father Cavanaugh and Father Burns. He had achieved a legendary fame as chaplain in the War. He brought some of Cavanaugh's eloquent persusiveness and some of Burns' administrative controls. In addition he brought a fine personality of his own, and seasoned the new era with a timely sense of humor usually difficult for college presidents to display.

Father Walsh had come as a boy to the minor seminary at Notre Dame and spent much of the time there under the inspiring superiorship of Father John Cavanaugh. In 1903 he graduated from Notre Dame. While pursuing his theological studied in Washington, he became the first student to enroll in the history courses at Catholic University and received his doctorate there in 1907. He studied economics at Johns Hopkins, and spent the summer of 1907 at Columbia University, which was to enter his life again forcefully with the Rockne coaching crisis of 1928.

Recognizing the history of Notre Dame, and the value of its traditions, Father Walsh's prime goal was to bring the students back to the campus. A temporary residence hall, derived from the barracks school of architecture, was ready for the Freshmen in 1922. The second hall, Sophomore Hall, enjoying the student categorization as one of the "cardboard palaces," was built in 1923. The two brought 362 students back to the campus.

Father Walsh's program received great support from the Alumni Association. The following is a letter to alumni from the association president, F. Henry Wurzer:

> Next to the loyalty to home and country, I know of no attachment in life that should be and is more inspiring and deep rooted than the love and respect one holds for his university.
>
> I say his university, because everyone should consider it in the same broad sense that he speaks of his home and his country. And this is especially true of the alumni of Notre Dame, because the interest that Notre Dame has always manifested in the welfare and success of its sons, no matter how far removed from it in point of time or space, is and has always been more personal and of greater reality than with any other institution of which I know.
>
> What would we do for our country in the hour of need? The answer is axiomatic: The utmost. Our loyalty to Notre Dame might well be as great.
>
> On a recent automobile tour of the East, I visited many of the larger and better known universities, with the result that I am the more confirmed in my conviction that Notre Dame, with the aid of its faculty and alumni, can advance from its present high position to one of the largest and foremost universities of the world.
>
> I am greatly pleased to learn of the proposed publication of The *Notre Dame Alumnus.* It will keep us all fully informed of the material and educational progress that is constantly taking place. And information of that kind renews interest and rekindles the old fires of interest in and affection for dear old Notre Dame. Next to information of this sort is to come in contact with the reality. Therefore, I must not pass this opportunity of asking, pleading, begging, every last Notre Dame man to come and join us at the University, first for commencement and the meeting of the Alumni Association this June, and next for homecoming in the fall.
>
> F.H. Wurzer '98, Pres."

Father Walsh recognized the significance of the Alumni Association, as evident in his first message in the new *Alumnus* magazine:

> It is a pleasure to send a word of greeting to all the alumni and friends of Notre Dame. I have always had the keenest interest in the former students of the University, and am pleased to note the growing concern for the school on the

part of the old boys. When I look back on the work that has been accomplished by Father Burns during the past three years, I begin to realize how much energy and how much support is needed to maintain the position that Notre Dame has reached as one of the leading educational institutions in America. Naturally one feels diffident about attempting to carry to completion big projects that have been initiated, and for a time directed, by others. I confess that I am no exception to this general feeling. There is one thing, however, that has emboldened me in my desire to bring to reality what Father Cavanaugh and Father Burns did so much to promote—a greater Notre Dame.

During the past few years the University has undergone many changes. These changes have affected both the material development of the school and the expansion along academic lines. The growth that Notre Dame has experienced has of necessity presented many new problems. Perhaps the most urgent matter before us at the present time is the question of caring for the large number of students now living in South Bend. To meet this situation we need new buildings on the campus and additional teachers and equipment in every course. This is a matter that may not be solved within the next few years, but a problem that unquestionably must receive serious consideration at once. This year an attempt was made in a small way to care for the overflow of students by the erection of a temporary dormitory building. As soon as conditions warrant it, work will be started on the Old Students Hall. This will mark the beginning of what I believe to be the most important era in the development of the University. An immense problem lies before the administration at Notre Dame. It would be almost presumptious to attempt to carry out our plans were it not for the fact that we believe the traditional isolation of Notre Dame has come to an end.

It is a regrettable fact that there has been comparatively little contact between the school and the alumni during past years. This condition, I believe, is about to disappear. The increasing number of our graduates and the growing prominence of our old students have made us realize more and more how extensive has been the influence of Notre Dame. Taken individually the Notre Dame graduate has been marked by his loyalty to his school. From now on we hope for unified action on the part of the alumni. What has been lacking up to the present—a direct contact between the school and the old students—can be largely overcome through the plan represented by this first issue of the alumni magazine. The homecoming in the fall and the alumni reunion in June should develop into open demonstrations of belief in Notre Dame. These occasions supplemented by the frequent exchange of views between school and old students, are certain to result in the creation of a wide-awake alumni group.

> Notre Dame wants you as her own, wants you to feel that each and every old student is as much a part of the school today as he was when professors and prefects made up the sum total of life's worries.
>
> (sig) Matthew J. Walsh, C.S.C.

Father Walsh's message pointed up two deeply significant points of alumni history.

I am sure that the alumni assumed a constant and close contact with Notre Dame from the graduation of the first class. And with the loyal alumni who came so frequently and contributed so much, whose names have dotted the pages we have written of early years, there had been "la vie intime." It was all personal, and because it was personal it was confined by the friendships and pressures, the proximities and the personalities of the changing University.

The new realization, rooted in the problems uncovered by the endowment drive, called for contact with all alumni. And beyond the personal, there had to be a less personal but also less fallible mechanism. The first of the parts of this new mechanism was the *Alumnus* magazine, published monthly during the school year and sent to all the Alumni Association members. Father McGinn, the alumni secretary was its first publisher and Alfred C. Ryan '20, its first editor.

The *Dome* of 1923 paid tribute to alumni, and to the Alumni Association:

> Notre Dame's tradition is her men. The measure of service to her is our gauge of a man and at the thought our minds leap to conjure up her devoted legions of such men. This expression of an alumnus might serve to express ideally the attitude and action of the members of the Alumni Association of the University of Notre Dame. Notre Dame has always known that she had in that body, composed of graduates and old students elected to the association, a group of men whose loyalty to the school which they so proudly claim can by no means be measured. Her appeals to them have been few. Until 1920 the fund for Old Students Hall was the only group appeal and the response was typical.
>
> When the two million dollar endowment and development fund was launched, the administration knew that they would find success in the appeal to the men of all times. The alumni responded to the best of their resources, and their activity resulted in its success. It will continue to be the alumni and old students that the University will look for the successful completion of her plans for increased service. That they will not fail her is Notre Dame's greatest assurance.

The new *Alumnus*, the immediate surge of Father Walsh's

broad programs, and the vitality of campus activities under the mature and experienced leadership of the returned veterans, and the new sense of purpose instilled into the high school graduates entering the University, spotlighted the spirit of Notre Dame, evolving from its origin in Sorin himself into the widening horizons of the new academic world.

Among items of interest covered in the new *Alumnus* was the use of "The Fighting Irish" to designate the football team. The national recognition given the quality of the game, and the flair of Rockne for national publicity raised the issue. The distinguished and elderly priest-professor-author, Father Arthur Barry O'Neill, C.S.C., LL.D. '17, wrote eloquently on the subject, and an excerpt follows because the interest has never subsided in team or name:

> This much being premised, it goes without saying that, as soon as Notre Dame entered the field of intercollegiate athletics, her athletes were dowered with other titles than the bare name of their school. The growth of the present honored and honorable designation is perhaps worth while explaining. In the early days of her football activities, the religion of the institution furnished an obvious—and not necessarily a contemptuous—substitute for the institution's name; her players were called "the Catholics," as they are still occasionally styled by reputable eastern papers "the Catholic collegians of Indiana." Three or four decades ago, "Catholic" and "Irish" were virtually synonymous terms. This fact, and the prevalence of Hibernian patronymics in the roll-call of the students, gave Notre Dame the racial distinction noted in the second popular name accorded to her players, "the Irish." As the years went on, it became more and more evident that our athletes were Irish, not only in religion and name, but in the salient and distinctive qualities that have ever characterized the soldiers of Erin—dashing valor, intrepid daring, contempt of danger, resolute courage and indomitable spirit. There is but one comprehensive epithet to cover all such qualities; and the world has not been slow in seeing how accurately it describes the athletes of Notre Dame. There are other Catholic and Irish football teams in this country; but from the Atlantic to the Pacific, from Portland, Me., to Portland, Ore., no one needs telling that to Notre Dame alone belongs the proudest title in the American athletic world, "The Fighting Irish."

In an early issue of Volume 1, of the *Alumnus*, Thomas T. Cavanaugh '97, expressed his views on loyalty in such an effective way that they have remained timely from one generation to another. Tom Cavanaugh was a verteran member of the association. He had been one of its faithful visitors to the campus, and one of the pillars of the Notre Dame Club of Chicago when the direction of the association rested there in exile by default. If you read his remarks from end to end, you will have a remarkably good definition of the distinctive relationship between a Notre Dame man and Notre Dame:

There are two things that the writer of this article actually dreads—one is double pneumonia, and the other is the conventional dinner of fellow alumni. From the viewpoint of the man in attendance who does not orate, these affairs from a speaking standpoint are never properly policed. On each and every toast list at these dinners is the old boy who wishes to recall the by-gone days. As a pest he qualifies as a full 100 per cent, but he's usually a good old soul, and the toastmaster is a good fellow, too, so in place of bringing down the gavel and parking him on the side-lines, he's allowed all kinds of time, with the result that he recalls and recollects until his memory backfires.

I never heard anyone recollect the Indians around Notre Dame, but I have heard recollectors start in at a period just following the wilderness, and work right along until they reached the Golden Jubilee epoch. The time the college burned is an old favorite; "Cap" Anson playing ball at Notre Dame is another one popular with the "back when" boys; athletic matches where a barrel of apples was the prize are occasionally recollected. These, and dozens of others, are always heard. They have actually evolved into standard practice, and deadly as they are, one manages to survive these dinners, and it's a certainty we will continue to attend them so long as we are subpoenaed. One refrains from declining to attend, really, from a spirit of loyalty, and this word loyalty brings up a matter on which I have a thought or two to express. Speakers at all alumni gatherings never fail to point out the loyalty due to the college from its alumni—and I might say in brackets, as 'twere, that this same thought is usually the prelude to a touch—all of which is orthodox. Get me right, mates, it's all right and this is sincerely meant.

There is, however, another side to this loyalty item that one seldom hears referred to, and that is the loyalty of a college to its alumni. I have been back to Notre Dame two, three or four times in a period of twenty-five years. These visits have been delightful, and why? It is true that many of the men of my intimate acquaintance at Notre Dame now rest in the cemetery, and this fact, naturally, throws a pall on one's visit. The best of good fellows—all of them—but taken. But new faces are observed. You meet the present generation and when these men are told you were at Notre Dame years back, your hand is grasped in genuine friendship and the old boy feels that he's sure enough back again with his own folks. The longer the time one is away from Notre Dame, the more keenly will one appreciate the sterling worth of the men of

Holy Cross and the splendid spirit that permeates every
individual of the Congregation. Their welcome is real and
genuine, and the same cheery, glad-to-see-you hospitality
goes out to the old boy who has made good in a big way as it
does to the men who have just about gone along and gotten
by, but not much else. The analogy of a college and a mother
of a family is right here thrown out in strong lights. The love
of a real mother is never divided—her sons who succeeds is
loved by her but not more or less than the son who fails.

To a man who has been away from Notre Dame for 25
years, nothing could strike him more forcibly than this genuine friendship felt by the men of Holy Cross toward the old
students. This sentiment is not confined to one or a few—it is
found at once in every man you encounter. Instinctively you
feel that right there at old Notre Dame are as fine a lot of
men you could meet, and they're pulling for you all the time,
and with you heart and soul at every stage of the game, and
at every turn of the road—a perpetual link of sincerest interest and unswerving fealty. And then an old picture—a word
picture—comes to mind and you see dear old Tom New-
combe lying in his last illness at Grey Friars, and responding
"Adsum" as he hears the chapel bell just as he did many
years before when he was back in school. The fine old soul
knew that as Grey Friars he was back among his own. Visit
the old school and you value as never before this exquisite
masterpiece of Thackeray.

I don't know how others feel about it, but to me it's a
tonic. All of us have encountered a million counterfeits in
our experience since leaving college. It's a bromide to say the
regular true blue, 24-carat man is seldom met. Now I am not
infallible—always—but it's my conviction that the old student
returning to Notre Dame will find more genuine friends and
sincere well-wishers among the Fathers of the Holy Cross
than is possible anywhere else—blood relatives and relations
by marriage not excepted.

And now, to add up my talk, as Chaucer might have put it,
the total is this: Notre Dame is very loyal to its old students,
and interested deeply in everything they are doing, pulling
always for a Notre Dame man's success, but never critical of a
failure. And as one whom, with no streets, public parks or
racing stakes named as yet in his honor, and no monuments
erected, etc., has been back to Notre Dame, and has had the
actual experience, my earnest advice to every man who ever
attended college there is to go back, and see for yourself if I
am correct.

When it comes to loyalty, first, hand it to the old college
and the men of Holy Cross—they are the salt of the earth.
Win, lose or draw—they are behind you to a man, and that's
loyalty.

There you have one of the great strengths of Notre Dame

from the days of Sorin—the continuing interest of the members of the Congregation of Holy Cross in the family of Notre Dame.

Then—and now—many colleges and universities consider the diploma as a discharge paper and with a cursory good-bye turn their backs on the graduate to concentrate on the internal purposes and pressures of the institution. When they find in after years that they need to appeal to their alumni, they frequently find it difficult to renew a relationship.

At Notre Dame, the integral role of the alumnus as a member of the family has been preserved. Clergy and lay faculty retain interest. Alumni are in fact a part of both those groups, a large part of the makers of the policy and decisions of Notre Dame. They are an equal power in the lay trustees of the University. The diploma here is not a discharge, but simply a passport to travel in the outside world, with the mutual hopes of frequent returns to the campus—another ingredient of the spirit of Notre Dame.

The effort to express the spirit of Notre Dame, with its postwar renewal of fervor, was evident in the campus publications. Commenting on the endowment campaign, the *Dome* of 1923 said:

> The dull red glimmer of the sanctuary lamp threw a faint shadow over the bended figure that knelt beside it. The little log chapel by the lake was almost hidden by the stately pines that rose by its side as the dusk gathered in the straggling rays of sunlight, and put them ro rest in the magnificent flame of departing day. The soft sweet sound of the Angelus rested calmly over the lake. All was silence save the fervent prayer that rose from that chapel some four score years ago.
>
> It was the prayer of an inspired man that the child of his mind might someday grow into a full and proud manhood; that this rude log structure might someday fulfill the purpose for which it was builded; that it might grow into a greater Notre Dame. Only those who are familiar with the purpose of this great university can in any way understand its growth. It is conceived in the fire of undying faith and sacrificial love.
>
> During the past year Notre Dame began an expansion drive. Headed by Father James A. Burns, then University president, and Father John McGinn, the country was canvassed, in order that the $250,000 received from the General Education Board and the $75,000 received from the Carnegie Corporation might grow to a million dollars. Thanks to the generosity of friends, alumni and students, the million mark was passed and during this past year a drive was begun for an additional and necessary million.
>
> Especially generous were certain districts, particularly

South Bend, Chicago, the East, the Alumni Association and
the Knights of Columbus. Of these South Bend donated
$252,138 and Chicago $197,386. A student drive raised
$27,066. Heading the student campaign was Father O'Hara,
as general with staff composed of Frank Blasius, Lewis
Murphy, Gus Desch, Eugene Payton and Jimmie Murtaugh.
The majors were Jack Higgins, Sorin; William Voss, Corby;
Frank McGinnis, Walsh; Cletus Lynch, Town; Eddie Anderson, Brownson; Roger Kiley, Carroll; and James Egan, Badin.
(These were all the halls in that year.) Very soon, the result
of the campaign will be seen in the increased teaching staff,
in increased laboratory equipment, in a new engineering and
a new commerce building, in a new gymnasium and more
residence halls. The santuary lamp still throws its faint red
gleam through the open doorway of that rude log chapel. The
Angelus still rises softly over the lake and a bended figure
bows down in thanksgiving—for his prayer for a Greater
Notre Dame has been answered.

The first issue of the *Alumnus* gave evidence of the significance of its function as an informing contact between Notre
Dame and Notre Dame men.

The second issue contained a warm greeting to alumni from
the venerated honorary president, Father William Moloney,
C.S.C. In a greeting from Father McGinn, the alumni secretary,
he made the interesting statement: "We are meeting at Notre
Dame to stimulate and advise. The faculty looked for a counsel
from the alumni." The issue reported alumni meetings in Cleveland and Toledo, addressed by Father Burns, Father McGinn
and Knute Rockne.

Frank Wallace '23, had an article in the third issue, on the
25th anniversary of intercollegiate debate. Wallace pointed out
that Notre Dame's debating teams rivalled the athletic record of
victory, and excelled any other college debating record in the
country. Notre Dame had won 44 of 51 debates, for a percentage of 86.2. The best known record of any other institution was
that of Bates College which had won 40 of 52, for a percentage
of 76.4 and was acclaimed by the Literary Digest as the intercollegiate debating champion. Father William A. Bolger, C.S.C.
was the debating coach.

The *Alumnus* pointed out as a seeming detail a principle
which has at once helped and hampered fund-raising at Notre
Dame throughout the subsequent years. In the first successful
endowment campaign, for the $2,000,000, the entire staff was
composed of Notre Dame alumni—Father Burns '88, director,
Father John McGinn '06, assistant to Father Burns, as was

Father Walsh '03. Earl Dickens '16, who had been secretary to Father John W. Cavanaugh, returned to the campus staff to aid the drive. Joseph C. McGinnis '19, directed the field work, while Alfred C. Ryan '20, edited the magazine and promoted the alumni and student participation.

The ability of Notre Dame men to organize a fund-raising program was demonstrated. Probably in this first effort no one thought of any other way. The arts and sciences of fund-raising had not yet produced the galaxy of experts. Alumni secretaries and alumni editors had organized (1913) before thought was given to the growing number of fund-raisers. All these joined together later (1927) in the American Alumni Council to channel for mutual progress the rapid development of the several professions to meet the greatly expanding needs of higher education.

When the later Rockne Memorial campaign was discussed, internal organization was anticipated, but it became necessary to bring in professional fund-raisers to please a group of trustees. The outside group proved not to understand the Notre Dame history or the Notre Dame man. Disappointing results were salvaged, in the end, by an alumni campus staff.

Similarly, in an effort to secure funds for Lobund, Professor Arthur Reyniers' distinctive research in the germ-free production of animals for scientific research, a program of great promise for which Professor Reyniers had himself been largely charged as fund-raiser, professional counsel proved to be completely inadequate.

And when the genius of Harry Hogan proposed the present Notre Dame Foundation, the trustees again wanted professional endorsement, which came only after futile and expensive efforts had been made to fit Notre Dame's fund-raising foot into the standard professional fund-raising shoe. It was an all-alumni staff that developed the outstanding success of the Foundation in cooperation with the University administration.

With the establishment of the *Alumnus* it became necessary to report and to define both the University and the association programs to the total alumni. This was a salutary recognition of the stature of both. It was also a salutary challenge to the programs. A professional tone began to appear. It marked, however, little change in the basic Notre Dame man. It was the same growing man, increasing in stature and in dignity, but now putting on the new garments of his new estate.

XXIII

The Quickened
Pace of Peace

The last American soldiers returned from the Rhineland in 1923. The soldiers bonus bill was enacted in 1924. Between 1920 and 1926, the number of degrees granted by American colleges and universities doubled. The war had expanded the political horizons of the United States, and expanded its educational boundaries.

Notre Dame was no exception to the spirit of progress and wider horizons. Father Burns had launched the endowment drive while the ink was wet on the peace treaty. Now, as Father Walsh began his term, he inherited the continuing building-fund campaign, with Father Burns directing. He was given the responsibility for consolidating the new status of the colleges of the University and for meeting head-on the applicants storming the admissions office. His administration was faced with both horizontal and vertical growth. And he was to bring to all this the traditions of old Notre Dame. The calm, intelligent, orderly and constructive manner in which Father Walsh met these challenges—spotlighted by the new national championship teams of 1923 and 1924 which Knute Rockne offered to the unprecedented postwar crowds—resulted in some obscuring of the variety and the scope of the accomplishments of the Walsh years.

The annual Alumni Association meeting in 1923 was called to order by F. Henry Wurzer on June 10. A proposal to change the provision for election of nongraduates to the association was withdrawn in favor of a motion to prepare a revision of the Constitution and By-Laws of the Association. The committee appointed was made up of Father John McGinn, Frank O'Shaughnessy '00, Aaron Huguenard '22 and F. Henry Wurzer

'98. (The presence of the recently graduated Huguenard on this committee points up the constant consideration the association has shown for the viewpoint of the young alumnus.)

The treasurer showed total receipts of $2,145, including $1,785 in dues, the largest amount collected in dues since 1908-09 when the reorganization occurred. Disbursements left a cash balance of $792. At this point, the University was supplying the *Alumnus* magazine, the alumni secretary and the staff salaries of those who—as part-time workers actually—kept the records, edited the magazine, and traveled in the interests of the clubs and the fund-raising campaign.

The treasurer reported that the final $5,300, of the association's gift of $60,000 in cash and securities to the endowment drive, had been paid in July, 1922. An interesting item in the disbursements was a $10 dues entry for membership in the Association of Alumni Secretaries (later the American Alumni Council). The campus staff was willing to learn and profit from all who pursued the same goals. Warren Cartier moved that the small balance in the Old Students Hall funds be transferred to the general fund, and the association treasurer's bond be removed. A detailed report of Old Students Hall funds and remaining unpaid pledges was given.

Father Maurice Griffin '04, Youngstown, O., was elected as honorary president. John H. Neeson '03, became president, the popular Philadelphia engineer receiving a unanimous vote. His opening talk reflected interest in a broader alumni program, in commencement and reunions, and in the Notre Dame spirit necessary to everything.

Vice presidents were Maximillian St. George '08 of Chicago, Frank Hayes '14 of Chicago, Ray J. Eichenlaub '14 of Columbus, O. T. P. Galvin '16 of Hammond, Ind., and Paul Castner '23, one of the greatest of Notre Dame's all-around athletes. Father John McGinn was reelected secretary, and Warren Cartier was again named treasurer. Trustees were an all-Chicago group, Thomas Cavanaugh '97, Frank O'Shaughnessy '00 and James E. Sanford '15. Angus McDonald '00, was elected as a lay trustee of the University, as then provided for, with Warren Cartier and C.C. Mitchell reelected to that same group.

President Neeson, Father Hugh O'Donnell, Tim Galvin and John U. Riley spoke of the need for appointing class secretaries and a committee consisting of Father O'Donnell, Galvin, and Al Ryan was appointed to secure such appointments. As the first class secretary under the newly approved program, Henry

F. Barnhart was announced as the secretary of the Class of
1923

Byron Kanaley '04, proposed a resolution asking all alumni
to cooperate with Father Burns in the building-fund effort, to
attend meetings being held throughout the country for this
purpose, and to contribute personally to the urgent drive.

The meeting commended the *Notre Dame Daily*, a student-
initiated newspaper published on weekdays to supplement the
Scholastic, whose weekly reports proved slow and inadequate
for the needs of the large, and especially the large off-campus,
student body. *The Daily* enjoyed the editorial direction of the
best campus journalist—Henry Flannery '23, later distinguished
Berlin correspondent and author, was its first editor. It was
published necessarily in a downtown printshop, where student
staff hours had to conflict with the campus curfew. The off-
campus production also posed a threat, administrators thought,
to the supervision implicit in the *Ave Maria* Press. And like one
of its counterparts, the *Juggler*, the first signs of financial
distress were utilized to discontinue the publication. A student
offer to guarantee the cost of continuing the paper was not
accepted. In the light of current campus journalism, both the
Daily and the *Juggler*—then the humor magazine—were sparkling, clean and responsible products of a well-qualified student
journalist training.

The October, 1923, issue of the *Alumnus* carried a significant
item. The number of students in the University then was 1855.
I have mentioned that postwar returning students—after World
War I, and to be repeated after World War II—brought maturity
to the student programs. Also, during these years, Father John
F. O'Hara, C.S.C. was battling the problems of wartime, and of
prohibition, with an intensified religious program as prefect of
religion, from his base in Sorin Hall tower. The *Alumnus* reports
that "the religious growth of the student life has resulted in the
relaxation of discipline and the granting of more personal freedom." Father J. Hugh O'Donnell, C.S.C. '16, was at this time
the prefect of discipline. Both Father O'Hara and Father
O'Donnell had been lay students while attending the University,
and were well acquainted with the threats to religious and
disciplinary administration. These two great members of Father
Walsh's team worked well together. Father O'Hara was an
ardent disciple of daily communion, as a source of spiritual
strength and moral courage, a practice he had adopted from the
enthusiastic encouragement of Bishop Chartrand of Indianapo-

lis, Father O'Hara's home town. Father O'Hara shared with Knute Rockne a prodigious memory for names and faces. It was this, and not a sometimes suspected trick, that enabled him to know almost to a man the student attendance at daily communion in the familiar basement chapel of Sacred Heart Church. Confessions were heard at all hours. Father O'Hara slept about four hours a night. His door in Sorin Hall was open for counseling or confession at any hour. The confessionals in Sacred Heart Church were occupied during all services in the church and many additional hours. Two of the priests who were always on call to aid Father O'Hara were Father Thomas Steiner, dean of the Engineering School, and Father Charles Doremus, teacher of French. Father Steiner's strong voice was the frequent leader of singing in the church. These three priests and Father O'Donnell probably knew the student body of Notre Dame more thoroughly and personally in these years of ferment than is possible for the administrators or faculty members or counselors of the usual campus. It brought back in the '20s that close-knit family spirit, the "vie intime" that the war had threatened. And it restored it in the face of much liberalized academic and disciplinary freedom, of a maturing student relationship and of a difficult off-campus residential situation. And all of it was done with unquestioned authority and with dignity.

Father O'Hara has been criticized in recent years for his use of statistics in promoting student religious participation. The statistics have survived but have been removed from their context. Father O'Hara had been dean of the College of Commerce. Statistics were a part of his education and his thinking. They were a vivid method of telling the story of campus Christianity in the daily *Religious Bulletin*, a single sheet which he founded and edited. And with half the students on the campus enrolled in the College of Commerce, the method was appealing and easily grasped immediately by this large segment of his target. The vernacular which was employed in the *Religious Bulletin* was a popular forerunner of the now popular vernacular relaxations in the liturgy. The success of Father O'Hara's methods is not as much in the speculation of posterity or the new theology as it was in the daily surge of most of the enrollment to the altar rails of church and hall chapels; as it was in the quotations nationally taken from his *Bulletin;* in the adaptation of the *Bulletinn*, or the *Bulletin* itself, in Catholic schools around the United States, but outstandingly, it seems to me, and I lived with the products for many years thereafter, in the Christian courage and integrity and leadership of the Notre Dame man. Father O'Hara himself was not one to rely on speculation. He instituted a Religious Survey, first of the students, later of alumni. You have to believe them.

In the fall of 1923, President John Neeson, in conjunction with Father John McGinn and Al Ryan who were developing an alumni program in many directions, proposed to the association an event which has subsequently become an alumni institution at Notre Dame, and a program of emulation by many other colleges. The program inaugurated in the spring of 1924 was Universal Notre Dame Night.

John Neeson's first letter, and the event as outlined in more detail in the *Alumnus*, belong in any story of the progress of Notre Dame and its alumni.

First, the memorable letter from President Neeson:

We are going to make it possible for every alumnus of Notre Dame to participate in a tribute to his alma mater and we hereby proclaim the Night of April Twenty-Fourth a Universal Notre Dame Night.

Gather the clans together, you men of the Notre Dame Clubs and put on your own show—a dinner dance, a smoker, a club meeting—we will leave it to your judgment—but make it worthy of yourselves and Notre Dame, knowing that at the same hour old friends are greeting you all over these United States. Nor do we exempt our members to whom distance from a club center is a barrier.. If you are not accessible to a local club, organize a group for a "Get Together Number" that night. Hold the function in your own home, if necessary, with your best friend as a guest. If he thinks enough of you to be your friend, he is a friend of Notre Dame.

We shall devote one evening to the "Old Days" to reminisce, to play and—to be serious. Discuss the problems that you know must be sorely troubling the successors to Sorin, which are our problems. Discuss the plans of the Notre Dame men, as a group, in your own city. What is our interest in the Building Fund and how can we best serve Notre Dame as an association? Just a suggestion. Nothing so stimulating, men, as coordination of effort; it gets one somewhere. And, if we know, as we will, that Notre Dame men the country over are, like us, meeting together in the spirit of the old days, the night of April 24—that's a thrill worth while!

Consider your engagement calendar for This Night as filled now. Let us know what you are doing about it. Keep the editor of the *Alumnus* advised of arrangements under way so that we may know through the columns of the next issue just what you propose doing to make this a memorable affair in the history of the Alumni Association of Notre Dame.

J. H. Neeson, President.

And now, from the *Alumnus.* As you read this, note how far-sighted were the hopes in this first proposal, and how much greater its implications than the fund-raising medium it was undoubtedly anticipated to be at that time:

The Universal Notre Dame Night has been heartily approved by the Administration at the University, the Alumni Association and the leaders of the larger Notre Dame Clubs throughout the country. It has been predicted that this night will be one of the most eventful in the history of the Alumni Association. It has possibilities that everyone can picture.

Consider what united support and interest will be aroused by the success of the movement. Notre Dame men will gather, perhaps for the first time since they left the campus. Old friendships will be renewed and strengthened, new friendships will be formed. Contacts will be established and the spirit of the University will be extended to points that have been neglected for years.

One of the finest things that can result from the inauguration of the Universal Notre Dame Night is the organization of Notre Dame men into club groups. Numbers are not so important as spirit. The spirit should not be lacking—we don't think it is! The alumni office on the campus is equipped and ready to furnish you with the corrected list of the men in your vicinity. It will furnish you with articles of association and assist you in every possible way to complete your organization. Get in touch with one or two other Notre Dame men in your community and start planning on your organization.

The local alumni club is the backbone of successful alumni service to the University. A meeting on Notre Dame Night is just the start. Local alumni clubs many times ask the question: "What can we do?" Here are some suggestions for consistent and continuing activity:

1. Meet and eat together at regular intervals. Maintain your association and contacts. There is something genuine and worth while in the fellowship and friendship of Notre Dame men.

2. Make sure that all Notre Dame men in your community are members of your club and readers of the *Alumnus*—in other words, in touch with the University. It will keep alive an interest that sometimes is inclined to lag but never disappears. Keep it active.

3. There are students in the high schools and preparatory schools that are prospective college men. If they're the right kind, Notre Dame is the right school for them. Maintain contact, through a special committee, with the schools, looking to promising students for future enrollment. The alumni office can furnish you with any literature you may desire.

4. Award trophies to high school teams or students for excellence in scholarship and proficiency in athletics. The

Cleveland Club is doing this. Yale, Michigan, California and Cornell alumni utilize this form of publicity to build good will.

5. Cooperate with the alumni office and the student clubs to book Notre Dame attractions in your town. They are representatives of everything Notre Dame.

6. Your direction of Notre Dame publicity in the local publications is advisable. Correct any misstatements about the University that may appear in the papers.

7. Entertain the University representatives when they visit in your community. The occasion may often arise and you will want to make the reception a fitting one.

8. Cooperate with alumni of other universities in the advancement of affairs of mutual interest, especially on the day of football games or other contests between the two schools.

9. Take an active interest in the Catholic affairs of your city. The leadership of Notre Dame men is naturally expected in this field.

10. Establish scholarships at the University for deserving boys, or make available to the President a loan fund to aid needy students.

11. Discuss alumni and University problems and pass your suggestions and recommendations along to the alumni office or the President of the University.

12. Create and stimulate the interest in alumni reunions at commencement and homecoming.

These are suggestions to which many local associations may add and from which others may subtract, or substitute, but they paint the picture of the possibilities that form the background of Notre Dame Night with its call to organize and reorganize.

So was born one of the great achievements of the association. And so was created perhaps the most effective public relations medium of Notre Dame for maintaining at least an annual close tie with its alumni, and for bringing into the sphere of the University a widening circle of friends who might or might not ever visit the campus itself.

In a frank estimate, eight alumni clubs were reported at this juncture to be well organized and functioning. On that first Universal Notre Dame Night, in April, 1924, 40 clubs, most of them newly formed in response to President Neeson and the *Alumnus*, held some type of observance, throughout the country.

The Universal Notre Dame Night will observe its 50th celebration in 1973 (its 50th Anniversary in 1974). Two hundred local Alumni clubs, some of them with as many alumni members as the national association boasted in 1924, will stage programs the University itself could feature with pride. The clubs have become microcosms of the University. The programs have aimed annually at stressing the spiritual, intellectual and cultural accomplishments and values of Notre Dame, to balance the already enthusiastic knowledge and appreciation of the more publicized athletic achievements.

Speakers from the campus have been sent with increasing numbers and distances to bring a direct contact, a breath of "la vie intime," to the clubs. Radio was enlisted in its prime, both network and local, to air programs bringing the familiar voices of the campus to scattered alumni. Television has proved expensive and has come into an era when the original concept of a single night had already been altered to multiply the use of popular speakers. This consisted simply of considering the night as not one date, but a valid observance on the night "or a date conveniently close" so that a campus speaker might, for example, arrange an itinerary through the South or Far West or East which would permit him to speak to five or six club functions.

The President of the University and the head football coach have always led the demand list for such occasions. But the clubs have enjoyed other administrators, deans, faculty members, and in the more revolutionary years student speakers to interpret the meaning of the barricades on campus which alumni never knew.

The alumni office, which originally used the *Alumnus* as the sole promotion for Universal Notre Dame Night, became involved in correspondence with ambitious club officers, found itself contacting radio on national and local levels, writing scripts for the radio programs, publicity for the press, and speeches for administrators and faculty members. The adoption of the "central theme" for a given Night aided this growing demand. But Universal Notre Dame Night could, in itself, have utilized the entire staff, equipment, budget and time the early alumni secretary and alumni office possessed.

Unaware of this great potential, or, most probably aware of the other equally great opportunities of this unfolding program, the association proceeded at once with the organization and appointment of the class secretaries. The classes of 40 to 50 graduates had hardly needed a unifying agent within themselves. But with the growth of the classes, and the accompanying explosion of alumni programs of all kinds, the adoption of the class secretary system became not only desirable but urgent. Just a single source for material for the *Alumnus* from each class was itself a reason. President Neeson, in the *Dome* of 1924, writes of the four steps of alumni organization. Step one was the *Alumnus*. Step two was renewed life and new organization of the local alumni clubs. Step three was the adoption of the class secretary system. And step four was the newly launched Universal Notre Dame Night.

This far-sighted ship of state was a large and powerful one. The crew was widely scattered and widely divergent in background and pursuits. But the two came together quickly and magnificently under the common cause of Notre Dame.

The same *Dome* of 1924 contained an article reaffirming the identity of Notre Dame as a "campus University."

> The primary purpose of the University of Notre Dame is to afford Catholic young men the opportunity for a Catholic education. The principles and ideals of the institution are distinctly Catholic. The Catholic student is here taught first of all his religion, that he may be well able to give an account of the faith that is in him, and he is carefully trained to live his life in conformity with the principles of his religion. The secular branches of study that have an ethical aspect are all taught from the Catholic point of view. But while the ideals and atmosphere of the university are Catholic, non-Catholic students are admitted and are left entirely free to practice their respective religions. There has always been among the students of Notre Dame a considerable number of non-Catholics, and some of the most loyal alumni and supporters of the school are not of the Catholic faith.
>
> A distinct feature of Notre Dame is found in the fact that it is a "campus school." Until a few years ago all the students lived on the University grounds. A rapid increase in the enrollment, however, made it necessary for some to live in South Bend. It is hoped that within a few years adequate facilities may be provided to make it possible again for all the students to live at the University. The solidarity resulting from the condition makes the school in a very true sense a large family, and to this close association of all the Notre Dame men is due much of the unique spirit of Notre Dame. This mode of life means to the student a larger circle of select acquaintances and friends, and it makes possible that give-and-take which helps so much to knock off the corners and to rid a man of the defects of character which tend to unfit him for leadership in his community in later life.
>
> The University of Notre Dame aims to train the student physically, mentally, and above all, morally, and to develop in him a strong Christian character, that he may become not only a leader in his profession but an enthusiastic and inspiring influence in every moment that tends to the betterment of his fellow-citizens.

In that same *Dome* of 1924, Al Ryan '20, the editor of the *Alumnus*, informed the students of the progress of the alumni publication from its inception in January 1923. The magazine had already presented the colleges of University to alumni and friends, in an unprecedented series of articles on their development. The *Alumnus* was the first monthly alumni publication issued regularly by any Catholic university and had already won recognition as one of the most representative alumni publications in the United States. Charles Donahue '25, was the circulation manager of the *Alumnus* then, another case of early involvement of young graduates in the Association programs.

Father John W. Cavanaugh '90, former President, in 1924 a popular and majestic figure on the campus as curator of the Dante Collection, expressed in this *Dome* of 1924, for students and alumni, perhaps the most eloquent definition of traditions at Notre Dame which exists. It added lustre to the revitalized Alumni Association, and should be familiar to Notre Dame men of all generations:

> Traditions are the real tapestries of all noble halls. Traditions claim and receive the plenary loyalty of all high and fine spirits. "Our Fathers Have Told Us" is a slogan of all reverential— that is to say, the best—minds. It is almost a touchstone of refinement in a man to be mindful of the cave from which he was digged and the rock from which he was hewn. In theology tradition is a fount of revelation; in education tradition is a fount of culture. You hear much of the Notre Dame spirit; do you know what it means except in athletics? Raucous screaming about it in print, frantic appeals to create it (as though it had not existed these 80 years), puerile zeal to "start" traditions, low-bred hanging out of the family lingerie in public—these things are the properties of the vulgar, the Great Unwashed. Once while visiting a new university I was importuned by students (as an ancient, who should know) to "suggest some traditions to start." These innocents will by divine arrangement go to their graves without ever understanding what a tradition is.
>
> Traditions are never started. They exist and grow strong long before anyone discovers them. They exhale from any distinctive group life as naturally and inevitably as perfume exhales from a violet. They are the fragrance of life and can no more be created than a new star. The old songs sung by generations of happy students without any thought of "starting a tradition"; the old jokes (the marble champion, the fake atheltic captain, pew rent and water-rent and the "holy hour" at the Grotto), the old stories about Brother "Bony", and Brother Hugh's "hawses" and Rockefeller Hall and the dead Caesar in Washington Hall who had to sneeze while

Mark Antony was delivering his funeral oration in the play,
the old atmosphere, the old dreams and enthusiasms, the old
"razzes" and "rough-houses" (in due place and season) the
old thrilling stunts handed down by word of mouth, the old
unaffected pieties and reverences when there were no statistics, the sturdy old contempt for "snitching" or for smelling
at another man's heels, the old scorn of unclean speech or
cheating or stealing or unfair self-seeking—these things are
such stuff as dreams and traditions are made of. Like epic
poems these things are never "started" or "made"; they
grow. They are the cream skimmed off the rich milk of the
college mind.

Hence the crudities among us who "import" traditions
(God help us!) from without, who lug in manners and customs and symbols and badges and nomenclature and clothing
and programs and sundry other oddities from alien schools,
are not normal, nor civilized. They are not creative but
merely mimetic, and they are fully entitled to all the respect
due to industrious monkeys. Only I submit they ought not to
monkey with an historic and picturesque school, that has
gone on these four-score years facing sometimes hostility—
often coldness and occasionally (as in mid-west athletics) low
theological prejudices—doing its own work in its own way,
fighting its own battles, meeting its misfortunes and calam-
ities with a level eye and a stout heart, and with never a
thought of borrowing old clothes from the neighbors.

Perhaps we elders are to blame for not indoctrinating
freshmen more zealously in Notre Dame traditions—for not
telling them that the pioneers on winter mornings often had
for coverlets the snow that had sifted in through the chinks
of the log hut during the night; that Sorin and Granger at one
time possessed only one hat between them (poverty!) so that
when one was seen abroad on the campus the other was
known to be for most excellent reasons at home; that once
the students must have gone supperless to bed had not the
arrival of an unexpected gift from a friend relieved their
distress; that while the foundations of our resplendent art
traditions were being laid by the purchase of pictures many
years ago the horses were once actually unyoked from the
plow to be sold for debt. (Saints and fools do such beautiful
things and the saints get away with it.) Perhaps we ought
more often to recall the old missionary days when after long
journeys in sub-zero weather the priest had to be lifted out of
the sled and his feet thawed back to life; when teaching
brothers returning from a hard year's work in the mission
schools walked forthwith into the harvest field to garner
wheat against the next year's bread; when in the old Argo-
naut days of the "foolish 1840's" three grave and reverend
brothers set out pathetically for the gold fields of California
in the desperate hopes of gathering enough bullion to lift the
college debt. They got no gold, the splendid old heroes, but

they were willing to do that terrible thing—to leave the peace and safety and refinement of their monastic shades—to endure not only the privations and perils of the Argonauts but (worse still, sometimes!) to endure the Argonauts themselves—in order to save our alma mater from the auctioneer. No, they found no nuggets of gold, but they left after them golden memories. Their superb failure is one of the most thrilling traditions of Notre Dame, and the sheen beneath thy feet, sweet Lady of the Dome, is all the brighter for their adventure.

And the heroic memories are not the distinctive glory of priests and brothers alone. There was Professor "Joe" Lyons—Lyons of the sunny smile, the shy manner, the heart of gold, who took no vows but practiced them all, and whose days were one unending procession of kindnesses to the simpler as well as the great. There was Professor Edwards— "Jimmy" alike to the ungodly and the affectionately reverential, whose library, and museum, and bishop's hall and archives are merely his monument and not the whole story. And, thanks be! there is still "the Colonel"—one William Hoynes, of jovial and beneficient repute, favorably known in Rome and Chicago (among other places) doctor of laws as well as expounder of them. Knight of St. Gregory, these recent years, but a true knight always, who is a very lively tradition indeed but who would have to admit, if indiscreetly questioned, that he is not of today or yesterday! And the colonel, who went into the Civil War as a "mere stripling" (ouch! these historical dates!) who was sent home to LaCrosse when a Southern bullet ploughed across the top of his skull, leaving the trough of the wound to this day, as the most honorable of decorations; the colonel who most wickedly and disobediently intruded himself by stealth once more into the army before he was half recovered—well the colonel may perhaps stand as a symbol not only of the professors' devotedness but also of the patriotic devotion that sent our priests to the front as chaplains, our nuns as nurses, our battalion of students under Col. Lynch to the ranks, and that later gave Notre Dame the singular distinction of the only G.A.R. Post made up exclusively of priests and brothers . . . ,

Here, then, in the midst of Father Walsh's quickened pace of peace, from the flowing pen of a past President, who for decades had known Notre Dame from a young seminarian to its acclaimed President, we have the heritage of a statement of our tradition. It is dated only in detail. In principle, it had come with Soring, and it will go only when Our Lady of the Lake snuffs out the moon at her feet and her crown of 12 stars.

XXIV

To The Moon

The 17th annual meeting of the Alumni Association was called to order in Brownson Recreation Hall on June 15, 1924, by President John Neeson. The first annual Universal Notre Dame Night had just been written into alumni history. The *Alumnus* was entering its second year, restoring close communication between the campus and the world-wide family of Notre Dame men.

Two long-time friends who played important roles in University progress were listed among the deceased of the year, Maurice Francis Egan and Father John Talbot Smith.

A constitutional committee, chaired by F. Henry Wurzer, appointed in 1923, had presented a proposed Constitution in the May *Alumnus*. On request of Father John McGinn, who reported a receipt of a number of recommendations for change in the proposed constitution, which the committee felt should be considered, the meeting discussed deferment of adoption. On motion of Byron Kanaley, the report of the committee was adopted and action on the proposed final draft deferred until the next annual meeting with the same committee, Henry Wurzer, Aaron Huguenard, Francis O'Shaughnessy and Father McGinn retained until that time.

Warren Cartier read the treasurer's report. He asked that the $250 restriction on checks cashed without the signature of the president be removed. A new record, in the collection of dues for the year, had been offset by the expenses of the alumni office and the *Alumnus* magazine. He urged more widespread payment of dues, and that these dues be sent directly to the alumni secretary, with receipts mailed from the alumni office. Byron Kanaley, with a second from Clarence "Chick" Bader

'19, moved the adoption of the treasurer's report and recommendations. Discussion of dues concluded that the payment of dues began with the association year—June to June—and that notices for payment should be sent out regularly by the secretary.

The committee on class secretaries reported and its report was adopted for immediate action. Father McGinn reported on the increased activities of the office.

Father Michael Shea '04, Yonkers, N.Y., popular author—with his brother John '06—of the "Victory March," was elected honorary president of the association.

Hugh A. O'Donnell '94, New York City newspaper executive with the *Times*, was the unanimous choice for president. His vice presidents were James V. Cunningham '07 of Chicago, John P. Murphy '12 of Cleveland, Edward A. Roach '13 of Oak Park, Ray T. Miller '14 of Cleveland, Mark Duncan '15 of Chicago and Donald Gallagher '24 of Ogdensburg, N.Y.

Father John McGinn then nominated Alfred C. Ryan '20, who had become acting secretary to the position of secretary, and a unanimous vote resulted. The same unanimity reelected Warren Cartier to his deeply appreciated treasurership. New trustees for two-year terms were A.A. McDonnell of St. Paul, Grattan Stanford of New York and Stanley Cofall of Philadelphia.

Father McGinn, active in the ongoing building fund campaign, asked for greater participation. He reported that a mail campaign was being conducted among alumni, because the scattered nature of the Notre Dame alumni did not permit the direct personal contacts which the major cities enjoyed. Response to these mail appeals was requested as a necessary measure of cooperation for the drive's success.

I am going into some detail during these early '20s, because they were the transition from the volunteer years of the association—largely staffed, directed, and supported by the University—to the development of a staff and office, still on the campus, but no longer staffed by the University or directed or supported by the University—in theory. It took a little while to achieve the latter goal.

The office, under Father McGinn and Al Ryan, had already instituted the *Alumnus*, published the first *Alumni Directory* in eight years, installed a card file of 12,000 alumni and nongraduate former students, organized or reorganized 15 local clubs, appointed class secretaries, and revised the Constitution.

Collection of dues in 1923 amounted to $1,800 from one form
letter appeal. Contacts with hundreds of alumni not previously
contacted was reflected in the magazine and in the office
correspondence. The 1923 commencement and reunion had
been the best since the 1917 diamond jubilee. The first specific
class reunions brought back 300 alumni, compared to the 50
who had attended the traditional general reunion in 1922. And
the association had affiliated with the national professional
Association of Alumni Secretaries.

This was a very sound foundation for the Alumni Association. In basic principles, we have been building upon it successfully ever since. Some of its provisions at the time I am writing
of were already implemented in part. Some were promising
shoots still of delicate structure and some were seeds planted
with hope and conviction.

The immediate preoccupation of the alumni and the men in
the alumni office was still the building fund of $1,000,000
which was not completed. Father McGinn was deep, with
Father Burns, in this project. Al Ryan, in addition to the
campaign duties he still retained, was also acting as business
manager of athletics under Knute Rockne, a job of growing
magnitude as the ticket problem overflowed Rockne's pockets
and, on the crest of the national championships of the Four
Horsemen teams of 1923 and 1924, taxed the box offices of
Ebbets Field, N.Y. (for the first Army-Notre Dame game to be
played in New York City), Lincoln, Neb., Pittsburgh and St.
Louis, in 1923; Princeton, N.J., at Princeton and the precedent-
shattering Rose Bowl game on Jan. 1 in Pasadena against Stanford. Box office rose from 197,000 in 1923 to 265,425 in
1924, which was before the 53,000 Rose Bowl attendance was
added.

No wonder the budding professional demands of the campus
programs still needed volunteers. Vincent Fagan '20, a classmate
of Al Ryan, and faculty member, contributed much unsung
labor to the *Alumnus* magazine. The talented architect also had
a talented literary pen, evidenced in his later collaborations with
his brother-in-law, Joseph Casasanta '23, University band and
glee club director, in several of the popular Notre Dame
marches. Even I, a Senior in 1924-25, was drafted to do a
"campus news and views page" in the *Alumnus*, a happy proximity when editorial succession came shortly, and to which I
attribute my unanticipated and undefined career. It took years
to find out what an alumni secretary really is—and years more

to achieve general understanding. But the traditional willingness and interest of the Notre Dame man in aiding Notre Dame never wavered. Al Ryan was in history the first lay alumni secretary, and he and Father McGinn should be forever commemorated as far-sighted and practical founding fathers of the strong Alumni Association developed after them at Notre Dame.

As I have underscored, the *Alumnus* had already, in its first year, brought to all alumni a story of the various colleges of the University and their development over the years. But the academic structure was not singled out. Al Ryan and Father McGinn, and Vince Fagan in outstanding measure, were aware of the men whose work and whose identities were not always recorded in administrative or academic records, but who were so vital a part of "la vie intime." For example, the brothers:

> The average alumnus is quite unfamiliar with the origin of the brothers or the wonderful work the brothers have done over 80 years. . . . . He does not know how important a work the brothers have always undertaken, not only in teaching, but in the administrative work of the University. In fact he knows little or nothing about that part of the Community that has been so modestly in the background, but still so essential a factor in the upbuilding of Notre Dame.

> An interesting memorandum of the occupation of some of the brothers of this earlier time of Sorin has been preserved. Associated with the primitive bake shops are the names of Brothers Vincent, Joseph, Michael, Augustine and John the Evangelist. The first carpenters were brothers Francis Xavier and William. Brother Patrick, the prototype of the ever popular Brother Matthias, was in charge of the refectory. An interesting little story is to be found in the archives of how one night he had no food to serve to his brethren, for the cows had beaten the monks to the evening repast. The good old porter, Brother Cyprian, was in charge of the shoe shop, Brother Augustus conducted the tailor shop. Brother Benoit, the ancient predecessor of our friend, Brother Terance, was the locksmith. when the printing office was established, Brother Joseph was placed in charge.

> Students of the college and Industrial School were together in recreation, and the latter came into the college study hall. In those days, Brother Francis de Sales, the old warrior of the first Empire, held the post which has since (1869) been so long and so efficiently occupied by Brother Benoit, whom he resembled both in strictness of discipline and partiality to snuff.

> Of the early teachers, the author of the *Golden Jubilee* tells us, "Brother Gatien was a genius, an incomprehensible Frenchman! He was capable of doing anything and everything. He was at that early day the intellectual soul of the

institution. Peace to his ashes!" Father Gillespie writes of the
great work of Brothers Edward and Gabriel in the steward's
department and of the accomplishments of Brother Francis
de Sales as procurator of the college. How Brother Basil took
hold of the band and sounded the first notes of the Philharmonic Societies is another of his themes. The work of
Brother Vincent in the direction of the novitiate, and of
Brothers Lawrence and Paulinus in running the farm, comes
in for its share of praise.

Professor Lyons has preserved for us the names of some of
the officers and professors of the University at the time of
the silver jubilee. We find Brother Gabriel, secretary, and
Brother Celestine, assistant secretary, Brothers Basil, Leopold
(still living), and Joseph Calasanctius, professors of music;
Brother Phillip teaching English and bookkeeping; Brother
Francis de Sales, professor of Geography and history; Brother
Claud, professor of Hebrew; Brother Simeon, teacher of the
Irish language.

Such was an early *Alumnus* tribute to traditions. And, of
course, long after this era, the University was continuing to
benefit from the extension of the dedication of both religious
and laymen in the many facets of activity its programs called
for.

In 1923 Rockne himself recognized the expanding demands
of his athletic programs. He brought George Keogan in as head
basketball and baseball coach, succeeding Walter Halas, brother
of the legendary George Halas. It was said of Walter, in lapses in
charity which extended in several directions, that he was hired
under the illusion that he was George. Keogan, while never
developing a warm affection for his overshadowing director of
athletics, nevertheless produced some fine teams and was a
distinctive part of Notre Dame's athletic tradition until his
death. When the addition to the old Gym was built in 1924, and
a hardwood basketball floor, with galleries for spectators,
added, some of the most stimulating sports events were lost
from history. But the science of the game, and relations with
opponents, improved substantially. The dirt floor in the original
Gym was a terrifying surprise to opponents, and few major or
return games with established basketball teams were possible.
But for sheer gladiatorial combat, it drew a student crowd that
rocked the suspect rafters of the Gym.

Professional dining facilities were looming on Father Walsh's
building horizons. But the sisters continued to cook for the
Brownson and Carroll refectories, in the separate kitchens behind the Administrative Building. Carts trundled the food from

the vats to the students, through sleet and snow, with much dust, and a growing legend that bracketed the poor nuns with the Borgias. A Class A rating might have been hard to come by under the circumstances, but many of us who ate in those old dining rooms with the platters of meat, the pitchers of milk, the square pies, and the home-baked bread, have lived to long for those days again. Malnutrition was unknown.

The sisters also presided in the laundry, where they were regularly accused of rending shirts and ripping off buttons. When the later and modern laundry building was dedicated to St. Michael, there were irreverent references to the appropriate implications of a sword wielded among the helpless laundry bags. But there were nuns who remembered boys by the hundreds by their laundry numbers.

And the sisters directed the Student Infirmary, as they happily still do. But there were not the modern facilities then, or the more extensive professional staff. The students were convinced that the traditional substitute for the later two aspirins was castor oil or salts, a remedy frowned upon for injuries which hampered locomotion. One long-time attending physician, an authority on respiratory diseases, was pictured by his patients in their letters home as a more colorful and questionable medic than Doc in the current *Gunsmoke* series.

But returning alumni, remembering these personages and practices, in the light of maturity, were their most frequent visitors and ardent admirers.

The lay faculty still retained a number of wonderful men, whose teaching was supplemented by their example as gentlemen and men of faith. Some lived on the campus—Edward "Heine" Maurus in Sorin Hall, Francis X. Ackerman, who had a less charitable apellation based on a genial disposition and perhaps on the fact that occasional stimulant was desirable to get him to the "temporary room" he had occupied for 40 years on the 4th floor of the Main Building, and George Shuster, brilliant English teacher, who was to return to Notre Dame in later years. Professors such as the tobacco-chewing engineering teacher William Benitz; the precise teacher of biology Regidius Kaczmarek—who anticipated current sex education with annual lectures aimed at removing the threats of South Bend's social evils, including prohibition, from the lives of students; the ever courteous Jose Caparo, genius in the field of electrical engineering; John M. Cooney, the Kentucky gentleman, who could measure with equal skill the quality of the bourbon from his native state or the quality of the men of Notre Dame, and who admired both—these men lived downtown, supporting families on salaries which were far from their academic stature, and who reflected a dedication to Notre Dame equal to that of the religious themselves. These were exemplary men, who were thanked many times in retrospect and sought by alumni on all occasions.

There was a fallacy long extant that the relative financial poverty of Notre Dame extended into its intellectual resources as well. If anything, the situation was more like inverse ratio. The religious, many of them highly endowed in their fields of teaching through the insistence of Father Zahm and Father Burns, could have been matched with the professors of any college or university. Because they were priests or brothers, and because they were not available in the academic marketplace, they were too often removed from consideration before comparisons of merit even began.

The case for the laymen was more difficult to explain or to be understood by outsiders. Most of the lay professors were alumni. They were well trained and competent. A number of them had enjoyed advanced studies away from Notre Dame before returning. The low salaries they received, even in the generally low scale prevalent in higher education, was judged inevitably by outsiders to mean a lack of ability. The success of their alumni in the competitive world beyond the campus should have been answer enough, but the evaluation was for the most part made without including the vital factor of product performance. As alumni secretary, I saw the success of product comparison.

There was also the problem of limited personnel study and assignment. A case I recall well because he was a good personal friend, was James Hines, a professor of history. Hines was a gentle, scholarly man. He had no stomach for discipline. And he loved the students of Notre Dame. The prompt and ruthless reaction was a campus orientation of new students that "Goof" Hines' classes were a cinch, good grades and little discipline. Few of the boys who sat in his classes were really there to learn. The truth of the experience, as I have shared it with many in later years, is that Hines was an excellent teacher of history. In addition, he had a scholar's zest and rare ability to match the somewhat colorless chronology of history with the colorful dramas of those same periods that made them come alive— particularly infusing Shakespeare and the history of Europe.

Many of us are convinced that Hines, a mellow man, occasionally earthy as an academic Falstaff, would have been of great value teaching graduate classes, where ideally the juveniles of the campus have become appreciably matured. I cite this instance mainly because the tendency to grow by belittling those against whom we are measured can result in injustice to others and illusions to ourselves.

During the second consecutive undefeated season in football in 1924, when Stuhldreher, Crowley, Layden and Adam Walsh were almost everybody's All-Americans—Red Grange, the Galloping Ghost of Illinois, crowded Dan Miller, the Fourth Horsemen, from his deserved spot in the Four Horsemen All-American backfield—and Knute Rockne was embarrassing sports writers by outshining the traditional old generals of the American gridiron, the enthusiastic Alumni Association presented a car, a Studebaker Bix Six, to Rockne at the Homecoming Game when Georgia Tech, a popular rival, was defeated 34-3 before a capacity crowd of 22,000 on Cartier Field. (I was mellow myself—two years later I married a classmate of Red Grange's.)

In 1922, Georgia was the scene of a revival of the Ku Klux Klan, and the movement was spreading around the country noticeably in Indiana. Father Walsh and Father O'Hara were anxious to have Notre Dame combat the movement in some way. Rockne and Bill Alexander, the nationally popular coach of Georgia Tech, believed that a game between Notre Dame and Georgia Tech, home and home, would help to bring about better understanding and tolerance. The first game was played in Atlanta in 1922, Notre Dame winning 13-3, the second and third games were played at Notre Dame. Although Notre Dame won these first three games, the caliber of the Tech teams and the character of Coach Alexander dictated a continuing series. The series has continued, and in spite of a 19-3-0 record in Notre Dame's favor, the rivalry, broken in 1970, will be resumed with five successive games beginning in 1974. This series in its inception stands out as bringing with it a strong example of the bridge, the beacon and the crossroad that universities can be.

In March, a map of the student body origins showed 48 states and 40 foreign countries represented. It was pointed out that this distribution provides a skeleton structure for alumni growth, so that no matter where a graduate may go, he will find Notre Dame men there before him with a fraternal welcome. Notre Dame had already achieved its distinctive universality, the national identity marked by the majority of its students coming from outside the state of Indiana.

In the spring of 1925 the alumni of Catholic colleges formed what was to become the National Catholic Alumni Federation. Notre Dame was among the 12 colleges which sent delegates to the first meeting. This was an organization which had a fine potential. Its major problem was that it was launched as a federation, and there were frankly few Catholic alumni organizations to federate. In addition to that, the few that there were—Notre Dame included—were not in a financial position to subsidize the new federation. But from the years of its existence, with the Notre Dame alumni secretary serving a term as its president, much that was fine in Catholic alumni thought was presented at the biennial conventions of the federation, and the proceedings of those meetings make rich reading.

In the spring of 1924, an addition to the rear of Science Hall added 17 classrooms and seven laboratories to ease the student overcrowding of academic facilities. Kervick and Fagan, professors of architecture, who had entered into a practicing partnership, were given the assignment to design the long-awaited Old Students Hall and two other residence halls. They presented a plan for three such halls and in the summer of 1924 the foundation was laid. This was the first residence hall to be built under the spur of the building campaign, and according to agreement as previously noted, was to be the Old Students Hall the association had planned since 1908. By the time the hall was completed, it had been named Howard Hall, with Morrissey and Lyons Halls as its projected neighbors. Since it was dedicated to Judge T.E. Howard, one of the great lay alumni teachers and pillars of the early association, there was no argument from the alumni. Morrissey was named after Father Andrew Morrissey, the outstanding alumnus-President of the University, and Lyons Hall after the legendary Joseph A. Lyons, prototype of the dedicated alumnus-lay-professor at Notre Dame.

I have said several times that comparisons are not valid. But it should not preclude the observation that the budget allotted Kervick and Fagan for the three halls, $500,000, was modest. It involved curtailing many of the decorative features they hoped to incorporate. But it did not preclude the production of three very attractive, functional residence halls, with one of them, Lyons Hall, containing in its Lyons Arch one of the architectural gems which has enjoyed professional camparison with some of the far costlier designs of later Halls.

In the fall of 1925, the enrollment was limited to 2,500.

On June 14, 1925, Hugh A. O'Donnell called the annual meeting of the Alumni Association to order in Washington Hall—the site marking the increase in numbers occasioned by the Class of 1925 and its 315 graduating members, a University record. Two of the great pioneer alumni of the Eastern seaborad were among the deceased alumni reported—Joseph M. Byrne '79, and Rt. Rev. Luke J. Evers, his classmate. But by this time the Notre Dame Club of New York and the Notre Dame men in New Jersey were assurance of the permanence of the University's programs in the East.

F. Henry Wurzer '98, chairman of the constitutional revision committee, reported on the new Constitution. In the discussion before adoption, Wurzer moved that the new provision establishing directors be made operative immediately to avoid the election of the six-man vice presidential group of the older rule. The motion was seconded and passed. Warren Cartier moved that Article VIII covering dues be amended to add a section establishing a life membership of $100, which would give the association an investment fund, and a reliable dues income from those members. This was also passed. Father McGinn moved amendments providing for election of friends and benefactors of the University to the association through nomination by the board of directors and balloting at the annual meeting, and for the ex officio membership for honorary degree holders. These amendments were passed, and the new Constitution was moved for adoption by Wurzer, seconded by James Fogarty '00, and passed.

The secretary's report was read and adopted, detailing the work of the office and the magazine. Warren Cartier read the treasurer's report, showing another record collection of dues, but a total amount still adequate to meet the increasing expenses. He said that the increased activities of the association could not be pursued without greater payment of dues. He recommended that the *Alumnus* magazine not be sent to members who had not paid dues for three years. His report was accepted by the meeting.

Daniel J. Murphy '95, Rockaway, N.J., and Byron Kanaley '04, Chicago, were elected to the Board of Lay Trustees of the University.

The election of officers brought Father Michael Moriarty '10, Wooster, O., to the honorary presidency. William P. McPhee '90, Denver, was nominated for the presidency and elected unanimously. McPhee praised Hugh A. O'Donnell, and the association's accomplishments, and promised to further them during his term.

Daniel J. O'Connor '05, was named vice president. And the newly created board of directors was selected: Joseph M. Haley '99, Fort Wayne, for a term of four years; Edward C. McHugh '13, Cincinnati, O., a term of three years; Thomas J. McKeon '90, Duluth, Minn., a term of two years, and John P. Murphy '12, Cleveland, O., for a term of one year. A new member of the board was to be elected each year thereafter, for a four-year term.

This was the historic group which launched the long and invaluable direction of the Alumni Association under the newly acquired Constitution.

Warren Cartier was reelected treasurer, with a vote of appreciation and Alfred C. Ryan '20, remained the secretary. The association then elected to the University Board in Control of Athletics Frank E. Hering '98, M. Harry Miller '10 and John H. Neeson '03.

In December of 1925, Al Ryan gave an excellent address to the new National Catholic Alumni Federation in New York City. He pointed out the necessity of full-time alumni secretaries on the campus, complete records of alumni, an alumni directory and magazine, and the organization of alumni clubs and classes. His thesis then was "Remember that a moderate amount of organized alumni loyalty is worth more than an unlimited amount of unorganized good will."

This was Al's swan song to alumni work. Essentially a businessman, and one who was still handling several major job responsibilities with outstanding results, outside opportunities became too inviting to resist. The campaigns were winding down. The Alumni Association was winding up, with increasing energies along a well-charted course.

A special meeting of the new alumni board was called in January to discuss the association's future.

I had been brought back to the campus in September, 1925, from a job on the *News-Times* in South Bend. I was to handle publicity for the University, and, for some measurable activity, teach a course in journalism under Dr. Cooney.

Rockne's publicity as a coach was threatening to swamp the institution. In addition to that, he had for some years enjoyed the practically professional services of Arch Ward and Frank Wallace in their student years. And when I began to read other University publicity stories in the *Chicago Tribune* which I had not yet even heard of, I realized that the school was not yet ready for a centralized publicity bureau. Nor was I. Similarly, teaching a quarter, facing men about my own age, with such imminent talents as Walter Wellesley "Red" Smith and Walter Trohan, I felt inadequate in the Cooney tradition.

So when the alumni board, undoubtedly in a quandary, knowing of my association with Al Ryan and the *Alumnuss*, asked me to take his place, I jumped at it. What new graduate, offered a magazine to edit, with other responsibilities not yet defined enough to be frightening, would turn it down? As for the University, I suppose, like Mt. Everest, I was there.

And so the University went on to better things, and the long romance between the alumni board and me was begun. I will affirm many times in the pages ahead that this group, year in and year out, contributed more to the progress of Notre Dame than any other off-campus group. I am sure that its success is in the fact that it was never really an outside group. It was the open channel, the magnetic force, that kept alive the "vie intime" which lies at the roots of Notre Dame's distinctive record of alumni loyalty and achievement.

The method of election of the board assured the continuity and the experience necessary to good government. In the University's own tradition, the various board years tend to be identified by the presidents of those years. And the presidents, who had been schooled by their terms on the board, were able leaders. One negative aspect I'd like to point out immediately was the tendency of the presidents to measure their competence by the calendar year they were in that office. As a matter of fact—a point I constantly sought to make to past presidents— few projects of the association could be realized within a one-year span. The value of the board and its excellent continuing leadership was that no projects of merit died with a president who proposed it. Many of the finest programs of the association and the University came from the persistence, the continuity, and the consideration in depth given to proposals. The board was constantly alert to both the initiated and invited suggestions of class and club officers. It was always sensitive to suggestions by the University for mutual development. The Alumni Association's progress is the cumulative contributions of many dedicated men, unified by the outstanding continuous leadership of the board of directors.

I had returned to Notre Dame with a deep admiration for Father Walsh. This was not because he had hired me, although I used to assure him in later years that this was the outstanding act of his administration. It was because he was a man of great stature, an administrator of purpose and performance, a priest of manifest character and grace and the possessor of a sense of humor which I have always found is an essential ingredient of dedication to an institution.

As a student, I had seen Father Walsh avert what might have been a bloody and bitter page in Notre Dame's history. The Ku Klux Klan, chafing under the opposition of Notre Dame, decided to stage a massive parade in South Bend. Indiana was then under its most deplorable domination by Klan leaders. On a Saturday, when the parade was to be held, cars and street cars from the area began bringing in the rather guileless and harmless members who were the Klan's basic strength and source of income. The students in small "hospitality groups" met these trolleys or stopped the cars and offered to escort the members, with their robes under their arms, to the meeting place nearby—wherever the car was stopped. The disillusionment of the Klansmen was quick, not too violent, and ended with the welcoming group returning joyously to the campus with the confiscated robes and hoods. This was intended to prevent other Klan demonstrations in the area. But the Klan leadership was unwilling to accept the defeat. On the following Monday night, students on the campus were suddenly alerted that the Klan was launching a parade in downtown South Bend. The evacuation of the campus was startling and masses of students marched to the city. Plans had the most unfriendly segment of the South Bend police force on duty. And the Klan members whom the students faced were not the neighboring farm and small-town innocents, but an imported assortment of goons who led the students into a funnel-like trap, where serious physical action quickly began. The odds were immediately recognized as impossible, and the potential realized. Into this difficult situation, where the irresistible force of spirit was willing to attack the immovable object of armed force, President Walsh swept in the familiar University car. Calling the students to assemble on the Court House lawn, he used his military experience to point out the futility of the fight and the dangers of casualties. As a priest, he summoned the virtues of charity and tolerance. And as President of Notre Dame he ordered the students back to the campus. So steeped were Notre Dame men of that day in all these areas that they followed his leadership. It was magnificent. It was close.

The bridge and the beacon again were there. The incident helped Indiana to regain its political stability and eliminate the Klan. The crossroad, however, showed how dangerous the barricades can be when manned by emotion only.

The January, 1926, *Alumnus*, my first editorial effort, contained comments on Al Ryan, in the total inadequacy of words then or since to spotlight his real value to the Alumni Association. And they launched the first of 42 years of exhortation to the alumni which were to make them feel as though their postal life was one long series of appeals from the alumni secretary.

It was. When I took the job, even the most loyal of the directors were kind in their suggestions that I would make contacts that would help me when I decided to follow Al's example and enter business or professional life. I have always appreciated that friendly counsel, because I was among the first and the few who identified alumni work as a professional challenge, requiring competence and conferring dignity and stature of a very satisfying nature. With Notre Dame as my alma mater to serve, the continuity of the years which followed was inevitable for me.

As for the Alumni Association and the University itself, the launching pad first established by Father Sorin in 1842, and prepared with the brilliant science, the imaginative arts, and the magnificent spirit of his successors, was now ready.

We were off together on our trip to the moon—not the moon of dusty craters and no life, but the moon at Our Lady's feet and the life of a world to come.

This was the confidence of inexperience, as I expressed it then, in a simplicity totally unaware of the significance of the transition being made:

Alfred C. Ryan, Ph.B. in Com. '20, is now just one of the Notre Dame alumni. Perhaps Al had this day in mind when he organized the alumni body of the University into one of the leading associations of its kind in the country. Notre Dame's alumni body is recognized as the outstanding national group of Catholic college men. During Mr. Ryan's administration the number of Notre Dame clubs throughout the country increased four-fold and the interest and activities of those

which already existed were invigorated by the new life that
the secretary brought to his work.

The Notre Dame *Alumnus*, which was begun as a feature
of the Endowment Drive, was taken over by Mr. Ryan and
made into one of the leading magazines of its type in the
college world. The *Alumnus* is a member of the Alumni
Magazines Associated and the alumni secretary of Notre
Dame is a member of the Association of Alumni Secretaries,
the only Catholic college or university represented.

Universal Notre Dame Night, which for two years has
made the world acquainted with Notre Dame alumni, and
Notre Dame alumni acquainted with each other, and everyone familiar with Notre Dame, was begun by Mr. Ryan. The
history of those two nights is familiar to the alumni and is
testimoney enough of their success.

These are things of matter; concrete evidence of the benefits which accrued from Mr. Ryan's regime. But an even
greater heritage of his work is the Notre Dame spirit. He
didn't discover or begin Notre Dame spirit. Father Sorin and
his little band brought that to Notre Dame in 1842, and it
has grown and waxed strong with the years. the students have
had it and it has bound them like a chain. But with its alumni
it was as though the links had been separated, one link going
to California, another to New York, a third to Mexico and a
fourth to the Philippines. These links were the same strong
bonds, potentially, that had bound their owners as students,
but actually, in their separateness, they lost all their binding
power. "Al Ryan, through his *Alumnus*, his Universal Notre
Dame Night, his Notre Dame clubs, and his own personality
and efficiency, took all these scattered links, reforged them
through class reunions, molded them with the strong but light
chain of the Notre Dame student body and produced a bond
that holds the whole world within the unity of Notre Dame
spirit.

For a man who effected such changes within so short a
time, it is not to be wondered that the gates of opportunity
opened wide and revealed so much that he yielded readily.
He left behind him only cause for praise. The house was set
in almost perfect order. His record is one of rapid and
constant progress. The Alumni Association has lost a brilliant
secretary, but the world has gained a Notre Dame man, who
will continue the constructive work from the outside that he
began in office."

"Ring In The New"

Personal mention of the editor by the editor isn't exactly
the thing, but so much of this work is dependent upon
personal contact that it is necessary for just this once to drag
in the persona non grata. Al Ryan built up a splendid organization through the aid of hearty personal support from Notre
Dame alumni. It is hard to step into his shoes, familiar only
with the alumni of '25 and '24, and expect or ask that same

support. But that is just what is being asked. It was this support that built the association to its present strength, and if there is to be further growth and harmony of architecture the material used in constructing must be the same. So if the alumni will carry on as though Al were still capably holding down the position, the new secretary will try to learn the craftsmanship of arranging the material in the same attractive style.

XXV

Bigness Is
Just Around the Corner

Fortunately, bigness, like prosperity, was not as inevitable as its champions—or its opponents—thought. In fact, so competent was the administration of Father Walsh that the marked moves toward bigness escaped both the inflated values of its admirers, and the damage to principle, tradition, or nature that frightened its enemies. Father Walsh's first move was the limitation of enrollment to 2,500. Pressures began almost at once to expand this figure, but the ceiling provided a shelter under which much of the post-World War I boom was analyzed and its gains consolidated. And it offered enough time during which plant and personnel were adjusted to meet the next growth pressures.

Father Walsh's first goal—after the residence halls were provided—was a major dining hall, which would reassemble the students, faculty and administrators under the original unifying and congenial aegis of eating. The Rockne successes brought pressure for a new stadium. But the dining hall was given priority. Cartier Field was expanded to seat 30,000, as a token of appreciation to the athletic program. The gymnasium boasted the new basketball court. But Ralph Adams Cram, Boston architect, who had impressed the campus in 1924 when he was awarded an honorary doctorate, was asked to design a suitable dining hall. His first design was on the side of magnificence. This was reflected in the cost estimate. As a result, in consultation with the Kervick and Fagan campus team who were familiar with the campus economy, modified plans were presented from which the present South Dining Hall emerged in 1927. The factor of professional direction of institutions on the campus, which were traditionally entrusted to men and women of faith, good will, but limited experience, entered with the dining hall. A competent hotel and restaurant man, Robert Borland, was hired to direct the new hall while it was still in the building stage. The result was kitchen equipment, furnishings, and the arrangement of major halls, central kitchen and dining adjuncts, producing from the beginning an efficient, impressive and economical three meals daily for what was then the entire campus population.

My real initiation into the true boarding-school philosophy came when I discovered that this magnificent, shining building, with its quality food, service and management, was the victim of the same old familiar charges of poisoning and discrimination that had been hurled at the innocent nuns of the old kitchens.

A growing campus water shortage was met with the discovery and utilization of a water supply under the northern campus. The resulting use of well water saved the jeopardized water of St. Joseph's Lake. W. J. Burke, Portsmouth, O., industrialist, thought the University should have a golf course, which would open the fast-growing sport to the students without taking them away from the campus. He offered to develop the course if the University would provide the land. The present Golf Course, then the domain of Brother Leo, whose cattle, hogs and grain were legendary in Midwest agriculture, was set aside. Burke died, but the University proceeded with the plan and has subsequently enjoyed a fine relationship with the family of the intended donor.

The east door of Sacred Heart Church, designed by Vincent Fagan as a memorial to the Notre Dame dead of World War II, was appropriately dedicated with a Mass on Memorial Day, 1924, celebrated by Father Walsh, President of Notre Dame and also the chaplain-friend-teacher of many of the men whose names appeared on the memorial plaque. Father Walsh's building program during his presidency totalled $1,650,000.

There was also action on the academic front. The College of Arts and Letters reduced the number of degrees from the seven it had offered in its departments, to retain only the collegiate A.B. The increasingly unpopular requirement of 174 hours for a bachelor degree was modified to 144. It opened the way to more electives. Latin and Greek were removed as requisites of the A.B. In the College of Commerce, Dean James E. McCarthy, "Big Mac" to the entire campus, was overcrowded in classrooms and understaffed with teachers. In 1926 Father Francis Wenninger, dean of science, organized the Academy of Science, limited to upperclassmen with averages of 85 per cent or better.

He ruled the college with rigid concern for his students. But his premedic students were admitted with amazing consistency to the medical schools of their choice. Father Wenninger brought the same rigidity to his post of master of ceremonies at campus liturgical functions. It evoked his lasting comment that if the participating priests paid as much attention to the liturgy as they did to their golf stance it would dignify the services greatly. The effect was minimal.

Martin McCue, the lay dean of engineering, had been at Notre Dame from his student days, receiving his first degree in 1879. He was eyewitness to the great fire, and to the faith and steadfastness of Sorin. He made a great contribution, as a competent teacher of engineering and as an exemplary Christian gentleman. He retired in 1928 after 49 years on the faculty. The enrollment in his college had doubled during Father Walsh's administration and the rumbles of the explosion of knowledge were beginning to be heard in that great field.

In 1923 Father Walsh had accepted the retirement of another venerable lay dean, William J. Hoynes, of the College of Law. He replaced him with Thomas F. Konop, a Wisconsin legislator. The attraction of the expanding field of law was reflected in the continuous growth of the Law School. Both law and engineering were the first such colleges to be established in American higher education, as you have already been reminded. The two-year Law course was extended to three.

Under Father Walsh, the total faculty almost doubled from 90 to 175. The salaries of the laymen, both individually and collectively, were becoming a critical problem of administration. The dedication of the older lay faculty, and the quality and permanence of new members, were poorly mirrored in the prevailing scale of pay. In spite of this, faculty members began to publish more. And there were few casualties in spite of the sacrifices entailed in staying. There were some adjustments of doubtful value—my own example being a class in metaphysics taught by the nephew of the famed Cardinal Mercier, a Belgium's war-time prelate. If you can imagine metaphysics being taught in a fractured and anguished effort to elicit American understanding with French thinking and vocabulary, you can imagine why it later took me some time to welcome the influx of scholars who came to the campus from the Continent in the disturbed '30s. Charles Phillips, a teacher brought from the war background by Father Walsh, was an inspiration to me as he was to most of the faculty and students. He was an enthusiast for the joy of learning and communicating. He wrote and spoke often, and his tower room in Sorin rivalled Father O'Hara's for patronage. For a year, I was his secretary, an experience I cherish.

The 1926 annual meeting of the association was called to order in Washington Hall by President McPhee. An unusual number of ballots, 800, had been cast for the election of officers under the new Constitution. After the Class of 1926 had been admitted to membership, and the list of deceased read and resolved upon, the results of the election showed Daniel J. O'Connor '05, Chicago, to have won the presidency by a very close vote. James E. Sanford '15, Chicago, was made vice president. Warren Cartier was the unanimous choice for treasurer and Al Ryan '20 was made a director to hold on to the knowledge and initiative he had contributed to the pioneer work of the association.

Warren Cartier '87, Ludington, Mich., whose long years since 1908 as treasurer of the association had brought Old Students Hall to fruition, tendered his resignation. Efforts were made to avoid accepting it, but on insistence it was reluctantly accepted with deepest appreciation for the hard work and achievements which the treasurer's long tenure had involved,—without the help of campus office or staff. Byron Kanaley '04, advanced the name of Walter Duncan '12, to succeed Warren Cartier, and the directors were empowered to select the new treasurer.

The treasurer's report detailed the association's financial condition in the contemplation of his resignation. He was disappointed in the small response to the life membership proposal. He cited the new commitments of the association as demanding an ordered and much larger financial program to support them. He had already met with the Alumni Board, before the meeting, to propose the adoption of a budgeted system of financing the association programs. The hope for a solution to the problems was also a prominent part of the retiring president's farewell address. McPhee was warm in his praise of the programs instituted and of the officers and alumni and the University, whose efforts had brought so much progress. But he, too, felt that the time was at hand for the introduction of business methods and strong alumni involvement.

President O'Connor in his opening address to the membership at this meeting gave evidence of the wisdom of his selection. He was an outstanding organizer and had given thought over the

years to the work of the association. It was reflected in the
almost instant quality of the steps he proposed to take with the
new board in making the association a continuing asset to Notre
Dame but at the same time a self-sustaining one.

The idea of the budget was advanced. This would include the
projected expenses of the association and would give alumni a
detailed statement of what their dues were needed to support.
The programs were widening the gap between their cost and the
relatively inadequate increase of annual payment of dues. The
operation of the association, President O'Connor pointed out,
was no longer dependent upon the decision of an annual meeting of an unpredictable number of loyal alumni, who could be
carried away by a current whim or emotion on these mellow
occasions. Its success would depend from here on upon a
continuous and planned direction.

The first budget proposed—which included the cost of printing the *Alumnus* for 10 months, the salary of a full-time
secretary, postage and stationery for class letters, etc., traveling
expense for the secretary to visit clubs and attend conventions—was set by the board at $12,000. It was projected, on the
base of the records to date, that only about $4,000 could be
expected from annual dues. This also projected an immediate
large deficit. The board felt that ultimately, by performance,
members in sufficient numbers could be made dues payers.
Other methods were suggested to meet the obvious immediate
deficit.

This brought up the first suggestion of annual giving, in
effect—the annual contribution by alumni according to means
and interest, rather than fixed dues. It was noted that other
alumni associations were adopting this method. The advocates
of the traditional and conventional dues were not easily moved,
but the idea was almost essential to meet the immediate gap
between projected income and expenses. The $5 dues remained,
but a request for additional amounts from able alumni was
accepted. The board was asked to propose a plan at the next
annual meeting which would do away with the need of such
additional solicitation. Raising dues, a system of graduated dues
for years out of school, and other methods were suggested.
Aaron Huguenard '23, proposed the elimination of dues and the
permanent adoption of the annual voluntary contribution.
Many a hard year was to pass before that far-sighted recognition
of the one great successful approach to alumni giving was to be
implemented. It points up, however, how often the seeming

failures of alumni deliberations had within themselves the seeds of later success. Additional gifts from members present erased a $1,000 deficit shown in the treasurer's report. The action strengthened the idea of voluntary increases in contributions. The board was empowered to approach the membership accordingly, through the mails.

The board subsequently confirmed Walter Duncan '12, La-Salle, Ill., as the new treasurer of the association, a responsibility to which his considerable talents were dedicated in the difficult years ahead. It was 15 years later, in 1941, when the Alumni Board was finally given the green light for the Annual Alumni Fund, the system of annual contributions to the University by alumni, from which the Alumni Association budget, submitted by the alumni board, was to be the first expense.

In this simple system, the psychology of alumni giving to the University raised their sights generously, as against the little understood and traditionally negligible expenses of the association, which had occupied University office space free, entertained alumni returning for reunions at University expense, circulated a magazine which had perhaps mistakenly been initiated by the University at its own expense.

The new alumni office, in the meantime—and the new alumni board—were prolific in ideas and programs for developing a wider interest among alumni. I have never ceased to wonder at the frequent statements that capital is so often in search of ideas. It seems to me my life was lived in a climate where ideas were constantly seeking capital. In any event, the office and the secretary, were sorely pressed, and the treasurer usually in despair.

Father Walsh's administration, constantly striving to lose nothing good from the Notre Dame heritage, saw many of the old personal ties between campus and alumni severed by death. Father Alexander Kirsch, who had come to Notre Dame in 1873, who was ordained in 1880, and who, after two years of science study at Louvain, came back to the Notre Dame faculty, was such a priest. He was an ardent scientist, stern in requiring quality from his students. His classes in anatomy and zoology were bolstered by his occasional summers at the famous Woods Hole center in Massachusetts.

Father John Scheier, who like Father Kirsch had been born in Luxembourg, was a competent Latinist. He was educated in the Jesuit schools in Luxembourg before coming to Notre Dame in 1882. Father Scheier was head of the Latin department, and, like so many priests on the campus, held the additional posts of prefect of religion and pastor of Sacred Heart Church, which from the origins of Notre Dame remained a parish as well as the University church.

Sister Martha, an Irish-born sister of the Holy Cross, was for 23 years director of the University kitchens. Her death in 1923 came several years before her familiar kitchens gave way to modernization. Sister Cecilia was the director of the Student Infirmary for 34 years, familiar to students who for good reasons or guile reported in sick. She was, as nuns so often are, the combination of tough-and-tender that produced good immediate results, and brought back her boys to visit her once-dreaded domain when they returned as alumni.

One of the oldest ties to go was Father Timothy Maher, a Tipperary lad who came to Notre Dame in 1846, to become a brother. In 1861 he decided to become a priest of the Congregation, and he was ordained in New Orleans with two other former brothers of the Congregation. For years, Father Maher was secretary of the University. He later became Notre Dame's postmaster. He died in 1925 at the age of 94, almost the entire span of "la view intime." Another venerable link with the past was Father Daniel Spillard, one-time prefect of discipline, whose entries in the "black book" are classics in the University Archives. Father Spillard was a graduate of '64, ordained in 1869. Father Spillard served pastorates in South Bend, Notre Dame, and Austin, Tex. He was for a time superior of Holy Cross Seminary, and president of Holy Cross College. His last post was as a chaplain at Saint Mary's. He was 87 at his death. A comparable life span was enjoyed by Father Thomas Vagnier, whose parents had moved to Notre Dame and lived near the Mission House. He taught in the preparatory department before his ordination in 1867. He held several pastorates in Indiana but his last and longest post was as chaplain at Saint Mary's, from 1895 to 1919.

One of the colorful brothers of Notre Dame died in 1923. Brother Columba was a shoemaker on the campus. But he had achieved a growing fame, against his own modesty, as a "miracle worker." He was known as a man of deep faith and almost constant prayer as he worked. His intercession was sought by many and reports of cures began to grow. He was equally modest about an older distinction. He had been Father Sorin's nurse during the founder's last illness. Brother Philip Neri was another legendary brother who had served for years as a teacher of the then vital course in penmanship in the commercial department. In later years he became the landscaper of the campus, developing what has long been the beauty of the Main Quadrangle, marking its diverse trees and setting off the buildings which surround it. Another landmark for alumni passed with the death of Brother Cajetan, who for 46 years had supervised the Minims, Father Sorin's "Princes," in St. Edward's Hall. It was in a sense fitting that Brother Cajetan's death, one of the gentlest and most exemplary of men, was accompanied by the closing of the Minims chapter in Notre Dame history.

I have pointed out how often the distinctive richness of Notre Dame life, and the unselfishness and dedication which have fostered its progress, are found in obituaries of Notre Dame men. This was a period of such evidence.

Father Burns had pursued the goal of the $1,000,000 building fund. He reported that the money received toward the fund had come mostly through the interest and cooperation of alumni. Father Hope, in his *Centennial History*, believed that this credit should be modified because most of the money came from non-alumni. I would like to record my own belief that Father Burns was right, and the situation reflected a strength which was almost lost in misinterpretation. Notre Dame alumni were, in the first place, usually from modest backgrounds and often the first generation to attend college. They seldom graduated to inherited or established wealth or position. But they were enjoying widespread success in their own progress toward prominence. Their wealth was still very limited but their power to enlist the interest and support of others was becoming a major asset. This was a strength used by all other fund-raising programs. It was then, and has remained, an essential part of Notre Dame's own programs. Even the great increase in participation and amount of alumni giving could never have produced the support for the phenomenal growth of recent years.

In the September 1926 *Alumnus*, President O'Connor outlined the functions of the Alumni Association for the membership. The board had already endorsed this program.

1. Publishing the *Alumnus* magazine, for universal contact with alumni.

2. Organizing the local alumni clubs.

3. Homecoming, Universal Notre Dame Night and reunion planning.

4. Issuing an Alumni Directory.

5. Maintaining a Placement Bureau for alumni.

6. Helping clubs establish scholarships.

7. Assisting in student and University activities.

8. Representing Notre Dame at conventions of national alumni organizations.

These suggestions were accompanied by an urgent request to alumni to make the necessary contributions to finance them. The courage of the convictions of the association administration at the time was reflected in the earlier notation that the budget for the year was projected to face an $8,000 deficit of its total $12,000.

The *Alumnus* also carried another article, which was voicing the enthusiasm of the secretary, a proposal made by an Amherst professor at a convention of alumni secretaries, that continuing education should be a part of all alumni programs. This early seed is only in very recent years beginning to bear the fruits of its inevitable good. But it was a continuing theme of the magazine and the board throughout. The Center for Continuing Education, given to Notre Dame by the Kellogg Foundation in 1965, was heralded by the Alumni Board because it gave the impetus to a major program, initiated, as it has to be, by the University administration and faculty.

Another very important chapter in Notre Dame and Alumni history was carried in the *Alumnus* with the announcement by Knute Rockne that J. Arthur Haley '26, would become the graduate manager of athletics. This responsibility had been one of those held by Al Ryan. Art Haley had been a member of the short-lived S.A.T.C. at Notre Dame in 1918, and returned to graduate from the College of Commerce. He had a fine mind for business, and brought order to the football ticket situation, which had outgrown the casual handling of Rockne himself and the partime attention Al Ryan could give to it. Between Rockne, Ryan, the Faculty Board of Athletics with its alumni representation and Art Haley the alumni were given a preference in the purchasing of football tickets which has persisted through the years. With the present broad allocation of one-fourth of the stadium to alumni, and the present five-game sell-outs, the alumni are responsible for an estimated half-million dollars in annual football revenue from this segment alone, a sum not counted in the report of annual alumni giving. Similarly, to cite a somewhat related situation, alumni parents of the several hundred sons in the current student body, are responsible for another million dollars and more of revenue. At the start of the Notre Dame Foundation, many alumni parents asked to have their tuition credits included as gifts. But the misleading aspects of this dual book entry were apparent. This substantial income from alumni is also not a part of the annual alumni giving report.

The Alumni Board, in the fall of 1926, was urgent in its request to establish the Annual Alumni Fund. There was reluctance to abandon the long-familiar system of dues. Requests for additional gifts were only partly successful But the widening of association programs continued. The 40 clubs which had reported on the first Universal Notre Dame Night, including some optimistic projections of such organizations in many communities, had grown to 43 clubs in 1926.

The board, in its own inexperience and with its usual friendly cooperation with the secretary, announced a change in the June reunions. The recently adopted 5-year plan was abandoned to install a new program which sounded impressive in its principle. The Dix Plan, begun at Princeton, provided for the rotating reunions of groups of four consecutive classes, so that in a 20-year span, each class would have had at least one reunion with every other class with which it had been on the campus. This was a complicated plan for the alumni, who preferred their organization programs to be easily understood and easily enjoyed. The recognition of the failure of the Dix Plan to take hold, and the restoration of the five-year program, was one of the early evidences of the board's wisdom.

The alumni office, in spite of its burdens and its financial limitations, announced the opening of a placement service. The scattering of alumni across the country, and the communication and time aspects of the placement problem were evident from the start. But the persisting recognition by the Alumni Board of the value of a service to the alumni from the campus resulted in the expansion of the placement program within a few years, especially after William R. Dooley '26, joined the office staff. Ultimately the establishment of the Placement Office under Bill Dooley became a responsibility of the University, from which appropriate move it has grown in stature. The emphasis was soon switched from the almost impossible problem of placing scattered alumni, to the strong program of bringing corporate employers to the campus to interview seniors. The encouragement and selection of major large corporations has resulted in better jobs with better companies in the national pattern which is still a hallmark of Notre Dame.

Not all of the changes at the University survived that era of growth. Prof. James Hayward, in an article in the *Alumnus* in February, 1927, pointed out the rosy future of the Department of Agriculture, anticipating 300 students, based on the affiliated farm properties of the University, and the fact that Notre Dame was the first Catholic university to offer a four-year course in agriculture. The national character of the enrollment was offered as an advantage to the students, and University freedom from political pressures reflected the growing involvement of farmers in American politics.

The 1926 Summer School had enrolled 905 students, and alumni were urged to study the possibilities it offered for advanced degrees. The Summer School, though peopled primarily by sisters, was actually coeducational. But in 1927 the announcement was made that courses would no longer be open to lay-women.

In April, 1927, the *Alumnus* reported the alumni giving as falling short. Apparently some alumni regarded the voluntary amount as giving the affluent a chance to advertise themselves. The *Alumnus* tried to explain the difference and repeated the essential value of broad-based giving, even in the small amount of the $5 dues.

In May the *Alumnus* announced the coming alive of the placement service, with questionnaires to be filled out, card files of applicants and employers, and an appeal to the clubs to cooperate in this program, which was most often one that could best be solved on the local level.

The 1927 football ticket applications, for the first time, were marked "alumni," offering eight tickets in the preferred section of Cartier Field, and additional tickets in the non-alumni section if desired.

The June reunions featured a luncheon arranged by the campus Monogram Club for the returning Monogram alumni. This Monogram alumni reunion has since become a valued and permanent part of each reunion.

The annual meeting in 1927 was held on June 5. Detailed reports from the secretary and the treasurer were read and approved by the meeting. Ballots for officers had become so numerous that the meeting approved an advance appointment of tellers to count the ballots before the meetings in the future. Walter Duncan moved that the retiring president of the association automatically become a member of the board for a one-year term, thus adding the value of his continuing experience to the new board. This was agreed upon, and has proved most effective.

The Constitution was referred back to its writers, Messrs

O'Shaughnessy, Huguenard, Wurzer and Father McGinn, to repair an omission.

John P. Murphy '12, Cleveland, was elected president. James F. O'Brien '13, Detroit, was made vice president, Walter Duncan, treasurer. The move creating the post for the retiring president left a vacancy in the board of directors and George Maypole '03, popular Chicago politician, was named to the 4-year term.

A motion by Byron Kanaley '04, is of significance in the light of its subsequent long years of constructive recognition of the lay faculty by the alumni association:

> Inasmuch as the Alumni Association ended its year with practically no debt, and inasmuch as interest in the association has been stimulated (the Alumni Fund and the gifts of the Chicago and New Jersey Clubs are evidences), be it moved that the Alumni Association of the University of Notre Dame award an annual prize of $500 to the member of the lay faculty who will have performed the most meritorious service during the year, the prize to be financed by a permanent lay faculty foundation of $10,000 to be freely subscribed by the members of the association.

Fortunately, provision had been made by alumni to underwrite the award for its first five years. And to Byron Kanaley himself is due the realization of the $10,000 projected foundation which has kept the annual award alive, honoring an illustrious list of lay professors annually in the ensuing years.

A motion to raise dues was discussed favorably and recommended to the board. The Alumni Board, feeling that the alumni preference in football tickets would attract additional members, did not raise the dues as suggested.

The growing inter-club potentials in programs were recognized when Father Michael Moriarty '10, a popular priest in Wooster, O., and member of the alumni board, extended to all alumni an invitation to join the Cleveland Club in an annual summer pilgrimage to his parish in Wooster. The Cleveland Club, after Father Mike was gone from Wooster, tried to revive this principle by inviting all the clubs in the Ohio and adjoining states to organize a summer reunion at Cedar Point, the fabled site at which in earlier years the Dorais to Rockne pass had been developed, where hundreds of alumni had worked, and which was being modernized in the wake of the Disney trend.

The Alumni Board continued to encourage the development of clubs and classes. When the first Committee on Alumni Clubs reported, in 1924, it said that its first approach found eight clubs "questionably active." At the time of the report, 32 clubs were active in 20 states, largely the result of Universal Notre Dame Night, which it predicted (accurately) would result in many more clubs as the alumni population grew.

In 1924 there were clubs in Akron, Boston, Calumet District (Ind.), Chicago, Cincinnati, Cleveland, Columbus, Denver, Detroit, District of Columbia, Fort Wayne, Green Bay, Indianapolis, Kansas City, Lafayette, Ind., Los Angeles, Milwaukee, Minneapolis, New York City, Philadelphia, Rochester, N.Y., St. Joseph Valley, Ind., St. Louis, Syracuse, Western Pennsylvania, Western Washington, Toledo and Youngstown. The work of these clubs in presenting the University in balanced perspective to America cannot be explained or appreciate in the depth it deserves. We have noted that for 14 years Father John W. Cavanaugh was a one-man public relations program for Notre Dame. Knute Rockne took up that identity from 1919 to 1931. Both found invaluable channels for their national influence in the alumni clubs from coast to coast. When they were gone, the clubs became invaluable in public relations.

The optimism stemming from the treasurer's report in 1927 was commendable as spirit and good intention. It failed to recognize the austerity by which this achievement was attained. But I was a casualty of the same optimism. After returning to Notre Dame in 1925, I lived for two years in Sorin Hall. This great experience—I had lived only one year on campus previously, as a Senior in Corby—paid great dividends in acquainting me with hall life, and with the Classes of 1926 and 1927, Seniors then being housed in Sorin. At the same time, I was eating my meals in the Brownson Refectory, at a lay faculty table, where I learned the nuances of the borders between students and lay faculty, between lay faculty and clergy—most of the negative ones being a nurtured mythology.

At any rate, in 1927 I was married, and moved off-campus, to discover what the lay faculty members meant when they discussed the tortured process of paying their bills.

In addition to taking a wife, I had been voted a secretary. It became very hard to support both. The 1927-28 association budget was proposed at $8,700. This was to pay salaries, mailing costs, *Alumnus* publishing cost, office supplies and travel.

The University itself received a major financial boost with a $400,000 bequest in the will of Frank Phillips, a former student at the brothers' high school in Fort Wayne, and for two years a student at Notre Dame. He was also the brother-in-law of William P. Breen '77, distinguished pioneer alumnus in the association's development. Breen-Phillips Hall resulted from this benefaction, as did the Breen Chairs in the Law School.

The Alumni Board was zealous in its increasing responsibilities. Dan O'Connor was appointed to develop the placement program. Joseph Haley was made head of the committee to study the needs of the colleges. Al Ryan was asked for suggestions to increase the effectiveness of the *Alumnus* and George Maypole was charged with a plan for a student loan fund.

The national climate was good. Morris Starrett '21, wrote an article showing that 621 football monograms had been awarded, 241 of them under Rockne. Sixty-eight Notre Dame men were head coaches or assistants in universities and colleges about the country. Fifty-nine of these were products of the thorough schooling under Rockne.

The alumni secretary's immaturity showed with an announcement that he was instituting a 16mm moving picture service, showing campus development, to be available to the clubs. Without time, talent or funds, the idea, despite all its merits, fell fatally short of its expectations.

The St. Joseph Valley Club proposed a stadium at Notre Dame, to cost $800,000 and to seat 50,000 spectators. Rockne previously had asked the South Bend Chamber of Commerce to consider a municipal stadium which the University might rent. In the absence of action, Judge Gallitzin Farabaugh '04, through the club, proposed such a stadium, to be financed by the sale of box seats. Father Walsh, involved in the major programs which produced facilities for almost 900 students on campus, and the unprecedented new Dining Hall to feed them, backed away from the stadium project, but it was immediately at hand for his successor. A laundry building was badly needed. The compromise course was installation of $50,000 in new equipment and the hiring of the first professional manager.

The lay trustee portfolio showed an endowment figure of $1,104,325 earning 6.09 per cent. Investment was 82 per cent in real estate bonds and mortgages, 15.7 per cent in preferred stocks, the balance in bonds and utilities. The board appointed two committees to study the stadium proposal. Chairman Albert Erskine headed the finance committee and the committee on site and architecture included Father James Burns, Father Thomas Irving, Father Thomas Steiner and Knute Rockne.

Academic life was burgeoning. An article in the *Alumnus*, by
Brother Alphonsus, listed four pages of current faculty and
alumni publications, books and articles in a wide variety of
publications.

To bolster association finances, the alumni office suggested
that clubs might undertake individually the sponsoring of projects such as issues of the *Alumnus*, or representation at conventions. The response was not great, but it helped greatly. A
feature on the Notre Dame Club of New Jersey pointed to their
balanced program as a proper textbook for other clubs. The
Notre Dame Club of New York entered a major development
stage with the opening of club headquarters in the Fraternity
Club.

Father Walsh's years were aided by the beginnings of some
really major benefactions. The Phillips bequest has been noted.
James J. Phelan, Boston lay trustee, gave $5,000 for a student
loan fund, and other gifts brought this to $7,500. The Rowley
family of San Antonio established a memorial scholarship with
$12,000, commemorating their son, killed in an accident while
returning to the campus, in November of 1925.

A vital principle of philanthropy was exercised when Boetius
Sullivan, Chicago, offered to build a radio station at Notre
Dame and at Illinois, pioneer opportunities at the time. When
asked if he would finance their maintenance, he said he could
not, and Notre Dame declined the offer. The state university
accepted.

Student publications had moved from the traditional *Scholastic*, and the short-lived *Daily*, and the popular *Juggler*, to the
establishment of a Knights of Columbus publication, a Department of Chemistry magazine, *The Catalyzer*, and the *Notre
Dame Lawyer* in the Law School.

Perhaps the most embarrassing situation of Father Walsh's
administration was what became known as the "Columbia incident."

Knute Rockne, after the sensational success of his Four
Horsemen teams and their consecutive national championships,
was inevitably besieged by offers from other schools, and by
offers from business. His own salary was unbelievably modest
for his accomplishment and national stature. It was then, and
has remained, a University policy to try to keep salaries comparable. In the case of the coaches, because of the national
claim of uncertain tenure, allowance has been made for them to
accept outside emoluments. These were not nearly so frequent

or so substantial as they are now. Rockne was financially
embarrassed by the demands made upon him. He was also
disappointed that the stadium had not had greater acceptance
by South Bend and Notre Dame. His teams of 1925, 1926 and
1927 were excellent, but defeats by Carnegie Tech, Nebraska,
Army (2), and the prospects of a poorer record in 1928,
disturbed him. Under all these pressures, in a visit to New York
he permitted negotiations with Columbia University which resulted in that school's announcing the signing of Rockne as its
new coach. The loyalty that was in Rockne, and his appreciation of the values at Notre Dame which offset many of his
problems, caused him to deny the alleged signing. He referred
the controversy to Father Walsh. Recognizing the principles
implicit in the involvement, Father Walsh, to the consternation
of many alumni, stated only that Rockne was free to accept any
offer to better himself if he chose. Rockne did not choose, and
restored Notre Dame and his own image to the football hall of
fame.

At the June meeting of the alumni association, the treasurer
reported that income from alumni had exceeded any previous
record, totaling $10,235, which left a balance of $662.

At the suggestion of president John P. Murphy, the alumni
office set up a "carnival" for the 1928 reunion alumni in the
west wing of the new Dining Hall. It demonstrated disastrously
that such an event was not a proper part of either reunion or
fund-raising for alumni. The good idea and the good intention,
were turned back to the parish and other fraternal groups which
had undoubtedly profited from them.

Donald M. Hamilton '12, was the first non-Catholic to be
elected president under the new board structure. Professor
Edward Maurus '93, was made honorary president. William A.
Draper '07, Evanston, was named vice president and Walter
Duncan, treasurer. The directors for the year were Draper,
Ryan, Maypole and Miller, with John Murphy added ex officio.

Father Walsh's term expired in the summer of 1928. He left a
larger and a more sophisticated University. He had quietly and
modestly moved Notre Dame into the mainstream of American
higher education. He returned, with personal joy, to teaching.

XXVI

Ups and Downs

Father Charles Leo O'Donnell, C.S.C. '06, Kokomo, Ind., in 1928 became the 12th President of the University of Notre Dame, the 11th in alumnus to serve in that position. He was 44 years old and had already served as a chaplain in World War I, as Provincial of the Congregation of Holy Cross, and for two years preceding his presidency as Assistant Superior of the Congregation. He was an established poet, his secular rating in this profession undoubtedly held back by his identity as a priest, and by his concentration on the beauty and art of religious poetry. His style was deceptively simple. It was a pleasure to look at the serene surface of his poems and then suddenly discover the power and majesty of the current beneath. This major contribution of his career was frequently likened to the delicate and beautiful poetry of Sister M. Madeleva, C.S.C., who proved to be a similarly effective administrator of neighboring Saint Mary's College.

When Father O'Donnell succeeded Father Matthew Walsh, the academic surge of the postwar years heralded the accession of a recognized "intellectual" to the direction of Notre Dame. Father O'Donnell's years as editor of the *Ave Maria* under Father Daniel E. Hudson, C.S.C., had given him not only a highly polished literary style, but an aesthetic demeanor which did not have the congenial welcome with which his predecessors had greeted all comers. He was indeed an intellectual, in the better sense.

Being a poet was a factor which perhaps aided Father O'Donnell through the always strong factor of surprise in becoming one of the greatest and most astute builders in University history. He was one of the most articulate and effective de-

264

fenders of the academic stature of Notre Dame and the President who, in that sometimes critical period of transition, then and for all time gave intercollegiate football its proper place in American higher education and the first class citizenship it so richly deserved in the Notre Dame family.

When the Alumni Board met on July 7, president Don Hamilton appointed Frank Hayes '14, a Chicago banker, who had espoused the cause of annual alumni giving, as chairman of a committee to study the needs of the Alumni Association, and to devise methods of meeting these needs. Hayes was a keen student of the annual alumni fund plan. The alumni secretary, meeting the men in charge of these funds, in the conventions of the newly federated American Alumni Council, and seeing the rapid progress of their programs, was an ardent participant in this study. Hayes concentrated on the plan in effect at neighboring Northwestern University. He was a friend of its dean of business, and Northwestern at the time had the outstanding national program in higher education for both alumni and general fund-raising. He also included Dartmouth College which, like Notre Dame, was a private men's college with strong alumni tradition. The headstart of Dartmouth alumni in wealth and power was no deterrent to the far-sighted Notre Dame planners. Cornell's program, another leader nationally, was familiar to the secretary.

As an aid to the projected expansion of fund-raising, and for better communication generally, Father O'Donnell consented to inaugurate a President's page in the *Alumnus*. President Don Hamilton of the association also joined in the approach to the annual giving program, which had been voiced in the first meeting of the Alumni Board by Aaron Huguenard.

In November, Frank Hayes wrote a lead article in the *Alumnus* detailing the "Living Endowment Plan," as it was generally known because it represented not capital gifts but the equivalent annual interest on such capital gifts. The plan permitted the institution to avoid the frequent and flamboyant capital drives for large gifts, permitted the donor to retain his capital, and at the same time gave the institution equivalent results. In more mature years, I have realized that many of the Congregation members may have been concerned that the term "Living Endowment" might obscure the great Living Endowment principle of their own unremunerated services, which were still a major factor in Notre Dame's fiscal survival among its competitors.

The Alumni Association, under the new system of directors, had established the historic fact that the association had a continuing loyalty and relationship to the University, and would strive to increase alumni support of the University programs. But it had added the new dimension of an autonomous association which had a loyalty and a continuing relationship with its members, and an obligation to develop for them programs of benefit to alumni. In the continuing sense these were identified as the class structure, based in the secretaries and focused in the reunions, and as the newly created Universal Notre Dame Night and the expanding network of clubs. In the spiritual and intellectual areas, they were the visits of religious and lay faculty and administrators to the clubs, the development of club retreats, the use of the *Alumnus* as a medium for such stimulus, and—developed much later, but urged then—a program of continuing education for alumni, preferably emanating from the Notre Dame campus through the faculty.

The board realized from the beginning that alumni interest and support, no matter how deep loyalty might be, was only one side of a two-way street. University interest in, and support of, alumni was the other. The material support which the University had generously extended to the growing association, and still was, was deeply appreciated and had sustained alumni ties and enthusiasm to an obvious degree. There was fear that a self-sustaining association, as projected, might lose the essential two-way programs. Efforts became deliberate to avoid this.

The *Alumnus* further announced the introduction of a page of book reviews by Father John W. Cavanaugh. The magazine stressed emphasis on features involving traditions and familiar campus personages. It introduced articles on new programs and new personalities. When the *American Midland Naturalist*, founded by Father Julius Nieuwland in 1909, celebrated its 20th anniversary, Professor Henry Froning outlined the outstanding career of this great alumnus and the benefits which had accrued to Notre Dame in prestige and outside support as a result.

Father O'Donnell announced a gift of $100,000 for scholarships in honor of Leonard M. Anson. The scholarships, restricted to students from Merrill, Wis., opened impressively a new era of scholarship aid based on cooperation with the donor's wishes.

Imbued with family spirit and academic fervor, the *Alumnus* carried an article criticizing a change in the policy of the

Department of Journalism. It was written by the editor in what was of course calm objectivity, but credited anonymously because of obvious implicit prejudices. Father O'Donnell's brilliant caustic tongue respected the anonymity, but clarified who determined academic policy.

Father O'Donnell, in an early message to alumni, indicated his familiarity with alumni of other institutions, and added: "The university whose graduates are done with it once they are graduated, if any such university exists, would seem to be in the most desperate situation of all."

The 1929 Universal Notre Dame Night, having failed to interest network radio, launched a program to enlist local radio stations individually. Prepared material from the alumni office was supplied, and the local alumni clubs were invited not only to aid in enlisting the stations, but to be involved in the material, which varied, including some simple factual accounts and also a few skits concerning persons and events in the University history. Response was generally good although no Hollywood scouts or network offers came to the office.

The big news of 1929 was that the new stadium at Notre Dame was definite. It was to seat 60,000 and would cost $750,000. The 1929 home games, in view of the stadium construction near the Cartier Field site, would be played in Soldiers Field, Chicago, where Southern California in 1927 had gathered the largest crowd in football history up to that time— 120,000. The Navy game in the same location in 1928 had drawn a similar crowd. Chicago had always been the alumni population center and a strong Notre Dame source of support for all the University programs. The few really good seats in the huge stadium at that time produced headaches in ticket distribution but these were offset by the pageantry and the previous two fine wins for Notre Dame plus expediency and the unprecedented gate receipts.

An all-alumni Stadium Finance Committee, consisting of J. Arthur Haley '26, G. A. Farabaugh '04, Herbert E. Jones '27 and Knute Rockne '14, announced a plan for the sale of box seats on a ten-year basis, which would provide revenues for the immediate beginning of the stadium. Response from St. Joseph Valley business and industry, from leading families and from alumni of a much wider Midwest area, lived up to expectations and the stadium was begun. The Osborne Engineering Co. of Cleveland had been selected as the most competent builders of stadia. They proved a wise choice, in quality, in cost and in scheduled performance. The Notre Dame Stadium has been a constant source of good to the University. Its maximum visibility for every spectator in it made it an instant success with fans. The return of the home schedule, and the more important teams that the attractive stadium and its revenues found on the home schedule, has been a visible factor in the preservation of the unity of the students, faculty and alumni as well as the unity of the campus with the surrounding community and campus ties with alumni and friends from the entire country. It moved "la vie intime" into big production, as had, on the local scene, and more limited scale, the new Dining Hall.

With prescience that Rockne was unlikely to repeat the low ebb of the 1928 season—which was still a winning one, 5-4-0—and to quell the rumbles of critics over the University's investment in a major football field which was solely for the football games of the fall, Father O'Donnell announced: "There will be no radical change in Notre Dame, least of all in the spirit of the school. That spirit is so deeply rooted in tradition and the tradition itself is so strong that Notre Dame men of the future will simply be men of another generation—the hallmark will not change."

At the annual meeting on June 2, 1929, John W. Eggeman '00, Fort Wayne lawyer and judge, was elected association president. The huge football hero of an earlier day was a happy choice for this year of the new stadium. The venerable Mark Foote '73, Chicago alumnus who had known Sorin and the early Notre Dame, was elected honorary president. James E. Deery '10, Indianapolis, became vice president, and T. Paul McGannon '07, New York, joined the board of directors, with its continuing members, retiring president, Don Hamilton, and Al Ryan, George Maypole and M. Harry Miller. Walter Duncan retained the treasurership.

The meeting attempted to collect contributions to make up a deficit. The deficit resulted from two major causes—the absence of an appeal along the lines of the "Living Endowment" principle tacitly agreed upon, and the deliberate incurring of debt by the board to avoid abandoning new programs, or development of the older ones.

Judge Eggeman, in his opening presidential address, quoted Father Charles O'Donnell's statement that "Notre Dame will be the greatest Catholic University in the world." He pledged that the Alumni Association would take steps to make this prediction come true. The association was already showing its effectiveness toward this goal. The defeat of Alfred E. Smith for the Presidency of the United States in the 1928 elections had convinced Catholics that a President from the faith was still removed from the national prospect. Undaunted, the University awarded Smith its Laetare Medal to express its endorsement of his character and his campaign. And the New York Alumni Club made the presentation one of the great events in the long history of such presentations. A message of congratulation from the successful opponent of Smith, President Herbert Hoover, was a highlight of the meeting. Through club interest, the National Broadcasting Company aired the program to the nation.

Athletic Business Manager Art Haley announced that for the 1929 home games in Soldiers Field—Wisconsin, Drake and Southern California—alumni would be assigned a section beginning at the 50-yard line on one side of the field, and extending until all orders were filled. This actually included, as Haley pointed out, only 15,000 seats between the goal line and the 50-yard line, and with the preference allocation of eight tickets to each alumnus, it became a major headache for the ticket office, as it remained for many other teams in Soldiers Field until the current renovation for the professional games of the Chicago Bears.

The fall of 1929 was memorable for other things besides the Soldiers Field games. The Minims were absent from the campus for the first time. The Preps left in 1921. The mantle of responsibility now fell solely on the University students. St. Edward's Hall became a welcome haven for 207 of these, who would otherwise have been relegated off-campus.

The *Alumnus* magazine, conscious of the need for broad interest and for the rich general traditions of the University, featured the retirement of Father Daniel E. Hudson, for 55 years editor of the *Ave Maria*. Never officially connected with the University in an academic capacity, he inspired faculty and clergy, supplied a sanctuary of continuing education for many of the literary faculty, especially the religious, who lived and congregated in the Presbytery behind Sacred Heart Church. His sponsorship of many of the leading Catholic authors who had emerged during his tenure was known to all, as was the errorless nature of the popular *Ave Maria* weekly.

To reassure an increasing non-Catholic enrollment, the *Alumnus* pointed out that one of the first students at Notre Dame was a non-Catholic. His sister attended Saint Mary's, then in Bertrand, Mich. Some of the ecumenism faded, however, with the added information that the sister had had to run away from home to become a Catholic, but all ended happily when the family became the founders of St. Patrick's Parish in South Bend.

Reminiscing about old Cartier Field, as the new stadium rose, the *Alumnus* recalled the games on an open field in 1886, when only contributions from faculty members saved the Athletic Association from ruin. In 1899 the University wanted to build an enclosed field, but an appeal to the alumni did not bring enough general return to pay the costs of the mailing. It was then that Warren Cartier responded. The circumstances magnify the significance of his gift—also the revolution in attitudes the years have brought.

The world-wide economic depression began in the fall of 1929. It was to last in effect until 1937. The prospects for Father O'Donnell's administration looked bleak. A student enrollment drawn from the entire country, usually from homes enjoying the relative prosperity of the postwar '20s, seemed certainly in jeopardy. Moreover the budding field of philanthropy had hardly planted roots on the Notre Dame campus.

Neither the Alumni Board nor the University seemed to lose momentum in the face of the crisis. The board, meeting in Chicago on Nov. 16, after the historic stock market crash in October, seemed undaunted, as it authorized another girl to assist in the growing work of the alumni office. And—a move whose vision lost something in the economic pressures of the immediate years ahead—the board authorized a council of delegates from the local alumni clubs to meet in conjunction with the 1930 commencement. This group ultimately passed through a biennial program of such club councils to become the present extremely effective Alumni Senate,—an expansion and extension of the two-way communications between alumni and campus, which had become a growing and difficult task for the small Alumni Board.

If this were a biographical effort, a chapter could be written about the heroic girls who first joined the association staff. My first secretary was Eleanor Engledrum, whose uncle Jack had been a student at Notre Dame in its early years. Now Mrs. Charles Scoglund, and back on the campus in the Computer Building, she was reminding me only recently how she had to go to the campus Postoffice then and buy stamps on credit for the alumni office, an illegal procedure only made possible by her charm, her fast exit, and the brothers' charitable confidence in University backing. My second secretary was Mary Cass, now Mrs. Robert Cahill, wife of the business manager of athletics, Robert Cahill '32. Both these girls fitted into the pattern of the office during that pioneer stage with invaluable competence. Personnel tests in shorthand and typing might have barred them forever, but in their ability to win the friends and influence people that the office needed desperately, they were close to the little group of miracles I have mentioned. A third girl who handled the very vital launching of the mailing and records section of the association, and who deserves similar praise, was Alicia Przybysz, now Mrs. Thomas Perry—Tom is an alumnus—who is presently a member of the Athletic Office staff. These girls, and those who followed them, made me an ardent believer in the competence of women, in their understanding of the complicated problems of organizing an all-male association, and in their dedication to Notre Dame and its purposes, far and above the call of the modest pay received. The pay was actually immodest, but mothers liked their daughters to work on the campus, and the competitive markets were closing like the banks.

In another direction, Father O'Donnell demonstrated a similar determination of the University to progress. He announced the construction of a new Law Building, to meet the rapidly expanding needs of the Law School. Membership in the Association of American Law Colleges dictated its broader facilities, and the University felt that its distinction as the pioneer Catholic Law School in the U.S. should be recognized properly. The new building, designed in the now familiar collegiate gothic, was estimated to cost $400,000. It intimated the possibility of the great economical benefits that might accrue from building under the competitive conditions of the depression, if such building could be financed. This realization was to become one of the greatest contributions to Notre Dame's progress, and one of the most memorable phases of the O'Donnell administration.

The *Alumnus* persisted in its espousal of continuing education for the alumni. The American Alumni Council was strong for the movement. In 1913, when the alumni offices first organized, there were 25 Alumni Associations, with 75,000 active alumni reported. In 1929, the newly federated council had 250 member colleges, with the original 25 alumni magazines now totaling 125, and with 800,000 alumni involved. Notre Dame had been a part of this dynamic group for five years. A statistic which intrigued the University was that of gifts

to colleges in 1929, amounting to $150,000,000 half of which
had been given by alumni. (Today, 3,534 alumni administrators
represent 1563 member institutions.)

In the face of the growing depression, Father O'Donnell
published a major statement of the needs of Notre Dame. It
included a comparative listing of endowments of colleges.
Faculty salaries were in urgent need of added funds. Eminent
lecturers, always a strong tradition at Notre Dame, were becoming more expensive as campus competition for their appearances
grew. The high costs of graduate school programs and research,
both essential to quality education in a major university, were
advanced as readily recognized arguments for endowment and
larger current giving. The Art Gallery was listed for $1,000,000
to meet the items needed to perserve and enlarge its quality.
Student loan funds were wholly inadequate to meet the growing
demands of students whose parents had suffered from the
depression. A new engineering building, a new commerce building, and a new fieldhouse were among the formidable listings.

Like Sorin viewing the ruins of fire, Father Charles O'Donnell
surveyed the crumbling American economy and, taking a page
from his predecessor, forged promptly ahead with the new brick
of buildings and the new mortar of intangibles which together
make a great University.

The *Alumnus* announced that beginning June 1, 1930, the
association would appeal to its members under the principle of
the "Living Endowment," as studied and reported on by Frank
Hayes '14, and approved both by the Alumni Board and the
University.

An editorial in the *Alumnus* emphasized the historic service
of Notre Dame to alumni and the association. The inadequacy
of the goal of the first successful Endowment Drive was already
evident. Not only had the University afforded the association an
office, but absorbed association debts for publishing the magazine, payment of salaries on occasion, office equipment and
travel. If these programs were mutually beneficial, their reality
as a deplorable relationship still existed, and the University was
being faced now with increasing pressures of its own. Father
O'Donnell had pointed out the years that the University had
picked up the whole expense of intercollegiate athletics, a
substantial income from sports being of very recent and still
inadequate consideration. The stadium under construction was
evidence of the University's continuing endorsement of athletics, a popular and important common denominator of alumni
interest.

The annual meeting of the association in June mirrored an optimism in sharp contrast to its national environment. The "Living Endowment" was reported as a fact of alumni life, beginning immediately. The year had already broken records with $12,285 in dues, and $1,500 in advertising. The *Alumnus* had been increased in size to incorporate the volume of University, club and class news demanding publication. The Alumni Board had held two interim meetings, underlining the promised value of the board in constant and competent direction of the association. The first Council of Alumni Clubs brought delegates from 14 clubs. Four new clubs were on record. The association and the Athletic Department announced a vital change in football tickets preference for alumni. Preference was to be given only to alumni whose dues were paid for the preceding year. The preference was to close by Sept. 15. Alumni limit for the Army game in New York was set at four tickets. The club delegates heard J. Arthur Haley '26, on football ticket policy and Byron V. Kanaley '04, on the program of job placement for young alumni. Charles Molz '24, Detroit journalist, spoke on charging dues in the local clubs, and E. J. McErlain, veteran South Bend alumnus-banker, spoke on the scholarship program at the St. Joseph Valley Club. Recommendation was made that the traditional scholarship form be abandoned in favor of student loan funds. Clubs were urged to aid in the selection of outstanding student candidates for Notre Dame in their community. Frank Fitzsimmons, Chicago Club delegate, was appointed to draw up a suggested basic program of organization which all clubs, and prospective clubs, could consult for their individual club organization direction. "Living Endowment" was launched with a gift of $500, 17 gifts of $100, and more than 50 of $5 to $50.

The item of advertising income can be disposed of promptly, if you are curious. Nationally, and at Notre Dame, alumni magazines, with their selected readership were suddenly believed to be the advertiser's dream because of their high average reader purchasing power. A separate organization was set up outside the American Alumni Council, with its endorsement, to provide access to the booming expenditure for advertising in the national media. It was soon discovered that the small circulation of each magazine, and the unquestionable fact that alumni read most of the leading newsstand media, plus technical discrepancies in size, rates, periods of issue, and paper used, made the project unpalatable to advertisers and agencies. After honest effort, the usual discovery—as at Notre Dame—that the cost of

274	Onward to Victory

carrying the advertisement exceeded the ultimate revenue from it, practically ended the experiment. Promotional and public relations values of the space were far more profitable to association and University.

With the stadium under construction and relations with South Bend important, the June ballot of the association contributed significantly with the election of Father John W. Cavanaugh, C.S.C. '90 as honorary president (still a great favorite in community activities). Frank E. Hering '98, South Bend alumnus, former athlete and football coach at Notre Dame, now a leader in the popular Fraternal Order of Eagles and editor of its nationally prominent magazine, and a civic leader, was elected president of the association. Frank Hering was a editor of great competence. He was a nationally recognized authority on fraternal organization. He was an eloquent orator. Under his interested guidance and understanding leadership I learned much of the "trade" of alumni organization, editing, programming and fund-raising. Hering was a non-Catholic. He had no children, and his interest in Notre Dame and its students had remained after his campus ties had given way to his career with the Eagles. He was known favorably to most of the nation as the "Founder of Mother's Day," a title which seems to be historically accurate in principle but disputed by Anna Jarvis on the strength of her later persuasion of Congress to declare such a National Day.

William J. Granfield '13, Springfield, Mass., a member of Congress, was elected to the Alumni Board as vice president, and Peter McElligott '02, New York Club pillar, to a four year term on the board, joining Walter Duncan, George Maypole, Harry Miller, Paul McGannon and John Eggeman on the 1930-31 board.

One of the little items of great significance in the September 1930 *Alumnus* was the appointment of Robert B. Riodan '24, as the first lay registrar in the history of the University. He succeeded Father William A. Molon C.S.C., Bob Riordan was a veteran of World War I. He had returned to Notre Dame and completed a course in journalism under Dr. John M. Cooney. A man of magnificent character, Bob was enthusiastic about God, Country and Notre Dame. He was later, for country, to give up his life as a result of a volunteer return to duty in World War II. But in the meantime, he brought to the registrar's office a military organization, philosophy and aggressiveness, which did much to offset the anticipated decrease in student enrollment. In-between his graduations and his death he had married, become the father of nine lovely children, made a major contribution to Notre Dame's progress in his administrative post, and established a coordination between the registrar and the alumni secretary which was of lasting value. His wife, Dorothy Stoddard Riordan, was a dynamic person and a much admired leader among the faculty wives. One of Bob's annual responsibilities was the military arrangements for the Memorial Day Mass, a chore which became increasingly difficult, especially the firing squad—described on one occasion by Chet Grant to Riordan's chagrin, as having produced "desultory firing." Bob Riordan and I enjoyed a close personal relationship, based on our mutual devotion to Professor Cooney. In the lowest ebb of the enrollment crisis—still not as critical as projected—Bob and I, encouraged and accompanied by our wives, drove for several weeks through the East, visiting high schools and prep schools which had been basic contributors of students. The military academies were Bob's prize targets. We took quite a bit of criticism for previous lack of contacts with these schools, and our wives could not have found the exhausting trip as enjoyable as it looked. But from that trip on—we never really went into other possible factors—enrollment turned upward again and acquired a permanent pressure of surplus applicants, except during World War II.

The Congregation of Holy Cross and the University were backing the new Living Endowment program of the association. Local clubs seemed more active.

Father O'Donnell announced a great benefaction to the University, the gift of $200,000 from Edward N. Hurley, non-alumni member of the Board of Lay Trustees, for the erection of a building for the College of Commerce. Hurley, vitally interested in commerce, especially foreign trade, had long been involved in the creation and development of the Notre Dame program. The gift added to the optimism of Notre Dame's future, while the rest of the nation pursued an unhappier course. A Chicago architect, Graham, was retained at Hurley's suggestion.

Possibly unrelated to this trustee gift, which was a forerunner of many to follow, the University announced the increase in the Board of Lay Trustees from 12 to 16. Two of the newly created four members would be alumni, to hold the 50-50 balance.

Father O'Donnell had been constantly concerned with the academic progress of the University and its academic and cultural impact. Frederick Kenkel, a leader of the Central Verein, a German society for the advancement of social science, was the 1930 Laetare Medalist. The presentation of the medal was made by Father Francis Wenninger, dean of the Notre Dame Science school, at the diamond jubilee convention of the Verein in Baltimore.

Hilaire Belloc was one of Father O'Donnell's first hopes as a distinguished visting lecturer. Disappointing factors prevented the realization of this mutually desired goal. He did succeed in bringing to the campus for six weeks the great and popular Gilbert K. Chesterton. Guglielmo Marconi, inventor of wireless and radio, was awarded an honorary doctorate at Notre Dame in a special convocation in 1933, recalling the fact of Prof. Jerome Greene'e first successful duplication in the United States of Marconi's accomplishment. William Butler Yeats, Irish literary giant, was a campus lecturer. But Father O'Donnell's own stature was itself a constant stimulus to faculty and students. Among Chesterton's comments I like to recall was one made to me in an interview. I had mentioned the movement for continuing education among alumni. He said he was very interested in this and would like to come back to Notre Dame to take part in such a program.

The fund-raising program was reflected in recommendations in the *Alumnus* for gifts to Notre Dame through estate planning. Features continued to cover the history and traditions of Notre Dame, the University's present problems and virtues, and the now quite explicit plans for its growth in the years ahead. The Law Building and the Commerce Building dramatized the realitites of what had been dreams only a short time ago. A minor, but symbolical, contribution to the growing concept, was the design of a new University coat-of-arms at the request of Father O'Donnell. Designed by a Harvard artist, the official insignia, which remains a part of the University Seal, was carried in its gold and blue designs as a color insert in the *Alumnus*.

In February, 1931, some evidence of increasing financial pressure was the appointment of a layman, Clifford Collins, a Boston accountant, as business manager and comptroller of the University.

The Notre Dame alumni secretary was named general chairman of the 1931 convention of the National Catholic Alumni Federation, being held in Chicago at the invitation of the Notre Dame Club of Chicago. The Notre Dame secretary also held a similar post that year for the American Alumni Council, whose convention was being held in Atlanta. This also was the year a second son was born. Happily, there was youth and faith all around me and no time for worry or pessimism. It was a full year.

In March, 1931, the University carried the announcement that Maginnis and Walsh had been retained to design two large residence halls near the campus entrance. Similar in collegiate gothic design, materials and size, to house 500 students, the total cost was estimated at $800,000. In appreciation of alumni support, one of these halls was to be called Alumni Hall, in keeping with the long planned Old Students Hall of the association's earlier dreams, a dream deferred when the expected fulfillment was abandoned for a change in name to Howard Hall, as mentioned before.

The 1929 season had witnessed a national championship football team, but it had also witnessed the illness of Knute Rockne, sometimes coaching his champions from a wheelchair. The 1930 season had witnessed the opening of the new stadium, Rockne had requested that the new stadium be called the Notre Dame Stadium, shutting off the natural efforts of admirers to designate it in his honor. The schedules for the near future were outstanding. Revenues continued good. The 1929 game attendance was up some 130,000 above the 1920 figure, and the 1930 attendance, in spite of the economic reverse, dropped very little.

In April, against the preceding background of progress, the *Alumnus* announced in bulletin form the death of Knute K. Rockne '14, in a plane crash in Kansas. The following issue of the magazine was devoted entirely to the campus, national and world impact that the death of this great alumnus made.

The details of Rockne's life and death are familiar to all alumni and friends. Books have been written on this alone. The press has contained unprecedented coverage of a man who was, indeed, a legend in his own time and a legend whose interest has continued through generations since his death.

Immediately, newspapers, through their sports columnists and pages, began the discussion of commemorating Rockne and some of the columns were opened for contributions. Hundreds of small contributions began pouring in from alumni and friends, and from strangers—the "synthetic alumni" who were largely the creation of the brilliance of the Rockne era of Notre Dame football. The University appointed a committee with the cooperation of Frank Hering and Father O'Donnell to study a

fitting memorial. A statement was made that no funds would be
solicited and that the memorial would be created from the
voluntary contributions.

Father John F. O'Hara, prefect of religion, had sent out his
first *Religious Survey of Alumni* questionnaire. Life seemed to
be going on. But the fears that the public relations values of
football, its increasing revenues, and the loss of the coach who
dominated sports in America, and whose influence was extending into other fields, would bring substantial problems to Notre
Dame must have existed. Rockne had begun an association with
the Studebaker Corporation which augmented his income and,
with outstanding performance in the field of sales, seemed to
secure his future. When he decided to fly to the West Coast, it
was in pursuit of arrangements based on the filming of a story
about Notre Dame, hinging on his remarkable career and the
teams he had produced. It would have been another lucrative
area.

Alumni Association respect on the campus, and appreciation
for the *Alumnus*, reached an important milestone in that spring
of 1931, when John F. Cushing, a 1906 classmate of Father
O'Donnell, wrote to the President:

> Being deeply impressed with "The Needs of the University"
> as so clearly set forth by you in the *Alumnus* of January,
> 1930, and because I find at Notre Dame the conditions that
> make for the two-fold training of great engineers in all the
> departments of engineering, a technical training that ranks
> with the best and a training in character nowhere excelled,
> and because I feel I owe Notre Dame a debt of gratitude
> which I can never fully discharge, I ask you to accept from
> me a gift of $300,000 toward the erection of a hall of
> engineering to serve the immediate needs of the College of
> Engineering, and to meet the expectations of older men like
> me who confidently look back to Notre Dame to produce the
> men that are to carry on.

Notre Dame had allowed John Cushing to complete his last
year of engineering study when family finances could not afford
it. This was the debt to which he referred, the 1905 favor of
Father John W. Cavanaugh. Some of his classmates were now
partners in his business. And his firm hired Notre Dame men
periodically. His sons has come to Notre Dame. These were the
bases for his confidence in the training.

The commencement address in June, 1931, was given by
Angus McDonald '00, distinguished president of the Southern
Pacific Railroad. He had been a football monogram man in

1899. As an alumnus and later a lay trustee, he had been a patron of the sports program, an ardent admirer of Rockne. The choice for the commencement honor was fitting. Among the things McDonald said, of alumni import, were these: " ... There are thousands who, like myself, think today of Notre Dame as a home of great teachers. It is not so much a place where all that is known is taught, as a place where great minds, generous hearts and noble souls are gathered to offer their wisdom, their love and their faith towards the development in young men of the worthy ideals of right living and perfect manhood."

The miracle probably was, at that time, that Notre Dame and the Association had come so far, were so free from crises until Rockne's death, and met that crisis so effectively, in a sense, without losing stride toward the greatness already on the horizon.

XXVII

Depression

The economic depression which gripped the United States was not without a brighter side for Notre Dame. With no serious decrease in enrollment, the University suddenly found its regular income possessed increasing purchasing power. Faculty salaries, which had been a major hardship in the period before the crash, now loomed as credit priorities in the South Bend community. The University and its faculty attained first class citizenship in the neighborhood.

In the silence of curtailed business and industry, the noise of construction on the Notre Dame campus made waves heard across the nation. The St. Joseph Valley building trades have credited the University as almost the sole means then of their survival. And the magnificent buildings which Father Charles O'Donnell completed along the southern front of the campus, east of the South Dining Hall, remain an impressive monument to his administrative ability and to the economic wisdom of his advisors, including the lay trustees.

But there were other areas of depression which did not spare Notre Dame.

The administration did not have faith in the ability of the small contributions coming in toward the Rockne memorial to achieve a major goal. The fieldhouse need was an urgent one. So, in 1931, the University announced the formation of a Rockne Memorial Association, its goal to be some $800,000 to erect a Memorial Fieldhouse to commemorate Knute Rockne and his broad interest, as director of athletics, in all campus sports—varsity and interhall—and in the physical development of the individual non-athlete student. A committee composed of Frank Hering, J. Arthur Haley, G.A. Farabaugh, Vitus Jones,

A.R. Erskine, Paul Hoffman, Clifford Collins, Father James Burns, Father Michael Mulcaire (University vice president), J.E. Armstrong and Father Charles O'Donnell was appointed. This was a committee with all the necessary know-how to pursue such a program.

With the prospect of fund-raising emphasis, and in recognition of his studies and advocacy of the "Living Endowment Plan," Frank Hayes '14, was elected president of the association at the 1931 reunion, with Clarence E. "Pat" Manion '22, South Bend, as his vice president. Father John MacNamara '97, a diocesan priest from Mt. Clemens, Mich., and a long devoted alumnus, was named honorary president. Walter Duncan remained as treasurer, Frank E. Hering was retiring president, and directors were Harry Miller, Paul McGannon, John F. O'Connell '13, Chicago and Robert E. Lynch, '03, Green Bay, Wis.

The *Alumnus* pointed out editorially the great eras of the association—1868-1908, 1908-1923, 1923 to this point in 1931 when a great new era seemed to open. Frank Hering, in retiring, outlined weaknesses in the association. He recommended a reorganization of the association, to give the alumni board more authority. He suggested the creation of districts, recognizing local clubs and alumni population needs, each to have a district governor. A committee was appointed to draft amendments to the Constitution to pursue this suggestion. Two things stood out as familiar handicaps—the association's programs had to be financed entirely by the alumni, and the 1931 treasurer's report showed total receipts of under $15,000—a little short of the year's expenditures. The secretary's report explained the expense increase—new staff and equipment necessitated to adopt the "Living Endowment" plan. Special issues of the *Alumnus* had been published to recognize the dedication of the Stadium, and to memorialize Knute Rockne. Seven new clubs had been organized. The second Council of Local Clubs was convened at the 1931 commencement-reunion. The alumni office had cooperated with Father O'Hara in his first religious survey of the alumni.

The problem was clear. A sound and expanding association program was in need of more money. The most experienced leadership to promote the "Living Endowment" was now elected to office. Alumni ticket preference in the new Stadium would be given to alumni contributors. The committee for local clubs, chaired by Frank Fitzsimmons, and including Father J. Hugh O'Donnell, C.S.C., Dudley Shively, South Bend; Henry Dockweiler, Los Angeles; Joseph Nulty, New Jersey; Alfred Slaggert, Saginaw; Hugh O'Donnell, New York; George W. Burkitt, Texas and Patrick E. Burke, New Orleans, gave a concrete report. Three model constitutions, one for large, one for medium and one for small clubs, were submitted. And the committee had drawn up 21 sound suggestions for club activities.

Conditions had never seemed better for the association to realize its potential. Instead, the Rockne Memorial Committee, chaired by A.R. Erskine, announced that the Rockne Memorial could not depend on the contributions from unofficial sources, and that it had employed professional fund-raising counsel to organize a nationwide campaign. A national organization was detailed, with Erskine as chairman, Frank Hayes as a chairman of organization, Art Haley as treasurer and chairman of lists, Father Mulcaire as chairman of speakers, Paul Hoffman as chairman of ways and means with J.E. Armstrong as secretary. Sixteen geographical districts had been organized. Plans for an $800,000 fieldhouse were announced.

President Frank Hayes issued an appeal to alumni to continue paying dues, but it was evident that the major program of the association had in effect been suspended by the imposition of the Rockne Memorial campaign. On top of this frustration, the professional counsel attempted to put the national standards formula fund-raising shoe on the Notre Dame foot. The first segment of the gift campaign was to be for very large gifts—of which few were likely under the circumstances from a still young, largely modest economic alumni body. The circle of afflu-ent friends of Notre Dame was not yet that wide. The broad-based small gifts were, by formula, to be sought last, as a cleanup campaign. This unpopular plan brought no fund-raising success, but it brought rumbles of complaints—the Stadium should be re-named Rockne, the fieldhouse was not a proper symbol of Rockne's great career in football, and—most damaging—Rockne had made millions for the University through his teams, why should a memorial to him be a burden on contributors outside the University? After raising only about 25 per cent of the goal, and in the face of worsening economic conditions and the rising rejection of the memorial program, the campaign was sus-pended. Later, when the depression years were improving, and when Father John F. O'Hara, C.S.C. had become President, a home-grown committee, consisting largely of the campus mem-bers of the original organization, succeed in raising as much in a modest revival of the effort as the original had achieved with all its fanfare. It was still only half the need, but in tribute to Rockne, and in recognition of the merits of the building as planned, the present Rockne Memorial was constructed.

The economic reverses had had another constructive result. Alumni who had been caught in or who witnessed the transient nature of material wealth were more than ever aware of the values Notre Dame had taught. The request for the *Religious Bulletin* from alumni was the largest single response Father O'Hara received to his survey questionnaire. And his encouragement of the Communion Breakfast as a local club event blossomed into a major national program soon after. Retreats were also suggested as club programs, and although they proved difficult to time in the small membership clubs, many were held, some annually.

In 1931, "The Spirit of Notre Dame," the moving picture for which Rockne was flying to the West Coast when he was killed, was announced as continuing as a tribute to his memory. Mrs. Rockne and Father Lawrence Broughal, C.S.C., went to the West Coast to aid in the historical facts of the picture. The Four Horsemen, and other prominent monogram men, including men from the 1929-30 teams, offered their services in the picture.

A national recognition of Notre Dame's academic side came in December, 1931 when Du Pont announced the discovery of synthetic rubber which was developed into neoprene, the result of basic research by Father Julius Nieuwland '99.

Falling back on its non-fund raising activities, the *Alumnus* pointed out to its readers the growth of the campus publication. Their variety and quality were tributes to student competence. The University was also the home of Father Nieuwland's high regarded *American Midland Naturalist*, the Catholic weekly magazine *The Ave Maria*, and the *Annals of Our Lady of Lourdes*, an adjunct to the Grotto of Lourdes on the campus.

One of the results of Father O'Hara's religious survey of alumni was that, from a high 20 per cent response, there was a high alumni regard for daily communion as the outstanding feature of their life on the campus.

The *Alumnus* pointed out the expanding pressures of the office, in contacting 42 class secretaries and a new record 66 local clubs. The clubs had been intensively cultivated by the Alumni Association, and were greatly stimulated by the biennial Council of Clubs. Dues had not increased. A meager $5,000 from the "Living Endowment" in 1931 had been turned over to the University. Father O'Donnell announced that this fund would be used for the main altar in Alumni Hall, for the cataloging of the Dante Library and for a course of lectures by Hilaire Belloc then under negotiation. Father O'Donnell expressed pleasure for this first year's "Living Endowment" help, and the allocation told alumni how significant such unrestricted University annual income could be.

The financial plight of the association was so discouraging to the June meeting of the Alumni Board that future progress and planning was left entirely to the new board. Five new clubs had been organized—Sioux City, Kane County, Ill., Kansas, Bridgeport, Conn. and Waterbury, Conn. A new program of sending names of student applicants to the local clubs or to individuals in non club areas was instituted. Contacts with high schools were increasing. The first building given by an alumnus had been dedicated as the John F. Cushing, C.E. '06, Hall of Engineering. Father O'Donnell, in his alumni banquet speech, was optimistic about the University. He recognized the pressures of the recent endowment campaign among alumni, the association's modest appeal to alumni for the Lay Faculty Award fund, the approach to alumni in the sale of boxes in the new Stadium, and most recently the Rockne Memorial campaign. He announced the official discontinuance of the Rockne Memorial campaign. None of these had helped the association's operational budget and were in almost direct conflict with the "Living Endowment" which President Frank Hayes had purused so valiantly. Possibly the most discouraging development came when Frank Hayes offered to come to the campus as director of the "Living Endowment," at a salary small by comparisons with his previous banking post. Father O'Donnell, sensitive by nature and disliking anything which bordered on begging or "huckstering", let it be known he thought Hayes' motive in pushing the "Living Endowment" was to create a job at Notre Dame. The opportunity was lost and the board faced a difficult dilemma.

The spirit of alumni progress had also been evident when the reunion weekend featured a general gathering of Commerce alumni, at the invitation of Dean James E. McCarthy, to signal the opening of the College of Commerce, which had been dedicated appropriately on May 17 at the meeting of the lay trustees, of which the donor, Edward N. Hurley, was a member.

But the flesh was still weak.

The Alumni Board that met this critical 1932-33 period was composed of Father John W. Cavanaugh, C.S.C., with his experience and serenity and persuasiveness, as honorary president;

Clarence E. "Pat" Manion, popular alumnus, lawyer, a rising figure in Hoosier politics and an eloquent orator, as president and Timothy P. Galvin '16, Hammond lawyer, orator, and a leader in the Knights of Columbus, as vice president. Directors were Frank Hayes, James E. Sanford '15, T. Paul McGannon '07, John F. O'Connell '13, Robert E. Lynch '03 and Hugh A. O'Donnell '94. In an effort to involve the new alumni, discouraged by the economic world they were entering, George Higgins '32, was made a director for a one-year term.

The Summer School attendance dropped slightly. But the association gave support to the newly organized Women's Club of the Summer Sessions. Sister Agnes Alma, O.S.D., of Newburgh, N.Y., succeeded Sister M. Fidelis, O.S.U., of Toledo, as president of the alumnae organization.

This is not an autobiography, but this was the year that pressures came close to the breaking point on both personal and association fronts. With three small sons and responsibility for a costly serious and long illness in the immediate family, with the expanding of programs that increasingly pinched the association budget and with the University conscious of still deepening depression around it, at one point Pat Manion and I agreed that the situation was intolerable. We advised Father O'Donnell that we proposed to close or seriously curtail operations of the Alumni Association. It was in the great tradition of "la vie intime" that we were told in kind and reassuring words that we could not be allowed to do that and that the University would find a way to extend the help we needed to continue.

The *Alumnus* gave up the separate covers which had marked a progress pleateau, but retained the news of the clubs and classes for an alumni readership more than ever mindful of the values of Notre Dame and fellow Notre Dame men.

Frank Lloyd succeeded Clifford Collins as comptroller, when ill health forced the competent Boston creator of the campus office to retire. Visiting lecturer William Butler Yeats brought a great reputation to the campus but his secular approach to Ireland left many of the ardent priests and scholars on the campus cool to his fame.

Some of the tradition of Notre Dame, in fact one of its richest assets, was contained in the *Alumnus* story on the death of Martin McCue, long-time dean of Engineering. Remaining on the campus, in the winter of 1932, Professor Francis Ackerman had 46 years of service; Professor William Benitz, 37 years; Professor Knowles Smith, 27 years; Professor James Hines, 25 years; Francis Kervick, 24 years; Col. William Hoyes, 50 years; Professor Edward Maurus, 40 years; Jose Caparo, 25 years; Professor William Farrell, 26 years, and Professor Robert Greene, 31 years. This was the Notre Dame which transcended its colleges and departments. These were men dedicated to an institution first and to a discipline second. These were, with many before and after, the familiar men who taught the alumni of Notre Dame "not only how to make a living, but how to live."

When Col. Hoynes died in this year, Father Cavanaugh in his eulogy reminded his bearers that while the colonel was dean of the Law School, the net income to the University from all sources was seldom as much as $20,000. Col. Hoynes, he said, had worked for a salary similar to that usually paid to domestic help. Yet he had saved and given to the University $30,000 in savings and investments from these lean years, to aid in the education of priests of Holy Cross. After his death it was discovered that the colonel still had unsuspected resources. He had been sensitive to the neglect of some of the younger priests during his last years on the campus and, with probably a professional tongue in cheek, he left no will. His beloved profession used up most the estate funds in the litigation which followed.

In May, 1923, the *Alumnus* announced another major page in alumni giving. Augustus Meehan '90, Chattanooga, created in his will six scholarships to Notre Dame, which were to be awarded on a competitive basis to students in six Southern states—Georgia, Tennessee, Kentucky, Alabama, South Carolina and Virginia. These were states from which relatively few students came to Notre Dame, and the bequest established a constant representation by at least six outstanding boys from this great Southern area.

The Alumni Board expressed its appreciation to the University for its help in the 1932 Universal Notre Dame Night. The response had been stimulating to the University in the light of continuing depression conditions.

The 1933 commencement, in spite of the depression, was outstanding. The Fourth Annual Council of Clubs was held. Class Reunions were regularly scheduled, and the Class of 1928, which was to remain one of the most active and effective classes in the years to follow, made its Fifth Reunion memorable by setting a new reunion record of attendance with 100 members registering.

Feature of the commencement was the golden jubilee of the Laetare Medal. John McCormack was the popular selection for the medal, and headed a brilliant program in the Gymnasium which featured former Medalists Charles D. Maginnis, Dr. Stephen Maher, Margaret Anglin, Dr. James J. Walsh, Jack Spalding and Edward N. Hurley. Alfred E. Smith, Father Charles Coughlin, Governor Paul McNutt and Indiana Senator James Watson, were among other distinguished guests. Father Charles L. O'Donnell was present at only part of the ceremonies because of the illness which was to bring about his death a year later.

A popular young Irish priest, Father Michael Mulcaire, C.S.C., had been vice president under Father O'Donnell. A brogue and a temper tended to obscure the doctorate he held in economics and the effectiveness of his administration of his service as chairman of the Athletic Committee and in other important campus areas. The unerring ability of the campus to condense an image, however harsh the result, designated the administration of O'Donnell and Mulcaire as the "Poet and Peasant." Only the poet was appropriate. In any event, as Father O'Donnell's illness recurred, the Congregation chose to make Father O'Hara, former dean of commerce, a fine administrator and a priest of national regard, a popular figure among alumni and students, vice president of the University, replacing Father Mulcaire.

There was unrest in other areas. Heartly "Hunk" Anderson and Jack Chevigny, hero of the 1928 "win one for the Gipper" legend, had been made coaches of football, succeeding the irreplaceable Rockne. Both had assisted him and were dramatic in their devotion to Rockne while he lived. To bolster this difficult transition Father O'Donnell had brought back Jess Harper who had guided an older Notre Dame into big-time football. Harper, a successful cattleman after leaving Notre Dame, was not up to the changed world of college athletics to which he returned. Anderson emerged as the senior and logical head coach. The spirit, and perhaps the preparation, of Rockne carried the 1931 team to a creditable 6-2-1 season, marred by the unfortunate and allegedly unnecessary loss to Southern California 14-16 in the last minutes of a game in the new Stadium, and with a loss 0-12 to traditional rival Army the following week in Yankee Stadium. Rockne's death and the depression combined for a loss in total attendance in 1931 of 108,000. These figures continued to slide downward as the 1932 team had a 7-2-0 fall, losing to Pittsburgh 0-12 after scoring 177 points against its first three opponents, Haskell, Drake and Carnegie Tech. When the 1933 team played to total attendance of 178,000, the lowest since 1923, and in a 3-5-1 record lost to Carnegie Tech, Pittsburgh, Navy, Purdue and Southern California, tying with Kansas and recording a season's total of only 32 points against a rather creditable low opponents 80, the administration took reasonable alarm.

The 1933-34 association officers had been chosen with Byron Kanaley '04, as honorary president; M. Harry "Red" Miller '10, Cleveland, president, and Frank C. Walker '09, vice president. Directors were: Arthur Carmody '15, Shreveport, La.; John F. O'Connell '13, Chicago; Robert E. Lynch '03, Green Bay; Hugh A. O'Donnell '94, New York; Fred L. Steers '11, Chicago; Francis A. Werner '33, New London, Wis. and retiring president Manion.

The secretary, in the absence of any appreciable association income and the assumption of $5,000 debt by the University, was asked to assume the dual role of secretary-treasurer, and the years of helpful, competent, and often thankless, service of Walter Duncan were ended, with expressions of deep appreciation.

Four new clubs were reported—Dallas; LaPorte, Ind.; Okalahoma City, and Rhode Island. The alumni secretary had made one intensive six-week tour among high schools during the year, covering 15 alumni club meetings on the same circuit. Later, the secretary and registrar made a second six-week tour as reported earlier. The drop in payment of dues was offset to some extent by hundreds of letters from alumni telling of their regret in not being able to respond and their appreciation of the association program. It was a key factor in the University's continuing cooperation.

One of the phenomena of the depression was the 1933 booking of the Notre Dame Glee Club by a circuit of theaters, opening with an appearance at the Capitol Theater in New York, and closing in the Hippodrome in Cleveland, Ohio. Joseph J. Casasanta '23, was the popular director of the club. The tour received excellent reviews. The Glee Club had achieved national recognition with its first sound recording in 1926, in Hollywood, for the sensational new development, sound pictures. The campus competition in music between the Glee Club and the slightly more restricted Moreau Seminary Choir resulted in two consistently high quality singing groups. Joe Casasanta was

also the director of the band, which achieved high musical
ratings. It was in 1935, when the marching bands of the Big Ten
made a memorable impact on Notre Dame authorities, that the
Notre Dame Band was asked to incorporate the military adjunct. Casasanta was not happy with the devaluation of music,
as he viewed it. In addition to his work with the Band and the
Glee Club, Joe Casasanta, in the old tradition, taught regular
classes in the Department of Music. And in an area above and
beyond the call of duty, he composed the music for most of the
marching songs of Notre Dame which followed the original
"Victory March" of the Sheas. Like the famous brothers, Joe
was a product of Massachusetts.

Another long tie with the past was spotlighted by the golden
jubilee of Brother Cyprian, C.S.C. With a stern demeanor, and a
drill sergeant's teaching techniques, Brother Cyprian had turned
out generations of able accountants who competed successfully
with the alumni of the nation's top colleges. In addition to this
demanding task, Brother Cyprian had been in charge of Washington Hall, supervising its recreational hall, and the use of the
theater for visiting lectures, concerts and dramatic events, and
the more challenging rehearsals and performances of the campus
organizations. Few alumni exposed to Brother Cyp as students
failed to look him up on campus visits.

Father E. Vincent Mooney '16, a former athlete and popular
rector, the priest who baptized Knute Rockne in 1925, was
appointed director of the new Catholic Youth Bureau of the
National Catholic Council of Men in Washington, D.C. This
appointment recalls two important pages in University history,
of alumni involvement and interst, and passed over rather quietly in the manner of campus revolutions in days past. The first
was the Boy Guidance program of graduate studies instituted at
Notre Dame in the mid-'20s by the University in cooperation
with the Supreme Council of the Knights of Columbus. It was a
course designed to provide large boy organizations badly needed
leaders who would have had Catholic training. It was largely the
concept of Brother Barnabas. Funds soon became a problem
with both the Knights of Columbus and the University, and
details were allowed to end what could have been a major
contributor to the prevention of the rise of juvenile delinquency
just as that national problem was beginning to assume major
proportions. But the relatively few alumni of that program
proved over the years the inherent merits of its purposes and its
quality. Catholic organizations were not yet coordinated to

absorb the graduates, but the Boy Scouts, Boys Clubs, Red Cross and similar groups, including the Knights of Columbus, profited from the experiment. Father Mooney had been one of the enthusiasts.

The other quiet revolution hinged about a program which the Congregation undertook at St. Thomas College, St. Paul, Minn., in conjunction with the archbishop. I have no documentation at hand but the problem as alumni generally understood it involved an original agreement that if the Holy Cross priests could revitalize the College and Military Academy at St. Thomas, the archdiocese would turn it over to the Congregation, for due consideration. Father Charles O'Donnell's administration at Notre Dame was dealt a serious blow when Father Matthew Schumacher was assigned to St. Thomas as its president in 1928. With him went Father William A. Bolger, the University's leading economist. Father Thomas Crumley, a philosopher whom Harvard had sought, Father William Cunningham, outstanding authority in Catholic educational circles, and Father Vince Mooney, the latter to be commandant of the Military Academy. At the end of five years, in spite of the depression, Thomas seemed to be a sound opportunity, and the priests assigned there urged the foreclosing of the option. A new archbishop had succeeded in the meantime and the expected permanent arrangement was, for whatever private reasons, cancelled. The Holy Cross priests involved were withdrawn from St. Thomas but echoes of the revolution carried throughout their remaining years.

For practical administration, Father John O'Hara became the Acting President of Notre Dame in the fall of 1933. The new responsibilities again called on his administrative talents and his broad grasp of Catholic educational principles. The duties reduced his contacts with his beloved boys, who had found him counselor and confessor on a grueling schedule that began at 5 A.M. and frequently did not end—including his preparation of the *Religious Bulletin*—until 1 or 2 A.M. He was one of those rare geniuses who had unbelievable vitality which required only a few hours of sleep. This, and his prodigious memory, would have given those who now wish to stamp out cigarettes a bad time. Father O'Hara was seldom without one. This is only a token instance arguing against his reputation as a rigid disciplinarian—in Father John W. Cavanaugh's administration, cigarettes were not allowed on the campus (it said in the rule book). The students' nickname for Father O'Hara indicated the informal respect which the boys attached to his prefect of religion role. He was called "The Pope," and he almost made it. Father O'Hara was himself informal, answering his own phone and doorbell after he was Cardinal Archbishop of Philadelphia. As prefect of religion at Notre Dame, his door in Sorin Hall was always open to a student who needed him.

His new duties brought him now more contact with alumni, his students of earlier times. A meeting of the St. Joseph Valley Club heard the new vice president admonishing alumni to "Be good Notre Dame men. The three subdivisions are: Be courteous, be loyal, be Catholic." He assumed that the academic University would make them competent in this discipline. He added, "Speaking for the administration I want to tell you that I shall be tickled to death to receive any and all suggestions on how to run the University, the barber shop or the steam plant . . . my private view of executive work is that it consists largely of the ability to recognize and the courage to carry out some other fellow's sound suggestions. I have no particular ambition to be a big-shot, but I want to do the best I can for Notre Dame."

The *Alumnus*, through Father John W. Cavanaugh's page, kept alumni steeped in the older traditions. Father Sorin's many journeys to Europe to secure help for Notre Dame were told. As was the remarkable story of the Curé of Ars prophecy to Father Sorin, on one of those visits, that "Notre Dame would go through 75 years of hardship before blossoming forth in its full strength and vigor." Father Sorin was not alive, but Father John W. Cavanaugh was President, when the diamond jubilee celebration in 1917 bore out this earlier assurance.

In February, 1934, Father O'Hara, as Chairman of the Athletic Board, was instrumental in bringing Elmer Layden '25, to Notre Dame as head football coach and director of athletics. Elmer had been the 165-pound full-back of the All-American Four Horsemen, and had coached at Duquesne in Pittsburgh. He inherited the problems of the transition from the Rockne era, and of the low ebb of the national economy. His recruiting was limited. His players were required to have full entrance requirements and to pay an entrance fee. They were given jobs as part of their scholarships and were required to work at these jobs. The eligibility requirements were those of the surrounding Big Ten and were strictly enforced. Like Rockne, Layden had been an outstanding track man. His administration of athletics was broad and constructive for all branches

of sport. His overall football record, 1934-40, the span of
Father O'Hara's administration, was 47 games won, 13 games
lost, 3 games tied—a highly creditable .783. But Layden made
contributions of even greater and more lasting values. His public
relations with Notre Dame opponents was outstanding. Professional jealousy or just plain caution had not allowed Rockne to
test the competition of some of his major confreres—Zuppke,
Yost and other reluctant Big Ten and intersectional conference
leaders. The anti-bowl policy made it even more difficult. Layden became very friendly with Yost and Zuppke, obviously not
because he lost easily. His 1935 victory over the Ohio State
team in Columbus was recently voted the most outstanding
football game of the century. The Michigan rivaly, suspended
since 1909, was resumed in 1942 shortly after Layden's term.
Illinois was already a frequent opponent by that time. He had a
dozen All-Americans on his seven teams. He built back attendance at Notre Dame football games to a season's average of
415,000 against the 350,000 three-year season's average of his
predecessors. Only Rockne's 1929 and 1930 teams had drawn
more attendance than Layden's 1940 season. He was a popular
Alumni Club speaker. Layden's contributions to Notre Dame
and its athletics was a major one. This is after discounting any
classmate prejudices.

The Alumni Board in 1934 stressed alumni involvement in
contacting prospecting students for Notre Dame. Here was a
valuable contribution to the University which cost the alumnus
nothing but time and effort.

Father O'Hara, Dean McCarthy, Dean Konop and Father
Bolger spoke to the 1934 National Catholic Alumni Federation
convention in Chicago, based on the theme of "Social Justice."
The *Alumnus* published these talks, and pursued continuing
education as a desirable program for alumni, to emante from
Notre Dame.

A major step forward in association administration was announced in 1934. Wiliam R. Dooley '26, joined the alumni
office as assistant alumni secretary and managing editor of the
Alumnus,. Three girls and a parttime student were assisting.
More intensive pursuit of the magazine, clubs, classes, placement and records followed. Bill Dooley was a Cooney journalism alumnus, a man of great talent and great integrity, devoted
to Notre Dame and its teachings. His corporate experience
attracted him to the placement service, which the depression
and office pressures had combined to obscure. His competence

in this work led eventually to his selection as director of the University Placement Service, when Notre Dame recognized the status and importance of the program. Bill's death was another of the serious losses to the University and the association's programs.

Father Charles L. O'Donnell died on the morning after June, 1934, commencement, in the sixth year of his Presidency, as though faithful to his responsibilities to the end. The commencement was outstanding, with the apostolic delegate and Secretary of State Cordell Hull as featured speakers.

The poet-President had written:

> ". . . . . .when I go otherwhere -
> An unreturning journey - I would leave
> Some whisper of a song in these old oaks,
> A footfall lingering till some distant summer
> Another singer down these paths may stray -
> The destined one a golden future cloaks -
> And he may love them, too, this graced newcomer,
> And may remember that I passed this way."

Notre Dame remembers.

XXVIII

An Era
of Persisting Pressures

Before pursuing the narrative of Notre Dame alumni development, let me repeat here that I am not undertaking a history of the University. Father Arthur Hope's *Notre Dame—100 Years* does a very thorough job on the history of Notre Dame from 1842 to 1942. I am skipping lightly over the athletic history, because books have been written on its many phases and heroes. The press, radio and television have informed alumni of the past, present and future glories of the sports tradition. Books have been written on Father Zahm, on Cardinal O'Hara, and one has just been published as I write this, dealing with the 20 years of Father Hesburgh's administration. Father Charles O'Donnell's poems have been collected and edited by his nephew, Father Charles Carey, C.S.C. '31.

What I wish is to trace the involvement of alumni—on and off the campus—individually and in the Alumni Association, as they have contributed to the University of Notre Dame. Even with this limited purpose, much will be of necessity missed. First, there is too much to relate in detail. Second, many fine contributions have been shrouded in modesty, or in mistakenly defined cause-effect relationships. Again, my major goal is to put the alumni into the proper perspective of their roles in bringing Notre Dame through the years of growth and change. The identity of past alumni performance is of the essence of the University today. But even more importantly, without this clear image of the alumni role as it is an integral part of Notre Dame, the future of the University can be greatly and adversely affected by challenges which could not prevail against the cumulative strength and momentum of the very tangible force we refer to as "Notre Dame spirit."

294

Father O'Hara, as he assumed the presidency, was given a strong right arm in the person of his vice president, Father J. Hugh O'Donnell, C.S.C. '16, a football monogram man, who had filled a lively and demanding term as prefect of discipline, followed by a term as president of St. Edward's University in Austin, Tex. Father O'Hara and Father O'Donnell were popular with alumni, and few administrators have been better acquainted with the members of the association. The dynamic qualities of both men guaranteed the progress of Notre Dame, even in the dark depth of the depression.

Graduate work was trying to flourish in the limited facilities of many departments. Father Wenninger, dean of science during Father O'Hara's presidency, was the personal patron of the successful premedical program. And he fostered the pioneering work of James Arthur Reyniers '28, whose talents in the field of biological engineering led to the perfection of germ-free animals and conditions, which are now moving scientific and medical research and practice ahead in many areas. The experiments were begun in fruit jars in the basement of old Science Hall. Reyniers was persuaded to remain after his graduation. Father O'Hara in 1937 erected the Kirsch-Wenninger Building to house the Laboratories of Bacteriology, popularly identified as Lobund. At the same time, Professor Theodore Just was pursuing the work of the great Father Nieuwland in botany, and editing the *American Midland Naturalist*. Reyniers was later charged with so much of the responsibility for fund-raising connected with his research that, in spite of new facilities, and the designation of his laboratories as an institute, he resigned to continue his experiments in Florida. The progress at the University has continued under the direction of former associates and students, and brought in eminent researchers from around the world. The present Lobund program is housed in the larger facilities of the Galvin Life Sciences complex, commemorating the generous interest of the Paul V. Galvin family. In an effort to assist Reyniers in fund-raising, a professional in the field, alledgedly a specialist in the area of science, was employed. The program failed, discouraging both Reyniers and the University, and widening the gap that the dual pressures of research and public relations had created between Reyniers and his alma mater. Just before his death, Notre Dame awarded him an honorary doctorate (1967).

In 1933 Father Philip Moore, C.S.C. '24, returned from France where he had spent three and one-half years in the Ecoles des Chartes, pursuing medieval studies. His appointment

as secretary of the Committee on Graduate Studies resulted in
the advent of many competent professors, in the opening of
new avenues of graduate study leading to doctorates in philosophy, physics, mathmatics and politics, and in the later creation
of the Medieval Institute. Father Moore instituted the *Publications in Medieval Studies.* It was in this era that brilliant young
faculty members often built new equipment which the University could not afford to buy for them.

The Alumni Board elected in 1934 for the ensuing year was
composed of alumni well acquainted with the new University
President. Frank Walker '09, one of the prominent members of
the Franklin Roosevelt New Deal family, was the honorary
president of the association. Timothy P. Galvin '16, Hammond
attorney, was the new president, an alumnus whose Catholicity
was reflected in his prominence in the Supreme Council of the
Knights of Columbus. Bernard J. Voll '17, an active civic leader
in South Bend was vice president. Directors were Grattan Stanford '04, Robert E. Lynch '03, Hugh A. O'Donnell '94, Fred L.
Steers '11, James E. Deery '10, retiring president Harry Miller
and the representative of the Class of 1934, James S. Kearns.

The June meeting heard the enthusiastic report on the 10th
Universal Notre Dame Night, now an institution. "Living Endowment" was muted in the stringent economy of the year.
Payment of dues remained low. Alumni clubs were bursting
with ideas, but sharing the national association's support problems.

The *Alumnus* continued to inspire alumni with the articles on
Notre Dame of the past. N.J. Nealis, a student in 1885, wrote to
Father O'Hara, telling of his memory of being a member of the
Hoynes Light Guards, when that group provided the escort for
the transfer of the body of Orestes Brownson, on its arrival
from Detroit, to the crypt of Sacred Heart Church. Father
Sorin, Nealis added, once took Nealis' father and two small
sisters on a walk about the campus. The little girls' feet became
cold, and Father Sorin himself bathed the chilled feet in a basin
of warm water. The humility of Notre Dame's founder made a
lasting impression.

Sister M. Frederick, C.S.C., succeeded Sister M. Agnes Alma
as president of the women's club in the Summer Session of
1934. Committees on literature, monthly bibliographies of
interest, studies in the teaching field, the *Alumnus Directory*
and a social committee for the year, projects of merit, were
doomed to the serious curtailment of the depression. The Uni-

versity entertained the alumnae at a dinner in this summer, and the *Alumnus* offered to publish book reviews of interest to them, if they would contribute the reviews.

Father O'Hara appointed Thomas J. Barry '25, as director of academic publicity, to relieve the increasing pressures on Joseph S. Petritz '32, already recognized as one of the outstanding sports publicity directors in the college field. Academic publicity as a job was still a bit vague to administrators and faculty. During several interims, between the directors who succeeded me after my original effort in 1925, I was frequently asked to take over the office again until a successor was found. This was of course to be done without added compensation or interference with the increasing burdens of the alumni office. The survival of the University and the Alumni Association, in the face of such juggling, joins the little miracle category. I was young enough to try, and employment at the time carried with it two old traditions—one was not questioning the employer, the other was supporting your family.

The Gogebic Range Club, Ironwood, Mich., was organized in the summer of 1934, after a joint dinner of Saint Mary's and Notre Dame graduates. The good-neighbor policy between Notre Dame and Saint Mary's really predated coexchange and coeducation.

The low state of the economy caused the discontinuance of the *Juggler*. Father O'Hara had frowned frequently on the contemporary humor, in spite of editorial effort to avoid anything in poor taste. Other schools, some of them suffering from excesses in such humor magazines, took this same opportunity to suspend them. The rebirth of the *Juggler* has found its nature altered to a literary magazine. The *Alumnus*, in an editorial (by an old member of the *Juggler* staff), mourned the demise.

In the fall of 1934 the association sent to all Alumni Association members a geographical *Directory of Alumni*. The pall over alumni everywhere was lifted substantially by this service, the reestablishment of old ties between classmates, all enduring similar economic hardships.

And alumni were again stimulated when the Alumni Board, after a November meeting in Chicago, issued through President Tim Galvin a program of activity—continuation of student contacts, continuation of the *Alumnus*, a program to locate and involve non-graduate former students in the association and the clubs, the continuation of Universal Notre Dame Night, to include national radio if possible, visits to clubs by members of the board and by district governors, resumption of effort to collect dues, bringing the intellectual facilities of Notre Dame to alumni through the magazine and campus speakers at club meetings, utilizing the commencement weekend to further alumni programs, and continued affiliations with the professional alumni organizations.

A sad note for alumni was news of the death of Warren A. Cartier '87, whose loyalty was reflected in the history of the Alumni Association from his graduation in 1887 until his death. He had given generously of his resources, time and talents.

In January, 1935, Notre Dame announced a major conference on aeronautical science. The conference was to pay special tribute to Albert F. Zahm '83, pioneer in this now rapidly developing field. Dr. Zahm, a member of the Smithsonian Institute in the field of aeronautics, attended the conference, as did World War I ace Eddie Rickenbacker and Col. William Bishop, his Canadian counterpart. The Bendix Corporation and South Bend aviation industry enthusiasts took a prominent part in the conference.

The appointment of Fred Steers '11, to a committee of the Amateur Athletic Union, offered an opportunity to point out the great service that Steers, a non-Catholic, who had been instrumental in bringing Rockne to Notre Dame, had rendered Notre Dame's sports programs. Steers, a friend of Avery Brundage and administrators of the Big Ten rules, was instrumental in keeping Notre Dame's standards in conformity, and encouraging competition between Notre Dame and Big Ten teams in all sports.

With Father O'Hara and Father Hugh O'Donnell cooperating, the alumni office edited and published an illustrated *Alumnus* supplement showing the campus in its current scope and explaining in text what alumni needed to know to counsel high school students.

The 1934 football banquet reflected the great and lasting influence of Knute Rockne. Principal speaker was Will Rogers, who had earlier intended to come at Rockne's invitation, and who accepted this posthumous opportunity to pay his respects to the great coach. Rogers himself died in 1935 in a plane crash.

And on March 22, another strong alumni tie with the past was transferred to the intangible with the death of Father John W. Cavanaugh, C.S.C. '90, President of Notre Dame from 1905 to 1919. The May issue of the *Alumnus* was a memorial to Father Cavanaugh. The "vie intime" was underscored again with the concurrent death of Brother Leopold, at the age of 98 after 72 years of service to Notre Dame. My generation knew him as the little old man who raked leaves in the large yard of Columba Hall, in our time the "pest house," haven of students with contagious diseases. Brother Leopold as a printer had helped start the *Ava Maria* magazine under Father Sorin in 1865. He taught the University choir for 30 years. But the alumni who knew him most familiarly were the generations who had bought milk or lemonade and cookies from him in the campus candy store. His was another good memory, and his alumni visitors had been legion.

The 1935 Universal Notre Dame Night featured a coast-to-coast broadcast through the cooperation of the Studebaker Corporation. In addition 132 individual radio stations, in the United States, Mexico, Cuba and Rome, consented to recognize the program, usually in conjunction with local alumni or clubs.

Alumni attendance at the June reunions was greater than ever before. It brought up the necessity for developing the Friday night class dinners, separate from the general banquet. Only 16 clubs were represented at the sixth annual council, but this hard core paved the way for revived club activity when the economy should recover, already a trend. Seventy-nine clubs were nominally in existence. Three special editions of the *Alumnus* had been published. In its programs the association was progressing but a $15,000 deficit, covered by the University, was an unhappy note.

The annual meeting of the association appropriately elected Dr. Albert Zahm, honorary president; Bernard Voll, president and Albert J. Galen '96 of Helena, Montana, and George Shuster '15, vice presidents. Directors were Hugh A. O'Donnell '94, Fred L. Steers '11, James E. Deery '10, Don P. O'Keefe '03, Joseph M. Byrne '15, retiring President Tim Galvin, and the new class director, Thomas G. Proctor '35. The latter was the son of Robert Proctor '04, Elkhart.

In 1935, construction was begun on a badly needed Student Infirmary. The structure, designed by Maginnis and Walsh, has remained a major asset to the campus, in both form and function, under the direction of the Sisters of Holy Cross. An original suggestion that the new structure might house guests was soon abandoned as the increase in student need was compounded by the growing occasions and numbers of campus visitors. The Alumni Board was a favored group which was permitted the use of the Infirmary facilities for meetings. This hospitable and congenial contact with the sisters persisted until the Morris Inn was constructed. The on-campus deliberations of the board were productive of the close contacts with administrators, faculty and students which were becoming an important factor in board decisions.

As though the Infirmary's new home had relieved him of a long period of responsibility, Dr. Francis J. Powers, University physician since 1910, died on Sept. 17. He was an alumnus— B.S. '94, M.S. '99. He had taught in the College of Science until 1904 when he entered Northwestern University Medical School.

President Bernard J. Voll announced the emphasis for the year would be revitalization of the clubs and the classes. He felt that the many fine programs of the association could prosper only if strong club and class organization provided bases for them. The friendly, informed, and frequent contacts between the alumni office, President Voll, and the greater administrative liaison of Father Hugh O'Donnell with the association added a strong progress factor.

Father O'Hara announced the advent of six prominent European scholars. The world depression, the growing international spirit in the world, and political unrest in Europe combined to make such prominent men available. Christopher Hollis, English economist and author, was the first. Desmond Fitzgerald, Irish statesman and writer, was the second. Jacques Maritain was expected but health prevented the engagement. The University now has a Jacques Maritain Center where Maritain's voluminous writings are being indexed and cataloged. Etienne Gilson and Arnold Lunn were others announced, as was a return visit by G.K. Chesterton, which did not materialize again because of ill health.

Feature of the sports year was the legendary football game with Ohio State in Columbus. I am sure more alumni can give you score, line-ups and names involved in that classic than can recite the Gettysburg Address. The Notre Dame Club of Central Ohio (Columbus) has never since lost the momentum gained from its organization of that incredible weekend.

In an address on campus radio, by Father Thomas T. McAvoy '25, historian, 1935 was pointed out as the real centenary year of Notre Dame because it was the date, in 1835, when Father Badin and two Sisters of Charity abandoned their orphanage on the Notre Dame site and gave the property to Bishop Bruté of Vincennes. When the bishop visited the property later in 1835, he commented, "The 625 acres of land surrounding the mission house make it a most desirable spot and one soon, I hope, to be occupied by some prosperous institution." Except financially, his vision was embodied in Notre Dame on this 100th anniversary.

Father O'Hara, whose business background and interest sensed the impending economic recovery, outlined Notre Dame's immediate needs. One was the completion of the Rockne Memorial program. Two residence halls were still needed as were a biology building, a fine arts building and a number of specific amounts for research projects and personnel. Notre Dame's clerical faculty was being bolstered by the return of four C.S.C. priests who had completed studies at California Tech, Massachusetts Institute of Technology, University of Chicago and John Hopkins.

The December 1935 *Alumnus* carried a story on the origin and development of the Law School, first Catholic law school in the United States, and with it published the first directory of Notre Dame lawyers. The list provided a strong national identity of the distinguished Notre Dame men in the profession and began a valuable exchange of professional interests.

On Dec. 9, 1935, Notre Dame's lavishly decorated Gymnasium was the site of a convocation honoring the new Commonwealth of the Philippines. The January *Alumnus* published a special supplement containing the addresses. Guest of honor and the recipient of an honorary doctorate was Franklin D. Roosevelt, President of the United States, in the first campus visit by a chief executive. Principal speaker was Hon. Carlos P. Romulo, outstanding Philippine journalist, subsequently one of the leading world statesmen, and a popular and articulate spokesman in the United Nations. The oratory of Romulo stole the show on that historic date at Notre Dame. He also received an honorary doctorate. Another major contribution to the occasion was the appearance of His Eminence, George Cardinal Mundelein of Chicago. An occasional visitor in earlier years, the cardinal had fallen victim to an episcopal weakness which was to plague Notre Dame's relations with the hierarchy on many later occasions—a feeling that the University of Notre Dame, which was pouring Catholic leadership back into a diocese, had no claim on the Catholics of that diocese through rare appeals for voluntary support. Father Hugh O'Donnell was chairman of the committee planning this major occasion. The alumni office was represented on the committee, and William R. Dooley assisted Thomas Barry in the extraordinary publicity pressures of such an occasion. The Athletic Department was enlisted to handle the clamor for tickets, and parking. Superimposed over all the arrangements—a new experience for Notre Dame—were the incredible security measures of the Secret Service. Father O'Hara pointed out that the historic presence of a C.S.C. priest, later Archbishop Peter Hurth, for 20 years in the Philippine Church, and the fact that many students and alumni were from the leading families of the Islands, created a community of interest for the convocation.

On November 22 and 23 of 1935 an Old Timers' reunion on the occasion of a football game with Southern California brought back three members of the first varsity eleven, Judge Patrick Nelson of Dubuque, Col. Frank Fehr of Louisville and Edward Sawkins of Detroit. The Notre Dame team of 1935, which had lost to Northwestern and tied Army after its magnificent performance at Ohio State, roused its tired talents to defeat Southern California 20-13 for a memorable homecoming.

The January 1936 issue of the *Alumnus* began to identify the phrase, "Greater Notre Dame," in conjunction with a statement from Father O'Hara of continuing needs, listing at the same time current gifts to the University. The death of Sister Lourdes, C.S.C., who worked for 49 years in the campus kitchens from 1878 to 1927, was a reminder of how far the University had already come.

Bernard Voll, in his presidential letter to alumni, called attention to the centennial in 1942. The alumni association had five years in which to recover economically, he said, and to develop its programs to a degree in keeping with this great occasion. The placement of young graduates to advantage was urged as the most immediate problem, and also as a far-reaching contribution to Notre Dame's future. He also broached another popular project, the provision by alumni over a period of years, either through payments to the University or through insurance, for the education of their sons. The economic status of the average alumnus was still considered moderate. Parents who had just begun to intimate inherited wealth and power had been decimated by the depression. The Alumni Board considered this program for the next several years, as did the University. The ultimate decision was that the project might answer a problem for alumni, but it could create multiple problems for the University and the association neither of whom were in a position to risk. Alumni were urged, however, to look ahead in their own planning.

Father O'Hara's concern over modernism and the disintegration of principles was evident in his proposal for a two-year course in Apologetics for Catholic writers which would produce graduates equipped to oppose the trend with the same sophistication and professional competence with which the threat to our society was making considerable headway. He asked for ten gifts of $1,500 each to start the program, and for a number of smaller gifts which would be called the Father Daniel E. Hudson, C.S.C., Scholarships, toward the same end, in memory of the highly regarded editor of the *Ave Maria* magazine.

Alumni clubs were growing—new ones appearing in Harrisburg, Dubuque, Central New Jersey, Northern New York State, Flint and Muskegon, Mich., and in Miami, Fla.

The death of Father Julius Nieuwland, C.S.C. '99, recalled the world stature this modest scientist had achieved in the limited laboratories of the campus, first in the Main Building, then in what was a new Science Hall. His accomplishments indicate the great expectations which have accompanied the present great new Nieuwland Science Hall, built for the college in 1952. Father Nieuwland's older Science Hall became the unbelievably renovated LaFortune Student Center, through the generosity of Joseph A. La Fortune '16. Father Nieuwland's banjo would still feel at home there.

Arthur J. Hughes '11, Chicago attorney, became president of the Alumni Association in 1936. He was a man of professional competence, but also a man deeply ingrained with Catholic principles and disturbed by the growing threats to the ideals long held by the Judaeo-Christian traditions of the Western World. He did not immediately project a program but asked alumni to continue their interest and cooperation for opportunities he felt were imminent. Bernard Voll, at the annual alumni banquet, stressed to the large alumni audience the board's concerns in the areas of placing graduating seniors and in the pending study of the advance payment plan for educating sons. The secretary reported the continuing debt incurred in pursuing the promising and worthwhile projects of the association. Only $7,000 was contributed in dues during the year. A deficit of almost $2,000 existed, in addition to which the University was paying the printing costs of the *Alumnus.* The seventh Local Club Council advanced club organization substantially. The need for structure, in modification of the traditional transient and spontaneous administrations, was reflected when it was decided that undergraduates on the campus, in the growing number of corre-

sponding geographic clubs there, must secure permission of the
alumni club counterpart, for home town functions. Friction and
debts had arisen without this cooperative provision. The Chicago club had pioneered a local alumni club *Alumni Club
Directory* for its 1,200 members which accelerated its programs.
Cleveland reported success in its annual retreat. Club Communion Sundays were reported, some to commemorate Mother's
Day, others to remember the anniversary of Rockne's death in
March. Clubs were urged to approach local colleges and universities for speakers, in pursuit of continuing education.

In September, 1936, encouraged by Father O'Hara's concern
for current attacks on fundamental principles of Church and
state, President Arthur Hughes sailed for Italy to lay before
Pope Pius XI a proposed program of the Notre Dame Alumni
Association for combatting these erosive forces. The program
had the prior approval of Father O'Hara and Cardinal Mundelein. Father O'Hara commented: "Mr. Hughes will pledge our
allegiance in the fight for conventional institutions of society
without which no group can hope for existence as a social unit.
I speak of the four necessities—the home, education, the rights
of private property, and the rights of the state." The eyes of the
world were on this movement, the first of its kind to be
undertaken officially by an alumni association. This was not an
impulsive gesture to secure publicity or prestige. In Spain, at the
time, the Civil War was witnessing a major confrontation between the encroachment of communism and the somewhat
suspect, and perhaps unfortunate, fascist defenders. In the
United States the power of the communist ideology, control of
large segments of the communications media, and the calculated
intellectual appeal to American campuses, were already evident.
Francis Wallace '23 in Hollywood as a successful author, was
eye-witness and victim of the occupation of that vital center of
influence by the leftists. Part of their reason for victory was
that unorganized and uninformed nature of their opposition.
This was the climate in which the program organized and
pursued by Hughes and the association was launched. In the
light of resources and preparation, we were Don Quizote perhaps. But Arthur Hughes should be remembered as the alumnus
who dared to reach for the impossible star.

Cavanaugh Hall, first of two adjacent residence halls, named
for the late Father John W. Cavanaugh '90, was completed and
opened to 196 freshmen in September. Its next-door neighbor,
Zahm, was opened a year later, named in honor of Father John

A. Zahm '71. "La vie intime" was being continuously preserved by these hall tributes to the great Congregation figures who had paved the path for their need—Sorin, Corby, Walsh, Morrissey, Dillon and now, Cavanaugh and Zahm. The lay involvement confronted students daily with Lyons, Howard and Alumni. The broad campus contained halls named for Badin, the proto-priest; Moreau, the founder of Holy Cross; Dujarie, founder of the Brothers of Holy Cross, and St. Edward, patron saint of Father Sorin. Patriotism was tangible in Washington Hall. The cross of Sacred Heart spire, and Our Lady on the Dome placed the purpose and the principles of Notre Dame above all else.

The enrollment was back to 2,950, the largest since 1931, close to the 3,000 ceiling thought then by many to be a desirable permanent limitation. Alumni clubs continued to grow. New ones were Tri-State (Indiana, Illinois and Kentucky around Evansville and Vincennes) and Central New Jersey.

On Oct. 25, 1936, Eugenio Cardinal Pacelli, Papal Secretary of State, on the first visit of such a papal representative to America, came to Notre Dame. He was accompanied by Bishop Francis Spellman. The procession, in a drenching Indiana rain, stopped first at Sacred Heart Church. The picture of Pacelli kneeling in the sanctuary was widely used when he later became Pius XII. In Washington Hall a ceremony marked the award in special convocation of an honorary doctorate, making him an alumnus of the University *honoris causa*. The citation was read by Father J. Leonard Carrico, C.S.C., director of studies. The cardinal responded in English, a bit hard to understand, but the students in the hall understood him perfectly when he concluded by suggesting a holiday for Notre Dame—and for Saint Mary's. In spite of the inclement weather, Cardinal Pacelli was graciousness and dignity personified. The future Cardinal Spellman, possibly envisioning pneumonia for his important companion, was more difficult. Many attempted pictures that might have brightened University publications were nipped in the bud by the hovering bishop. The visits of celebrities were bright pages in University history but the campus committee in charge usually breathed a sigh of relief when the day ended.

President Arthur Hughes reported to the alumni on his visit to Pius XI. The Holy Father had not only approved the association undertaking, but, in a private audience, had bestowed upon it his blessing and his hope for its success. In pursuit of the program, President Hughes called upon the 85 Notre Dame

Clubs to implement it. The basic feature of the program was the enlistment of the intellectual training which alumni could contribute to the leadership of American citizens in recognizing and opposing the inroads of atheistic communism, and to the national organizations which expressed the wish to participate in such opposition.

The first major program was the arrangement of meetings of as many clubs as possible on Jan. 25, 1937. The meetings were to be centrally accessible, should be as brief as possible and should entail no cost to outside friends. They were to explain the nature of the Notre Dame program and the reasons for it. Educators, religious and members of local patriotic groups were to be invited. On the campus, the key meeting featured Father O'Hara, Arthur Hughes, Professor Daniel O'Grady and a student from Spain, Sebastian Bonet. The Notre Dame meeting was sponsored in the University Gymnasium by the Notre Dame Club of the St. Joseph Valley.

Other University progress continued. The priests of Holy Cross were moved into a renovated Corby Hall which now included a dining room. The *Religious Bulletin* observed its 15th anniversary. It was now edited by Father John T. Cavanaugh, C.S.C. '23. It was being mailed to 5,000 schools as well as many alumni and religious. Its readership was estimated to be no less than 150,000. Father Cavanaugh, who had been secretary to the unrelated Father John W. Cavanaugh, C.S.C., for a part of his presidency, had been graduated as a lay student. He had served as president of the Student Activities Committee and had worked after graduation for the Studebaker Corporation before returning to the seminary. His knowledge of the student mind was similar to Father O'Hara's, who had been a lay student with a background of foreign and business activities before entering religious life. Father O'Hara had grown up in the consulates of Uruguay and Brazil. Father Cavanaugh had been on one of the coveted Orient freighter summer jobs as a student. He says that his knowledge of the Orient was confined entirely to the hold of the ship. In any event, the *Religious Bulletin* and the *Religious Survey* continued to contribute to campus spiritual life, and far beyond.

J. Edgar Hoover, director of the Federal Bureau of Investigation, spoke at Notre Dame on Jan. 11, to a crowd of several thousand in the Gymnasium. He was pleased to learn of the Alumni Association program against communist infiltration in America. "There can be no higher ideal for the student of Notre

Dame, or any other university in America, than that he should consecrate his life to the virtue of justice. We need that virtue." It followed logically that Notre Dame alumni were welcome in the FBI numbering at one time 102 agents.

Father J. Hugh O'Donnell, C.S.C., announced the first reunion of all Notre Dame men who had worked and resided in old St. Joe Hall, now Badin. He conjured memories of Brothers Boniface and Florian to attract attendance, and promised the alumni residence in their old hall for the reunion. The tradition of working students remained—817 were now reported working, 300 of them under the National Youth Administration program. Many parent savings had been lost in the depression.

In the spring of 1937 President Hughes devoted three months full time to the association program, a unique and major contribution, visiting half the Notre Dame clubs. Accompanied by the alumni secretary, visits were made for the first time by association officers to the Notre Dame clubs on the West Coast.

Tradition was given a spotlight in the *Alumnus* with the listing of 14 current faculty members of long tenure—25 to 50 years. The priests were Father William Bolger, Father Charles Doremus, Father Matthew Walsh and Father Thomas Irving. The lay professors were Francis X. Ackerman, Knowles Smith, John Cooney, James Hines, Edward Maurus, F. W. Kervick, William Benitz, R.M. Kaczmarek, Robert Greene and Jose Caparo.

More than 800 alumni attended the 1937 reunion, indicating the strong interest in the association and its programs, as well as in the University. The Friday registration showed half the total attendance, a new opening day record More than 50 St. Joe Hallers returned, the boys who had begun as waiters and clerical staff in the University.

Father O'Hara, at the banquet, reported a good year. He recalled the economic problems of Father Sorin as a source of hope for the future. He praised Art Hughes and the association for the active program against subversion. Hughes thanked Pius XI, Cardinal Mundelein and Father O'Hara for their encouragement, and the clubs for the help and pleasure they had extended on his visits. The secretary's report showed that 35 per cent more alumni had paid dues than in the preceding year but total income was still only $11,000. Clubs were growing—Northern Louisiana, Sandusky and West Virginia were among the new ones. "Living Endowment" was still at low ebb as an effort. Contact with high schools was flourishing. A second illustrated publication for alumni counselors and prospective students had been edited by the alumni office. A new law directory had been published. The Eighth Annual Local Club Council was convened at this reunion with optimism expressed for continued club development.

The fiscal gap between successful programs and unsuccessful financing for them continued to stretch.

Father James A. Burns, C.S.C. '88, was elected honorary president of the association in 1937. William E. Cotter '13, New York City, was chosen as president to succeed Arthur Hughes. Cotter was one of a select group of alumni who had enjoyed the educational opportunities of Notre Dame for his entire academic life—Minims, Prep and University. He had, as Jesse Harper's athletic manager, finalized the Army game contract for the celebrated 1913 meeting at West Point. Harry F. Kelly '17, Michigan attorney general, was elected vice president, as was Charles Mooney '26, Cleveland. Directors were James E. Deery, Don P. O'Keefe, Joseph M. Byrne Jr., and newly-elected Francis McKeever '03, Chicago. Art Hughes remained on the board as retiring president.

In the fall of 1937 the University announced the establishment of the Julius A. Nieuwland Memorial Fund. Its immediate objectives were a chair of organic chemistry, $125,000; a visiting professors' endowment, $125,000; five $25,000 research fellowships, $125,000; a lecture foundation, $50,000; a library and research materials fund, $75,000, and a chemistry laboratory building, $500,000. In an address in Washington, D.C., in 1934, Francis P. Garvan, president of the Chemistry Foundation, announced that a cartel which had been pushing rubber prices upward had been halted "because of the fear of encouraging the development of duprene." Garvan said, "In other words this discovery (synthetic rubber) even now is possibly saving us $375,000,000 a year." The Nieuwland Fund seemed a modest target against this national contribution his genius had achieved.

In the same fall, the resumption of the Rockne Memorial effort was announced with $150,000 on hand from the 1931 campaign. The University appropriated $200,000 and the estimate based on the plans left another $200,000 to be raised. Only 409 alumni gifts had been recorded in the campaign of 1931. There were now 17,000 alumni in the records. Father Hugh O'Donnell, Elmer Layden, Frank Lloyd, Arthur Haley and J.E. Armstrong were appointed a committee to secure the needed funds.

President Cotter authored an article pointing out why Notre Dame needed outside financial support and why alumni were the logical spearheads of such support. He repeated the advantages of the "Living Endowment" plan. But it was necessarily obscured, as the *Alumnus* printed lists of contributors, many of them alumni, along with the side-by-side campaigns of the Nieuwland and Rockne funds.

"La vie intime" scored again, with a feature on the four generations of Coquillards. The first Alexis Coquillard greeted Father Sorin on his arrival in 1842. A second Alexis Coquillard, nephew of the fur trader, was the first student enrolled at Notre Dame. His son, Alexis Coquillard, Jr., was enrolled in the Mimims and remained at Notre Dame as a student for 13 years. Now, the fourth generation, Alexis Coquillard Coquillard III, was currently a student.

President Cotter, in the spring of 1938, was making a study of the financial plight of the University and the association. Among his comments was this, "And you naturally wondered, as I had suddently wondered, what has Notre Dame used for money? My study this year of the progress of Notre Dame in the light of its history and its resources leads me to believe that a miracle has risen in Indiana." He pointed out, however, that the tremendous resources of other institutions, and the growth of the challenges to Notre Dame, made it doubtful that progress could continue on faith alone, and the continuing dedication of administrators and faculty.

In May, 1938, 100 radio stations assisted in local Universal Notre Dame Night programs. A nationwide NBC program was partly lost when a program in the University Gymnasium, featuring Elmer Layden, was lost between the Gymnasium and the Stadium transmitter. Fortunately in other feeder centers, Father O'Hara, John McCormack, President Cotter and the band and glee club were heard.

The 1938 graduates were still encountering placement problems. The placement program was being intensified, in spite of economic pressures. President Cotter, in his final report, commented on the increased duties of association officers, and the varied demands on limited office staff and budget. He pointed to the new separation of the Senior class banquet from the alumni banquet as an instance of the growth.

The Ninth Annual Club Council found only 14 of 90 clubs represented. President Cotter stressed a broader representation as essential to the future. Northern Iowa and Scranton, Pa., were new clubs. Total association income was $12,286 in spite of a small increase in alumni participating.

It was a persistent dilemma.

XXIX

Prosperity Is Just Around...?

The "Living Endowment" plan, still cherished by its advocates, was buried as a program, but a spark of life occasionally emerged. The *Alumnus*, grasping at straws, pointed out that alumni contributions to the Nieuwland and Rockne funds during the year were $13,789, more than the total payment of dues. On June 1, the University announced that student enrollment for the following fall was 23 per cent ahead of the same date the previous year. The tangible values of the alumni programs were becoming more visible.

In May, 1938, spotlighting the newly established Department of Aeronautics, National Air Mail Week was the occasion for observing the 50th anniversary of the experiments of Dr. Albert F. Zahm '83, which had contributed to the first success of the flight of man.

In June, the Alumni Association elected its officers. Father Matthew Walsh, C.S.C. '03, became honorary president. Ambrose O'Connell, '07, Alexandria, Va., executive assistant to Frank C. Walker '09, Postmaster General of the United States, was named president. O'Connell and Walker were both alumni of Father William Bolger's debating teams. Joseph B. McGlynn '12 of East St. Louis, Ill., and James M. Phelan '17 of Sacramento, were chosen as vice presidents. Directors were Don O'Keefe, Joe Byrne, Jr., Frank McKeever, the newly elected Edward F. O'Toole '25 of Chicago, the Senior Class member John C. O'Connor '38 of Indianapolis and retiring president Cotter. O'Toole had had active volunteer placement experience with the Chicago club and for his entire term worked with Bill Dooley and the alumni clubs in the development of an efficient placement service.

Father James A. Burns, the retiring honorary president, also retired during the summer as Provincial of the Congregation of Holy Cross. It marked 50 years of service to Holy Cross and to Notre Dame, which had contributed outstandingly to the growth of both. He was succeeded as Provincial by another alumnus and friend of the Alumni Association, Father Thomas A. Steiner, C.S.C., '99, former engineer, dean of the College of Engineering and a familiar figure in the confessional and in hymns in Sacred Heart Church.

During the same summer, Father Wesley Donahue '07, retired after 12 years as Superior General of the Congregation of Holy Cross. He, too, was one of Father Bolger's debaters in the heyday of that activity.

On the 40th anniversary of the Department of Architecture, Professor Francis Kervick wrote an article on the history of the architecture of the University itself. He praised the vision which had created Notre Dame Avenue, and the arrangement of the college buildings as the campus expanded. He pointed to the Main Building, built in amazingly short time, from the plans of W. J. Edbrooke, architect of the United States Treasury. He called attention to French influences in many of the buildings, especially those behind the Main Building, referred to often as the "French Quarter." Most of these had been designed and built by Brothers Charles and Columbkille, C.S.C., carpenters in the tradition of their patron, St. Joseph. Kervick commented on the French influence in Sacred Heart Church, designed by Patrick Keeley, who had also designed the heralded, and thoroughly English Cathedral in Charleston, S.C. Boring and Tilton, New York architects, designed the 1917 library. Diversity of architects continued, but the variety of buildings continued to create an imposing campus, with a sense of beauty and of unity remarkable in the light of this changing pattern of structures.

The Rhode Island Club recognized the importance of the feminine involvement in Notre Dame programs by creating the Notre Dame University Guild. The Rockne Memorial Committee presented an article on the general importance of alumni giving in American higher education. The University had begun construction of the beautiful Memorial, on the west end of the southern mall. The Postoffice and laundry buildings which Father O'Hara had erected at the beginning of his term were meshed into the campus picture without fanfare, as was an extension to the Chemistry Building. The alumni office called attention to its growing pressures as the only keeper of records of Notre Dame alumni, and the only regular channel of contact. The contacts with the alumni through the magazine and the clubs and the classes, together with the task of contacting the 1,349 high schools represented in the student enrollment, were of constant weight and importance, and continuingly increasing.

In February, 1939, the University gave up the second effort of the Rockne Memorial campaign. Alumni had responded better than in the first effort. But the Memorial had become a reality, the need was debatable among alumni and friends for a sum which was being realized each season by the football revenues, and the irritant factor of the warmed-over campaign seemed unprofitable. The second effort, however, had raised more than the first.

A colorful figure from a long period of service joined the valiant rows in the Community Cemetery when Father John Farley, sometimes called King or Pop, a dedicated rector of Corby, Walsh and Sorin Halls, a former athlete of prowess, and a strict but respected disciplinarian, died. The amputation of a leg in his last years had not impaired the presence, the spirit or the popularity of the King.

In December, 1938, the New York Alumni Club, under the presidency of Daniel J. O'Neil '25, had held its first Communion Sunday in honor of the Feast of the Immaculate Conception. The appropriateness of this activity for a Notre Dame club was immediately evident, and it later became the Universal Notre Dame Communion Sunday, held on the Sunday nearest Dec. 8. Since the Immaculate Conception is the patroness of the United States, the opportunity to spotlight the proper relationship of religion and citizenship has remained great 'Many outstanding programs have been presented under this universal plan. The pace of the first meeting was hard to sustain, featuring as it did an address by Father O'Hara broadcast from the American Congress in Lima, Peru, and the live presence of the eloquent Msgr. Fulton J. Sheen.

In June of 1939 the *Alumnus* called attention to the increasing conflicts in interests and in numbers between the alumni and the parents and guests of Seniors during the commencement-reunion weekend. It also reported the success of the separate Senior banquet in May. And it pointed with concern to the major expenses which the University now incurred in preserving the almost 100-year-old tradition of campus hospitality.

The Rockne Memorial was dedicated on June 3, with Charles

"Gus" Dorais '14 as the appropriate main speaker, the Rockne family present, and Father Michael Shea '04, whose *Victory March* had been such an integral part of Rockne's career. For the first time, Notre Dame announced the retirement of four professors, Ackerman, Maurus, Benitz and Greene.

Association officers for 1939-40 were named. Professor William Benitz was fittingly named honorary president. Daniel E. Hilgartner '17, Chicago, was made president, with Henry C. Wurzer '25, Davenport, Iowa, and Keene Fitzpatrick '13, San Francisco, vice presidents. Directors were Joseph M. Byrne Jr., Francis McKeever, Edward F. O'Toole and the newly elected John T. Higgins '22 of Detroit, along with retiring President Ambrose O'Connell. The Tenth Annual Council of Local Clubs adopted the placement program as their top priority. A committee was appointed to prepare a handbook, updating suggestions for local alumni club programs. Father O'Hara's talk at the alumni banquet stressed the growth of graduate work in chemistry, physics, mathematics, philosophy, politics and apologetics.

In the fall of 1939, William R. Dooley '26, assistant alumni secretary, managing editor of the *Alumnus*, director of the association's placement program, and—in the old tradition—graduate manager of University publications, made a milestone report on the placement program, after a 15-month study. He defined the difficulties of placing a widely scattered alumni demand with a central office. He introduced the advantages of having corporate recruiters interview graduating Seniors on the campus, cutting off many of the placement problems at the start. And he urged the departments which had often placed their own graduates to continue and to intensify that practice.

The 1939 Summer School was the third largest in history and the largest since the depression of 1931. Tradition was augmented during this session when the sisters choral group sang a Gregorian Mass in Sacred Heart Church.

Arthur Hughes '11, had been made president of the National Catholic Alumni Federation in 1938 following his outstanding year as president of the Alumni Association. Now, in 1939, the Federation chose the Notre Dame alumni secretary as its president, to succeed Hughes. The truth was, unfortunately, that few Catholic colleges had developed enough alumni organization to cooperate with or direct the federation program. We used the honor during this period at Notre Dame to point out the strengths of the Notre Dame program as recognized by outside

authorities, with more force and effect than modesty would
have permitted us internally.

In November, the alumni board evidenced its stature when
President Daniel Hilgartner directed a study of the financial
needs of the association under Henry C. Wurzer '25, and another study of the programs for alumni clubs under Keene
Fitzpatrick '13. A third study, of the placement program, was
assigned to Edward F. O'Toole. O'Toole had worked with Bill
Dooley, and a rising volume of cooperation in placement was
coming from the clubs. President Hilgartner and the board felt
that the programs of the association were not sufficiently
understood by the members at large and that more education in
these programs would bring more support. An indication of the
new scope of association programs was the 2,500 attendance at
the rally in New York City, sponsored by the Notre Dame Club,
before the Army game. This involved as many people as the
total association had represented not many years before.

In December, Notre Dame received a combination of shock
and honor when President John F. O'Hara, C.S.C., '11, was
named titular bishop of Milasa, and military delegate for the
armed forces of the United States. The shadow of World War II
was shaping in substance in Europe. Archbishop Spellman,
under whose jurisdiction the Military Ordinariate functioned,
was familiar with the hard-hitting and successful program which
Father O'Hara had conducted for the very masculine Notre
Dame campus. The visit of Cardinal Pacelli had provided the
Vatican's endorsement. Notre Dame and the Congregation of
Holy Cross were honored—only a few of the Congregation had
risen to this honor, and it was the first for a President of the
University. Bishop O'Hara was consecrated in Sacred Heart
Church on Jan. 15, 1940. Forty-five bishops and archbishops
were in attendance in spite of a blizzard the preceding day.
Archbishop Spellman was the consecrator, and Bishops Noll of
Fort Wayne and Ritter of Indianapolis were coconsecrators.
Bishop O'Hara's new office was in New York, and this office
became in the war years following as busy as the tower room in
Sorin Hall had been, but on a world-wide scale. The government
took care of the education and health of the armed forces. The
U.S.O. offered them entertainment. It was up to the chaplains
to provide the spiritual strength and welfare of the services.
Sacrifice, dedication and limited material resources did not keep
them from a performance which renewed religion in the lives of
many, and served it in all. Directing the Catholic chaplains,

Bishop O'Hara was neither pietistic or naive. The result was a
program which met the needs of the men in service and which
frequently prevented or cut short programs which contained a
potential of moral erosion. Father O'Hara, as alumni continued
to think of him—and as he preferred it—was tireless in his travels
and in his communications with the many and far-flung men
under his care.

Father Tom McAvoy has published the magnificent biography of Father O'Hara, who went on to become the Bishop of
Buffalo, and the Cardinal Archbishop of Philadelphia—the first
alumnus and the first C.S.C. to receive the red hat. His career in
those posts was as effective as his Notre Dame years would
assure, but there was the frequently expressed, and assuredly
sincere, wish on his part that he could be back in Sorin Hall
ministering to the students he loved. In his farewell to his
students, he expressed a memorable measure of the Notre Dame
man, at the end of almost 100 years of University history:
"Retrospect would be easy, especially when in three decades of
work with Notre Dame men you can't recall one who was really
evil." But he told the students that their problem was of the
present and the future.

Father J. Hugh O'Donnell, C.S.C. '16, was named Acting
President to succeed Father O'Hara, and Father John J. Cavanaugh, C.S.C. '23, was moved from the post of prefect of
religion to that of acting vice president. The feeling of loss, as
after the death of Rockne, was great on the campus, but both
Rockne and Father O'Hara had left such vital programs that the
University hid its regret and moved ahead with new resolve.

Father O'Donnell had been an understanding friend of the
alumni office ever since his days as prefect of discipline under
Father Matthew Walsh. During the dark depression years, he
gave constant moral support to our efforts, and, I suspect,
influenced a few of the essential administration decisions in
favor of the association. He believed fervently in Notre Dame
men, as he believed fervently in their alma mater—a term he
used often. I might be prejudiced in my own description of
Father O'Donnell. In any event, I could never capture the
contradictions in him as beautifully as Richard Sullivan '30, in
his "Notre Dame: Reminiscences of An Era."

" . . . As a student he had played football. 'Pepper' was his
nickname. He strode along cockily, with a large chin, a
swinging of burly shoulders. I suspect now that internally he
was quaking under the dignity of his priesthood; for behind

his pompous facade he was essentially a timid man. The facade may indeed have been erected to hide the self-doubt. But his swagger, his resonant voice, his pompous manner—above all the office that he held (prefect of discipline)—were enough to arouse antagonisms. . . . He came back here (from Texas) in 1935. By this time he had dropped the front initial from his name. And he had, aged 40, acquired a kind of courtliness, a gracious, booming cordiality which some people felt was a conscious imitation of Father John W. Cavanaugh; but which, imitation or not, curiously became him. ⸱ . it seems to me likely that the final manner which in the late thirties struck me as completely becoming the man was the very manner which, in its earlier stages of development, infuriated so many of us in the late twenties. . . . He was extremely gracious in his elaborate way to all members of the faculty. . . . When in private conversation he spoke of Notre Dame gushingly as 'alma mater' I felt like cringing. Yet when he spoke of Notre Dame it was with an absolute and unquestionable, unselfish love; he was dedicated, he was given over; he had a childish terror of making any mistakes which would involve this place; he relied with a childlike confidence on God to prevent him from making such a mistake. As a character he was a remarkable combination of the simple and the grandiose. He was both obvious and indirect; he was both pretentious and humble. . . . He died of cancer a few days after commencement, in 1947; a man lacking wit and intellectual profundity, but largehearted, lumbering, and anxious: a good priest, according to the order of Melchisedech, and at the end a quietly heroic human being."

I hope you will some day read the context of Dick Sullivan's book, which captures so much of the character of the campus and the men of whom he writes. My contacts were closer and more frequent. I concur in the measurements of Dick Sullivan and some of them made the very ends we sought difficult to accomplish. But I saw a few memorable things done which, in my view, increase the stature of Father O'Donnell even beyond the high regard and ultimate praise accorded him by a distinguished member of the Notre Dame faculty these many decades.

In March, 1940, vice president Henry C. Wurzer reported on his study of the finances of the Alumni Association. Its growth and diversity were stressed. An interesting phenomenon was the fact that the younger classes were responding to the programs as well as, sometimes better than, the older classes. The alumni were not criticized by the study, but were urged to study the programs more seriously and to understand the need for their financial support, so that the association could be self-sustaining and independent.

Father Francis Wenninger, dean of science since 1923, with the exception of a year during which he received his Ph.D. from the University of Vienna after one of the greatest intellectual performances in the records of that great University, died on Feb. 12, 1940. His contributions to the College of Science were outstanding, as was his long service as master of ceremonies for the major campus liturgical programs.

In a report by Vice president Keene Fitzpatrick on the local alumni clubs the spread of activities in number and nature was noted, as was "growing recognition of the women as a factor in club programs, which marks the maturing of the club viewpoint." The latter point was followed shortly by the formation of a woman's auxiliary by the Notre Dame Club of the Twin Cities. Ninety-two clubs observed the 17th Annual Universal Notre Dame Night. Detroit was the key club, from which Bishop O'Hara, Harry Kelly, Elmer Layden and the Glee Club broadcast through the Mutual Network to all parts of the country. Philadelphia paid special tribute to the founder of the night, John H. Neeson '03. Father Eugene Burke, C.S.C. '06, presented Neeson with a replica of the Notre Dame Dome and a scroll greeting from the University.

In June, 1940, at a concerned alumni banquet in the east wing of the Dining Hall, Father O'Donnell called attention to the possibilities of United States involvement in the war already going on in Europe. "It might not occur to you, but the peaks of Notre Dame's history are shrouded in the mists of war. The Mexican War was fought when Notre Dame was in its infancy. The Civil War had just ended and the era of reconstruction just begun when Notre Dame celebrated her silver jubilee. As we approached our 50th anniversary there were fomented in Cuba the conditions that eventually led to the expulsion of Spain from the Western hemisphere. Of the diamond jubilee I need not speak. There are many men in this room this evening who were wearing their country's uniform when they received degrees at commencement in 1917. As I review our history, I am impressed with the thought of an apostolate of selflessness under the guidance of the Mother of God which can be attributed purely to the supernatural. No individual, no group of individuals, no single administration, can take to themselves the credit of Notre Dame's growth and development."

The 1940 banquet was also addressed by Ray Kelly '15,

national commander of the American Legion, and by Lewis J. Murphy '26, national commander of the Disabled American Veterans.

The alumni secretary's report showed the snowballing of association programs. The Class of 1939 had added 700 alumni to the records Eight issues of the *Alumnus* had been published that term. Placement had grown to an impressive program. Universal Notre Dame Night and the reunions demanded more time. The prospective student program had dictated another illustrated booklet edited by the alumni office, and 150 copies of the 1940 Dome had been sent to high schools with several students represented on the campus. Bishop O'Hara's consecration and a tie-in with the American Legion Convention in Chicago had been special events enlisting alumni cooperation. The sisters in the Summer Session were active, and a special news letter was being edited for them by the alumni office. Football highlight films had been sent to 40 clubs in the Spring of 1940. The survey of local alumni clubs was a special project, as was a new effort, an Alumni Association-sponsored luncheon on the campus for 70 sons of alumni currently enrolled.

Officers elected in June, 1940, to guide the association through the imminent critical year were Father Thomas Steiner, C.S.C. '99, Provincial, as the honorary president; Ray J. Eichenlaub '15 of Columbus, O., a legendary fullback of the Rockne-Dorais era, president, with Clyde Broussard '13 of Beaumont, Tex., and Thomas F. Byrne '28, Cleveland Heights, O., as vice presidents. Directors were Frank McKeever of Chicago, Edward O'Toole of Chicago, John T. Higgins of Detroit, and the newly elected director, William J. Mooney Jr., '15 of Indianapolis. Daniel Hilgartner remained on the board as retiring president and the '40 director named was Joseph Mulqueen of Havertown, Pa.

During the summer of 1940, the Provincial Chapter officially elected Father J. Hugh O'Donnell, C.S.C. '16, as President of Notre Dame, and Rev. John J. Cavanaugh, C.S.C. '23, as his vice president.

The 1940 Summer Session enjoyed the highest enrollment in its 22-year history.

A new building was constructed by the Congregation of Holy Cross to house the printing facilities of the *Ave Maria* magazine and its expanding activities. The 75-year-old structure built by Father Sorin had become wholly inadequate, as the Ave Maria Press handled other publications, including the *Alumnus* and the *Scholastic*. Father Patrick Carroll, C.S.C. '10, had succeeded Father Eugene Burke, C.S.C. '06, as editor of the *Ave Maria* who in turn had been the first successor to the venerable 50-year editor, Father Daniel Hudson, C.S.C.

Father Michael Shea '04, a secular priest in the New York archdiocese, who was coauthor with his brother, John '06, of the *Victory March*, died during the summer. By special permission he was buried in the Community Cemetery at Notre Dame, after services in Sacred Heart Church, among the members of the Congregation whose victory march in developing Notre Dame had been some part of the inspiration of his younger years. Father Mike had taught at Notre Dame for five years before entering the diocesan seminary.

South Bend and Notre Dame combined in one of the most glamorous events of the history of "Town and Gown" when the world premiere of "Knute Rockne, All-American." was held in the Palace Theater. Bernard J. Voll '17, was civic chairman for the occasion. Stars of Hollywood, led by Pat O'Brien, who played the role of Knute Rockne and still does, gave natives and students a first-hand look at the fabled Hollywood premieres.

A more significant event was the annual football banquet, sponsored by the Notre Dame Club of the University. Elmer Layden had achieved another good season, with a 7-2-0 record, losing to Iowa for the second year in a row, and to Northwestern. Georgia Tech, Carnegie Tech, Illinois, Army, Navy and Southern California were defeated, as was Amos Alonzo Stagg's College of the Pacific. And attendance, at 468,000, was 28,000 above any previous Layden total, and exceeded only by the Rockne championship teams of 1929 and 1930 which had exceeded a half million each.

Commenting on the season, Father O'Donnell said: " . . Perhaps no one is better acquainted with the policy of the faculty board than Elmer Layden himself. He receives his instructions and attempts to carry them out faithfully, both on and off the gridiron. His influence for good is wide-spread. So, Elmer, as long as you adhere to the board's instructions and direct our varsity teams in playing the traditional brand of Notre Dame football, you can rest assured that your tenure here is not in jeopardy. Moreover, a season resulting in seven victories and two defeats, combined with a record of past seasons, is a splendid tribute to your ability and that of your associates. All we ask is that, in the future, our teams play smart football, characterized by hard blocking and effective tackling, with that inimitable spirit so typical of Notre Dame. Do this, and you won't have to worry; do this, and the faculty board and the President will always support you. We don't expect the impossible season after season."

Francis Wallace, in his book *Notre Dame, Its People and Its Legends,* who was a nationally popular sports writer at the time, says that Elmer Layden had, to many, become conservative in his coaching, had not "won the big ones" in the Notre Dame tradition. This latter undoubtedly stemmed from the consecutive losses to Iowa. In any event, whether Layden envisioned the future of professional football, or read between the meaningful lines of Father O'Donnell's comments, he resigned in February to become the commissioner of the National Football League.

Father O'Donnell and Father John Cavanaugh, now chairman of the Faculty Board of Athletics, immediately hired Frank Leahy '31, outstanding coach of the Boston College football team, to replace Layden. The brilliant Leahy record at Notre Dame is known to alumni, second only in the success of his teams to Rock himself. In his senior year, on the 1930 championship team, Leahy had suffered a broken leg, and with the intensive drive characteristic of his entire career, he sat on the bench with Rock and absorbed the science and the detail, and some of the genius, of what was to be Rockne's last coaching season. Leahy brought with him the assistants who had helped him create the success at Boston College, and who proved equally effective in their new surroundings. Ed McKeever had played at Notre Dame, as had Bill Cerney, who was retained from Layden's regime. Joe McArdle and John Druze had been coached by Leahy at Fordham.

Father O'Donnell announced a change which in retrospect, assumes great significance. J. Arthur Haley '26 who had acted as business manager of athletics from 1926 to 1941, was made director of public relations of the University, a new post. It was a title which was to cause some confusion and concern in the years ahead, but the purpose of the new office and its director was clear from the start. Haley was to begin the vital public relations assignment of bringing prominent friends of the University closer to its family, by programs which neither the academic nor the alumni programs were prepared to effect. The concept and the appointment were one of the visionary moves in Notre Dame's progress which lend credence to some form of supernatural guidance. Frank Leahy's performance was public domain. Art Haley's new assignment was still only a hopeful concept, to be wholly shaped at Notre Dame.

Haley was succeeded in the athletic post of business manager by Herbert E. Jones '27. Herb had come to Notre Dame in 1921, on the two-year full work program, which was followed by a four-year college course. In his two-year full-time period he served as secretary to Father James A. Burns, C.S.C., then President. Herb's two older brothers, Gerald '22, and Willard '25, were known to the students as the lucky drivers of the University car—note the singular—and residents of "Cadillac Hall." This term, in the rich tradition of Notre Dame satire, was applied to the garage which housed the University car, and which had living quarters above it. Herb had been Art Haley's assistant from his graduation in 1927 until 1941. This is perhaps the logical spot to record that Herb Jones chose as his own assistant Robert M. Cahill, Class of 1934, who had been secretary to Elmer Layden, and who was a fellow resident of Dixon, Ill. The forty-seven Haley-Jones-Cahill years as athletic business managers have given Notre Dame uninterrupted progress and prosperity. Cahill succeeded Herb Jones when sudden death claimed Jones at the completion of one of his most cherished projects, the Athletic and Convocation Center. I would like to put forth this praise in neon lights, because during the 40 years of our concurrent efforts, the Alumni Association enjoyed the fullest cooperation of these alumni executives, and, in turn, the alumni provided their efforts with a loyal and constant following and policy approval in some pressure areas, as football grew to unprecedented proportions. We worked together closely.

In the spring of 1941, the alumni secretary reviewed in the *Alumnus* the conflict between program advancement and insufficient financial support. The association had grown from 3,000 to 11,000. Thirty-nine local alumni clubs had become ninety-three. The *Alumnus*, originally a small magazine with news hard to elicit, was now a larger-size publication, with clubs and classes and University news crowding its pages. Two hundred alumni came back for the 1926 reunions. In 1940 there were 926 returned graduates. The only staff increase in the 15 years had been Bill Dooley and a second girl secretary. The report, pessimistic in tone, proved to be most timely.

Father John J. Cavanaugh, C.S.C. '23, was named by Father O'Donnell as chairman of the executive committee to handle arrangements for Notre Dame's centennial year, 1941-42. A Centennial Committee was appointed, under Father John J.

Burke, C.S.C. '30, and consisting of Rev. Bernard J. Ill, C.S.C.
Robert B. Riordan, Clarence E. Manion, James E. Armstrong,
Paul I. Fenlon and the presidents of the Alumni Association and
of the St. Joseph Valley Alumni Club ex officio.

Two priests of Holy Cross died in this spring, with long lines
leading back to the "vie intime" of an earlier Notre Dame. One
was Father James French, outstanding orator and mission
priest, who had been a vice president of Notre Dame from 1893 to
1905. He had founded the nationally known Holy Cross Mission
Band, which gave parish retreats. The other priest was Father
Paul Foik, outstanding historian of the Church, and the first
librarian of the University Library dedicated in 1917. In 1924
he had gone to Texas to pursue his history of the Church in the
Southwest, at St. Edward's in Austin.

Foreshadowing the financial concerns of the new University
administration, Father Cavanaugh, as chairman of the Athletic
Board, revealed that the Notre Dame net annual receipts from
football had never exceeded a quarter of a million dollars, in the
relatively few years that there had been any surplus. The announcement was in reply to unfounded reports that the University received more than a million dollar yearly net from the
sport. This had hurt recent fund-raising effort.

The June commencement was a restless one. The alumni
secretary's report projected two major national and University
programs which would affect the association greatly. One was
the conscription for the Armed Forces. The other was the
upcoming centennial. Alumni already in service were becoming
a daily contact of the alumni office. The busy year was concrete
evidence of program progress. Clarence "Pat" Manion '22, was
named new dean of the Law School. The athletic prospects had
been vitalized.

But total Alumni Association receipts for the year had been
only $13,319. The alumni secretary, now with a wife, five sons,
and a growing staff and program, was crawling up the walls of
the alumni office to make ends meet.

The new University administration brought in a general
auditing firm, and for the first time the association was made a
part of the University audit.

When the frantic maneuvers of the association to meet its
costs with its income were put under the cold eye of accountants, I could have gone to jail. Not that there was serious doubt
of a return of service for dollar received—in fact almost awe at
the amount of service for the few dollars involved. But the

"how, when, where and who" of the simplest accounting procedure, when applied to my bookkeeping, defied any but supernatural explanation. Both Father O'Donnell and Father Cavanaugh were sympathetic. They were also smart. Another man
was added to the alumni office, Charles E. Cartier, a retired
business man from Ludington, Mich., not an alumnus, but a
brother of Warren A. Cartier '87, so long a part of Notre Dame,
and treasurer of the association. Charley became the competent
bookkeeper of the long hoped-for "Living Endowment" program.

It was the dawning of the long years of World War II. Also, it
was the dawning of the decade of Leahy's national champions.

But above all it ushered in the new era of prosperity for
Notre Dame, and financial security and respectability for the
alumni association.

XXX

The World War II Years

Peace in the world, however tenuous, permits me to express a long-held opinion that Father J. Hugh O'Donnell, C.S.C. '16, President of the University of Notre Dame du Lac, a priest and a patriot of fervor, should be credited with one of the great victories of World War II—over the United States Navy!

In the fall of 1941, the first unit of the Naval R.O.T.C. was organized on the campus, in response to Father O'Donnell's invitation to use the Notre Dame facilities. Father James D. Trahey, C.S.C. '30, was named University defense coordinator. The traditions of the Civil War and World War I were renewed on an even larger scale. The R.O.T.C. program was still a part of the regular University program.

The Navy liked the campus facilities. In February, 1942, it announced that Notre Dame had been chosen for a 30-day training program for 1,000 V-7 (deck officer) candidates. The dining halls, drill field and limited classroom space were to be used, along with Morrissey, Howard, Lyons and Badin Halls. Dining hall service was changed from the traditional family style to cafeteria. Four V-7 indoctrination classes of 1,000 men each, and one commissioned officers class of about the same size had been graduated between April, 1942 and October, when the Navy announced that Notre Dame had been declared the fourth midshipmen school in the country. This involved four months training on the campus, with commissioning at the end of this period, as ensigns of the U.S. Navy. The selection marked the fine facilities which the University presented for such training, and the rapport which Father O'Donnell had established with Capt. H. P. Burnett, U.S.N., the first commandant of the Navy program at Notre Dame.

The victory? Well, simply put, the Navy looked upon the
occupation of the facilities as reducing the University to a
civilian bystander basis. The program, I am sure, envisioned the
Navy officers housed in the Main Building and the Navy cars
sweeping through the Main Quadrangle. Father O'Donnell, with
the rare combination of courtesy and pomp which Richard
Sullivan has described, was most hospitable to the Navy administration. He would walk down the steps of the Main Building,
tossing his cape over his shoulder, greet the officers effusively.
But when the conference was ended, the officers would get
back in their cars and return to the modest and "temporary"
headquarters behind the Rockne Memorial where they remained
during the entire war years, and which still houses the R.O.T.C.
program. The University of Notre Dame, with its student enrollment decimated, its faculty and priests off to another war, still
functioned in the historic Main Building and its adjacent Sacred
Heart Church, awaiting another peace and reconstruction. Between the University and the Navy, and between the neighboring St. Joseph Valley, there was cooperation and understanding.
The period of dislocation for the University was to exceed even
the long dark years of the Civil War and the severity of the
dislocation was in many ways greater. Yet from its records, the
University not only repeated the outstanding performance in
the area of patriotism which had become a hallmark, but paved
the way during these years for the solutions of many of the
problems that were to shatter many precedents in the postwar
decades.

In the Fall of 1941, Father John J. Cavanaugh '23, vice
president, presented "A Case for Notre Dame" which once
more underlined the need of Notre Dame for alumni support.

This time the seed fell on more fertile ground—the result of
many new circumstances. Among these was the Alumni Board
elected in June of 1941.

Bishop John F. O'Hara, C.S.C. '11, was honorary president.
Harry F. Kelly '17, was the new president, with Frederick
Mahaffey '17, Indianapolis, and Alfonso A. Scott '22, Los
Angeles, as vice presidents. Directors were Edward O'Toole '25,
John T. Higgins '22, William J. Mooney, Jr. '15, the newly
elected Rev. Michael L. Moriarty '10, a popular secular priest
from Wooster, O., and retiring president, Ray J. Eichenlaub .15.

Following Father Cavanaugh's presentation, Harry Kelly and
the board began a plan which the *Alumnus* editorially indicated
in a "Stand by for Action" appeal. The board was preparing to

work in conjunction with Fathers O'Donnell and Cavanaugh to pursue the urgent program for financial support.

This Alumni Association program was announced by President Kelly in December, directed toward improved support of the University in its centenary year. Three major goals were listed for the "Centenary Fund." First was increase in participation by alumni. Second was an increase in the amount of annual contributions. And the third, a very major and far-sighted project, was the enlistment of non-alumni support. The local alumni clubs were asked to become actively involved in the new program. As a part of the anticipated growth, the University increased its Associate Board of Lay Trustees to 24 members, half of them continuing to be alumni. And the *Alumnus* remained a valuable source of support by printing a page of information on tax benefits to donors to the University.

On Dec. 7, 1941, while the Universal Communion Sunday of the Notre Dame Club of New York was being addressed by Myron C. Taylor, Presidential representative at the Vatican, the report came in of the attack on Pearl Harbor. In February, after studying the war's impact, Father O'Donnell addressed the students, asking them to remain calm under growing war conditions and to wait for information as against reacting to rumor. There was still hope expressed for the centennial program. The association moved ahead with plans for Universal Notre Dame Night and the reunions. The decision to continue the Alumni Fund was unanimous—a vital and far-reaching decision. The University announced the introduction of a three-semester plan to coincide with the Navy training programs beginning on the campus. In the light of campus revisions, the announcement of the reunion program for 1942 was modified to a one-day basis, with alumni having to be housed in South Bend.

Universal Notre Dame Night was featured by a national radio program, "Meet Your Navy," broadcast from the Gymnasium. Father Hugh O'Donnell was a featured speaker. Centennial plans began to look less feasible. Emphasis was moving to the significance of the publication of Father Arthur Hope's centennial history, *Notre Dame—100 Years*.

The early and curtailed alumni program in May found several hundred alumni on hand to continue the traditions. The alumni banquet was held, but there was a Navy flavor in its program, and a tension of war throughout.

Some changes of consequence were announced by the Alumni Association. The association would henceforth operate

on a calendar-year basis, and President Kelly and the board were
asked to serve the extra half year to establish the new plan. It
was evident already that travel, printing, the placement program as well as club and reunion traditions were facing serious
change and curtailment. Alumni were asked to turn their serious
attention to the new Centenary Fund and to consider that the
war effort of the government to sell bonds could be tied to
increasing contributions to the University by making the war
bonds payable to Notre Dame. Clubs were asked to continue
their programs, but it was admitted that many of the young
clubs, mostly of young alumni, would be so decimated by the
services as to be in effect suspended for the duration.

The *Scholastic* magazine observed its 74th anniversay, carrying thoughts far back into the Sorin era of traditions and
achievements.

President Kelly and the Alumni Board announced a plan to
strengthen the fund effort. In addition to the club cooperation,
class agents were appointed to stir up participation in each of
the classes. Continuing alumni spirit during these difficult years
was urged. A prompt response to this plea came from the St.
Joseph Valley Club, where Lay Trustees Frank Hering '98,
Ernest M. Morris '06, George O'Brien '93 and J. J. O'Brien
hosted a club meeting to begin a $25,000 Centenary Fund
campaign in the St. Joseph Valley.

The centenary year began with a full campus enrollment,
mostly Navy trainees. But in his opening sermon at the beginning of the school year, Father O'Donnell said, "Notre Dame
changes, but remains forever the same. Notre Dame still empha-
sizes the discipline of the spiritual, the intellectual and the
moral. Here you will always find applied the first principles
from which all true development proceeds. This is still the
Notre Dame of Father Sorin and his worthy successors." It was
a far cry from the glorious year of jubilee celebration hoped for,
but no circumstances could prevent the President of the University from the preservation of the University's essence. In
November, a beautifully written story of Notre Dame, by
Richard Sullivan '30, was heard on NBC radio. Alumni were
reassured, refreshed, and reminiscent. And the centenary history came from the University of Notre Dame Press on schedule
to contribute a lasting and major study of Notre Dame's first
hundred years.

Further encouragement came with the announcement of a
gift of $100,000 from I. A. O'Shaughnessy, to establish a fine

arts foundation at Notre Dame. The gift from the St. Paul philanthropist was particularly effective as a stimulus to the liberal arts, which had been overshadowed by the needs and techniques of war, and to the Centenary Fund. On this, Father O'Donnell wrote for the *Alumnus*, "Mind-power as well as man-power is necessary not only for winning the war, but also for winning the peace. The current propaganda that the liberal arts be suspended for the duration, if successful in its purpose, may well be the death blow to all that remains of the historical concept of Christian education in the United States. Then, insofar as American democratic institutions are concerned, we will have traded substance for shadow."

Publication of contributions to the Centenary Fund in the *Alumnus* by amounts and by classes indicated increasing alumni support.

The Notre Dame Club of Denver was cited as a fine example of wartime club activity. A club newsletter was being sent to all club members in service, and in the Denver club area, contacts were being made with alumni who came into the several camps nearby for training. All clubs were asked to follow the Denver example. Universal Notre Dame Night, because of travel restrictions, was changed by the board to the recommendation of a club communion breakfast on May 2, which would have been the occasion of the reunions on campus.

Two Notre Dame football seasons under Frank Leahy '31, had kept alumni interest and contacts alive with successful records in 1941, 8-0-1, and a third national ranking, and 1942, 7-2-2, with a sixth national ranking. The Armed Forces were beginning to make inroads. The 1942 team lost to Michigan in a revival of the series begun in 1887 and ended in 1909. Georgia Tech won the other game, with Wisconsin and a burgeoning Great Lakes service team providing the ties.

In June, 1943, the Alumni Association announced that the Centenary Fund, after two years, and in spite of the war, had passed the $100,000 mark in alumni giving. The Annual Alumni Fund, the "Living Endowment" hope of Frank Hayes and his successors, was here to stay.

The Alumni Association announced the immediate opening of the second Annual Alumni Fund. While the Centenary Fund had been considered successful, the fact remained that only one-third of the alumni had participated, and many clubs had not contributed special efforts. Prospects, in view of the failure of the first year of war to curb contributions, seemed good for continuing the long-delayed plan of annual unrestricted alumni giving.

Harry F. Kelly '17, who had been attorney general of Michigan during the two terms he actually served as president of the Alumni Association, was elected Governor of Michigan. The alumni board which succeeded the capable Kelly presidential tenure consisted of Father J. Hugh O'Donnell, C.S.C. '16, honorary president; Thomas F. Byrne '28, Cleveland Heights, O., an officer of the Ohio Bell Telephone Co., president; Gerald "Kid" Ashe '22, Rochester, N.Y., and E. Bradley Bailey '22, Jenkintown, Pa., vice presidents. Directors were John T. Higgins '22 of Detroit, William J. Mooney '15 of Indianapolis, Rev. Michael L. Moriarty '10 of Wooster, O., and the newly elected John T. Balfe '20 of New York City with Harry Kelley remaining as retiring president.

This was the board which rode out the remaining years of World War II, which nursed the rich promise of the newly established Annual Alumni Fund into unquestioned success and acceptance, which kept alumni interest alive in the face of limited contacts, which preserved the structures of class and club when their membership was gravely reduced, and which paved the way for the adjustment of both University and Alumni Association to some of the major problems of the coming postwar period, particularly enrollment and placement.

President Tom Byrne at once visited the campus and conferred with association and University administrators. Tom was an enthusiast whose optimism was contagious. He was an organizer. It was to be the first period in which the alumni office enjoyed the continuous active and personal effort of the association president in the pursuit of policies and programs. In view of the spiritual opportunities of the era, the association made formal the custom of Universal Notre Dame Communion Sunday, originated five years earlier by the Notre Dame Club of New York, and already a custom in a dozen other clubs. Its patriotic significance and its alumni family inclusion were submitted as strong assets.

On October 29, 1943, in Washington Hall, the University held its 100th commencement for the small accelerated Class of 1944. Harry Kelly '17, past president of the Alumni Association, veteran of World War I, now governor of the State of Michigan, gave the commencement address. A letter to Notre Dame on this very modest occasion of its centenary was received from one of its most illustrious honoary alumni—Pope

Pius XII. In even more somber note, it was announced that this would be the last formal commencement exercise for the duration of the accelerated program.

But even as the mechanics of the University were over-shadowed by the priorities of the war effort, the underlying University of Father Sorin and those who followed him emerged in unexpected places and strengths.

One of the most impressive of such instances came with the publication of a short comment on "Notre Dame spirit," that intangible but tremendous force which had manifested itself in so many ways, yet defied any rigid definition. The interest in this particular effort lay in the source. Its author was E. C. "Bud" Dollard, a handsome young officer appropriately cast as the public relations officer of the Navy program on the Notre Dame campus. When Lieut. (J. G.) Dollard presented a request to campus or city, almost everyone was prepared to give him South Bend or the University—except, as I have noted, Father J. Hugh O'Donnell. But the following message indicated that not only had Notre Dame not been taken over by the Navy, but that the Navy, at least in part, was being taken over by Notre Dame. The publication of the message appeared first in the South Bend Tribune:

Dear Bob:
Instead of sending you the Log this week I'll try and answer your question, and if a few other people see this letter, I'm sure you won't mind.
I've told you about the Navy here, but your question 'What is the spirit of Notre Dame?' has me a bit stumped. But here is a try . . .
Notre Dame is truly a way of life. To describe it is to challenge the powers of descriptive words, at least mine. You see, Notre Dame is the mist rising from the lagoons at dawn as the spirit awakens and pushes the mists skyward. It's the whispering 'amens' from the trees as the priests, young and old, say their morning prayers and give thanks for the things we're fighting to retain.
Or maybe Notre Dame is the nuns, who have dedicated themselves and their lives to a cause within our cause, Christianity in a democracy. It might be the shadows, as they drift lazily into the corners in rooms of men whose names are now legend. They're all gone now, but the shadows and fading rays of light are the sparks of time that keep their spirits aglow in the rooms they left long ago.
Or perhaps the spirit of Notre Dame is the grin on the face of the Junior, who delights in telling the Navy why he joined the Marines.

It might be the thrill of the Angelus at eventide, or the face of the statue in the grotto. Perhaps it's the kind old brother in Washington Hall, whose eyes have a way of shaking hands when he says good morning. Maybe the spirit of Notre Dame is the ancient Irish gardener, who always has his wife awaken him when it rains at night so he can hear God's gift to his 'children', the lawns and shrubs.

Some folks would say the spirit of Notre Dame embodies the unwritten words to the hymns the priest plays on the organ in the cathedral on quiet summer afternoons, when the breeze is gone. You have a feeling it, too, stopped to listen. Maybe it's the majestic dignity of the painted windows as they wait patiently for the setting sun to get behind them, each in turn, so that they may daily tell their part in the story of the Creator of all things.

Those things belong to you and to me, Bob. You'll receive those gifts when you come here and carry them always under that spot on your tunic, reserved for medals. And you'll leave this school and this earth, knowing and believing that . . .

Notre Dame is truly a way of life. Sincerely, Bud

The 75th anniversary of the Alumni Association was observed by the Alumni Board on Jan. 23, 1944 with the setting up of a major program. Its points were: (1) organization of the local alumni clubs to develop a Catholic lay leadership in the field of preserving the fundamentals of American democracy, (2) rewriting the Association Constitution, which, like the government, was pretty much suspended in the exigencies of these war years, (3) establishing the association programs on the calendar year, (4) reestablishing Universal Notre Dame Night, beginning with April 17, 1944, (5) officially establishing the Universal Notre Dame Communion Sunday, on or near the Feast of the Immaculate Conception, patroness of the United States, the occasion to be dedicated to the bonds of religion and citizenship in the United States, (6) launching the second Annual Alumni Fund immediately, (7) sending the *Alumnus* to all graduates in service and to all contributors to the fund, with a newsletter to be sent to non-contributors to keep their contact with the campus alive, (8) study placement, particularly in relation to the problem of the return of alumni after the war, and (9) secure as soon as possible a field secretary whose primary duty would be to develop the local alumni clubs.

The program should have gladdened the men who for 75 years had made heroic efforts to bring the alumni and the University together for the mutual benefits inherent in close contact and communication. It must have pleased especially the officers of all those years who pursued the ideals of alumni organization with few members and few resources. And in this dark year of war, the strength of the Alumni Association in the coming years of peace was insured by this clear call to action.

In recognition of the association's achievements and its future promise, Father Hugh O'Donnell, in reporting the allocation of the successful Centenary Fund, announced that the debts of the association to the University, during the earlier years of pressure, had been made the first charge against the fund, and the slate was cleared. In addition, the fund had aided the Graduate School, faculty travel expense, funds for the Library and the College of Law, and a fund for faculty advanced study. When the surplus of contributions over expenses became evident in this first fund, the University and the board wisely decided that the expenses of the Alumni Association should be a part of the general University budget each year, subject to the University accounting procedures. These expenses would constitute the first charge against the Annual Fund, with the surplus remaining in the University funds.

A significant part of this understanding was that the Alumni Board would continue to direct and create the programs of the association, the alumni secretary to be responsible to the Alumni Board. The assumption was the continuing loyalty and interest of the association in the University, and the right reason and common sense which had become a constant factor in the board's functioning. Only once, and in a mild way, stemming from the corporate backgrounds of several directors, did the question of autonomy—so often a wrench in otherwise good machinery—arise. The perspective was explained, and the relationships of board and University have continued to be amicable and advantageous to both.

In pursuit of the "Program for Progress" announced by the board, the *Alumnus* urged alumni to implement it on three suggested "fronts." First, they should refresh their own educational strengths, to extend their benefits to others, especially organizations which had social and political impact. Second, they must see Notre Dame as a vital institution to be constantly strengthened for its mission of proper education of top quality. The third front was the home of the alumnus. The family was the basic unit of a sound society, and the families of Notre Dame men should be exemplary. Bill Dooley, who had been managing campus publications, and the alumni secretary, who had been handling academic publicity, as extra war year efforts, were relieved of these duties to add direction to the new program.

In 1943, Frank Leahy coached the team ranked Number One nationally, with a 9-1-0 season, losing only to an all-star Great Lakes team in the final game, after a sensational victory over the equally star-studded Iowa preflight team the week before. On the heels of this success, Leahy and many of his staff enlisted in the Navy. For the next two seasons, Ed McKeever and Hugh Devore, with service-riddled teams, still produced outstanding results, 8-2-0 under McKeever and 7-2-1 under Devore. The sore thumb of both seasons was Army, with the legendary Blanchard and Davis, who poured on a 59-0 defeat in 1944 and a 48-0 defeat in 1945.

The March, 1944, semester opened with a civilian enrollment about one-fifth of the normal prewar figure. J. Walter Kennedy '34, who had become sports publicity director when Joe Petritz entered the Navy, took over the total campus publicity program. Kennedy is the commissioner of the National Basketball Association, as I write this, a former mayor of Stamford, Conn.

The *American Midland Naturalist,* founded in 1909 by Father Julius Nieuwland '99, C.S.C., and edited by him for 25 years, published an issue commemorating the University's 100th anniversary, and also the centenary of the birth of Edward Lee Greene, donor of the outstanding herbarium and botanical library of the College of Science. Another pleasant journey back to "la vie intime" came with the golden jubilee of Father Bernard J. Ill, C.S.C. Father Ill had witnessed the building of every residence hall on the campus and had witnessed the first football game with Michigan in 1887. He had been hall prefect, and treasurer of the University for many years. He was a staunch advocate of athletics and was a prodigious walker himself. He had been chaplain to the nuns on the campus for 17 years.

The first break in the war years came with the announcement that the V-12 program was cutting enrollment, and that Zahm and Cavanaugh Halls would be returned for civilian use. The Alumni Association urged alumni to renew efforts in student recruitment to take advantage of the expanded civilian capacity. The Alumni Board extended the second Annual Alumni Fund for a half year, to bring the fund into the general calendar-year pattern. Men in service were sent 5,000 questionnaires by the association to update its postwar preparation in the field of placement. Clubs were asked to use the Universal Communion Sunday to preserve or reestablish their identities.

In 1941, as a proper setting for the projected Annual Alumni Fund, Father Hugh O'Donnell had instituted an annual statement of University receipts and expenditures. In 1944, his third report indicated receipts of $4,585,989.63 from all sources, leaving only a net credit of $39,322 from miscellaneous small gifts.

The University announced the opening of an Office of Veterans Affairs, to coordinate the problems of returning service men. Bernard J. Voll '17, chairman of the association's vocational committee, met in October to hear a report on the service questionnaires. The University, in anticipation of peace, announced the reorganization of the graduate studies into an official Graduate School, with Rev. Philip Moore, C.S.C. '14, as its first dean.

Another obituary rich in history and campus folklore came with the death of Father J. Leonard Carrico, C.S.C., who had been at Notre Dame from 1908. He was a Kentucky gentleman of the old school, an English teacher of legendary precision, a dean of Arts and Letters for ten years and the director of studies until his death. He was, as Father Eugene Burke, C.S.C., said in his eulogy, "a man of high intellectual ideals. For a quarter of a century he was a kind of watchdog of our academic standards . . . If I might pick out one virtue that shone in him more brightly than others, I should say it was his passionate love for honesty and fairness." I can attest to this. I have seen nuns with tears in their eyes try in vain to coax a higher grade in their Summer School courses for mother superior, only to hear a delightfully soft voice reply with an irrevocable no.

The January meeting of the board of directors of the association in 1945 underscored all the points of the Program for Progress. It gave special emphasis to the mechanics of the association toward these ends. In the spring the University made a memorable announcement. The midshipmen school was to be closed. The Naval R.O.T.C. would be continuing University program. Lyons, Morrissey, Howard and Badin Halls would be returned to the University for student residency. The University midshipmen school had commissioned 8,510 Navy officers since October, 1942.

Father J. Hugh O'Donnell, President of the University, at the Universal Notre Dame Night meeting of the Notre Dame Club of Chicago—always a major event—made one of the milestone addresses in University history. After much campus discussion and much urging from Father Cavanaugh, Art Haley and the Alumni Board, Father O'Donnell said that during the immediate years ahead the University should have $25,000,000 to carry out programs which studies in four major areas indicated. These were the Graduate School, the rehabilitation of war veterans returning to or enrolling at Notre Dame, development of technology, engineering and science programs, whose prewar progress had been spotlighted by their contributions to the war effort, and the strengthening of the undergraduate courses, especially liberal arts and training for government service. The figure named was, for Notre Dame, awesome.

Another postwar story of great alumni interest was the appointment by the Vatican of Most Rev. John F. O'Hara, C.S.C., to be the Bishop of Buffalo, N.Y. Father O'Hara had made a brilliant record in his vital assignment to the Military Ordinariate during the war, with its challenges from the far outposts of the world where United States troops were stationed.

In August, 1945, student enrollment of civilians exceeded that of the curtailed Navy programs for the first time since 1943. Bill Dooley was developing a strong program in placement among the local clubs, and, with Director Ed O'Toole, fostered the first local alumni club placement office to be opened in Chicago under the auspices of that strong and veteran club. The board also requested a report from J. Arthur Haley on the significant work of his public relations office. Haley stressed the importance of the alumni in referring to the University possible non-alumni benefactors, whose existence might otherwise not be known, and in making and maintaining contacts with such sources of support.

The second Annual Alumni Fund, covering a year and a half in order to effect the callendar-year transition, had again exceeded the $100,000 alumni gift record. There was no longer any doubt of the effectiveness of the long-delayed "Living Endowment" principle, though the Annual Alumni Fund was its current designation. One of the major uses of the second fund was the establishment of the Father James A. Burns, C.S.C. Memorial Scholarships, to commenorate the former alumnus-President, and to extend aid to deserving boys needing financial help, as Father Burns himself had. In making the announcement, Father O'Donnell also added that "no head of any University could have had a more loyal and devoted alumni board than Notre Dame has had during this critical period."

In this dawning of the postwar boom, Notre Dame's total receipts for the fiscal year had been $5,000,000 and its total expenditures $4,989,909. With a few gifts, the credit balance was $50,251. In November of 1945, the Associate Board of Lay Trustees observed its 25th anniversary. Byron V. Kanaley '04, long a pillar of the Alumni Association and a founding member of the trustees, paid tribute to Father James A. Burns, its creator. The million dollar fund entrusted to the first board had finally begun to grow, and on this silver jubilee was nearing $5,000,000.

Most significant for the era ahead were announcements that P. C. Reilly, lay trustee, Indianapolis industrialist and philanthropist, had made the first million dollar gift to the University in its history, and that Notre Dame was the beneficiary in the will of Martin J. Gillen, a Wisconsin attorney for the steel industry, of properties which could exceed a million dollars in value.

The third Annual Alumni Fund, completed within the calendar year of 1945, closed with $94,284. In view of the period covered, it was considered successful and convincing. But the needs, as outlined by Father O'Donnell in his $25,000,000 presentation, were far from filled by this unprecedented generosity. And the *Alumnus* noted this in an editorial entitled "Notre Dame Is Still Poor." The editor again received, in the sonorous umbrage of Father O'Donnell, the presidential opinion that while Notre Dame needed support, it was not "poor." This was the dark day from which dates the substitution of "opportunity" for "need," and "limited" for "poor." Father O'Donnell was right in the long-term view. But in those pioneer days of creating instant generosity, the use of the blunt "poor" and the publication of names and amounts of gifts—anathema to professional fund raisers—achieved results that were long overdue and might have been much longer in the embryonic stage.

The campus was facing the varied problems of peacetime readjustment. Conflict based on the disciplinary system traditional for Freshmen just out of high school was immediate when applied to the returning veterans of several years of rigid training, world travel and frequently combat experience. Similarly the problems of married returned veterans, many living on the campus in temporary structures the Navy had left behind it, were different from any previous campus experience. The competition for acceptance between the returning veterans and the new high school graduates was intense. Father Louis J. Thornton, C.S.C. '29, who had returned from his duties in the Military Ordinariate under Bishop O'Hara, had assumed the difficult role of registrar, responsible then for admissions and housing. To balance the enrollment in 1945, he closed registration for all but returning veterans on April 11. The GI Bill, aiding veterans in resuming their education, brought not only a flood of Notre Dame veterans, in addition to the regular high school applications, but it also opened the doors of Notre Dame to many young veterans who had not previously been able to consider the resident boarding school. It was a period of extreme pressures, with constant regret for the many fine prospects who had to be turned away.

Two priests aided greatly in the solution of the above problems. One was Father Thornton and his competent handling of the various factors in assuring balance in college quotas, equitable treatment of veterans, and preserving the vital lifeline with the high schools through continuing acceptance of their graduates. The other priest was a personable, young, and newly ordained member of the Congregation, Rev. Theodore M. Hesburgh, C.S.C., originally of the Class of 1938, who had completed his studies in Rome. He had worked with young people in Washington, while at Holy Cross College, during the USO peak program in the capital during the war years, and was attracted to the problems of the young married veterans in their village called "Vetville." The conflict there between the traditional authority of the University and the mature background and needs of its residents was creating serious problems. Father Hesburgh, immediately popular with his adopted responsibilities, turned the whole climate completely around. The programs established were constructive, designed to solve the particular problems contained in the group, and became the spearhead morale programs of campus reconstruction.

The spring semester opened with the largest enrollment in the history of the University. More than half were veterans. Father O'Donnell announced to alumni the allocation of the third Annual Alumni Fund, which featured the establishment of Bishop John F. O'Hara, C.S.C. Scholarships in the Graduate School. In his report of the University's financial picture in the previous darkest year of the war, he said that total expenses of $4,207,213 had not quite been offset by total receipts of

$4,203,053, but gifts had increased the figure sufficiently to create a balance of $4,190.

In the Summer of 1946, Father O'Donnell retired from the presidency. He must have been greatly disappointed at the limitations the war had imposed on his administration of his beloved Notre Dame. But the death of Harry Truman, as I write this, reminds me that Father O'Donnell was another President of whom little was expected, yet from whom the exceptional exigencies of war produced much. He had made the magnificent gesture of patriotism in making the University one of the most productive of the Navy programs of the war. At the same time he had preserved the integrity, the identity, and the autonomous function of the University. He had balanced the precariously low budgets of those critical years. He had worked with the Alumni Association so effectively that the long-postponed "Living Endowment" had become during these years the outstandingly successful Annual Alumni Fund, which was to be the trunk of the money tree that opened the broad doors of the future to his successors in office. He had preserved the faculty of the University, so that they remained the hard core of loyalty and dedication which is of the essence of Notre Dame. Faculty members who had gone into service returned. And new faculty necessary to the new growth were attracted to the Notre Dame campus. The *Alumnus* said of Father O'Donnell on his retirement, "The alumni have always been a keen source of interest and encouragement to Father O'Donnell in his administrative posts at the University. He has recognized in them the institutional sine qua non of progress. And he has not only lent his talents and friendship to alumni success—he has demanded it, rightly and effectively."

Alumni organization owes a lasting debt to this 13th President of the University of Notre Dame, who was to die of cancer in gracious resignation to the will of God only a year later.

XXXI

Ever Changing,
Never Changing

The explosion of the atomic bomb on Hiroshima in 1945 signalled a new world, with ramifications still far from understood. It did not come as a complete surprise to the Notre Dame campus. Physicists, in the limited laboratories of that department, working with a home-built mechanism, had been studying the dawning era of atomic fission. Two of them, George Collins and Ed Coomes '31 who had been major figures in developing the research, were drafted immediately into the government war research program. Bernard Waldman, now dean of the College of Science, was another significant researcher and was among the select few who witnessed the first test of the ominous atomic bomb. The scientific background created at Notre Dame by Father John A. Zahm and Father Nieuwland, by Dr. Albert Zahm and Father Kirsch and Father Wenninger, found the University almost at home in the new world of the atom.

Rev. John J. Cavanaugh, C.S.C. '23, vice president under Father O'Donnell during the war years, was chosen President to succeed him in 1946. Father Cavanaugh was a bridge for the enduring Notre Dame. He had served the two-year secretarial apprenticeship under the elder Father John W. Cavanaugh. His brother, Francis P. Cavanaugh, was a priest of the Congregation, a teacher in the College of Arts and Letters, and for a time its dean. As a lay student, John Cavanaugh had been popular on both the Notre Dame and Saint Mary's campuses. He had become head of the Student Activities Committee when that first real effort at student government achieved such a mature stature after World War I that it proved to be premature as well.

But John Cavanaugh, who had left Studebaker after graduation and a promising career start, to return to the seminary to become a priest of Holy Cross, knew student thinking. He had a background of lay approach to Notre Dame problems. And he had absorbed and developed a gracious personality and a fluent manner of speech, which escaped the oratory of the elder Cavanaugh and the pomp of Father Hugh O'Donnell. It made him an articulate and attractive interpreter of the new programs and problems which the University of Notre Dame was to face during his presidency.

Action was the postwar national keynote. Urgency was felt in overcoming the lost years of the war, and an almost equal urgency developed quickly in the competition to master and spearhead the new world of science and technology which had dawned.

Major events began to happen at Notre Dame. The Brothers of the Congregation of Holy Cross, long affiliated with the priests and sisters established a separate province. The move recognized their rapid expansion in the national field of secondary schools, in their foreign apostolates, and in their publications. Under the first Brother Provincial, Brother Ephrem O'Dwyer, C.S.C., M.A. '24 who had been treasurer of the University, the new province prospered and now has itself subdivided into the Indiana, the Eastern, and the South-West Provinces. In the separation, the brothers assumed the responsibility for St. Edward's University, Austin, Tex.

June 28, 29 and 30, 1946 marked the resumption of the commencement and reunion programs in June. The return to two semesters was announced. Class reunions were not held as such, but the general alumni reunion attracted a crowd, and the alumni banquet heard President Tom Byrne outline the programs which the board had guided through the critical war years, and which now were demanding full alumni cooperation for successful expansion. The 10 points defined in 1943 were now more urgent than ever before. The Ninth Universal Communion Sunday was announced for the December Feast of the Immaculate Conception, falling on Sunday. The clubs had had a dramatic wartime experience to appreciate the need for close ties between religion and patriotism if America were to supply a proper world leadership.

The September semester opened with a record enrollment of 4,489 students. Only the R.O.T.C. program remained, an integral part of the University program. At a September meeting in

Cleveland, the Alumni Board voted to bring the club presidents to Notre Dame on Nov. 29 and 30, to discuss the prompt revitalization of the widespread Notre Dame Alumni Clubs, now resuming full membership potential, and faced with the influx of larger numbers of alumni as the larger postwar classes were graduated. Father Patrick Peyton, C.S.C. '37, whose miraculous recovery from an illness near his ordination had created in him a fervent apostle for Our Lady and the custom of the Family Rosary to honor her, was already winning great numbers of followers. In 1946, he announced the creation of the Family Theater in Hollywood, to enlist the services of the moving picture industry in promoting his crusade.

The Local Alumni Club Council on Nov. 29 and 30 found 77 of the 83 local alumni clubs represented on the campus for the revitalizing meeting. This response was in itself a new plateau of club achievement. The University and the Alumni Association presented, through administrators and Alumni Board members, the challenges of the war years, and the challenging opportunities of the immediate future, for both Notre Dame and the association. The delegates were articulate in their discussion of the programs, and in suggestions of their own for improving the clubs and the programs of mutual interest. The value of the Local Club Council was more evident in this first postwar assembly than it had ever been.

The *Alumnus* entered upon a renewed effort toward continuing education. An article by Professor Henry C.F. Staunton on "Worthwhile Reading: How to Do It," offered an outline of an approach to reading that met the requirements of any alumnus from the Beowulf students of Staunton's own courses to the bestseller and off-beat books of the liberal arts. The article remains, in my judgment, one of the most helpful guidelines to continuous reading, and the most effective tool of continuing education to be found.

Frank Leahy returned from the Navy in the fall of 1946, along with a dream team of veterans and former players from the war years. The Army game, with Blanchard and Davis still on the West Point roster, was a scoreless battle of giants that for Notre Dame fans did much to erase the previous two Army massacres, especially when the Notre Dame team went on to win its eight other games, piling up 271 points to the opponent's 24, and winning the Number One national ranking.

During the winter, Father Louis Thornton, registrar, emphasized a March 15 deadline for enrollment applications, directed toward alumni with sons to apply. "We in the registrar's office, like everyone else at Notre Dame, are very conscious and very proud of the Notre Dame family spirit and the Notre Dame tradition . . . we derive a special satisfaction, you may be sure, when we are able to enroll a student who will be a Notre Dame man for the second or third generation. Upon such a foundation does Notre Dame go ahead to greater glory."

And now, as the natural course of Notre Dame and the association moves on, we come to another of our miracles!

The wartime Alumni Boards, under President Harry F. Kelly from 1941 to 1943, and under President Thomas Byrne from 1943 through 1946, had among other achievements produced a new Constitution for the association, moving its procedures into the more sophisticated channels demanded by the expanding membership and programs.

First of these to be affected was the election of a brand-new Alumni Board on Jan. 25, 1947. Two nominating committees had each prepared a slate of 12 candidates—alumni in good standing (i.e. contributors). The 24 names had been placed on a mail ballot an distributed in December to alumni contributors. The board was to be enlarged to 12 members, elected for 3-year terms of office so that two-thirds of the board would be an experienced continuing majority for the operation of the association. In this first selection, four members were to be elected for three-year terms; four for two-year terms, and four for one-year terms, annual elections thereafter to be the selection of four new members, from a slate of eight, for four-year terms. The new board was a strong, representative body of alumni experienced in club and class activities, and coming from key areas, key classes, and key business and professional pursuits. The retiring president of the last wartime board, Thomas F. Byrne '28, was made honorary president, to retain his experience. J. E. Armstrong, alumni secretary and William R. Dooley, assistant secretary, were elected to ex officio posts on the new board.

In a tribute to seniority, and to a director of exceptional versatility and experience, the new board elected Harry G. Hogan '04 of Fort Wayne, a monogram alumnus, as president. The move was unprecedented, as Hogan had already served a term as president of the national Alumni Association in 1917. But he was a highly regarded attorney and a political leader of substance in Indiana. He was president of the Dime Bank of Fort Wayne, and a partner there in a tool and die company and a lumber company. He was ostensibly retiring from this multi-interests activity, which led to his acceptance of what he regarded at first as an honorary responsibility.

With him on this new postwar board were Francis Wallace '23, journalist and author; Robert T. Hellrung '30, St. Louis businessman; John J. Elder '30, Indiana businessman, a track star whose record 96-yard pass interception and run won the hotly contested football game against Army in 1929; Paul R. Mallon '23, Alexandria, Va., columnist and author; Louis P. Buckley '28, former teacher of economics at Notre Dame, a leader among the class secretaries and an economist of increasing stature among Catholic liberals; Daniel J. O'Neil '25, an executive with A.T.&T., holder of degrees in engineering and law, and an ardent follower of Father O'Hara from his prefect of religion days to the archbishopric; Harold E. Duke '30, Philadelphia businessman; Timothy J. Murphy '24, Hartford, Conn., businessman; Daniel D. Halpin '31, Haddonfield, N.J., business executive, who had been manager of the last Rockne national championship team of '30; Leo D. Kelly '21, Syracuse, N.Y., business executive, and Eugene S. Blish '34, Denver, Colo., manufacturers' representative. These were men still in the traditional voting pattern of electing national officers from class groups 15 to 20 years from graduation. (It has taken deliberate election method changes to achieve a more balanced class representation on subsequent boards.) They were men of business and professional competence. They were experienced in club and class functions. Several of them were from "Notre Dame families." They proved to be united in the dedication to the solution of the problems of the University suddenly unfolding to them, and in understanding them.

The Leahy powerhouse of 1946 drew the usual criticisms which attend success. One of the defenses of lasting merit, joining that of a previous President (Father Charles O'Donnell, under similar circumstances almost 20 years earlier), came from Father John J. Cavanaugh, now President of Notre Dame. "When we in American sports hold the winner under suspicion merely because he is a winner, we discredit many of the fine qualities that have made football inspiring—the will to win, extraordinary school spirit and devotion, heroic observance of training rules, indefatigable application on the part of coaches and players to the details of the game—and we come perilously close to the kind of dismal thinking that stigmatizes with suspicion the man who achieves outstanding success, a kind of thinking which is trying to spread itself over America and to make communism popular in our economic life by reducing the ambitions and possibilities of all men to mediocre and monotonous average stature."

These values of victory and success, inculcated and exemplified in the followers of Notre Dame from the example of Sorin, through two major world wars and a devastating economic depression, were still held in high regard on the campus, tempered as always by the theological and cardinal virtues.

The allocation of the successful fourth Annual Alumni Fund was largely to the continuation of the Burns and O'Hara Scholarships, and faculty benefits. A special series of lectures was financed by the fund, to introduce the newly established Medieval Institute at Notre Dame. The University, in a resumption of academic activity, announced the reopening and continuation of the Summer School, suspended necessarily by the war years, and at the same time revealed the establishment of a Summer Session in Mexico City, in conjunction with Mexico City College, open to alumni and veterans. This was an extension of the long-time Latin American relationships with Notre Dame, rooted in the travels of Father John A. Zahm, and in the later leadership of Father John F. O'Hara, encouraged in the first instance by President Theodore Roosevelt, and in the latter by Lay Trustee Edward Nash Hurley.

The new Alumni Board immediately launched the fifth Annual Alumni Fund, with strong encouragement from retiring President Tom Byrne, and Father Cavanaugh. The latter said, "The establishment of the Centenary Fund to augment our material resources at a critical, as well as at a historical, point in Notre Dame's life was a splendid manifestation of your generous understanding of the conditions favoring development. The participation of alumni in ever increasing numbers and amounts means a more and more significant future for the University and for Notre Dame men."

President Byrne quoted Father Cavanaugh, from a letter to Byrne, as pointing out that "Our Lady is never outdone in generosity," a statement borne out in the many decades of her obvious patronage of the University dedicated to her.

Harry Hogan, shedding any real or imaginary retirement slowing processes, endorsed the Alumni Fund. Recognizing its growth and value, he commented on the traditional need of money at Notre Dame, which the University had met with "requests modest to the point of humility." He repeated the

efforts of the Alumni Association, from the first University
Endowment campaign through the association efforts to establish the "Living Endowment" principle, culminating finally in
1941 in the Annual Alumni Fund, after 20 years of effort. To
foster the new financial expansion program, Hogan appointed
alumni governors for each of the states, to work with the
alumni clubs, but also to expand contacts with alumni outside
local club jurisdiction. Hogan became chairman of the new
board of governors, and secretary Armstrong its secretary.

The governors met with club representatives at the 1947
commencement. The clubs were assured that the new program
would not jeopardize their autonomy or identity, but would
actually add a new dimension to the geographical picture, both
for the association and for the University. At the alumni banquet in June President Hogan announced the mobilization of
alumni in an intensive program of fund-raising. He said, "Notre
Dame wants money only as a wholesome means to a sound
end . . . we must take off our hats to the past, but we must take
off our coats to the future . . . Our relationship to Notre Dame
must be on a 365-day basis." He added, "When I entered Notre
Dame nearly 50 years ago (1900), its athletic glory was a matter
of only a very local knowledge, but I know that this University
then had students attending from states throughout the union
and even from foreign countries. The great era of Notre Dame
athletics has been comparatively recent, yet Notre Dame has
been a famous institution of Catholic learning and culture for
over 100 years."

Harry Hogan, at retirement age, was, from his home and
businesses in Fort Wayne, and on tireless campus and alumni
club visits, a constant radiation center of organization for the
intensive new program. As alumni secretary, and personally
committed to the soundness of his belief in the necessity for the
new efforts, I was his campus booster station. My telephone
rang all hours of the day or night, in the office and at home,
with new ideas, and with frequent impatience at the limited
results a limited staff and academic institutional procedures
could produce. It is the recollection of this dedicated human
dynamo that brought me to this task of chronicling the Alumni
Association's development over its hundred and more years.

The total University needs were in Hogan's plans. On July 25
and 26, at a meeting of the executive committe of the board of
governors, sanctioned by the Alumni Board and the University
administration, Father Cavanaugh. and Harry Hogan issued a

joint statement announcing the creation of the University of Notre Dame Foundation. The Annual Alumni Fund was to be incorporated in this new program as a strong and established pillar of it, as was to be the existing Department of Public Relations under J. Arthur Haley. The Foundation would coordinate these programs, together with any other fund-raising pro grams within the University. Its two major purposes were to strengthen all existing efforts and to initiate new efforts toward essential support, from all sources, for University progress.

In the summer of 1947, Father Hugh O'Donnell died, a year after his retirement from the presidency. He was pleased with the strong new direction of the Alumni Association he had so long encouraged and supported. Speaking of Father O'Donnell, Father Cavanaugh said, "As President of the University for six and one-half most difficult years—in anticipation of war, while the war was on, and in the first stages of postwar readjustment—he distinguished himself by manifesting excellent judgment, foresight, and unusual administrative tact and ability."

The announced Summer Session opened in June, with an enrollment of 1,743, one-fourth of whom were sisters. During the war years, many of the religious orders who had sent Summer School representatives to Notre Dame, had turned to other colleges and universities, or had established provisions for such work in their own colleges. The predominance of women religious on the summer campus was ended, as was the unique spirit which had existed among the heterogeneous nuns of the Women's Club of Notre Dame.

The pressure program of Harry Hogan, alien to the academic processes, caused some stirs of anxiety on and off the campus. Alumni were too easily persuaded that raising money was their only role in higher education. And while administrators and faculty recognized the needs and the benefits of outside support, they had traditional inhibitions about becoming involved in its solicitation. The alumni office, the Foundation itself, and the Alumni Board took steps constantly to try to put the new program in proper perspective. Robert Hellrung '30, a veteran in local club organization, and now vice president for local clubs under the new board, stated his conviction that the new Foundation, and the work of the state governors and the new city committees would serve to strengthen membership and activity in all of the club programs.

By the fall of 1947, the Foundation, with Father Cavanaugh as its president and Harry Hogan and the alumni secretary directing its procedures, announced that already 100 city chairmen had been appointed in the first major test of the program. The $25,000,000 goal announced by Father Hugh O'Donnell earlier was the Foundation's first target.

In the face of enrollment pressures, the administration permitted the enrollment in the fall of 1947 to reach 4,767.

The presidents of the local alumni clubs were brought to the Notre Dame campus in November of 1947, to be briefed on the Foundation program, and to discuss and clarify its relationships with the clubs on the local level.

The Associate Board of Lay Trustees, in September, had received a thorough presentation of the Foundation plan to secure the $25,000,000 goal. The trustees not only endorsed the Foundation, but passed a second motion, that "The Board of Trustees feels that the Foundation, which was begun by the action and leadership of the Alumni Association and its president, Harry Hogan, is the greatest thing yet done by alumni for the University, and endorses, approves, and advocates the program evolved by the Foundation with Harry Hogan as chairman."

On Sept. 26, the Notre Dame faculty had been assembled, and the Foundation plan was presented by Father Cavanaugh, president, Harry Hogan, association president and Father Robert Sweeney, C.S.C., '30 a dynamic young priest who had been named by Father Cavanaugh as the University's special coordinator of alumni relations and who was instantly popular on and off the campus. As a result of the faculty meeting, James E. McCarthy, dean of the College of Commerce, was named chairman of the faculty committee to work with the Foundation.

Father Cavanaugh, in one of his presentations, had made a statement that the major programs of the University could be divided into three major categories—"enrollment, endowment, and prestige." This concept was easy to pursue, easy to understand. The club delegates in the November meeting leaned on it in their deliberations. They promised cooperation to the Foundation, as the arm of endowment. They determined to pursue an unusual path under the general heading of enrollment. They were enthusiastic in their role as prospective student contacts, but they added a new task, the discovery and enrollment, in the clubs themselves, of non-graduate former students. The multiple advantages to the three major areas of involving this large but unknown segment of the Notre Dame family was quickly evident. And the clubs readily recognized the already powerful role they exercised as public relations channels for the University—to alumni, to families of alumni and of present or prospective students and to the community. They precluded membership in the clubs for persons who had not had some campus experience, but agreed to study the formation of honorary or special groups for the increasing number of non-alumni friends of Notre Dame, as a tangible aid to the Foundation effort.

A constructive recognition of new Alumni Association stature, and a valuable tool in the expansion of its programs and responsibilities came through Harry Hogan's advocacy with the conversion of the Carrol Study Hall into combined offices for the Foundation and the Alumni Association, an efficient juxtaposition which has remained.

The new Foundation received a boost from E. M. Morris '06, president of the Board of Lay Trustees. He announced that a change in investment policy in the Board of Trustees had resulted in some increase in the endowment fund, now near the $5,000,000 figure, but that the stated needs of Notre Dame required an immediate campaign for greater and widespread support. He and his finance committee, including John C. Tully '11, Bernard Voll '17 and Thomas Beacom '20, had brought about the more liberal investment policy within the trustees, and now heartily endorsed the Foundation program as concurring with their own concepts.

The year-end report of the Foundation, scarcely under full organization status, was encouraging. Highlights were the 60 Foundation governors, the 160 city chairmen, the high percentage of alumni participation in the fifth Annual Fund, and the potential increase in participation and amount opened up by the involvement of non-graduate former students, many of whom were identifiable successes on the national scene, and some of whom had already been brought into the Alumni Association by its election clause.

On Jan. 11 and 12, the Alumni Board reelected the officers who had served in 1947, and who were in the midst of an outstanding vital, already successful program. Father Sweeney reported to the board his visit to 37 alumni clubs. Daniel J. O'Neil '25, who had organized the first Notre Dame Communion Sunday as president of the Notre Dame Club of New York in 1938, now a member of the Alumni Board, submitted a report on job placement and counseling which recommended added interest on the part of the University.

One of the first programs advanced by the Foundation to

dramatize the new dimension of alumni involvement was de-
vised around the effort of alumni to "Give Or Get $200" on an
annual basis. Because many alumni, probably the great majority, could not afford the personal gift increase to this unprecedented figure, the immediate alternative was to solicit friends,
business associates or other suggested sources of non-alumni
annual giving.

Harry Hogan was experienced and well aware that the sweeping segments of the Foundation program would not secure
instant success. But he was too experienced to let the doubts
and fears of others keep him from the constant sowing of seeds
of the Foundation which, largely after he had personally relinquished its guidance, resulted in its phenomenal harvests.

In Boston, on Jan. 22, 1948, Father John Cavanaugh and
Harry Hogan presided over the first regional meeting of 60
Foundation governors and city chairmen from the New England
states. Before a meeting of 300 alumni and friends on this
Boston pioneering effort, Father Cavanaugh pointed to the
youth of the Notre Dame alumni—almost 10,000 of a total
alumni body only slightly more had been in service. The University had provided facilities for the training of 25,000 Navy men,
some 12,000 of whom had been commissioned on the campus
but these were not Notre Dame alumni. The economic offset of
the average youth of Notre Dame's alumni body—unlike those
of the surrounding older Ivy League schools—was the unique
partnership which the whole nation felt with Notre Dame,
through the identity it held as a truly national Catholic University, and through the nationwide popularity and contacts of its
teams.

Harry Hogan pointed to the changes in the philosophy of
fund-raising in the postwar era, resulting in the creation of the
Foundation. He expressed the conviction that the new Notre
Dame, already unfolding, would make fund-raising a permanent
part of campus life. He also voiced another prophetic opinion,
that the work of the Foundation would produce a better
informed and better organized alumni group, to the advancement of the much broader benefits sought by both alumni and
University.

One of the benefits which Harry Hogan brought to the
campus was the corporate concept that expanded programs
meant expanded staffs and budgets. In line with the Foundation
growth, the foundation added John N. Cackley '37, Herman
Zitt '48 and Joseph DeMuro '48, to the staff. Zitt with Charles

Cartier, handled the increasing detail of contributions and records, while Cackley and DeMuro administered the multiplying details of 206 city chairmen and committees.

The 25th observance of Universal Notre Dame Night in 1948 offered a break in the financial pressures. The principal meeting was appropriately scheduled in Philadelphia, the home club of the night's founder, John H. Neeson '03. Father John Cavanaugh, Frank Leahy and Clarence "Pat" Manion, along with association president Harry Hogan, formed a major program for the occasion.

Under the studies of the Foundation and from the suggestions of many alumni and friends stimulated by the new program, many new suggestions for financial support of the University were being advanced through the Foundation committees and through the *Alumnus* magazine. Among these were gifts from corporations, gifts by wills and bequests, gifts through insurance, and the appeal of special gifts for special projects. This last suggestion had particular significance. Originally, the idea of "Living Endowment," at Notre Dame and other schools as well, was based largely on the value of unrestricted giving to the institutional administrators. This was true, but it weakened the force of the appeal in amounts. The concept of special gifts for special projects opened the door to major gifts for capital projects.

The alumni banquet on June 5 was highlighted by Father Cavanaugh's "state of the University" address. He detailed the increased stature and diversity of programs demanding attention. He reported the organizing of an Advisory Council for the College of Commerce, headed by Charles M. Regan '17. He said, "The Alumni Association, which was born in Notre Dame's silver jubilee year, and which has stood by in all emergencies since, has proved through its members to be the anticipated agency, the field force, the personal source, upon which the Foundation has to rise or fall. Response has indicated a rising well beyond the level of our hopes a year ago."

Harry Hogan informed the alumni that the Foundation was big business. He referred to the increasing competing fund-raising programs of other institutions. He cited the competition of other Catholic causes for the Catholic philanthropic dollar. He pointed to the generous, but very few, non-alumni supporting Notre Dame. He stressed the need for zeal in alumni solicitation. He called attention to the difference between the Foundation and ordinary big business—the Foundation does not work

for profit. And, too, since the Foundation is not the sole source
of University income, it must always have a program of convincing needs supplementing and strengthening the other sources of
support, e.g. tuition fees, interest from endowment, and the
auxiliary enterprise.

The reunion drew an attendance of 800, and the restoration
of the class reunions was begun. The Notre Dame Law Association was organized at this 1948 commencement, with 125 law
alumni present. Francis Jones '29, South Bend attorney, was
the first chairman, with Robert E. Sullivan '40, of the Law
School faculty as secretary.

The alumni secretary's report showed 107 local alumni clubs,
seven of which were new; the highly successful Local Club
Presidents' Council; the growing programs of Universal Notre
Dame Night and Communion Sunday; the Alumni Association
significances of the new Foundation; and the progress of the
placement program under William R. Dooley. A forthcoming
alumni dirctory was included in the program. As vice chairman
of the Foundation, the secretary's report also paid tribute to
President Harry Hogan for his great dedication to the University, and to Fathers Cavanaugh and Sweeney for their cooperation with the Alumni Association.

The 50th anniversary of the Department of Architecture had
been observed in May. Dramatic interest in the event rose from
the fact that the first student to enroll in the department in
1898, was Eugenio Rayneri, of Havana, later one of the Western
hemisphere's prominent architects and designer of Cuba's
capitol building in Havana.

The Class of 1928, under Bernard Garber and Louis Buckléy,
reported on the intensive survey of the class, the most comprehensive and revealing picture of alumni of Notre Dame after 20
years out of the University, to have been attempted.

Robert Cahill '34, football ticket manager, reported that
alumni, limited to two tickets each, had ordered more tickets
for the 1948 season than had been ordered for the previous year
with a limit of four. The problem of 14,000 alumni seats in the
Notre Dame stadium, with 15,000 alumni to order them, was
becoming acute. The two nationally ranked Number One teams
of '46 and '47 had not lessened the popularity or pressure.

The Alumni Association and the Foundation published a
Foundation Manual and *Guide for City Chairmen and Committees*, dealing with all phases of the Foundation, and statistics
of the Foundation and the Annual Alumni Fund. It was a major
tool in the growing program.

When the University opened its fall semester in 1948, the enrollment passed the 5,000 mark. Part of the increase stemmed from the acceptance of the usual size of Freshman class, but also from the unusual reduction of mortality among returning advanced students, in some part at least a contribution of the more serious older students of the postwar period.

The Foundation received its first major challenge in the fall of 1948 when Father John Cavanaugh announced the building of a new $1,750,000 science building, to meet the growing demands of the postwar interest in science, and to preserve the outstanding leadership of the University in this field. The Foundation was asked to raise $1,400,000 during the year 1949 to meet this challenge. The building was to be appropriately dedicated to Father Julius Nieuwland, C.S.C. '99, outstanding alumnus-priest-scientist and former dean of Science.

As Harry Hogan neared the end of his second year as president of the Association, he told alumni, "I feel that I am personally ending a chapter, a rich one for me. Many causes and many organizations have enlisted my volunteer time. But I have found in working for Notre Dame a spiritual motivation that has brought rewards beyond the usual satisfaction of civic or social group work . . . But if I am ending a chapter as president of the Alumni Association, I feel that in the University of Notre Dame Foundation we have begun a book, a great book."

Harry Hogan, another magnificent alumnus, was awarded an honorary doctorate by the University, which he accepted reluctantly in his unselfish dedication. Ageless in his vitality, he died in an automobile accident on April 1, 1966 in his home city, Fort Wayne.

XXXII

New Paths of Progress

The enthusiasms of the postwar years, the new emphases nationally on technology, the spotlight that was focusing on higher education as the hope of the nation's future, and at Notre Dame the advent of the Foundation as a means to unprecedented pursuit of these ends, created a new climate of academic life, and a new pace in its achievement.

The Alumni Board in the second year of Harry Hogan's administration had added four new members, for three-year terms, as constitutionally provided: Joseph M. Boland '27, former football star and coach, a popular radio sports announcer with the South Bend *Tribune*'s WSBT; Father Vincent Brennan '32, a diocesan priest from Butler, Pa.; Leo B. Ward '20, Los Angeles attorney and club pioneer there, whose office was a center for the many alumni moving to and through Southern California; and Arthur D. Cronin Jr. '37, a Detroit businessman, one of Layden's linemen in the legendary Ohio State games of 1935 and 1936.

A letter to the board from the retiring Hogan advised, "With the Foundation well established, the Alumni Board is in an excellent strategic position to take up both the purpose of fund-raising and the spiritual, cultural, fraternal, business and professional, social, and recreational activities of alumni life. From all of these high potentials came the factors that make our ultimate victory secure."

The new president, well equipped for this multiple-program challenge, was Francis Wallace '23, Bellaire, O., established author, sports writer and frequent campus visitor. Wallace, familiar with the association and University administrators, immediately set up an executive committee to study the programs

354

suggested in the Hogan letter. The board was of one mind that the paths ahead were many, all of value. Harry Hogan was made honorary president.

New board members elected for three-year terms beginning under Frank Wallace's presidency were William J. Sherry '21, Tulsa oil engineer; R. Conroy Scoggins '24, Houston oil executive; William B. Jones '28, Chevy Chase attorney, and Edward J. Beckman '16, businessman, a veteran of the New York Club programs, who had just moved to Lampasas, Tex.

The 1948 Universal Communion Sunday had been observed from coast to coast, from the Mexican parish observance of the Los Angeles Club, to the club event held at Mt. St. Joseph's in Baltimore.

One of the waves of the future was recognized, if not fully, when the *Alumnus*, in cooperation with the Department of Journalism under Professor Thomas Stritch '34, published an issue in which the postwar years on the campus were described in articles by students in the department. The seeds of new student power were also evident when study lounges were established in three Freshmen halls. The rector of Farley Hall said: "The study lounges are succeeding and the students run everything."

In harmony with the Foundation campaign for Science Hall, Universal Notre Dame Night in 1949 was devoted to the history of science at Notre Dame, a most attractive and enlightening review of the remarkable history of the achievements of the Zahm brothers, Father Nieuwland, Jerome Green and the currently highly significant developments in Art Reyniers' germ-free life experiments, and in the pursuit of atomic studies. So successful was the Night that the board began to consider the broadening of the occasion from the original one-night date, to include several days on either side. This would not interfere with the identity of the Night in the club community. It would permit campus speakers to make more than one club appearance each year. The only negative effect was in the speculative national radio program tying in the meetings. This tie-in, even when the broadcasts had been available, had proved to be a major publicity and public relations tool.

Father John H. Murphy, C.S.C. '35, former Superior of Moreau Seminary, had been chosen as vice president under Father Cavanaugh. Now, at the end of his first three years as President, and faced with multiple demands of both academic and physical expansion, Father Cavanaugh announced the creation of five University vice presidents to assist in the proper administration of the growing Notre Dame.

Father John Murphy was made vice president of public relations, in which post the Foundation was his responsibility; Father Howard Kenna '26, former prefect of studies, was named vice president for academic affairs; Father John J. Burke '32, was named vice president for business affairs, and Father Joseph A. Kehoe '33, was named vice president for student affairs. Father Cavanaugh's new executive vice president was Father Theodore M. Hesburgh '38, young teacher in theology, and the popular and effective chaplain of the University's Vetville.

Father Cavanaugh, with this very effective delegation of administrative responsibilities in the pressing and diverse channels of development, turned to the study of changes in higher education taking place all over the nation. In frequent talks with Maynard Hutchins and Mortimer Adler at the University of Chicago, along with Paul Hoffman, a trustee of both institutions, Father Cavanaugh discovered the interest in St. Thomas Aquinas which existed, under Adler's stimulus, at Chicago, and the interest in Great Books, which Hutchins and Adler were advancing as a major benefit to education, both on campus and as a continuing tool. He was exposed to the powerful impact of technological education, inevitable at Chicago, where Fermi and his associates had developed the wartime use of atomic energy.

The Alumni Board had decided that the class reunions would be more effective, and the commencements as well, by separating the two growing and diverse programs. The 1949 reunions were held a week following the commencement. Seven hundred alumni endorsed the board's decision. One of the events of the reunion program was a seminar, a forerunner of the serious programs added to the reunion weekend's regular features in later years. Faculty and administrators were more accessible to alumni contacts than they had been during the duties of the commencement weekend. The Seniors had for a number of years been separated from the annual alumni banquet, by both numbers and interest. The moves proved constructive.

Father Cavanaugh's suggestion of the broad guidelines of enrollment, endowment and prestige was reflected in the planning of the association. The June meeting of the board set the theme for Universal Notre Dame Communion Sunday as "the ties between religion and science," a particularly appropriate theme in the light of national focus on science, and the Foundation's Science Building program.

President Frank Wallace announced a program deeply endorsed by him and vital to the University, to be called the "prestige program." It was aimed at enlisting all alumni, the clubs and the classes, and the *Alumnus* magazine, in acquainting the nation with the quality of education and the quality of alumni of the University. The association budget for the 1949-50 year was set at $49,250, which included eight full-time and several part-time salaries, office expenses, the club council expense, and a $1,500 item for capital equipment (an Addressograph machine, as we were addressing all alumni mail in the alumni office).

The 1949 commencement, swelled by the graduation of returned veterans, moved the exercises to the Notre Dame Stadium, where a record 6,000 persons watched the 804 Seniors receive their degrees.

The board year under Frank Wallace provided a constructive transition from the intensive focus on fund-raising to the multiple programs of the association which would be necessary to maintain the interest and contact of alumni so essential to their participation in the Foundation effort. Wallace, who had been an effective ambassador for Notre Dame in the active areas of American sports, has remained throughout the years an effective missionary and interpreter of the University, not only in sports, but in the much broader University context from which the success in sports has sprung.

One of the major changes which occurred under Wallace was the outgrowth of years of effort and recommendation and of practical functioning by the Alumni Association in the field of job placement and counseling. Now the University, after several years of experimenting with a placement office under the priest-directors Rev. Francis P. Goodall, C.S.C. '20, and Father Robert Sweeney '30, announced the appointment of William R. Dooley '26, who had advanced the placement program of the association so constructively, as full-time lay director of the new Placement Office. The board endorsed the proposal to tie in the clubs and alumni with the new program, as they had worked well with the pioneering efforts.

The theme for the 1950 Universal Notre Dame Night was the prestige theme advocated by Wallace and the board as a major alumni contribution to Notre Dame. The board heard from Bob Cahill that even "alumni preference," the advantage given to alumni fund contributors, might no longer mean sideline seats, so heavy had the ticket demands of a rapidly growing alumni body become. The undefeated, once-tied (Southern California) team of 1948, and the undefeated and Number One ranked team of 1949 did not reduce the pressures for tickets. Notre Dame was playing regularly now to more than half a million people each football season.

When Harry G. Hogan retired as president of the Alumni Association and chairman of the Foundation, Father Cavanaugh created a committee to head up the Foundation's ongoing fund-raising efforts, including the Science Building program. Frank C. Walker '09, New York City, became chairman of the committee, which consisted of Father John H. Murphy, Father Theodore M. Hesburgh, J. E. Armstrong, J. Arthur Haley, John B. Kanaley '09, of New York City, John N. Cackley and Herman Zitt, with Father Cavanaugh as an ex officio member.

The Foundation reported that the hoped for $1,400,000 goal of the Science Building had not been achieved. But the stimulus of the Foundation was reflected in even greater significance. The Science Building fund had achieved $484,365. Mrs. Sally Fisher, widow of a former trustee, gave $1,000,000 to build the Fisher residence hall, costing $750.000, and to provide $250,000 for student aid. I. A. O'Shaughnessy gave another $100,000 toward his liberal arts fund. The Rockefeller Foundation gave $69,000 and E. M. Morris '06, contributed $78,500 from his foundation. The Kresge Foundation and the Damon Runyon Cancer Fund each gave $25,000 toward research. The estate of former trustee William J. Corbett provided $40,000 and the Michael P. Grace Trust $31,000.

The Foundation report showed a new high in the amount of alumni giving, a high percentage of alumni participation, and a doubling of non-alumni contributors. More than two million dollars in gifts and research funds had been received from outside the University. With Father Cavanaugh's report was listed the continuing urgency of the new Science Building, and other needs of the University in the immediate future. The Notre Dame Foundation had achieved a major breakthrough in the field of educational philanthropy, essential to the progress of higher education in the postwar years, and doubly vital to Notre Dame, which still reported a small endowment out of all proportion to the endowments of the colleges and universities with which comparisons were usually made.

This encouraging report was followed up dramatically when after the spring meeting of the Board of Lay Trustees in 1950, Father Cavanaugh announced the gift of $1,500,000 from I. A. O'Shaughnessy to erect a new Liberal and Fine Arts Building for that College, and a gift of $1,000,000 from E. M. Morris '06, to erect an Inn at the entrance to the campus. Morris was an astute business man and saw the value to the University of having on the campus facilities for housing the prominent men and women increasingly involved in the trustee, council and Alumni Association meetings, and the scholars, lecturers and parents of students, who visited the campus throughout the year.

At the January meeting of the Alumni Board in 1950, Leo B. Ward '20, Los Angeles, was elected president to succeed Frank Wallace. The new members of the Ward-directed alumni board were Dr. Matthew Weis '22, St. Louis, Mo.; Richard J. Nash '23, Chicago, Ill., contractor; John Q. Adams '26, Montclair, N.J., warehouse executive, and Harvey G. Foster '39, Newark, N.J., a high ranking agent in the FBI. Frank Wallace remained on the board as honorary president, which was no longer an honorary title, but a working retention of the experience and project leadership of the retiring president for an extra year. The practice accounted for some of the great unity of thought and purpose of the board and the continuity of its programs.

On Universal Notre Dame Night, dedicated to the prestige program, 105 Clubs observed the occasion and speakers from the campus joined local alumni in extolling the quality of Notre Dame education. The same theme was presented in the annual alumni banquet in June, when 970 alumni returned to the campus. As an academic feature of the reunion weekend, the deans of the five colleges held open houses and reviewed for their particular alumni group the progress of the college from the 1920 organization to the five colleges, to 1950. Seventy club presidents attended the Club Council held in conjunction with the reunion weekend. At the same reunion the Alumni Board announced the creation of the 50-Year Club, to continue the interest of the small but growing number and the enthusiasm of graduates after their golden jubilee reunion.

The reunion was also the 25th for the alumni secretary. The Class of 1925, always responsive targets of my appeals, gave me a Studebaker car on the occasion. It is difficult to estimate how many "downs" of the first 25 years turned sharply upward with this generous and deeply appreciated gift. It was a needed booster thrust for the seventeen years still ahead.

One of the great encouragements of the Foundation was the successful completion of a $500,000 fund-raising campaign in the St. Joseph Valley Club to augment the inadequate results of the first year of the Nieuwland Science Building fund. The campaign revealed that the people of South Bend, Mishawaka and the surrounding St. Joseph Valley understood the problems of the University, appreciated its value to the community—as dramatically underscored by the depression years—and were willing to participate in the Foundation effort. The fact that Father Julius Nieuwland was a member of the South Bend Belgian community when he became a member of the Congregation of Holy Cross added a dimension to the community campaign. Alumni were joined by non-alumni in the effort.

A new and valuable channel of alumni contact was announced in the new field of television, which undertook the live telecasts of Notre Dame football games. The Leahy teams had rivalled the New York Yankees in popular sports fan appeal. The live telecast brought thousands of alumni back, in effect, to the familiar campus and Stadium, and did much to relieve the growing pressures of the football ticket distribution.

The University began construction of the Science Building, and the efforts of the Foundation were turned toward a major campaign for a much less glamorous goal, the steam plant, utilities and generator, maintenance building—all essential to the sudden expansion of residence halls and classroom buildings. As continuing vice chairman of the Foundation, the alumni secretary was involved in both association and Foundation expansion.

The board received a fine report on the new placement program from its full-time lay director, Bill Dooley '26, so long a valued part of alumni boards. And the new Superior General of the Congregation of Holy Cross, Rev. Christopher J. O'Toole, C.S.C. '29, wrote to the association, "The alumni of the University of Notre Dame constitute one of the glories of Holy Cross . . . I thank them all, first of all for the splendid way they are carrying on the spiritual and academic traditions of Notre Dame, and for their great generosity in helping Holy Cross to meet the financial problems that arise in any large educational institution."

Father John H. Murphy, vice president of public relations, announced an operating deficit for the University fiscal year of $75,800, with total income of $7,817,500 and total expenses of $7,893,300. The importance of the Annual Alumni Fund as the source of substantial unrestricted funds was again evident.

The 1949 Universal Notre Dame Night had introduced to the local alumni clubs the "Man-of-the-Year Scroll," to be awarded to a prominent local alumnus or some local person close to the University, in interests or service. The 1950 Night had repeated the practice, and the Alumni Board now declared itself in favor of the award as a definite annual part of the club programs. The board also recommended a new *Club Manual*, for guidance of the expanding numbers of local clubs and the increasing number and scope of their programs.

The young Notre Dame Law Alumni Association held a meeting in New York in conjunction with a meeting of the New York Bar Association. Professional alumni of the other colleges, especially the College of Science and the College of Engineering, were advised to pursue similar affiliated meetings with their professional conventions.

The *Alumnus* magazine, never letting go of its advocacy of continuing education, printed an extensive list of suggested readings for alumni, prepared for the alumni by Rev. Robert Pelton, C.S.C. '43. When Bill Dooley took over the Placement Office, John P. Burns '34, became managing editor of the *Alumnus* and John Cackley expanded his Foundation duties to become associate editor. Burns was a nephew of Father James A. Burns, C.S.C. '88, former President, who had launched the University's first endowment campaign. The threads of history continued to weave through the years, and "la vie intime" remained still a way of Notre Dame life.

At the January board meeting in 1951 R. Conroy Scoggins '24, Houston, Texas, was elected president of the association. Leo B. Ward continued as honorary president. New board members elected for three-year terms were Joseph S. Morrissey '28, Cincinnati, O., former Rockne quarterback and now a coach; John H. Neeson Jr. '35, Philadelphia attorney and son of the former association president and founder of Universal Notre Dame Night; William C. Schmitt '10, Portland, Ore., industrialist, a member of the 1909 football "Champions of the West," with their first defeat of Michigan, and Luther M. "Mike" Swygert '27, Hammond, Ind., attorney.

In January, 1951 Harry Hogan received his honorary LL.D. At the same significant mid-year commencement, Arch Ward '19, who as a student had been in effect the first University publicity man, and whose brilliant career on the Chicago *Tribune* had been accompanied by many services to the University, also was granted an honorary degree, his own intended Journalism degree having been interrupted by World War I.

To assure cooperation with the Foundation, the Alumni

Association had formed a Foundation committee of the board, chaired by William J. Sherry. This committee informed the membership of the campaign for 100 per cent participation. Local clubs were asked to contact every member. And they were asked, additionally, to assume the solicitation of the broadening base of non-alumni small contributors annually. The *Alumnus* announced that with the "Living Endowment" principle firmly established in the Annual Alumni Fund, the names of contributors with accompanying amounts would no longer be printed, just names alone. The occasional criticism of the earlier procedure was far more than offset by the speed and the success of the transition from the ingrained $5 dues concept to the greater needs of a greater Notre Dame. From the $35,000 of the last three years of dues, to the $300,000 of the first three Alumni Funds, was an end that came awfully close to justifying the means.

For Universal Notre Dame Night in 1951, the usual corps of campus speakers in the various clubs was joined by the Mutual radio network and the Dumont television network to create a major observance, carrying the story of Notre Dame to alumni and friends nationwide.

The *Alumnus* did not lose sight of old traditions. An article in the spring issue listed 32 current members of the University faculty who together represented 800 years of teaching service. Dean of the list was Father Matthew Walsh, C.S.C. '03, former President of Notre Dame, who had returned to his teaching in history on retirement.

The Foundation executive committee, under Frank Walker, announced that the campaign for the essential funds to provide the campus utilities for expansion, would be pursued under the aegis of the Father John J. Cavanaugh Testimonial Fund, to pay tribute to the President under whose leadership so much of this expansion was taking place, and who was about to enter his last year in that office. Responding to this, Father Cavanaugh commented "The University is especially indebted, as you know, to the alumni, the trustees, the advisory councils and its growing circle of active friends. The workers of generations gone by and those who preceded me in this office made my job an enjoyable one. Their efforts in building the reputation and purpose of Notre Dame will always be respectfully remembered."

The Foundation added that if the $3,000,000 Cavanaugh Fund were completed within the projected year, the long-range 10-year program for securing $25,000,000 would be on schedule through its first four years.

An unsung hero of the Alumni Association program died in July, 1951. Vincent Fagan '20, had for many years been a member of the architecture faculty. As a partner with Francis Kervick, head of the department, he had helped design Lyons, Morrissey and Howard Halls. He had designed the World War I Memorial Door on the east entrance of Sacred Heart Church. With Kervick, he had advised Cram and Ferguson in the building of the South Dining Hall. With Dean James McCarthy and Coach George Keogan, Fagan completed a trio whose humor was the delight of campus and community. Vince was the lyricist, with his composer brother-in-law, Joe Casasanta, in increasing the repertoire of Notre Dame marching songs.

So that no prominent segment of alumni would be neglected, and no feeding hand bitten, the *Alumnus* published a complete roster of all Notre Dame All-Americans from Dorais and Eichenlaub in 1913, through Bob Williams and Jerry Groom in 1950. The heroic qualities of such earlier heroes as Louis "Red" Salmon and M. Harry "Red" Miller were too soon for these honors.

President Scoggins, at his first board meeting in that office, made a vital point. "There is a temptation to assume, because so much alumni activity is now blended with University activity, that we have lost ground. The contrary is almost unbelievably the case. The combined strength of the University and alumni programs has advanced far beyond the individual capacities of either."

There was indication that the strengthened and broader programs were timely. The pressures of the great football years, 1946-1949, were beginning to take their toll. Frank Leahy's health began to be of concern to his friends. And the dramatic successes of the postwar years had aroused the intense opposition and often undeserved criticism of contemporary coaches, teams, and writers. The 1950 season put a strange handwriting on the University wall—a 4-4-1 season in which opponents scored more total points than Notre Dame, with losses to Purdue, Indiana, Michigan State and Southern California, and a tie with Iowa. The 1951 team, with Leahy driving himself to restore winning football, achieved a 7-2-1 season, with losses to Southern Methodist and a 35-0 loss to Michigan State. And the old Notre Dame nemisis, Iowa, tied the game 14-14. Attendance had begun to move downward, not a mortal phenomenon as it had long since become evident that even the most successful football gate receipts were no longer a major part of the necessary income of the University to meet its expanding needs.

St. Edward's University, now operated by the brothers, but a reminder of the achievements of Father Sorin, was celebrating its diamond jubilee. And a refreshing breath from the past emanated from Hollywood, where Jim Bacon '37, already a rising film capital columnist, sent a story to the *Alumnus* recounting his meeting with Gary Cooper and a former Notre Dame student, an American Indian, Charlie Soldani, who had been a fellow student with Knute Rockne. When the students of that era put on the "Girl of the Golden West," Soldani was cast as an Indian, appropriately. His squaw was played by Knute Rockne. Soldani had left the University when he began receiving oil royalties from Oklahoma properties. Thomas F. Carroll '51, was added to the *Alumnus* staff as editorial assistant. Philadelphia welcomed Father John F. O'Hara, C.S.C., as its new archbishop. On January 11, Clarence Manion resigned as dean of the College of Law, having been on the University faculty since 1924.

The Foundation was now operating intensively with 49 regional governors and 232 city chairmen. This attention to the things that was Caesar's did not find any neglect of religion. As a tribute to Father Cavanaugh, the Alumni Association membership presented him with a spiritual bouquet of 7,500 Masses and Communions and 10,500 rosaries. What he appreciated deeply was the assurance of prayers from 43 non-Catholic alumni.

Another example of the persisting spiritual values of Notre Dame came with the publication of the letter in a national news magazine from the wife of a 1923 alumnus. "I hope that our daughter will be given the same happiness that began for me in the Log Chapel in 1933. It wasn't long before I realized that my husband's school had given him more than reading, writing and arithmetic. When his job called for a difficult decision, he made it with great integrity . . . In our family he has shown the sort of leadership we often read of as desirable . . . he often explains to the children the spiritual practices he learned at school; best of all, we like the way he lives what he says . . ."

I cannot miss this opportunity to comment that the Log Chapel mentioned above, a replica of the little chapel found by Father Sorin on his arrival, was the scene of many alumni weddings. Particularly during the depression years, it offered a small and inexpensive setting, but one rich in environment and spiritual tradition. The body of Father Badin, American proto-priest whose vision had in large measure made Notre Dame possible, lay beneath the floor, as did the bodies of Fathers

Deseilles and Petit, missionaries to the Potawatomis, whose dedication enriched the site of Notre Dame.

At the January, 1952, meeting of the Alumni Board, Harvey Foster '39, one of those non-Catholic alumni of outstanding character, was elected president to succeed Conroy Scoggins. Foster inherited a fast-moving and in-depth alumni program. Targets now included club presidents council, class reunions, Universal Notre Dame Night, local club involvement in job placement, club involvement in prestige and public relations projects, an additional project for Notre Dame families to hold Mass observances on Laetare Sunday, sustaining the enrollment at Notre Dame in quality and in geographical distribution, the *Alumnus* a vital vehicle of communication, the office records invaluable, was a working group, serious in purpose and broad in scope.

At a testimonial dinner for Father Cavanaugh, retiring President Scoggins pointed to the mutual development of the association and the University during the Cavanaugh regime. The 1951 Annual Alumni Fund showed a record 8,590 alumni contributing $329,379. Alumni were purchasing $300,000 worth of football tickets annually. Alumni sons were bringing $400,000 from alumni in tuition and fees. On the broader Foundation front, its revenues since its inception under Harry Hogan now totaled $7,000,000. On the academic side, the Graduate School enrollment had grown from 100 to 450 during Father Cavanaugh's tenure.

Universal Notre Dame Night in 1952 featured Father Cavanaugh as the speaker for the Notre Dame Club of Los Angeles. The Notre Dame Glee Club made its first appearance on the Ed Sullivan Show. And the advent of big-time publicity was marked by a major article on Father Cavanaugh in *Time* magazine.

New Alumni board members elected in 1952 included Lester W. Foley '24, Jacksonville lumber executive, who completed a remaining one-year term of John Q. Adams '26, resigned; Galvin Hudson '15, Memphis, Tenn., businessman; Ralph Coryn '22, Moline, Ill., attorney; John W. Courtney '25, Dearborn, Mich., manufacturers representative, and James G. McGoldrick '39, New York City attorney.

The *Alumnus* marked a 1952 change, when ill health removed John Burns, who was replaced by Richard Cody, a '52 journalism graduate. A $2,000,000 utilities campus construction program was begun, marking the assistance of the Foundation program. The reunion meeting of the Club Presidents Council brought 64 club delegates. At the alumni banquet, a testimonial to Father Cavanaugh, 750 alumni were present.

And now Notre Dame, after six of its most significant years, moved from the administration of Father John J. Cavanaugh into the unsuspected adventures of a new President. The Morris Inn, Nieuwland Science Hall, and Farley Hall were some of the tangible evidences of progress during the Cavanaugh years. Provision had been made for some of the buildings which were to follow. The Notre Dame Foundation was emerging as the most significant contribution of all. And to its direction, Father Cavanaugh was appointed by the new regime.

During his years in the presidency Father Cavanaugh, in retrospect, had played a role not unlike that of the later Pope John XXIII. He had become convinced that the imperative need of Notre Dame, and all Catholic universities, was stronger emphasis on academic strength. He aroused controversy with a major address in which he asked the question, "Where are the Catholic Salks and Oppenheimers?" He created resentment among many of the old-guard faculty of Notre Dame when he announced a need for a "distinguished professors program." For years the concept and goal of Notre Dame had been quality education, on the undergraduate level primarily, of young men within the philosophy of the Catholic Church. A priest of deep conviction himself, his stress on this secular aspect of education, his attention to the graduate school and research, and his application of the gadfly technique of the Great Books, created on the campus a climate of doubt. The purpose and the priorities of the University were opened up for discussion as the winds of change blew through the once tranquil campus. The identity of the faculty, who had once been assured that good teaching did not necessarily require ultimate degrees, publishing and research, or outside lecturing and consultantships, was now open to review. Alumni faculty members of distinction and dedication were particularly disturbed by the implication that they did not compare favorably with those imported from other backgrounds. And the Great Books principle of free discussion but no decision—stimulating in Great Books groups, but frustrating in academic structuring—presented for the first time at Notre Dame a campus in ferment over its own nature.

In spite of this turbulence, unusual as it was, most administrators, faculty members and alumni, believed that the new climate was designed to enliven the life of the campus and make its members more susceptible to the new volume of change dictated by a changing world. Progress and challenge had always been a part of Notre Dame. Only the scope of the new challenges was greater. There was one exception to this calm confidence in the inevitability of the usual and traditional evolution the exception was Father Cavanaugh's vice president, and now his successor, Father Theodore M. Hesburgh.

XXXIII

Decision and Development

Father Theodore Martin Hesburgh, C.S.C., became the President of the University of Notre Dame at the age of 36. Several earlier presidents had been appointed at even earlier ages, but in the years after the World Wars and the Depression he was the youngest in age and experience.

A native of Syracuse, N.Y., he had attended the college courses from Moreau Seminary for only two years, going then to Rome and Catholic University for his degrees. His return to Notre Dame brought a handsome young theologian to the faculty and student circles of the post-World War II campus, rumbling with the conflicts of veterans and non-veteran students, mature and immature young men, the impact of technological advance against traditional academic pursuits. He made a great contribution to the understanding, counseling and solving of problems of the young married couples in the campus Vetville—a totally new phenomenon in campus life. He became the apostle of youth and of change.

The purpose of this chronicle is to tell the story of the Alumni Association and its members. I have no intention of evaluating the administration by Father Hesburgh of his colorful years in office—in fact, it is still unfinished business.

The Alumni Association and alumni everywhere have been involved as never before. And a few editorial comments seem advisable, even before the simple continuation of the progress of alumni and association development.

From the deliberate injection of doubt, or inquiry, and discussion, during the Cavanaugh regime, there had begun to emerge a duality of Notre Dame identity. This duality had been so blended through the hundred years of Notre Dame history before World War II that it was practically indistinguishable.

368

As it began to show through in the new climate, it took on the first nature of a primary superstructure, reflecting the theological virtues of faith, hope and chairty, and the cardinal virtues of prudence, temperance, justice and fortitude, administered by the Congregation of Holy Cross under the evangelical counsels of poverty, chastity and obedience. It was a mission of education under God, dedicated to Our Lady.

With this superstructure, from the first concept in the mind of Father Edward Sorin, there has been, and continues to be, a secondary academic structure. The superstructure represents the unchanging; the academic structure has permitted almost constant change.

In its earliest manifestations the academic structure of the University incorporated the Manual Labor School, the Minims and the Preparatory departments. In its middle period, roughly the 1920s to the 1950s, it incorporated the undergraduate colleges, and the Summer School, with graduate departments advancing slowly through outstanding merit, as in the field of chemistry.

With the 1950s and 1960s, the focus, if not the volume, of the academic structure turned to emphasis on the Graduate School, and the socially responsive creation of institutes within the University, such as the Medieaval Institute, the Lobund Institute, the Institute of International Studies, the Center for the Study of Man in Contemporary Society, the Institute for Educational Programs, and the Urban Studies Institute.

The Graduate School now offers degrees in 27 departments, 22 of them leading to the Ph.D. The Law School is a separate academic entity with graduate status.

The Notre Dame academic structure, in the changes and pressures of the fifties and sixties, emerged as an almost secular institution. In fact, in 1967, the University of Notre Dame du Lac became a separate corporation, governed by a Board of Trustees, only a minority of whom are members of the Congregation of Holy Cross. By agreement, the President of the University remains a priest of the Congregation, and the actual government of the University is in the hands of a group of 12 Fellows, only half of whom are priests of the Congregation. The Fellows delegated the governance of the University to a Board of Trustees, to consist of the Fellows and an additional 24 to 34 members, elected by the Fellows for six-year terms. In legal effect, the University of Notre Dame carried out conditions expressed in the University *Register* of 1971-72 as follows: "A Catholic University such as Notre Dame must be a University in

the full modern sense of the word, with a strong commitment
to and concern for academic excellence. To perform its teaching
and research functions effectively, the Catholic University must
have a true autonomy and academic freedom in the face of
authority of whatever kind, lay or clerical, external to the
academic community itself. To say this is simply to assert that
institutional autonomy and academic freedom are essential conditions of life and growth and indeed of survival for Catholic
universities as for all universities."

This is a development of the more recent Hesburgh years, and
the autonomy of truly Catholic universities in relation to the
magisterium of the Church is still a subject of Vatican discussion.

But for my purpose, to go back to its beginning, Father
Hesburgh's administration launched a kaleidoscope of changes
and achievements unprecedented in Notre Dame history. They
have had unprecedented resources to implement them.

The new President almost immediately revealed a magnetic
personality, a flair for publicity and a scope of leadership which
has had honorary doctorates dotting the jet trails of his travels
like thirty beribboned knots in the tail of a comet.

He has been pictured in a parka at the South Pole, in
uncountable handshakes with Popes and Presidents, in the presidential chairs of the American Association of Colleges, and the
International Federation of Catholic Universities, and on the
cover of Time magazine. His "Thoughts for Our Times," covering many of his numerous addresses on special occasions of
academic and social significance, are widely quoted. His statements on campus governance in the face of student disturbances
are used extensively by his colleagues and the press. His championing of Civil Rights as member and recent chairman of the
Civil Rights Commission has been a national issue.

In fact he has reflected almost the personal superstructure-
structure combination of the University he heads. A theologian
and exemplary priest, he provides an articulate and impressive
representation for the Catholic Church and for Notre Dame. As
the most traveled President since Sorin himself, and member of
governmental and secular organizations, he is the very knowl-
edgeable representative of the secular University.

It would be naive, and so would I, to say that all this
late-blooming dichotomy is easy to understand. And the history
of dissent is evidence of its problems of administration. There is
among the alumni a continuing sense of loyalty and confidence

in the ultimate good to come from all this. I found it difficult to convince my colleagues from other colleges and universities that Notre Dame alumni did not fluctuate violently with the fortunes of Terry Brennan and Joe Kuharich, with the permissiveness of Father Hesburgh in campus programs, and his adamant statements on Civil Rights, or his dissent from Pope Paul's position in several current controversial areas, or his positive views on the war in Vietnam. Alumni loyalty never wavered. Financial support increased dramatically culminating in record generosity in the Summa program, 1969 to 1972, a $52,000,000 goal, over-subscribed by $12,000,000.

Father Hesburgh did what I consider a major service to Notre Dame and to all higher education when he defined the campus as a proper "beacon, bridge and crossroad," where the problems bombarding our beleagured world might find assistance and acceleration in their solution. The principle had existed in action on the Notre Dame campus from the days of Sorin. I think it has complete validity. But I think we may have to clarify that while all campuses can properly identify as "beacons, bridges and crossroads," it is not equally demonstrable that all "beacons, bridges and crossroads" are necessarily or exclusively colleges and universities. The distinction is important, to bring to the campus the constructive potentials of this new dimensional role, but at the same time to prevent the sometimes irrelevant distraction of the campus from the top-priority pursuit of its internal academic functioning.

Against this analysis, drawn from 41 years of interpreting Notre Dame to alumni, and from serving the alumni office during the first 15 years of Father Hesburgh's administration, I can now, I hope, more effectively continue for you the simple chronicle of the association progress.

Father Hesburgh plunged into the zestful administration of Notre Dame which has remained a personal trait throughout. The vice presidents appointed in 1952 to assist him were Father Edmund P. Joyce, C.S.C. '38, executive; Father James E. Norton, C.S.C. '29, student affairs; Father Philip Moore, C.S.C. '24, academic affairs; Father Jerome J. Wilson, C.S.C. '32, business affairs. Father John H. Murphy, C.S.C., remained as vice president for public relations.

The Congregation of Holy Cross established now a separate Eastern Province for its activities. Father James Connerton, C.S.C. '20, who had been president of the Congregation's King's College in Wilkes-Barre, became the first Eastern Provincial.

Old Science Hall, completely renovated into a most attractive building through the generosity of trustee and alumnus Joseph A. LaFortune, Tulsa oil man, was turned over to Father Norton as a Student Center, achieving a long-needed central facility for campus activities, and affording the off-campus students a campus base. The benefactor, Joe LaFortune, was a native of South Bend, and a former "day-dog" who understood the vacuum the new center filled.

Fifty local alumni clubs enjoyed campus speakers on Universal Communion Sunday, December 1952, the 15th anniversary of the custom.

Father John J. Cavanaugh, C.S.C. '23, now director of the Foundation which the Alumni Association under Harry Hogan had established through his cooperation, reported $2,000,000 in gifts and grants in 1952. The University's total endowment at this time was only $7,460,645, wholly inadequate to its challenges.

In January, 1953, the Alumni Board elected as president of the association John H. Neeson Jr., Philadelphia lawyer, son of a former president of the association and founder of Universal Notre Dame Night, John H. Neeson, Sr. '03. The association was observing the 30th Anniversary of the *Alumnus* magazine, and announced the 30th Annual Universal Notre Dame Night observance for April 13. High praise was given to Harvey Foster, now honorary president, for his excellent year as president, one of several outstanding administrations under non-Catholic alumni. Ecumenism, born on the campus with Sorin's arrival, had found easy expression in alumni organization at all levels.

New members in the Neeson board were Daniel Culhane '23, Washington, D.C., a graduate of the untimely Boy Guidance Course, a high executive in the Boys Clubs movement; Msgr. Joseph B. Toomey, Syracuse, N.Y. '26, a brilliant young diocesan priest, popular pastor and leader in Catholic Charities; John F. Saunders '31, Boston food merchant and club and Foundation leader in New England; and Dr. Leo D. O'Donnell, '17, prominent Pittsburgh physician and surgeon.

The first football season under Father Hesburgh was not a perfect one. Nor did the election of a president and a new board member from Pennsylvania save the Leahy fortunes. The University of Pennsylvania tied the Notre Dame team, 7-7, perhaps stimulated by recollections of the 60-20 defeat by Notre Dame in 1930, and a 49-0 defeat the following year. And Pittsburgh won its games, 22-19. The only other loss of the season was to Michigan State, 21-3. Despite these reverses, Notre Dame was voted Number Three in the national rankings in the sports-writers Top Ten, from which it had been absent the preceding two years.

At the 1952 reunions a meeting of class secretaries had been successful enough to dictate the establishment of this proce-dure, and the second meeting of the Class Secretaries Council was on the board agenda.

The calendar year of the Alumni Association and the Annual Alumni Fund were in increasing conflict with the fiscal year June-to-June University system. The Alumni Board also met a long discussed problem involving the University, when it set a reunion weekend fee, to provide basic compensation for the room, meals, beer and soft drinks provided by the University and the association. The 815 alumni back for the 1953 event were tangible endorsement of the fee's acceptance by the membership.

The Foundation, under Father Cavanaugh's direction, an-nounced a campaign to secure $450,000 annually from cor-porate gifts, to finance the "distinguished professors" program, which agitated the native faculty, since the project was to acquire such "distinguished" candidates from outside the Uni-versity. Three new alumni joined the Foundation staff, Alan Powers, Thomas Carroll and James W. Frick, all members of the Class of 1951. Youth was the overtone of the campus as never before. The radiation of enthusiasm was reflected in the crea-tion of eight new local alumni clubs.

Another indication was the entrance of 17 former lay stu-dents of the University into Moreau Seminary, the campus college seminary of the Congregation.

Accent on youth marked the 16th Universal Notre Dame Communion Sunday, dedicated to the success of the program of Pope Pius XII for the Centenary of the Dogma of the Immacu-late Conception, patroness of the United States. President Neeson urged especially the participation of alumni in the Marian Year prayers for the spiritual and moral welfare of youth.

Young graduates were asking about the "program" of the Alumni Association. They were given the following goals as answers; "to keep Notre Dame alive in the hearts of its alumni—the spiritual; to keep Notre Dame alive in the minds of its alumni—the intellectual; to keep Notre Dame alive in the minds of its alumni—the fraternal; and to keep Notre Dame alive—the financial."

A meeting of the Foundation governors and city chairmen, almost totally alumni, was called by Father Cavanaugh on Feb. 12, 1954. The discussion was to hinge on personal solicitation, and the involvement of corporation support, as well as the already established procedures. Faculty development—a broader term used to relieve the abrasiveness of the "distinguished professor" label—was to be the keynote of the 1954 campaign.

A tie with earlier history was spotlighted when Father Matthew Schumacher '99, C.S.C., celebrated his golden jubilee in the priesthood on Christmas Day. He had been director of studies at Notre Dame from 1907 to 1919, and president of St. Edward's University in Austin, Tex., thereafter. In 1928 he became president of St. Thomas College in St. Paul. When that program met an untimely end, Father Schumacher became chaplain, and professor of philosophy and religion, at Saint Mary's College, Notre Dame, where he remained for the 20 years that had elapsed before his jubilee Mass.

Retiring President John Neeson called attention of alumni to the 140 local alumni clubs now functioning, nine of them new during his presidency. The graduating class had passed the 1,000 mark for the first time. And youth moved into a position of strength with the news that 53% of the total 23,000 alumni were graduated after 1940.

The 1953 football team under Frank Leahy's coaching came back to achieve a 9-0-1 record, tied by Iowa, and playing for the first time before a season's attendance total of more than 600,000. But even the number two ranking in the Top Ten teams of the A.P. poll of sportswriters could not cover the serious tax on Frank Leahy's health. In a sweeping decision, Father Hesburgh made another commitment to youth with the appointment of Terry Brennan '49, as head football coach. Brennan, the hero of the 1947 win over Army in the Notre Dame Stadium, when the traditional rivals announced they were leaving the Notre Dame schedule, had made a great record as a coach at Mt. Carmel High School in Chicago. He was young, popular, from a Notre Dame family, unusually promising on his way to the legal profession. His image coincided remarkably with the Hesburgh image. The great Notre Dame career achievement of Frank Leahy, second only to Rockne himself, with 87 games won in 11 seasons, only 11 games lost, and only 9 games tied, remains a great contribution by an alumnus to a highly publicized and vital program of Notre Dame. Leahy's battle against ill health in the years since this changeover has deepened the respect for his courage and for the characteristic intensity with which he has insisted on an active career against the losing odds of his health.

The 1952 edition of *Who's Who In America* had called attention to the fact that 135 alumni were in the volume, including 27 priests of the Congregation of Holy Cross. It represented a tribute to the established quality of Notre Dame education.

The January Alumni Board meeting was brought up to date by campus leaders. Father Cavanaugh reported that in 1953 the University had received $2,170,851 through the Foundation in gifts and grants. Alumni participation was 47.7%, while 270 colleges and universities in the American Alumni Council had reported that their average participation of alumni was only 18%. A total of 9,184 alumni had contributed $364,320 to the 1953 Annual Alumni Fund, a far cry from the $15,000 total in dues from alumni in 1940, the last year before the Alumni Fund was instituted.

James G. McGoldrick '39, New York attorney, was elected president of the Alumni Association, succeeding John Neeson, who continued as honorary president. The four new members of the board were James L. Ferstel '48, Chicago attorney and son of a prominent Chicago alumnus, William G. Ferstel '00; Robert H. Gore '31, Fort Lauderdale, Fla., hotel and real estate executive, whose father had been governor of Puerto Rico, and whose brothers were alumni of Notre Dame; John E. McIntyre '31, South Bend, executive of the Sibley Machine Co., which was headed by Bernard J. Voll '17, former association president; and Joseph I. O'Neill Jr., Midland, Tex., monogram alumnus and former Philadelphian, now an oil executive.

In February, 1954, 63 Foundation governors and city chairmen met on the campus. They heard the various phases of the program outlined by Foundation staff members, and were briefed on the progress of the University under its dynamic new President. The Foundation program was being served by a new magazine aimed at the non-alumni contributors to the Foundations, who were not interested in the family details of class and club news and the Alumni Association promotions, but who were vitally interested in the history, status and future of the University and the programs to advance them. As the con-

tinuing Roman rider of both association and Foundation horses,
I was the editor of both magazines, with John Cackley '37, an
invaluable aid to the *Notre Dame* publication, of which he later
deservedly became editor.

The *Alumnus*, emphasizing many programs to offset and
balance the financial stress of the Foundation, pursued the
recurrent goal of continuing education. The Alumni Board,
encouraged by Father Cavanaugh and his belief in the Great
Books, proposed alumni discussion clubs, which would be open
to non-alumni. They asked Father Cavanaugh to pursue the
concept of such groups, and to make recommendations for their
direction from the University and the faculty, from where, as an
educational program, its direction properly must come.

A new University Bookstore, to relieve the crowded conditions that had prevailed for years in the Main Building, and
continued now in Badin Hall basement, was to be erected, the
gift of Mr. and Mrs. Romy Hammes, Mr. Hammes being a
Kankakee business man and philanthrophist, father of a Notre
Dame son, Gerald G., '53.

Ninety-five local alumni clubs observed and reported Universal Notre Dame Nights. Key program was the Notre Dame Club
of Washington, D.C., where the featured guests were Father
Theodore M. Hesburgh, C.S.C., President of Notre Dame, and
Richard M. Nixon, vice president of the United States.

The *Alumnus* paid editorial tribute to the volunteer workers
of the association—the alumni board members, the alumni governors and city chairman of the Foundation program, the class
secretaries, the officers of local alumni clubs, the alumni who
visit prep schools and interview prospective students, the alumni
members of the Associate Board of Lay Trustees, and the
alumni members of the advisory councils of the colleges, and
last but not least the alumni of the world, outside organized
efforts, who spend hours in simply talking about Notre Dame
and reflecting its teachings. The conclusion of the editorial—
"You may not have met all these workers. You must have met
some. I have met them all. There are degrees in their intensity
and in their results. And we seek constantly for more. But when
our Leader assembles our knights in the courts of Heaven, I feel
profoundly that the volunteer workers, who came to her cause
so heedless of their own gain, will be among the smiled upon."
And in his first letter to the alumni, President McGoldrick
pointed out that an association is only as good as its members
individually. He asked for the active participation of all alumni,

and the contribution of their experience. Members of the Alumni Board were assigned particularly local alumni clubs in an effort to bring the board closer to alumni throughout the country through club activities.

Eighty-seven local clubs were represented in June at the President's Council. They were asked particularly to use the helpful *Club Manual* for programming. The presidents joined in honoring former Alumni Director Joseph M. Boland '27, for his personal contribution to club development through the radio broadcasts of Notre Dame football games over the "Irish Network," radiating through 119 stations to all parts of the country from the key South Bend Tribune Station, WSBT. Boland was regarded as the most competent of the radio sportscasters covering Notre Dame games. His knowledge as former player and coach was augmented by an excellent voice, a fine mind and great fairness.

In the August-September *Alumnus*, James E. Murphy '47, authored a reminiscent story about the fire of 1879, 75 years before, and the great contribution made by Father Sorin in the example of Notre Dame's immediate and greater reconstruction. The University of Father Hesburgh was still administered from that Sorin-built Main Building, now surrounded by 50 other buildings. And the 300 students of the fire year had now become 5,400.

Another tip of the hat to history came from the Notre Dame Club of New York in a dinner honoring all its members who were out of Notre Dame 30 years or more.

Father Hesburgh announced a new residence hall to meet expanding campus residence demands. The new building was to be Pangborn Hall, a gift of Thomas and John Pangborn, brothers, prominent industrialists and Catholic laymen in Hagerstown, Md., and non-alumni.

The Notre Dame Club of Detroit instituted an innovation in club programs with "The friendly foes pre-season kick-off beer and pretzel party." The affair, a low-cost event appealing to young members, invited representatives from the Detroit alumni of all the opposing schools on the Notre Dame schedule for the upcoming season.

In a letter to alumni, president McGoldrick called attention to the sermon at the opening of the school year in 1954, delivered by Father Hesburgh to mark the 113th year of Notre Dame, in which Father Hesburgh said, "The time is ripe to make Notre Dame a new center of Christian culture." McGold-

rick pointed to the Summer Institute of Spirituality which had
brought 650 nuns, from most of the women's religious orders,
to the campus, and to the Religious Orders meetings of the
Mission Society, held on the campus under the aegis of Bishop
Fulton Sheen.

Academically, progress was reflected in the inauguration by
the College of Law of a *Journal of Natural Law Studies*, a field
in which Notre Dame was already widely recognized.

Notre Dame alumni everywhere were saddened by the death,
on Christmas, 1954, of William R. Dooley '26, for 16 years a
member of the Alumni Association staff, and for 5 years director of the University Placement Office. This office had just
issued a report of the year, showing 3,241 student job interviews, and 212 visits by interviewing corporations. In addition
to professional competence, Bill Dooley was a gentleman of the
John M. Cooney school, and a Catholic family man of the
highest distinction associated with Notre Dame husbands and
fathers.

Father Hesburgh reported the appointment of 14 "distinguished professors," under the Foundation's project for corporate contributions. These were divided into permanent appointments, semester appointments, and special lecture series. The
Marian Year had been observed on the campus with activities
throughout, in theological studies and programs, religious activities and artistic contributions.

In the preceding fall, the University Band paid special tribute
at half-time in the North Carolina game, Nov. 15, to the former
Band and Glee Club Director, Joseph Casasanta '23. Joe was
saluted as the composer of "Down the Line," and the popular
"Hike Song," and with Father Eugene Burke '06, as lyricist, the
composer of "When Irish Backs Go Marching By." He had also
written the music for the University's alma mater song, "Notre
Dame, Our Mother," with words by Father Charles L. O'Donnell, C.S.C. '06.

Dr. Leo D. O'Donnell '17, succeeded Jim McGoldrick as
Alumni Association president, in January, 1955, after a most
effective year of leadership by the former football captain and
New York barrister. New members of the board in 1955 were
John W. Brennan '27, automotive engineer, Royal Oak, Mich.;
J. Patrick Canny '28, Cleveland, O., railway attorney, former
Bengal Bout star and equipment room manager under Knute
Rockne, an avid follower of Notre Dame athletics and a pillar of
the Cleveland, club; Patrick J. Fisher '36, Indianapolis attorney

and labor arbitrator; and Joseph E. Whalen '29, Des Moines, Iowa, hotel executive. The Alumni Board now was adding annually as always men of stature, ability, and experience in alumni programs in their clubs and classes and in the affiliated Foundation organization. But now their problems were growing in number and significance; the relations with the University stronger and more vital, and their competent concern increasingly was evident in the steady growth of the association.

Reminiscence came to many alumni with an obituary in the *Alumnus*, written by Larry Stauder '29, former student and later colleague, of Professor Jose A. Caparo, professor of electrical engineering. Caparo had come to Notre Dame from Peru, South America, in 1904 at the age of 15. His quiet, pleasant manner covered what many asserted was a great genius in the field of electronics. In 1953, he had returned to his home city of Cuzco where he was honored. He returned to the campus in time for the Holy Week services of that year in Sacred Heart Church, services he had not missed for 47 years. He had taught at Notre Dame for 33 years, and was head of his department for 20. His family still remains in South Bend as a continuing contribution to the community.

Dr. O'Donnell pointed out the rapid expansion of the Alumni Association. Local alumni clubs, augmented by nine in the year passed, totaled 146. He urged alumni activities of their communities. He paid tribute to Father Hesburgh for the success of his first three years in office.

Nine hundred alumni were present for the 1955 reunions. The reunion features of the weekend were supplemented by a lecture on the germ-free life research in the Lobund center, and by a play written by Dr. Natalie White, a member of the Summer School faculty, which had received considerable acclaim. A generous gift to the alumni secretary, from the Alumni Board and members of the association, presented at the Alumni banquet, marking 30 years at the University, eliminated personal problems which had been cumulative, and permitted the continuation of a career at once challenging and rewarding. (Individual problems can get lost in the institutional euphoria of Notre Dame.) The expansion of individuals involved on the campus was evident in the appointment of Joseph F. O'Brien '49, formerly with the Whirlpool Corp., to the new post of personnel director, to guide the welfare of 1,000 non-academic University employes.

Father Alfred Mendez '31, C.S.C., later to become Bishop of

Arecibo, Puerto Rico, was named to succeed Bill Dooley as
director of Placement. And the Notre Dame Clubs of Florida
wrote a new chapter by establishing a state convention, under
the direction of Alumni Director Robert H. Gore Jr.. Father
Cavanaugh was their first campus speaker.

The College of Law announced the formation of an advisory
council, which, like the councils already existing in other colleges, included a good representation of Notre Dame alumni in
the profession. President Leo O'Donnell called attention to the
success of the dinner given by the Alumni Association and the
University to the Senior class. He urged its continuance annually as a way of winning the involvement of young alumni.
Father Hesburgh, as anticipated, was appointed for a second
three-year term. A change of great alumni interest came with
the resignation of James E. "Big Mac" McCarthy, dean of the
College of Commerce, to become associated with the Foundation program under Father Cavanaugh. McCarthy had been a
flamboyant dean, with wide contacts among faculty, students,
alumni and the South Bend community. The enrollment in his
college had grown from 400 students when he succeeded Father
O'Hara, to 1,500 as he left it. McCarthy was not considered
very "academic" but his college graduated many competent
young men who achieved later success in the business world.
Like Dean Konop's administration of the Law School, the
commerce graduates were given a valuable realistic approach to
their professions. A Chicago paper, reputed to be the major
reference work of the dean in his classes, may well have been a
more effective business textbook than many more learned volumes used in the traditional academic pursuits of the in-depth
degrees. Many official non-academic persons also had a lasting
effect on the campus, and were remembered by alumni. One of
these the magazine wrote of was a delightful Irishman, Eddie
Mahon, who supervised the supply room in the Department of
Chemistry for 43 years. Eddie had come to Notre Dame from
Dublin, as the result of a meeting with the elder Father John W.
Cavanaugh, C.S.C., there. Eddie and him family contributed
Irish songs and dances to many campus functions over the years.

The modern world of communications, and a center for the
"beacon, bridge and crossroads" concept, came to Notre Dame
with the building of a campus television station, WNDU-TV. Dr.
Leo O'Donnell stressed the significance of an address by General David Sarnoff at the dedication of the station, in which
the general said that the most important impact that could be

made upon the world of the time was sound morality. The campus station was an affiliate of NBC. Dr. O'Donnell urged alumni to contribute their efforts in programs of public relations and prestige for Notre Dame.

The University of Notre Dame continued to grow, holding to the principles of the 113 years of its existence, yet meeting the changes of an expanding world as they arose, with promptness, with effectiveness, with vision, and with courage. The Alumni Association had undergone, too, not a transition in principle but a transition in identity. In the first days of alumni activity, "la vie intime," the close ties, required little formal procedure, little actual time, and little actual material support, to advance the interests of the University. Now, the functioning of a carefully selected board of directors of the association, to meet several times yearly, in close consultation with the University administrators, faculty and students, was hard pressed to keep pace with the advances of American higher education as embodied in the successful conquests Notre Dame was achieving in challenge upon challenge.

At the end of its first three years the Hesburgh administration was embarked on a journey that was already meeting all the qualifications of its predecessors. The vast impact of the years ahead was still buried in the limited projection of another three years.

XXXIV

The Pace
of Progress Quickens

Father Theodore M. Hesburgh, C.S.C., with relatively little time spent on the campus before his election to the presidency, was not steeped in the history or the tradition of Notre Dame. His experience was in shaping the challenges of the future which were only surfacing in the administration of Father Cavanaugh. He was a priest of complete integrity and zeal, but he saw the urgent problem of the University to be the development of its secular competence. He was young, and he believed in youth. He had enjoyed the unusual maturity and sense of purpose of the students in Vetville. He believed that the University's selection of its Freshman class from an overflowing hopper of applications, and the national enthusiasm for higher education, would bring students to Notre Dame who could be approached in a manner like the universities of Europe, or the graduate schools. History and tradition were heirlooms to be revered, but the new administration was youth-oriented for a new world. It placed little value on looking back.

The election of Joseph I. O'Neill Jr., '36, as president of the Alumni Association, coincided with the forward thrust of the Hesburgh programs. Joe O'Neil was one of the World War II veterans who, in looking for a career of challenge, invested in oil properties that suddenly produced. At a comparatively young period in his life, O'Neill's horizons widened beyond any previous comprehension.

The *Alumnus* took stock editorially of the 30 years of the office and the magazine from 1926 to 1956. Alumni had increased from 2,400 to 24,000. The editor's first alumni board in 1926, had recommended placement services, and publicity

382

committees in the clubs, and now these were nationally functioning programs of substance and significance. In 1926, the income from alumni dues was $4,000. In 1955, alumni annual giving passed the $500,000 mark. This was after a 20-year delay in implementing the recommendation of the first alumni board for an annual unrestricted fund. In 1926, 20 local clubs reported meetings on Universal Notre Dame Night. In 1955, the number reporting was 115. The Seniors in 1926 had added 300 members to the association. The Class of 1955 numbered 1,000. The January *Alumnus* in 1926 devoted one column to news of two local clubs. The January 1955 issue devoted seven pages to 50 club reports. The January 1926 magazine carried six pages of news from 20 classes. The 1955 January issue contained 23 pages of news from 33 classes. The Alumni Association had instituted Universal Notre Dame Night in 1924, a Placement Service in 1933—which was now a University program—and Universal Notre Dame Communion Sunday in 1938. These had produced public relations and publicity values for the University and better jobs for its new graduates. In 1947 the Alumni Association was instrumental, through Harry Hogan, in having the University set up a major centralized fund-raising program, the Notre Dame Foundation. In 1948 the alumni secretary, working through the Foundation, had established the magazine called *Notre Dame* as a contact for non-alumni friends of the University. (This magazine later became the magazine *Insight*, and the *Alumnus* and *Insight* are currently one central *Notre Dame Magazine*, a contact with both alumni and non-alumni.) The Alumni Association revealed in this review that it had built well and steadily a base upon which the most challenging programs of the years ahead could be successfully launched.

The new board members elected in 1956 were Oscar J. Dorwin '27, Greenwich, Conn., a New York corporate attorney; Edmond R. Haggar '38, Dallas, Tex., clothing manufacturer; Eugene M. Kennedy '22, Los Angeles, banker, and Francis L. "Mike" Layden '36, Evansville, Ind., an executive with Indiana Bell, a brother of former coach Elmer Layden '25.

Father Hesburgh gave the Alumni Board a thorough briefing on Notre Dame at its January meeting. This Presidential custom had been a most constructive factor in board programming for a number of years. And the custom of having the University President deliver a "State of the University" address at the annual alumni banquet, provided another strong bond of communication and interest between alumni and Notre Dame.

The progress of the "distinguished professor program" and its broader application to faculty development was going well. The board was pleased with the progress of the Placement Office. The Foundation report for 1955 showed an outstanding performance by alumni with 52.5 per cent participation and gifts of more than $500,000. This achievement had placed Notre Dame in the top 10 of institutions receiving gifts from the Ford Foundation.

The 1956 Universal Notre Dame Night theme was "local leadership," an encouragement for alumni to continue to become involved in local civic, political and religious problems. It had been and continued to be a goal for all alumni.

The reunion weekend found 800 alumni returned. The organization of an association of the alumni of the University Band was begun at this reunion. The biennial meeting of the club presidents was also a part of the reunion weekend, briefing the local club leaders on the University and association efforts.

There was increasing concern that the University admission standards were becoming so high that many good candidates for Notre Dame, including alumni sons, were being rejected in favor of students with little interest in the institution, but high IQs. Father Louis Thornton, C.S.C., '29, who had handled the demanding pressures of the enrollment in the postwar years, was named by the Provincial Chapter to succeed Father Alfred Mendez, C.S.C., as Director of Placement. Father Thornton's experience as a lay student, as a young banker with the Guaranty Trust in New York City, as a member of the faculty of the College of Commerce, and as a strong disciple of Father John O'Hara in a study of the business world, gave him facilities in his new assignment which proved advantageous until his retirement from that office in 1970. The number and quality of interviewing corporations were increased so that Seniors were receiving top opportunities in national job selection annually.

In a move to restore the adequate housing which has always been a basic factor in Notre Dame education, Father Hesburgh announced the construction of two new campus residence halls. One was Keenan, a gift from Mr. and Mrs. James Keenan, Fort Wayne hotel man and former student in 1913, the other Stanford Hall, a gift in memory of Grattan Stanford '04, New York City attorney.

The Foundation marked its 10th anniversary. There continued a little feeling that the Foundation was not a proper part of the alumni program, because of its intense stress on fund-raising. An editorial pointed to the concurrent increase in Notre Dame's prestige and public relations during the decade; to the growing number of active clubs, to the reflection of individual alumni achievements in the *Alumnus* pages, to the increased value of the Notre Dame diploma, and to the recognition of the Foundation record by the Ford Foundation and by the American Alumni Council.

Father Hesburgh had launched self-study programs which had brought changes in the College of Arts and Letters and in the Law School. He now asked the College of Engineering to do the same. A boost to the academic program came with the announcement of five new fellowships and scholarships in chemistry, from five different corporations.

Football had enjoyed a good season in 1955, 8-2-0. Statistics published nationally showed that in the 25 years since Knute Rockne's death, Notre Dame still ranked first of the top 25 teams, in the percentage of games won and lost. Even more appreciated by Father Hesburgh in his emphasis on the intellectual was an independent survey made by *Sports Illustrated* magazine, which confirmed an earlier report that the academic status of the Notre Dame athlete was higher even than the University had revealed, and considerably more favorable in comparison with similar records of other schools.

The Alumni Association's Constitution had never kept pace with the demands of its growth. But in the serious scope of the major programs now under way, the board presented a new and better adapted instrument. The interest of the alumni was reflected in an overwhelming 3,241-88 vote for the revised document.

The Brothers Province was thriving, to the extent that they announced the creation of three provinces, the Midwest, Eastern and South-West. At the same time the Holy Cross Priests Province was enjoying an overflow of candidates, with the older Moreau Seminary housing only two of the four classes in the seminary college training program.

To offset this overcrowding, Father Hesburgh announced that the Province was building on the Notre Dame campus a new $3,000,000 Moreau Seminary to house 200 men. Because the University used a third of the priests ordained, Father Hesburgh asked the Foundation to assume a $1,000,000 goal toward the new building. Father Alfred Mendez, who had moved from the University staff to become director of province development, was in charge of the new campaign. Father Hesburgh said, "We have never really had enough Holy Cross priests at Notre Dame, especially in recent years as the number of students and classes and halls has grown. But now, at last, our prayers are being heard, and the candidates are entering the Holy Cross Novitiate in such numbers that any two classes will practically fill the present seminary."

President Joe O'Neill urged continuing alumni cooperation in the placement program. And he urged alumni to cooperate with Father Richard Murphy, C.S.C. '31 the new director of admissions, who was faced with personal interviews with each prospect, and a need for well selected candidates from which to choose. O'Neill suggested that full slates of active class officers, as already existing in several classes, would improve that program. And he asked for more response to the continuing education program which the association, through Father John Cavanaugh, was trying to move.

In the football season of 1956 the "commitment to youth" received a set-back in the eyes of the football world, when Notre Dame dropped to a startling 1-8-0, a complete reversal of the 1955 performance. A list of old rivals defeated Notre Dame—Southern Methodist, Purdue, Michigan State, Oklahoma, Navy, Pittsburgh, Iowa and Southern California. Nevertheless almost 600,000 fans remained loyal.

J. Patrick Canny '28, Cleveland, O., railroad attorney, succeeded O'Neill as president of the association. New board members elected were Leo J. Vogel '17, Pittsburgh, Pa., engineer; Raymond Durst '26, Chicago industrialist; Jules K. de la Vergne '33, New Orleans architect, and William E. Cotter, Jr. '41, Duluth, Minn., corporate executive and son of the former association president.

The *Alumnus* spotlighted some academic changing factors. Total enrollment was now 6,022, with 5,348 undergraduates. Catholics still totaled 96.7 per cent, although in the Graduate School the percentage was 79 per cent. Married students numbered 411. There were 44 Oriental students and 28 black. All 48 states and 36 foreign countries were represented. Of 641 faculty members, 105 were religious, including 82 C.S.Cs.

The Alumni Board's Committee on Prestige and Public Relations, with Joseph Whalen, John W. Brennan and Oscar Dorwin, reported that while the general progress in this area was encouraging, the achievements of many alumni still remained unknown. They advanced a ten-point working program for clubs and individual alumni to follow in bringing these achievements into public view.

The forward thrust of the campus was fretting under some of the old traditions. Washington's Birthday exercises, instituted by Father Sorin, were now modified to a program of the senior class at which a Patriot-of-the-Year award was made, in this first instance to Senator John F. Kennedy.

President Canny, in a letter to alumni, pointed to the fine balance which traditionally exists at the University in its total program. "The idea is that a man—or a University—can't over-develop one phase of his personality without injuring others. To put a name on it, the quality Notre Dame stresses is balance. One result of this is that the student begins early to learn maturity in judgment and self-confidence in his dealings with other people; to take, in other words, a balanced view of life. One aim of the Alumni Association is to cultivate continuation of this balance."

This was, in a mild form, the first voice of concern. The Alumni Board was observing through alumni outside and its contacts inside the campus that the very valid and valuable emphasis on the intellectual life of the University created by Father Cavanaugh and Father Hesburgh might be a cause of the weakening of the spiritual and athletic traditions, joint pillars of Notre Dame, and common denominators of alumni contact.

That the mind of the University had not stilled its heart came with the 1957 reunion when David Van Wallace, Class of 1927, paralyzed by a diving accident in his Sophomore year, a frequent visitor to campus events in the car and cart provided by the Notre Dame Club of Detroit, was given an honorary bachelor of science degree, the degree he would have received 30 years before.

More than 800 alumni attended the reunion. The Monogram Club held its annual meeting and golf day the day before the reunions started. "Informal hours" were introduced by the colleges, to bring returned alumni into their facilities for updating by members of the faculties.

Fuel for the Cavanaugh—Hesburgh intellectual concern was fed by a survey which listed the 10 best American universities. Not one Catholic university was among them. Controversy was beginning to take shape on Catholic campuses generally, and especially at Notre Dame, where the concern had been vocal for several years. The *Alumnus* called attention to one reservation, in an editorial—"I am sure that every Notre Dame man would like to see the University of Notre Dame listed among the top ten universities—by whatever yardstick the future may use. And we are working toward that goal with generous alumni participation. But it seemed to me that reunion classes and their experiences proved that there are things we would not wish to sacrifice in the competition."

Another rumble still unvoiced officially, was concerned with the unfortunate and unnecessary but frequent connotation of the hoped-for future with poor past performance. The immediate challenges and policies were, and continue to be, in many instances, greater and different. But the relation of the University to its challenges, at all points in its history, does not justify unfavorable comparisons. The commemoration of the 100th anniversary of the approval of the Congregation of Holy Cross by the Vatican offered endorsement to this defense of history. The Alumni Association sponsored a Field Mass in the Community Cemetery. Alumni of all years, reading the simple names and dates on the uniform headstones, were vividly reminded. Father John Wilson '32, C.S.C., said at the Mass, "This occasion, this quiet, peaceful place, these gray stone crosses marking the graves of our beloved dead—all these things combine to preach a sermon more eloquent than human words. They speak of a century's accomplishements more effectively than any recitation of deeds."

The Notre Dame Club of Dallas wrote an original page in club history with a family novena honoring the Blessed Virgin and dedicated to world peace. Three Dallas parishes participated on the campus of Jesuit High School.

President Canny urged alumni to participate in the Annual Fund, the only tangible yardstick for measuring alumni interest. He urged those active to solicit others.

John Laughlin '48, South Bend journalist alumnus, joined the *Alumnus* as editorial assistant. A fine contribution to alumni and public relations came with the filming of a 16mm color moving picture of the Notre Dame campus, done by Owen Murphy, a student at Notre Dame in 1915, and narrated by Joseph M. Boland '27, whose voice was pleasantly familiar to all alumni through his Irish network football programs. The film was a feature of more than 50 local club meetings on Universal Notre Dame Night. It was used on television in 43 cities and in later club events. It was prepared with prep schools in mind and made available to them. It was a vivid picture of the modern campus.

The diamond jubilee of the Laetare Medal was observed in 1957, another tie of distinction with Notre Dame of the past and the spectrum of lay leadership in the Church in the United States. Six thousand students enrolled in the fall, as the prestige and public relations, and the preparatory school contacts committees of the Alumni Board functioned. In his opening sermon to the students, Father Hesburgh said, "Man must not allow himself to be seduced by the material benefits of science to the exclusion of the deep spiritual values that he cherished long before the advent of modern science and its accompanying technology." The Vatican had recently appointed Father Hesburgh as a representative to the new International Atomic Energy Agency. The *Alumnus* editorially asked alumni to work toward the new Notre Dame image of both campus and alumni, still suffering from the nostalgic hob-nail shoes, corduroy pants and football spirit—good in themselves in time and place but obscuring the great progress now ongoing.

On July 4, young couples once of Vetville, now alumni, held their first reunion, with their popular chaplain now the University President. In his last letter to the alumni as president, Pat Canny expressed his sense of gratitude for the privilege of being a Notre Dame man. He expressed pleasure in the growth and influence of the Alumni Board and Notre Dame men everywhere, and in their generous support of Notre Dame and the principles it stands for. He asked that alumni response to the new Seminary Fund be particularly generous in gratitude to the Congregation of Holy Cross.

Francis M. Layden, '36 was elected president of the association to succeed Canny, who continued as honorary president. New board members elected were Joseph R. Stewart '22, Kansas City Insurance executive; Charles E. Rohr '30, Cleveland restaurateur; James H. Sheils '35, New York City attorney, and John C. O'Connor '38, Indianapolis attorney.

The football fortunes under Terry Brennan had recovered and in 1957 a 7-3-0 season attracted 621,000 fans. The Alumni Board enjoyed a first showing of the 1957 football night films, which had become very popular with Alumni clubs and many other organized groups throughout the country. The Alumni Board and the class secretaries were briefed on the University, the association, the Foundation and their current stresses.

The University now announced a major program for the future, involving financial needs of $66,000,000 over a 10-year period. President Layden pointed to this unprecedented effort as requiring total alumni material, and moral, support for its success. To step up Foundation efforts, John Cackley '37, was appointed assistant director of the Foundation under Father Cavanaugh, and editor of its magazine *Notre Dame*. Armstrong remained as alumni secretary and editor of the *Alumnus*, with Laughlin as managing editor.

Alumni were expressing concern over the "bigness" of Notre Dame. The *Alumnus* offered editorial reassurance with the treatment of "bigness" by Webster, which is not only size, but "strong and mighty," "pregnant, swelling, teeming," "important," "imposing," and "magnanimous." All of these actually become a great University it asserted. The small club, the small class, the small donor, remained as vital links in the chains of the University. Alumni stature was reflected in alumni appointments to the new Advisory Council of the Colleges of Science and Engineering.

A dramatic campus event occurred in 1958, the ending of the 115 years of service on the Notre Dame campus by a devoted group of Holy Cross nuns, who had once numbered as high as 100. In addition to kitchens and laundry, they had cared for the Minims, and served as proofreaders for the Ave Maria Press. Father Hesburgh said at the Mass in the old convent marking the event, "You can never leave the hearts and affectionate memories of the priests and brothers of Holy Cross and the administrators, faculty, and students of the University of Notre Dame. You have been golden threads woven forever into the tapestry of her life." Five nuns remained, to direct the Student Infirmary.

President Mike Layden stressed the significance of the new Foundation 10-year program to alumni. He pointed out the fact that the first Endowment Campaign and then the $25,000,000 University program announced by Father Hugh O'Donnell, had been dramatic and formidable in their eras, but had been achieved. The goals of the new program—faculty development, non-teaching staff security, financial aid, research grants, and physical plant expansion—were logical parts of Notre Dame's progress, and if tradition continued would be met by success.

A momentous change marked the summer of 1958. It was apparent that the impressive program outlined by the Foundation would require competent leadership. In a reversal of the policy which had resulted in limited six-year terms as Presidents-Superiors for all the priests from Father John W. Cavanaugh to this time, the superiorship of the Religious Community of Notre Dame, with its six-year limitation, was separated from the presidency of the University.

Following this change, Father Theodore M. Hesburgh, C.S.C., already a star in the firmament of higher education in the United States, was reappointed by the Congregation to the presidency of Notre Dame without terminal date. Father Hesburgh has always referred to his position as a "one-year contract." Twenty-one years in the position gives evidence of the Congregation's intended provision, that leadership would not be sacrificed to technicalities of religious life.

Father Chester Soleta, C.S.C. '38, was chosen as vice president of academic affairs and Father George Bernard, C.S.C. '45, of student affairs. Father Richard Grimms '33, was named Superior of the Community to succeed Father Hesburgh. The *Alumnus*, pointing to the presence at the 1958 alumni banquet of Father Matthew Walsh, C.S.C. '03, and Alfred C. Ryan '20, under whose auspices in 1923 the association's office and magazine were begun, spotlighted the lasting ties and the continuing development of Notre Dame. Unity had not been sacrificed to the great growth, which 1,000 returned alumni were seeing around them. A proposed alumni Mass at the campus Grotto of Lourdes, celebrating the centennial of Our Lady's appearance to Bernadette, was forced inside by Indiana rain, but the beauty of Sacred Heart Church with its Lady Chapel lost nothing of the majesty of the commemoration.

Father Hesburgh, in a special convocation of alumni in Washington Hall, outlined the new long-range program and his hope for continuing involvement of alumni in its achievement.

In July, the biennial Council of Local Alumni Clubs was held on the campus, an event which had become of a size and significance counseling separate convening. There were now 167 local clubs. The delegates were briefed on association and University programs affecting them, but most intensively on the new $66,000,000 challenge.

The Summer Session of 1958, enrolling 2,500 students, was the largest in its 40-year history. President Layden gave special attention in his message to alumni to the importance of the small club, the small class and the small gift. They were valued in themselves. Their participation was an endorsement of Notre Dame from which others were moved to become involved. And they constituted a structure on which the growing numbers of alumni and friends could continue to be built most effectively.

The spiritual program was marked, and a new form of activity introduced, when the *Alumnus* announced a tour to Lourdes, during this centennial year, which would be assisted by Notre Dame alumni and the Notre Dame Club in Rome. It was also pointed out that the established association programs of "religion and citizenship" and "prestige and public relations" had changed in relation to the changes in the Church as well as in society, and that alumni efforts had played a part. For Universal Communion Sunday it was proposed that a spiritual bouquet be prepared for Father Hesburgh, to invoke success in the program ahead, and for the continuing success of Notre Dame.

President Layden commented on a changed tradition, the new list of "outgoing faculty." The 55 faculty members leaving or taking a leave of absence reflected the developing concept of "loyalty to their disciplines" among the Notre Dame faculty, rather than the traditional and transcending "loyalty to the University." President Layden praised the clubs for suggestions for progress being mirrored in increased activity in the alumni office. And he expressed alumni sadness following the death of Pope Pius XII, the first Pontiff to have visited Notre Dame personally and to hold a doctorate from it, conferred on that occasion upon the then Cardinal Pacelli.

The March, 1959, *Alumnus* carried a letter of appreciation from Father Hesburgh to the association for the spiritual bouquet of more than 12,000 Masses, rosaries and communions for the success of his long-range program.

William E. Cotter Jr., 41, was elected president of the Alumni Association, the second alumni son to hold the same presidency held by his father in an earlier year. New directors elected were James J. Byrne '43, Detroit businessman; Paul J. Cushing '31, Oakland, Calif. engineer, son of the donor of the Engineering Building, John Cushing '06; Walter L. Fleming, Jr. '40, Dallas businessman, and W. Edmund "Red" Shea '23, Dayton attorney.

In 1958 the football team, under Terry Brennan and his staff, suffered another disappointing season, 6-4-0. Army, Purdue, Pittsburgh and Iowa won their games. There was no organized alumni protest or demand for a change. But Father Hesburgh, not too knowledgable or concerned in the area of sports, was impatient with the gathering criticism of the young coach and was aware that his search for excellence at Notre Dame, once spurred on by football success, was now possibly losing that source and example. In an about-face, apparently, from his commitment to youth and young alumni, he replaced Brennan with Joseph L. Kuharich '30. Brennan's career record at Notre Dame in five seasons had been 32 won, 18 lost.

In his last season, Brennan had an all-alumni staff—Jack Zilly, Bernie Witucki, Hugh Devore, Bernie Crimmins, Bill Fischer and Bill Walsh—with one exception, Henry Stram, currently, in 1973, coach of the professional Kansas City Chiefs. During Leahy's tenture, to relieve his pressures, Father John Cavanaugh had appointed Edward "Moose" Krause '34, one of Notre Dame's all-time great athletes, as director of athletics, a post he still holds. Bob Cahill '34 was football ticket manager, Herb Jones '27, was business manager of athletics and Charlie Callahan '38, was director of sports publicity. It was a strong organization, administering one of the great traditions of Notre Dame, a source of vital revenues for the University, and a great channel of contact and public relations throughout the country. It was too significant an asset to risk losing. So the coaching of the football team was turned over to an older alumnus, Layden-coached, from the ranks of pro football.

Father John Cavanaugh reported that the Foundation, in 1958, had received $3,030,052, the largest single year receipts except for 1956 and 1957, when Ford Foundation grants brought the total above that figure. The 11,688 alumni contributions amounted to $694,620.

On Nov. 17, the new Pope, John XXIII, announced the elevation of Most Rev. John F. O'Hara, C.S.C. '11, Archbishop of Philadelphia, to the cardinalate, the first Holy Cross priest to achieve this distinction.

The Fides Publishers, an on-campus group, celebrated its 15th birthday. Fides had been created to provide printed material for the lay apostolate, by returning World War II veterans under the inspiration of Father Louis Putz, C.S.C. '32. Works produced already included series in religion for high schools and colleges. Vincent Giese '50, Eugene Geissler '41 and William McCullough '27 along with Burnett Bauer '38, were among the pioneers. They were encouraged in their early efforts by the Ave Maria Press and by Francis "Bill" Fink '30, of *Our Sunday Visitor*.

President Bill Cotter outlined for alumni the increasing work load of the board of directors. There were now 12 committees

on the board, and each director served on three or more of
these commitees. He commented on the pride of alumni in the
fact that in 1957 and 1958 eighteen Notre Dame students were
Woodrow Wilson Fellows, making Notre Dame the fifth in the
nation in this academic distinction.

An editorial in the *Alumnus* pointed to the great adjustments
the Alumni Association had frequently had to make. From
1929-39, the association budget was inadequate to implement
its ambitions; from 1940 to 1950, World War II and its after-
math were radical changes. And the Foundation organization in
1947 had demanded Alumni Association strength and leadership to insure its strong establishment within the University.
There was reassurance that the old association purposes and
programs were still alive and strong and would be adaptable to
the new challenges. As if to endorse this belief, golden jubilees
of three of the great priests of alumni history were observed—
Father Cornelius Hagerty, C.S.C. '06, Father Eugene P. Burke,
C.S.C. '04 and Father Thomas P. Irving, C.S.C. '04. President
Cotter urged alumni to identify more often as needed Catholic
lay leaders, at the same time that he praised their Top Ten
national achievement in financial support.

Continuing education was announced as receiving a constructive boost with the agreed publication of a series of articles by
outstanding faculty members, as special inserts in the *Alumnus*
magazine, under the categoric title of "The Sublime Tradition."

The June reunions found not only monogram alumni, but
more alumni generally, coming back to the campus on Thursday
for the long weekend. Campus changes, and the introduction of
added features in the weekend program, required more time.
The Alumni Board, pressed by the diversity and volume of work
asked for a field secretary for the 170 local clubs—a request
made earlier and often. the board was told that the enlistment
of non-graduate former students in University and alumni programs was succeeding.

The *Alumnus* editor, writing in a faculty publication, asked
the University to preserve "la vie intime" in which alumni were
a part of the campus family, and not as so often labelled in
other institutions a "public." And he asked the faculty to keep
considering the student a person rather than a number in a card
file. One of the Holy Cross priests, answering later, pointed to
the fact that in 20 years of constant student enrollment increase, the number of Holy Cross priests on the campus in

University posts had risen from 59 to 68, with a resulting higher ratio of student-to-priest relationship.

President Cotter, at the alumni banquet, expressed alumni gratitude for the many early years in which the University initiated and preserved alumni contacts. He complimented alumni now for their generosity to the Foundation programs. The board had asked for a new survey of alumni, and Cotter asked cooperation in response to it. He asked cooperation and understanding for the University admissions program, now directed by Father James Moran, C.S.C. '17, who had stated that the University sought "the well-balanced student, not the young man who is scholar alone or athlete alone, or whose records show abundance of social activities alone."

In the fall of 1959 Father John J. Cavanaugh '23, was granted an indefinite leave of absence for reasons of health, and was succeeded by Father John H. Wilson, C.S.C. '32. In September, Frank Walker '09, an earlier interim chairman of the Foundation, died.

In response to the Alumni Board request for a field secretary, and to strengthen the contact between alumni and the Congregation of Holy Cross, the University appointed Father Thomas O'Donnell, C.S.C. '41, as University liaison with the local clubs and the association. Father O'Donnell was an active, talented, popular young priest, and was a great aid to the alumni spirit during these years of transition. He had a head start in alumni relations from his earlier post as assistant to Father Cavanaugh in the Foundation program.

The first of the "Sublime Tradition" articles appeared in the December *Alumnus*. Entitled "What America Stands For," it was prepared by the highly respected former member of the Hungarian diplomatic corps, Professor Stephen Kertesz, now a professor of political science, who had succeeded the late Waldemar Gurian as chairman of the University's committee on international studies. Universal Notre Dame Communion Sunday speakers were asked to explore clarification of the First Amendment of the Constitution, in the face of confusion arising from its freedom of religion too often ending in freedom from religion.

Now in 1960 there was the young University President, with a new unlimited horizon for his administration. There was a new Pope, stirring the Christian world with new hope. The Foundation was launching a new long-range program.

And there was still little real indication of the impact the 1960s were to have on the world and its institutions. Knocking seemed instead to be heard at doors of new opportunities.

On the young campus, we entered the revolution without even knowing we had manned the barricades, on either side!

XXXV

"Dissent" of The Holy Ghost

Theological interpretations became one of the major problems of the 1960s. I think the one which had perhaps the most widespread effect was a wrong interpretation of Pentecost—replacing the word "descent" with "dissent." Under this misguided aegis of a new freedom, dissent became the order of the day—not the traditional reasoning dissent of a democracy, but the dissent of everyone about everything; not dissent based on logic or purpose necessarily, but dissent for the sake of dissent. It follows from this explanation that no institution and no person was free from this wave—from Pope John to Dr. Spock.

Tradition and the pace of progress combined to delay the engulfing of Notre Dame. History and biographies, in fact, can not really be written except by looking back at events and people. Causes cannot be properly defined until effects are complete. Changes at Notre Dame have been many and major. But I am sure you share with me the conviction that we can only now complete the chronicle of the campus, leaving objective analysis for the years to come. If a little prejudice or a little nostalgia should show through the objective effort, please write it off as personal.

The awesome $66,000,000 goal of the Foundation, and the loss of Father Cavanaugh as its experienced director, had almost frozen its mechanisms. To restore function, Father Hesburgh announced that the first major goal of the long-range plan would be $6,000,000 for an adequate new Library. The attractive and functioning building of 1917 had been constructed for 1,027 students and 40,000 volumes. The University now listed some 380,000 volumes in main and scattered libraries, to serve 6,000 students. This project was immediate, easy to understand

and universal. It reflected dramatically the aspirations of Father Hesburgh for the academic future of the University.

Joe Boland '27, former Alumni Board member and known to all alumni, died suddenly. His Irish Network had been eliminated by the decision of the University to accept an offer from ABC to cover the Notre Dame games through the growing facilities of that network. Practical considerations for the change have not erased alumni convictions that the caliber of Boland's coverage of Notre Dame football was never equalled.

John C. O'Connor '38, was chosen president of the Alumni Association to succeed Bill Cotter Jr. New board members elected were Maurice Carroll '19, St. Louis architect; George Connor '48, Chicago, All-American, outstanding member of the Chicago Bears, and now a radio and television sportscaster; William P. Mahoney '39, Phoenix, Ariz., attorney, former Notre Dame track star and coach, and Harry Mehre '22, Atlanta, Ga., monogram football star of the Rockne era, now a popular coach and columnist in the Southeast Conference area.

Some changes were reflected in the Universal Notre Dame Night of 1960, when the traditional close ties of "la vie intime," based in the common experiences of life on the campus, were loosened to bring into the Notre Dame "family" the families of alumni themselves, the football fans long dubbed "synthetic alumni," Catholic leaders whose goals were so closely tied to the objectives of Notre Dame and the Alumni Association, corporation executives increasingly interested in Notre Dame as a source of young business leadership prospects, and increasingly contributing to the University, the parents of present students, and the long-time highly respected recipients of honorary degrees and the prestigious Laetare Medal.

The *Alumnus* boosted its now familiar cause of continuing education with the second of the "Sublime Tradition" series, "Casual Reading for Fun and Profit," a delightful treatise by one of the truly "distinguished professors" of the new program, John T. Frederick, a fascinating teacher and a man of substantial academic and literary stature beyond campus boundaries.

President O'Connor, in a letter to alumni, pointed to the assurance by the Alumni Association that alumni would work toward half the $6,000,000 Library fund, in the three-year period assigned to it.

The 1960 reunions reflected the in-depth approach of alumni in current and traditional programs. The old customs continued, but open houses in the colleges were supplemented by forums on business trends, civil rights, liberal arts leadership and admission policies. A Washington Hall convocation of alumni heard Father John Cavanaugh discuss the need for Catholic emphasis on the intellectual life.

Spiritual life was reflected in the pilgrimage of 96 alumni to Lourdes and Rome, and in the consecration of Father Alfred Mendez, C.S.C. '31, as Bishop of Arecibo. The new bishop had been director of placement at Notre Dame, and director of the Moreau Seminary building fund. And the most outstanding contributor to the spiritual life of the modern Notre Dame was lost when John Cardinal O'Hara, C.S.C. '11, died in Philadelphia on Aug. 28. He had asked to be buried without distinction in the Community Cemetery of his Congregation. As a compromise with his great contributions to Notre Dame and to the Church, he occupies instead a chapel adjoining the main altar of Sacred Heart Church, whose basement chapel was the radiation center of his concern for the religious life and strength of thousands of Notre Dame men.

The 1960 commencement was memorable. Honorary degrees were conferred on President Dwight D. Eisenhower, and on a gracious intellectual of the Church, Giovanni Cardinal Montini, later to become Pope Paul VI at the death of John XXIII. The stature of alumni was recognized at this same brilliant commencement, when an honorary doctorate was given to Dr. Thomas Dooley '48, the hero-doctor-author whose work with refugees from communism, especially in Laos, had moved the western world. At the same time, the traditional distinction of the Laetare Medal was conferred upon Dr. George N. Shuster '15, a popular teacher at Notre Dame, later an outstanding writer on the impressive staff of *Commonweal* magazine and still later president of Hunter College in New York City. Shuster had also been the United States Commissioner in Bavaria following World War II. He was now returning to his alma mater to assist the challenging administration of Father Hesburgh.

President John O'Connor urged all alumni to read Father Hesburgh's address at the alumni banquet on the challenges to alumni and to Notre Dame of its opportunity for greatness. He urged the Class of 1960 to become acquainted with alumni of older generations so that the unity of Notre Dame men and spirit would remain unchanged. He asked cooperation for the new Library, the details of its 14 floors now outlined by its architects, Ellerbe and Co., who had done the O'Shaughnessy Building, Stanford and Keenan residence halls, and the North Dining Hall.

The third "Sublime Tradition" brought alumni face to face

with problems that were to haunt them for years to come. Professor John J. Kane treated "The Squeeze on the Catholic Schools," and, in an accompanying article, Professor Donald Barrett wrote on "The Population Panic."

Recognizing in Father Hesburgh one of the dynamic young college presidents of the era, attuned to the forward thrust of their own purposes, the Ford Foundation, which had made several significant single contributions to Notre Dame, now chose Notre Dame as one of a pioneer small group of higher educational institutions, to receive a contingent gift of $6,000,000 if the University could raise $12,000,000 within a three-year period which it had already set for the Library campaign. This offer doubled the goal of the Foundation campaign, but promised to triple its results.

The *Alumnus* had entered now upon a conscious effort to preserve the unity which had been the basic hallmark of Notre Dame. The religious were beginning to feel a lessening influence. Their numbers had not increased proportionately, and the brilliance of the President of the University did not offset the rise of the lay professor and the off-campus influence of trustees, advisory councils and alumni on University programs. To assuage this feeling, the magazine thanked the people who, over the years, had done so much for Notre Dame entirely apart from financial contributions. These included 1,574 priests and brothers and 1,449 sisters as well as all alumni whose prayers and service had been such a major factor in progress. Father Hesburgh's academic advances were becoming national news, spotlighted by the Ford grant, and editorially hailed in major papers, coast to coast. Universal Communion Sunday broadened the thought of alumni and involved them in a growing movement when it was focused on the Ecumenical Council which had been summoned by Pope John XXIII. As John O'Connor said in summing up his year, the health of the Alumni Association in its traditional and in its new programs was a good omen for the challenges ahead.

Walter Fleming '40, Dallas, Tex., was elected president of the association to succeed John O'Connor. New board members added were John P. Dempsey '49, Philadelphia broker; Patrick Dougherty '50, Minneapolis corporation president; William H. Fallon '37, New Rochelle attorney, and Oliver H. Hunter '43, New Castle, Pa., of the F.B.I.

The retiring president praised the University for its publicized national achievements in the academic areas of the Rhodes,

Wilson, Fulbright, Danforth, National Science and Marshall fellowships and scholarships. But he assured alumni of the continuing balance of students in admissions, in campus activities and in goals. The board endorsed the Library campaign, urging alumni to give generously and to solicit non-alumni friends. Universal Notre Dame Night in 1961 was to be centered around the theme of "Personal Responsibility." This program gave support to the President's Committee on National Goals and to the 1960 meeting of the Catholic Bishops, whose separate reports dealt with the essential quality of individual responsibility in American life.

To encourage alumni and to explain some of the problems, the *Alumnus* reviewed the 35 years of experience of the editor in the multiple channels of the association, with their rapid growth both in number and in scope.

The Notre Dame Foundation reported $5,719,651 in gifts and grants in 1960. The number of alumni gifts dropped slightly but 10,976 alumni still gave a total of $625,169. The Foundation suffered a serious loss when John N. Cackley '37 resigned as assistant director after 14 years on the staff to become director of development at an eastern university. Jerome Parker '30, was appointed to succeed him. Father John E. Walsh, C.S.C. '45, former head of the Department of Education, was made director of the Foundation. On his staff were, besides Parker, Alfred Perrine '41, John MacCauley '41, William F. Murphy '38, Richard Bowes '38, Allan Powers '51 and James W. Frick '51. Dean Joseph O'Meara of the Law School announced a program to secure $50,000 annually in scholarships for the college. President Walter Fleming asked alumni to make Notre Dame, to see and appreciate the magnitude of the changes.
tide of appeals from Church and secular causes.

The Foundation announced a 179-city rally, featuring a film message from Father Hesburgh. Joe O'Neill '36, former association president, was general chairman of the rally. Walter Fleming urged alumni to come and bring their families to Notre Dame, to see and appreciate the magnitude of the changes and the challenges.

Father Jerome Wilson, C.S.C., led a second alumni pilgrimage to Rome, where Vincent McAloon '34, an unusual and dedicated layman of the Third Order living and working there, acted as guide and counselor. The 1961 reunion indicated to the alumni office that alumni would go only so far in the mechanics of big business. An effort to secure pre-registration by mail found rugged individualism intact. But the attendance, and the involvement in the serious programs such as "The Political Maturity of American Catholics," and "Racial Tensions," and the Notre Dame oriented "Peace Corps Mission to Chile," directed by Professor Walter Langford '30, augured a new depth. John Witucki '57, joined the Foundation staff, and John Janowski '51, was appointed to succeed Jon Cackley as editor of the magazine, *Notre Dame*.

The old Navy Drill Hall, a temporary assembly center from World War II, was razed. The announcement of a permanent assembly center, a gift of Alfred C. Stepan '31, Chicago chemicals executive, was made by Father Hesburgh. The Center, with a new and attractive geodesic dome, would be a feature of the north quadrangle. The University also announced the construction of a $2,200,000 Radiation Laboratory, to be financed by the Atomic Energy Commission. Administrative changes included Father Charles McCarragher '32, as vice president for student affairs. Father McCarragher, who had been called "Black Mac" in his days as prefect of discipline, now proved to be another apostle of youth. The Student Center began to reverberate with the liberation of various student activities. Dr. William Burke, popular lay faculty member, became dean of freshmen, in an effort to introduce the University and the transcending nature of Notre Dame to its students before they entered the demanding and separate channels of the colleges. Allan Powers resigned from the Foundation staff to take a similar type of job in Detroit. His place was filled by James D. Cooney '59, an eloquent alumnus of the University Theater and communications arts, a move of great later benefit to the Alumni Association as irresistible forces began to move immovable objects.

William P. Mahoney '38, Phoenix, Ariz., was elected president of the alumni, giving another year of the spirit of the great Southwest to the leadership, as he succeeded Texan Walter Fleming. New members of the Alumni Board were Albert D. Castellini '24, Cincinnati attorney; Philip J. Faccenda '51, Chicago lawyer and business executive; Peter J. Kernan '49, Detroit, Ford company executive, and Adam J. Walsh '25, legendary center of the Seven Mules football champions, and coach.

Football, under Joe Kuharich, was not following the traditional paths of champions. The first season, 1959, produced 5 wins and 5 losses. The second season dropped to a disappointing 2-8-0 with wins over California and Southern California to open and close the season. Kuharich and his staff knew football. It became apparent that they may not have known the new Notre Dame student and athlete. In any event, this symbolic beacon of excellence seemed to lose something in the translation from coach to player. The names of some of the Kuharich players still are prominent in pro football—the potential seemed traditional.

The *Alumnus* was feeling the push of the student tide. It began a series of articles by the secretary of the senior class, to cultivate the class it is true, but also to try to bring to alumni the changing student thought patterns. Terry McCarthy, '62 secretary, wrote, "This year a change in disciplinary policy greeted the students, a change which is the result of years of discussion, planning and study. The most obvious innovations are the abandonment of restricted study time, and morning checks, along with the installation of hall chaplains . . . It is felt that self-discipline can mold character much better than enforced discipline." Many thought it could—some were not so sure it would.

Universal Notre Dame Night was asked to spotlight John XXIII's Encyclical, "Mater et Magistra," an appeal for lay involvement in the Church, and in harmony with the urging of the Alumni Association for a number of years. President Fleming was pleased with the success of the committee system of the busy Alumni Board, and anxious for full alumni participation in the first Ford Challenge program nearing successful completion. The "Sublime Tradition" series showed itself abreast of the times with an article on "The Race Myth and the Christian Conscience," by sociology Professor William D'Antonio. President Bill Mahoney, a disciple of the new order, pointed to the new urgency on the campus, its scope, the loss of some personal touches of the past, the increased sophistication of the student body, and the introduction of the new dialogue Mass. An *Alumnus* editorial pointed out that, in a sense, the "image" of Notre Dame is shaped by each individual alumnus, based on his own era, his contacts, and his acquaintance with the programs of the present.

Alumni began to show more often and more prominently in the news. President Mahoney was appointed ambassador to Ghana in 1962. Edwin O'Connor '38, Boston author, won the Pulitzer prize for his "Edge of Sadness," after an even better known work, "The Last Hurrah." Three alumni were appointed Federal Court judges—George Beamer '29, South Bend, William

B. Jones '28, Washington, D.C., and Stephen Roth '31, Flint, Mich. And the Notre Dame alumni secretary was elected national president of the American Alumni Council, the professional organization of alumni association executives from 1600 colleges and universities of the United States and Canada.

In the face of an unprecedented dropping of visible religious interest on the campus, Father John J. Cavanaugh, C.S.C. '23, former President, and former prefect of religion under Father O'Hara, who had edited a *Survey of Religious Surveys*, was named director of student religious life.

An editorial in the *Alumnus* reached back to persuade alumni of the need for their participation in the association programs. "Father Sorin didn't come by way of Madison Ave., nor did he have professional fund-raising counsel, but he knew the value of involvement. From the reluctant Bishop of Vincennes to the suspicious settlers in Lowell and South Bend and Laporte, Niles and Kalamazoo, each found himself involved in helping the struggles of the new college—a college with which some of them were in neither religious nor intellectual sympathy."

The Foundation, moving at top intensity, added three more alumni to its staff, which was being reduced often by offers from other institutions which had watched Notre Dame's phenomenal financial progress. The three new men were Edward L. Recker '48, Donald R. Ross '53 and Dennis F. Troester '57.

The intellectual student life, and the rising wave of student social consciousness were reflected in a column by the secretary of the Class of 1963. He pointed to summer activities in the ROTC programs, to projects in Mexico similar to those of the Peace Corps, to student work in Ciudad de Dios in Peru helping the Maryknoll missions there. He also reported the opening of the student owned and operated WSND-FM station. And he described for alumni the "stay-hall" program which students had requested, whereby students who elected might remain in the same residence hall year after year.

A new Cartier Field was announed, on the east side of the campus, beyond the encroaching new Library. It featured track, tennis and practice football facilities. It also featured a baseball field named in honor of veteran Coach Jake Kline. Lights were installed on the football practice fields.

Revolution and tradition now seem to be competing. An independent student government, the student columnist says, now has a budget of $26,000. In the same column he reports "coffee hours" instituted by students to promote better relations between faculty and students.

The Florida State alumni convention moved to the Bahamas. And the final presidential letter from Bill Mahoney was from the United States embassy in Ghana. He praised the Holy Cross Brothers in their Ghanaian schools. Other alumni were involved in Ghana in N'Krumah's efforts to advance that nation. Paul Doody '57, was secretary of the Fulbright Commission; George McNerny '57, was head of the Catholic Relief Services, Gerald Meyer '58, was administrator of the National Health Institute research in tropical disease, and Jim Griffin '59, was editor of Ghana's Catholic newspaper.

The Kuharich football fortunes continued to baffle coach and fans. Two seasons, 1961 and 1962, produced only 5-5-0 records, in spite of players like All-American Nick Buoniconti and Quarterback Daryl Lamonica. A change was inevitable, in the national identity of the sport at Notre Dame and in line with the demand for excellence generally. As an interim solution, the 1963 coaching responsibility was given to Hugh Devore. Hughie Devore remains one of the great players in Notre Dame history and one of its best liked coaches. But the task given him was insurmountable, and he produced a 2-7-0 season. A scheduled game with Iowa was cancelled upon the death of President John F. Kennedy. What football fans noted in the season following Devore's short tenure was the high caliber of his recruiting.

The football situation, once catastrophic, lost significance rapidly as the wave of campus unrest, already advertised from Berkeley and Columbia, hit the Notre Dame campus.

The spring had seemed just the usual stepped up pace. A review of the 40 years of the alumni office and the magazine brought the association members up to date, and underlined the extent of the development of those decades. Vatican II had had 12 Holy Cross priests among its delegates, including eight bishops. And 24 of the hierarchy at the council were holders of honorary degrees from the University.

Father Edmund P. Joyce, C.S.C., announced that the Ford Foundation Challenge program had met its goal, insuring the gift of the additional $6,000,000 from Ford. He praised the alumni for their participation. The theme for the 1963 Universal Notre Dame Night spotlighted the centennial of Father Corby's memorable and historical role in the Battle of Gettys-

burg. Father Tom O'Donnell was chairman of the University
program held at Gettysburg in July on the 100th anniversary of
the Battle. The success of the Foundation program brought
added staff members. Thomas J. Kernan '55, was appointed
field secretary for the 190 local alumni clubs. James V. Gibbons
'53, was appointed assistant public relations director under J.
Arthur Haley '26.

Father Hesburgh had cabled the alumni board from Switzer-
land, for its February meeting, an appreciation of the association role in the Challenge success.

The student "stay-hall" request, which had assumed the
identity of the "demand" now common on campuses, was
rejected by the administration. Students began in earnest to
copy their aggressive counterparts elsewhere. The "Student
Manifesto," stopped from publication in the *Scholastic*, appeared in an underground student paper. Poor taste began to
dot student writings and speeches. A new demand appeared,
that Father Hesburgh be removed as President and made chancellor, presumably to act outside the University, and a more
liberal President elected who could identify with modern students. This was harsh treatment of the President who had
actually been the first to identify enthusiastically with students,
and to champion their interests. It was also a more blatant
revolution than the campus had experienced. Father Hesburgh
wrote a letter to the students on "the Winter of Discontent,"
during their Easter-break, in which he said, ". . . Worst of all,
the lifelong dedication of hundreds of valiant priests and brothers, over the course of 120 years since the birth of Notre Dame
was brushed off (by student writers) in several pen strokes. For
their penance, I would ask these writers to walk down the long
rows of crosses in the Community Cemetery and ponder the
difference between what this silent brigade has given to Notre
Dame and what they themselves have loudly contributed by
their thoughtless and tasteless words. . . . Neither do I consider
faculty and students equal partners in the educative process
here, since students by definition are here to study under the
direction of the faculty, and to learn. . . ."

The *Alumnus* recognized the growing unrest by carrying a
thoroughly prepared article on "Academic Freedom," from the
American Alumni Council, with an accompanying article by
Father John Walsh, C.S.C., relating the principles of academic
freedom to Notre Dame. Father Walsh recognized constant

pressures but called for constant efforts at Notre Dame to preserve academic freedom.

Oliver Hunter '43, New Castle, Pa., became the second FBI alumnus to be chosen president of the association. New board members in 1963 were George A. Bariscillo '44, Asbury Park, N.J., attorney; Paul I. Fenlon '19, Notre Dame, Ind., lifetime lay professor in the University; Morton R. Goodman '30, Los Angeles, a Jewish alumnus and attorney, and W. Lancaster Smith '50, Dallas, Tex., attorney, a monogram man.

In the summer of 1963, Cardinal Montini, LL.D. '60, became Pope Paul VI, succeeding the short but significant reign of John XXIII. The winds of change were already whistling, not only through the open windows of the Vatican but through the halls of Notre Dame.

An *Alumnus* editorial, meeting alumni concern over rapid changes, under the heading of "The Belabored Point," asserted that the tremendous changes in the form of the University— physical, curricular, and student life-style, had not changed the primary and enduring purpose of the University. President Hunter repeated this assurance at the alumni banquet to the 1963 reunion alumni.

The Gettysburg program in July was an outstanding one, featuring the first Field Mass a the monument of the eternal flame there. Gen. and Mrs. Dwight Eisenhower were among those present. John Gleason, alumnus head of the Veterans Administration, was designated by President John F. Kennedy as his representative at the ceremonies. Father Hesburgh, Archbishops O'Boyle and Shehan, and Bishops Leech and Connor graced the observance. Notre Dame Clubs, under the banners of the clubs in Philadelphia and Harrisburg, had been invited to the tribute to the Holy Cross chaplain of the Civil War. The association program of religion and citizenship was advanced by this.

As an outgrowth of the football situation, the Alumni Board requested that the president of the association be made an ex officio member of the University Athletic Board. There had formerly been alumni members of this board. Now, the board was administrative and faculty, as in most colleges and universities. But the usually alumni heads of the athletic program, Father Joyce as chairman, Ed Krause as director of athletics, and the various coaches, were actually annually in discussion with the Alumni Board.

Universal Communion Sunday in 1963 was directed toward

the growing theme of "Federal Aid to Education." Clubs were urged to involve as speakers authorities on this subject.

The *Alumnus* paid tribute to the leaders of the Challenge I program—I. A. O'Shaughnessy, Peter Grace, Joe O'Neill, the 170 City Chairmen, the 3,500 Committeemen and the 23,500 contributors. It said that the success had "demonstrated the association to be a mature, integral, substantial part of the University and its life. . . . We need not put away or even regret the joys, the fraternal instincts, the enthusiasms of our past. Even then, a close look finds them surging around a maturity and a purpose that cirumstances could not until now implement. Rather, we should mellow all these good and desirable qualities in the new plateau of a stature we will never again lose, a new breadth and depth that is in itself a new basis of promise."

Three alumni, George Shuster '15, Archbishop Paul Hallinan '32 and Father Richard Butler, O.P. '42, were honored by the Newman Clubs of America for their contributions to religion in public education.

With Notre Dame opportunities for progress recurring and increasing, and on the heels of the outstanding success of the Ford Grant program—in which 76 per cent of our alumni had contributed $6,000,000, or half the matching fund sought to meet Ford conditions—it seemed logical, if a bit formidable, when Father Hesburgh announced that the Ford Foundation had offered a duplicate of its first grant, under similar conditions. In the light of experience and a widening circle of alumni and friends, the Foundation launched a Challenge II program, to achieve a $20,000,000 goal. Faculty development was listed for a $6,500,000 allocation of this goal. But alumni and friends who were interested in the athletic tradition brightened when $5,000,000 was to be allocated to a badly needed athletic and convocation center. Other projects of the new Challenge were student aid and two new and needed residence halls.

With all the programs, all the magazine features, all the speakers from the campus and meetings on the campus, the noise of the winds of change threatened still to create waves that would drown the tradition, the spirit, the nature of Notre Dame. Like at many other embattled institutions of higher education, the processes of success seemed suddenly intertwined with the processes of survival.

XXXVI

The Incredibility Gap

"Credibility gap" is a term which has been used in many of the situations in which our revolutionary society has found itself. The Notre Dame society in which I now found myself functioning, apparently within the framework of a 120-year old University rooted in the American educational and the Catholic intellectual traditions, and with 40 years of personal experience including all of the traditional successes in the programs which were my responsibility—created a situation I can only describe as the "incredibility gap." Changes were occurring with no visible means of support. You read the orthodox and looked around you at the unorthodox. Students were selected, sophisticated, responsible—they looked nondescript, their expressions were often execrable, their actions were often irresponsible. I began to find difficulty in interpreting Notre Dame to alumni. It was difficult to interpret it to myself.

One of the reasons for this difficulty is found in the paragraph above. It arises from the fallacy we are all heir to, generalization. The purpose of Notre Dame was now more difficult to identify in the academic kaleidoscope. The attack on the traditional principle of "in loco parentis" had buried that concept in a wave of doubt and fear. "La vie intime" was seldom now a conscious concept, because the segments of campus life were militant in self-interests.

I think one of the greatest challenges to reason stemmed from the fact that the brilliant beacon, the two-way bridges and the crowded crossroads made it difficult on occasion to determine their relationships with the University. And there was even too much urgent business at hand to enjoy the luxury of study and reflection.

The alumni, in 1963, had contributed $1,258,956. In the first year of Challenge II the amount of alumni contributions increased to $2,102,299. This was the first time alumni, without including the honorary degree alumni, had passed this $2 million dollar annual mark. In 25 years, the total income from alumni had increased from $15,000 to this financial miracle of $2,000,000—and in the context of annual support.

Philip J. Faccenda '51, Chicago, was elected president of the association, one of the youngest alumni to have held this national office. Newly elected members of the board were Thomas P. Carney '37, Indianapolis, then with Eli Lilly and later with G. D. Searle, pharmaceuticals executive; Dr. Bertrand D. Coughlin '26, St. Louis, Mo., proctologist; William V. Cuddy '52, White Plains, N.Y., attorney, and Herbert V. Sampson '50, Omaha, Neb., an executive of Northern Natural Gas. It was taking more sophistication just to identify our board members. The old educational pattern, however, seemed to have been adequate in preparing alumni to meet many of the challenges of the times.

President Faccenda reported a new look in board committees. Association affairs now were handled by executive, club, class and inter-alumni committees; involved with the University were Prep School and Admissions, Placement, Prestige and Public Relations, and Alumni Fund and Foundation Committees. Concerned with the board and association programs were Committees on Religion and Citizenship, Nominations, Budget and Finance. Concerned with the campus were the Committees for Athletics, Academic Affairs and Student Affairs. The Alumni Association in 40 years had brought its officers from a popular reunion election to honorary posts, to the serious program of a 40,000 member world organization, where even the board members were commenting on their workload. My most difficult task was to convince these board members that their feeling of limited achievement in their three years should be offset for them when they saw the tremendous progress of the Alumni Association under their cumulative leadership.

Retiring President Hunter praised alumni for their success in the Challenge I program, and urged support for Challenge II. But he urged alumni attention to the rising incidence of student unrest. The resignation of John Jordan '35 as basketball coach had stemmed from such student activism.

The theme for Universal Notre Dame Night was designed to

reconcile the still suspect concept of the "distinguished professor" with the dedicated faculty of longer service. It was titled "Great Teaching."

In 1964 the first reunion of former alumni board members, from the 40-year history of the board, was held. It was a recognition of past success and a kick-off endorsement of Challenge II's new program. Father Hesburgh, Father Joyce, Ed Krause, Father John Walsh and George Shuster were among the speakers trying to underscore the bonds of history and tradition with the programs and progress of the turbulent campus. The alumni secretary, now a veteran eye-witness of a lot of history, stressed two persisting principles in the association's advancement. One was the consistent record of alumni initiative, and the other was the traditional "vie intime" inherited from the University of Sorin, a continuous close tie between Notre Dame and Notre Dame men, individually and in their association. A personal highlight of this reunion of 100 dear and vital components of my career was the gift to the Armstrongs of a trip to Hawaii. This was the booster shot that carried me through Challenge II and the remaining years of incredibility.

The past received two accolades, one with the publication in the *Alumnus* of a list of dedicated current faculty members who had taught 25 years or more, and the award of a monogram blanket to Sister William, of the St. Mary's Hospital in Rochester, Minn., who had been an enthusiastic angel of mercy to Notre Dame patients at the Mayo Clinic for 50 years. Her patients had included Knute Rockne, Frank Leahy and several University Presidents.

Dedication of the Memorial Library, new landmark among the libraries of American higher education, brought to the campus the involved heads of major universities, welcoming a constructive interruption of the spreading turbulence of American students. Another academic thrust came with the introduction of professional fraternities on the campus. The Colleges of Science, Engineering, and Business Administration advised alumni of their qualifications for membership.

National recognition of alumni association progress came at the Denver Convention of the American Alumni Council, when Notre Dame received the grand award for alumni giving to the University, including a $5,000 cash prize. An award was also given for direct mail efforts resulting in the 90 per cent attendance at the Alumni Board reunion.

In an intensive effort to understand the swirl of progress, the board instituted contacts with young priests and with the faculty and students, beyond the traditional and effective briefings of the administration.

In 1964, Father Hesburgh faced another of the major decisions in athletics which had interrupted his academic pursuits in the Brennan and Kuharich cases. This time the search was exhaustive, in an effort to bring the symbolic football program back to its historic perspective on the campus. The choice was the coach at Northwestern, Ara Parseghian. Parseghian, a non-Catholic in the early Rockne tradition, and a non-alumnus in the earlier Jesse Harper tradition, has achieved the goal of the administration. In his first year, 1964, he brought Notre Dame, which had been 2-7-0 in 1963, to an incredible 9-1-0 season. If the overall morale value of football in Notre Dame's public relations had ever been in serious doubt, the doubt vanished. Attendance increased more than 100,000 and future interest was guaranteed by the dramatic ending of the season, which was undefeated until the last minute and a half of the Southern California game in Los Angeles, when a field goal margin brought the only defeat.

A Notre Dame alumnus achieved the highest political recognition yet accorded, when William E. Miller '35, New York attorney, was nominated for the vice presidency of the United States on the ill-fated Barry Goldwater ticket.

Reunions in June reflected the increase in numbers, diversity and stature of alumni. Bus service around the campus for returning alumni spotlighted its expanding size. Open houses in the colleges were repeated. A kiltie band supplied music, in the absence of the school-year University musicians. A special alumni convocation to mark the dedication of the Library, brought alumni into the magnificent facilities of the 14-story structure. Father Hesburgh and Alumni President Faccenda addressed the group. The awards of the American Alumni Council were presented by that organization's executive director from Washington, D.C., Jack Johnson. The alumni banquet featured Father John Walsh on Challenge II, Dean Thomas Bergin on the Kellogg Center for Continuing Education, which seemed to implement the long alumni stress on such a program, and the new center of alumni interest, Coach Ara Parseghian. Alumni expectations rose, and the Parseghian record at this writing is—74-15-4, with Notre Dame in the Top Ten eight of the nine years. More than 40 All-American ratings have recognized the consistent accomplishment.

"A Century of Science at N.D." was announced in the December, 1964 *Alumnus*. The new Radiation Center building, and a new building adjoining the Library to house the Computer-Math program, were highlights of the observance. Enrollment in the College of Science had reached 600 undergraduates and 328 graduate students. A committee of faculty members included also Jim Gibbons and Jim Murphy of Public Relations, and Jim Armstrong from the alumni office. Alumni of the college who had achieved distinction in the field were to be awarded citations by the College during the June, 1965, reunion.

President Faccenda had proposed a workshop for the Alumni Board and the University, to review the upcoming 100th anniversay of the Association and the prospects and challenges facing alumni in the dawn of its second century.

Another of the thriving institutional offspring of the first little band of Holy Cross Religious was announced by the Brothers of Holy Cross. A new center was to be built across the highway from Notre Dame, including the Provincial House, and a Junior College. The brothers were now teaching 28,500 students in 55 schools, principally secondary, but including the St. Edward's University in Texas. They staffed 37 high schools in the U.S., and 11 in countries abroad in Asia, Africa, and South America.

Lancaster Smith '50, Dallas, succeeded Phil Faccenda as president. New members of the board were Ambrose F. Dudley '43, former coach, the founding promoter of the Liberty Bowl football game, originated in Philadelphia, now moving to Memphis; Joseph H. Carey '32, Detroit, Mich., automotive executive; Thomas W. Carroll '51, former assistant to Art Haley, now a corporate junior executive in Kansas, and Charles J. Patterson '47, Framingham, Mass., vice president of the Perini Corp.

President Smith, with the rise of football, was an easy victim of the incredibility gap, because in the Texas environment alumni did not hear too many student activist proposals, and believed very few of those they heard, assuming almost total immunity from them on the Notre Dame campus. Lanc Smith was a serious and multi-interested president of the association. He praised Director Mort Goodman for his success in stopping the proposed showing of a film based on Notre Dame football, a farce called "John Goldfarb Please Come Home." The complicated trivia was approved in an appeals court reversal, but with public exposure it died of its own weakness. The incident indicated, however, that widespread public interest and support is not a path to privacy. The bridge, beacon and crossroad does not enjoy the climate of the older academic cloister.

James W. Frick '51, who joined the Foundation staff after graduation, was made the first lay vice president of the University, succeeding Father John Walsh in the Public Relations and Development Office. The Foundation, the Alumni Association, Public Information, Public Relations and Placement, were coordinated under this office. Frick's outstanding competence in the programs of the Foundation during the two Ford Foundation Challenge programs made him a logical leader in the demanding expansion program. At the same time Francis McGuide '25, was named vice president in the newly created post for research, and Thomas P. Stewart '57, of the lay faculty, was made associate vice president for academic affairs.

Student government, with expanding interests, expanding budget and expanding ambition and power, instituted the first committee on Negro enrollment. The association vice presidents, Goodman, Bariscillo and Fenlon reported to the board on their program fields in the winter workshop. The basic comment was on the new freedom of expression on the campus.

John Laughlin resigned from the *Alumnus* staff and John P. Thurin '59, former *Dome* editor, was named to become managing editor of the *Alumnus* and editor of the magazine, *Notre Dame*, as well. James D. Cooney, also '59, had been a logical choice for the Alumni Office for some time, working on the Foundation staff. He now joined the Alumni Association as assistant alumni secretary.

The alumni secretary was battling to preserve the unity of the University and the Alumni Association. In an editorial he commented, ". . . while the programs of the Alumni Association must keep step with, in fact lead, the creation of sound and productive alumni, another dogma, it seems to me, must be a function of the Association: fighting a protective rear-guard action against the aggressive pursuit of progressive impersonalization. Stroganoff, or ordinary stew,—the beef is vital. Whatever the blend of the future—and our faith is unlimited in it—we should never omit basic ingredients."

Sister Suzanne Kelly, O.S.B., became the first woman to receive a full-time faculty appointment during the regular school year. Brother Raphael Wilson '48, a research scientist, was appointed director of admissions. The *Alumnus* softened the criticism of Notre Dame's four-years costs, now hovering around $11,400, by citing a substantial number of private universities whose costs ranged from $12,000 to $14,000. The Foundation staff acquired three more alumni members, as opportunities elsewhere siphoned off the fine young workers who had met the Challenge I and Challenge II goals,—Deon Sutton '31, New York, David Shanahan '58, Lima, O., and John Crowe '62, son of alumnus and former coach Clem Crowe '26, one of the legendary families of Notre Dame men. The University's world influence was spotlighted when a program of assistance to the official Catholic University of Peru, from the Ford Foundation, named Notre Dame its administrator. The Memorial Library, through Father Philip Moore, C.S.C. '24, Victor Schaefer, librarian, and Francis Wallace '23, acting chairman, announced the creation of a Sports and Games Section, to become a world research center in materials dealing with all forms of sports and games.

The 40th reunion dinner of the Class of 1925 featured the Four Horsemen. Al Ryan '20, George Strickler '25, George Vergara '25, "Hunk" Anderson '22, Father Joyce '38 and Coach Parseghian were speakers at the class dinner, which also paid tribute to the long and valued services of John P. Hurley, class secretary and Henry C. Wurzer, class treasurer. More than 1,100 alumni returned for the 1965 reunions.

One change in the Church caught up with a fine association program. Universal Communion Sunday had come under the criticism of pastors seeking to abolish corporate communions as hampering the new liturgy and the family spirit of the parish programs. The 1965 suggestion was that it be held on a weekday, Dec. 8. I have not been unmindful of the Korean War, and now the Vietnam War. Neither was really a declared war, neither possessed the rationale, the glory or the national acceptance of the remembered World Wars I and II. Notre Dame men responded, but there were also Notre Dame men increasingly vocal in the rising tide of opposition to the new Vietnam demands.

Academic changes and student life changes were many and rapid, still short of the demands and pressures of a dissenting and aggressive student body, the latter often bolstered in their activism by the new school of young activist faculty members.

A major University step in meeting new student freedom was the creation of a coexchange program with Saint Mary's, whereby Notre Dame students could take classes in some of the educational courses offered there, particularly in special education, and Saint Mary's girls could augment their studies in the Colleges of Science and Business, or Arts and Letters, on the Notre Dame campus. The program brought the first regular school year presence of large numbers of girls on the campus. The University had also followed a university trend by establishing a year of studies at Innsbruck, for Sophomores. More than 7,000 students were now enrolled at Notre Dame. Campus curfews were extended. A senior class bar, in an off-campus location, was sanctioned in an effort toward responsible recognition of the legal rights of most Seniors, freedom to drink.

In the face of the emphasis on the "structure" of the academic Notre Dame, the inevitable loss of attention to the spiritual values of the "superstructure," the unbridled freedoms and misinterpretations of Vatican II in the Church itself, and the always quick and perceptive ability of students to detect administrative vulnerability, were generally evident. It seemed a particularly inopportune time to discontinue the *Religious Bulletin*. But St. Thomas' philosophy, Cardinal Newman's integral concept of religion and education, and Father O'Hara's merchandising approach to campus religious life were all in disfavor, with students and with some faculty.

In a major move to tighten the bonds between the founding father and brothers and the dynamic University rushing forward in the vanguard of American higher education, the Alumni Association established the Edward Frederick Sorin Award, for service to Notre Dame in the great tradition of its founder. It was inevitable that Father Theodore Hesburgh, in the forefront of university presidents, in favor with the Vatican and the White House, a recipient of countless honors, and of the generosity of foundation and corporate gifts, who had brought Notre Dame to new heights in a few short years, should be its first recipient. He was also a member of the Congregation of Holy Cross, at that point in campus history indistinguishable from the University itself.

The kaleidoscope showed the *Alumnus* alternating six issues with four issues of the magazine, *Notre Dame.* Controversy over the Vietnam War was stirring up students and faculty. A major "Epilogue to Vatican II" was held in the Center for Continuing Education on the Notre Dame campus, and 24 of that council's fathers discussed the implications and the impacts of Pope John's convocation. The voices of dissent began to be heard in the winds of change, especially from the theologians.

Two echoes of an older Notre Dame, but never an un-changing one, came with the death of John Shea '06, co-author of the "Victory March." Another came with the retirement of Zigmunt Kucharczuk, "Ziggy" to 37 years of student waiters and special events in the Dining Halls. Ziggy took the daily pressures and the special events with efficiency and composure, even the 7,000 meals to be served three times daily during the Navy programs. Another Notre Dame tradition in the making was ended when Charlie Callahan '38, nationally known sports information director, who succeeded J. Walter Kennedy '34, in the position, left Notre Dame to handle this position for the Miami Dolphins. Alumni have followed Charlie's competence in that post from the ordinary sunshine seasons to the 1973 Super Bowl.

The Alumni Board meetings now usually found some inci-dent of student activism a part of the agenda. It was all "part of the times," incidents normal to the involved students of this generation, inevitable in the "permissive society," an off-shoot of a new student "affluence." But no matter how it was all explained, no matter how small a minority may have been identifiable parties, no matter how persistent the faith was in the majority of students and teachers, there was a growing air of incredibility that the Notre Dame campus, the University, its nature, its purpose and its traditions, could reflect the extreme turbulence besetting other national campuses.

In February, 1966, the association brought 42 class agents to the campus, to discuss the vital tradition of the class organiza-tion and its significance in the present and future University. The agents were to be responsible, in part, for the participation of the members of the class in the Foundation program. Alumni in the St. Joseph Valley were leaders in a $250,000 campaign toward the new Athletic and Convocation Center, which would have facilities of great community value.

Academically, Notre Dame announced a year abroad program in Angiers, France, in conjunction with the Catholic University of the West in that city. The program was open to Notre Dame and Saint Mary's students. Father Louis Thornton announced that the Placement Office had affiliated with the American College Placement Council program, based in Bethlehem, Pa., known as GRAD, whereby students and alumni could be con-tacted promptly through computerized records of employers and prospects.

Two deaths brought a sense of loss and many memories to

alumni. One was that of Father Charles Miltner, C.S.C. '11, at
the age of 80. Father Miltner had revolutionized the program in
Arts and Letters as its dean. The other was Harry G. Hogan, the
versatile Fort Wayne alumnus, whose post-retirement contribution to the University in the form of the Notre Dame Foundation was multiplying each year the wisdom of his plan, and the
competence of his performance. Results in its 17 years of
existence were nearing $40,000,000.

Universal Notre Dame Night was asked to tackle the "Role of
the Catholic University in the Modern Age." That subject is still
relevant, still not satisfactorily defined. But Notre Dame met it
more than half way, in the persisting tradition of leadership.

So many fine programs had sprung from the national alumni
organization. One of these was highlighted when Don Miller '25,
one of the Four Horsemen, and Ara Parseghian, football coach,
addressed the 35th annual St. Joseph Valley Club Communion
Breakfast honoring the memory of Knute K. Rockne.

Thomas P. Carney '37, succeeded Lancaster Smith as association president. Carney had shown a facility of dialogue with the
often difficult student representatives from the various campus
activities. In a letter to alumni, he commented, ". . . most
alumni are interested in preserving traditions, most students are
interested in breaking them. . . . There is an aliveness on the
campus today that is impossible to describe. . . . The student of
today and the alumnus of the past have one thing in common,
they are typical in that, almost invariably, they put progress
ahead of peace . . . I have implicit faith in the character of the
present Notre Dame man. Whether we understand all his reactions or not, he is going to bring as much credit to Notre Dame
in the future as have the illustrious graduates of the past. With a
little effort, I think we can understand him."

Ground was broken for the Athletic and Convocation Center.
Alumni giving to Challenge I continued to be generous, with
gifts from alumni-owned or directed corporations increased.

The University announced the successful completion of the
total Challenge II campaign, with its contingent second gift of
$6,000,000 from the Ford Foundation. Notre Dame's position
in higher education was now one of leadership and prestige.
Gifts and grants to the second campaign had amounted to
$22,084,291, more than 10% above the goal.

New Alumni Board members elected were Richard A. Rosenthal '54, president of the St. Joseph Bank in South Bend, a
former basketball star; William D. Kavanaugh '27, Washington,

D.C., an officer of American Cyanimid; William F. Kerwin '40, Green Bay, Wis., warehouse executive, and Leo V. Turgeon, M.D. '42, Los Angeles physician.

A faculty panel offered a seminar to alumni at the 1966 reunion, on "The Problem of Population." The controversial subject did not draw too well from the 950 alumni on the campus. It was decided that it was basically a family type discussion, and this was the nature of subsequent successful sessions in Club cities. During the summer, Father Louis Putz, C.S.C., was made superior of Moreau Seminary, and the former local club liaison priest, Father Thomas O'Donnell, was made his assistant. An echo of older Congregational ties was heard with the death of Father Matthew Schumacher, C.S.C. of the Class of 1899, at the age of 87.

In a letter to alumni, President Carney said, "With the increased stature of the University it is increasingly important that every alumnus, regardless of his year of graduation, continues to contribute to its growth. We take contributions of money for granted . . . However, other contributions are required also. The University cannot continue to grow without a vigorous, interested and informed alumni body."

The fall enrollment in 1966 reached 7,333. All off-campus students were permitted to have cars. And the curfew was removed from all but Freshmen students. A department in the *Alumnus* was begun to meet the new volume of voices of dissent. It was called "Alumni Ask," and was not without reservations on the part of the veteran editor. Like most "letters" columns, it is a channel for individual expression. But like most, too, it attracts the articulate extremists. It is not a vehicle, usually, for the voice of compromise. More often it tends to polarize. But in an era of "freedom of the press" already loosening profanity and obscenity on long protected readership, who could argue with a voice from Notre Dame alumni?

A survey of the 1966 reunion attendants showed that alumni were moving rapidly into the higher brackets of business and professional life and leadership. Practically all alumni were satisfied with the preparation for religious life and with the religious life on the campus. With the exception of the Class of 1941, the majority favored the University disciplinary pattern. Classes from 1936 through 1961 said the most important thing Notre Dame had done was to teach them to think for themselves.

The University was approaching its 125th anniversary in 1967. The Alumni Association was at its centenary. Challenge II was successfully concluded. Bernard J. Voll '17, lay leader and Trustee, was named the second recipient of the Edward F. Sorin Award of the Alumni Association. The *Alumnus* featured a debate between Professor Edward J. Cronin '38, favoring emphasis on teaching, and Professor Gerald Massey '56, favoring emphasis on research. The issue was a live one on most campuses, and of great interest to alumni. The association had reached a real contributing maturity. As President Carney expressed it, " . . . a triumvirate consisting of administration, faculty and students, all working for the same goals, certainly makes up a powerful team . . . we now believe that our alumni, through the alumni office, the board of directors, and the local clubs, can make contributions to the University comparable to those of the administration, faculty and students. We believe alumni should be equal partners in the University operation."

In January, 1967, the University announced that it would no longer be under the control of the Congregation of Holy Cross, but a separate corporate entity, governed by a Board of Trustees and Fellows. Alumni were reassured . . . "the essential character of the University as a Catholic institution of higher learning cannot be altered except by concurrence of at least two-thirds of the (12) Fellows (the Fellows are the executive group, with six priests of the Congregation and six lay members). Furthermore, the President of Notre Dame will continue to be a Holy Cross priest, appointed by the predominantly Lay Board of (30) Trustees."

President Tom Carney had made a great effort to understand and unite the old and the new Notre Dame. On his retirement as president of the Alumni Association, he was made a member of the University Board of Trustees. Edmund C. Stephan '33, an attorney-alumnus, Chicago, was made the first chairman of the new trustees.

Ambrose "Bud" Dudley '43, was chosen to succeed Tom Carney as president of the association. New board members were Leonard H. Skoglund '38, Chicago corporate executive and monogram football men; Edward G. Cantwell '24, Columbus, O., head of the Cantwell Machinery Corp.; Edward B. Fitzpatrick '54, New York business executive, and John J. Reidy, '27, Cleveland attorney.

An article in the *Alumnus*, by the new president, actually a speech delivered to several organization meetings of patrons of sports, entitled the "Lost Image," decried the publicized deterioration of students on the American campuses, suggesting that students trained in the discipline of athletics could offer constructive leadership to the campuses, even outside the athletic programs. It triggered a violent controversy between the revolutionists and the traditionalists. Extremists were most vocal, but apparently the airing of views was constructive.

At the same time, the announcement was made of the exploration of a merger with Saint Mary's. George Shuster '15, explained to alumni, "No one is thinking of absorption, coeducation or second-class citizenship on either campus. We have in mind, rather, a condition of cooperation into which both institutions can grow, undertaking jointly those educational and administrative tasks which they cannot do as well separately."

The Alumni Board now created a new body, composed of club presidents, to be called the Alumni Senate. The concept stemmed from the great value the board placed on its own meetings and briefings with the administrators and faculty and students of the University and the conviction that the new senate would multiply this beneficial process to reach thousands more alumni through the clubs. In one sense, it was an extension of the Club Presidents Council. But it was created for a wider purpose, to serve as an extension of the Alumni Board itself in translating the University and the association on the local community level, and bringing back to the University and the association the grass-root thinking of alumni everywhere.

The report of the 1966 Annual Alumni Fund showed $2,165,699 from 13,709 alumni, both new records for a single year. The percentage of participation was 50.95. A survey of Notre Dame clubs, as compared with a national survey of other college alumni clubs, made by the American Alumni Council, showed that Notre Dame clubs enjoyed more activity by a greater membership participation, by a substantial margin. And from their beginning, Notre Dame clubs had paid their own way in their programming. This was a unique feature in the national survey, a tribute to club loyalty and generosity.

The new University governance became effective in May. A new *Faculty Senate Manual* was presented to the trustees. Student government was definite and firm in its identity.

Father Hesburgh, in an address to the Notre Dame faculty, described his idea of the reality of the Catholic university, and his ideal of Notre Dame as a beacon, a bridge and a crossroad.

The University announced a grant of $4,700,000 from the

National Science Foundation, to provide expanded facilities to house the Life Sciences and a new Lobund center. The foundation report for 1966 showed a total of $10,180,547 in gifts and grants. Local clubs on Universal Notre Dame Night observed the theme, "Notre Dame, 125 years."

In every way, 1967 seemed the ideal year for me to retire. In the first place, the University, with some urging from the Alumni Board, had set up a retirement program for non-teaching administration officers. In the second place, the Alumni Association was observing significant anniversaries and embarking on significant new programs. In the third place, alumni generosity had long since paid off all Alumni Association debts to Notre Dame and was now a flourishing and respected part of the future; in the fourth place, no urgent campaign had yet been announced to succeed Challenge II's success.; in the fifth place, activities and concepts all pointed to young thinking. I was not unfamiliar with change, or opposed to it, but sometimes it was hard in long perspective to understand its advantages. In the sixth place, I had begged, borrowed and stolen Jim Cooney from the Foundation as a qualified successor. It was becoming more difficult to march to my own drummers, and most unlikely that different drummers would change that.

It was the time and place and the opportunity to stop the University, while an old commuter got off. It had been a wild and wonderful ride.

XXXVII

"I'm Stuck Like a Dope"

You fans of "South Pacific" recognize in the title a line from "The Cockeyed Optimist." As I come to this spot in the chronicle, "with a thing called hope," it is not a real conclusion of anything. I have taken the opportunity to record these thoughts, not as a work of nostalgia, but as a weapon of progress for those presently in charge, and those to follow them. Unless we know where we have been, and how and why we were there, and who led us there, we will have trouble charting a continuing path that does not bring us unnecessary hardship, or find us ultimately lost.

My retirement, personally, was a weekend of unceasing wonder. As I realized how much was being done for me by those immediately around me, my suspicions were confirmed—if most pleasantly—that I could no longer emcompass the scope of the day-to-day operations of the Alumni Association as a one-man band. But the headaches and heartaches of 42 years were erased by the rewards that accumulated as the weekend wore on. Assembled family, future trip, named scholarship, luxury car, and words that taxed even my calloused modesty, were deeply appreciated, even more as more than five years of tranquillity have given perspective to the recollection.

I like to believe that what happened to me was only a part of the general realization after 100 years of the significance of the alumni of the University, to Notre Dame, and to each other. I like to keep the conviction that the strength of organized alumni as an integral part of Notre Dame, a continuing segment of "la vie intime," not only was apparent on that occasion, but has remained, and will remain and grow, as a vital part of the projection of the Notre Dame of the future.

The five incredible years of enjoyment which have followed retirement have given me an assurance objectively about Notre Dame and its strength that I was never able to feel as deeply and confidently in the constant pressures of progress.

The five years have witnessed the phenomenon that haunts all retirees—the University has not only survived, but has continued on its fantastic journey into destiny as if with lightened burden. Jim Cooney has not only handled the Atlas-like assumption of the weight of the alumni world, but is juggling new programs with great dexterity and gracing the communications channels with eloquence and wit.

I have found, for example, that the climate of campus revolution was in fact a small, if very real, experience on the campus. The majority of students, and the majority of faculty, persist in the basic nature and purpose of education. Even the erosion of traditional Notre Dame and Catholic education is less than the blatant evidence of isolated instances could lead us to believe when we faced it directly.

I still regret a feeling that some changes have been made to satisfy demand for change. I still regret that the channels of communication were allowed to be largely taken over by the dissidents—a procedure outlined in a revolutionary manual for American campuses, which included also the injunction to gain control of the student body budget. These two minority actions alone have resulted in much of the shock to religion, tradition, good taste and patriotism that has kept the campus in an air of seeming turbulence which it has never actually suffered. The majority, as elsewhere, has been unfortunately silent. Administrators allowed some of the conditions to develop partly because they did not believe they could survive, and partly, in some instances, because they were afraid that actions in the framework of an older system of discipline would trigger the violence that accompanied revolution on many other campuses.

The fact that in the past September some 200 American colleges and universities were looking for new presidents, while Father Hesburgh remained for a term exceeded in length only by that of Father Sorin himself, should indicate that the substance of Notre Dame is not always reflected by its current shadows.

As I left office, alumni gave the new editor of the *Alumnus* a resounding vote for the continuing priority of the class news in the magazine. But editor competence, especially in the developments under John Thurin, had already given the format of the

Alumnus and of the non-alumni magazine *Insight* an added professional attractiveness which won then, and in the years since, awards in the quality competitions of the American College Public Relations Association and the American Alumni Council. The University itself received a rating of eighth among the top one per cent of American undergraduate schools, exceeded only by universities with far greater endowments.

One of Jim Cooney's prompt and effective programs has been the closing of the communications gap between the student and alumni groups, national or club. Jim had already done fine work on this. Now, as a part of his new program, in the house just south of the Stadium, he is godfather to an "Alumni Club," in which mellow conviviality among the graduating class, with occasional dropin alumni visits, makes a smoother transition from the insufferable sophistication of the Senior to the inevitable beginners class as alumni.

Philip J. Faccenda '51, former president of the alumni, attorney and business man, who brought his family to South Bend and became an assistant to Father Hesburgh, is now a vice president and counsel. Phil's move was in the new tradition of the successful young who willingly trade material success for a chosen preferred life-style. The move permitted retaining some interests and did not actually exclude material success, but it did bring to the University a dedicated young and experienced executive with a strong alumni perspective.

Controversy was not allowed to wane. Father McCarragher, in a reversion to more familiar years, stated that "the resolutions of the Student Senate and the Hall Presidents Council are only recommendations." This was in answer to a Student Senate resolution of separate and distinct student rights. The articulate minorities carried the innovations of a legal approach to "due process," and the concurrent abdication of the principle of "in loco parentis," to enough extremes that, as I write this, the Student Senate and the Hall Presidents Council, along with a Faculty Senate which seemed prone to procedural entanglements, are debating dissolution within themselves. The extremes of the new student politics resulted in a rejection by the once silent majority, when they elected as 1972 student body president a student whose campaign was a ridiculous spoof of the whole student government, to the extent of the election of the candidate's cat as Student Vice-President.

Former President Tom Carney said of the students, "I am not sure we can ever understand the students that come after us,

nor do I think it is completely necessary that we understand
them. But this I do know. I know it would be good if we
learned to trust them." And another association president, the
put-upon Ambrose "Bud" Dudley, urged personal alumni
understanding, "It is my hope that we will continue to question
one another and tolerate one another, and begin where those
before us have left off, so that all of us may perhaps have an
inkling at least of things that are really great."

Two Alumni Board members made memorable comments on
the undergraduate situation. One, when the trend was first
evident, was Mort Goodman's incredulous statement that the
"inmates were running the institution." The other came from
Bud Dudley, when he heard an administrator say that he was
afraid of the students. Bud recalled an earlier administrator
saying that "One man with guts is a majority." The student
unrest as it now looks to me, and it is not yet over, stemmed
largely from a small group of activists, drawing encouragement,
support and example from a national pattern, offering vicarious
and novel excitement to a larger but uncommitteed segment of
students, and enjoying the traditional unwillingness of the
unsympathetic majority to join any administrative efforts to
stop the trends.

The University, basking in the national spotlight of the two
Ford Foundation Challenges, involving actually two major
capital gifts campaigns, but still in the throes of rising costs,
expanding needs, and a vanguard competition with schools of
far greater financial resources, had to continue its efforts. With
a bold move that had fund-raising experts gasping and alumni
startled, Notre Dame announced a campaign to raise
$52,000,000 over a five-year period. It was only then to be
followed by a moratorium on capital campaigns. It was to be
called Summa. The fact that this imaginative and unprecedented
capital campaign, the third consecutive effort, was oversub-
scribed by $10,000,000 in less than the time allotted to it, has
been a tribute to the understanding and the stature of the
University and of its alumni and friends. It has also been an
evidence of the persisting faith in the ultimate destiny and the
original purpose and nature of Notre Dame. And, let me add, to
the competence of James W. Frick, '51.

The third Father Sorin Award went to Archbishop Paul
Hallinan, '32, who was serving as national alumni chairman of
Summa, and died during that program. He had been in the
Vatican II Council, and a constructive force for the Church in

Atlanta and the South. It was a distinction for me to have my name replace his in the Summa program for alumni.

The *Alumnus* carried four student-authored articles on the new "student power." A veteran faculty member, Frank O'Malley '32, wrote an accompanying article. He commented, "Our students today will not long endure academic structures set up out of sight and out of range of their living presences and pressures, structures which in the concrete situation may be found irrelevant or untoward." This is another reason for some success among the revolutionaries—they were partly right in their rebellion.

Richard A. Rosenthal '54, young South Bend banker, was chosen association president to succeed Bud Dudley, who remained as honorary president. Rosenthal brought a monogram student background, youth, success in business and proximity to the job, all of which were assets in the era of controversy. New directors elected were Donald F. O'Brien '42, Houston, Tex., a vice president of McCann-Erickson advertising; W. Jerome Kane '38, Seattle, a Boeing Aircraft executive; Walter M. Langford '30, South Bend, faculty member and long-time active association and club leader, and Francis J. "Fritz" Wilson '28, Pittsburgh clothier.

The rumbles of coeducation were being heard. Negotiations with Saint Mary's were reported in progress. A third Catholic women's college had declined an offer of affiliation and a similar proposal for Barat College was being discussed. But nothing appeased the demanding students. Reflecting a national token of unrest, 200 students demonstrated outside the Placement Office in the Main Building against the interviews to be conducted by Dow Chemical with student job applicants. The group, including a few faculty members, priests, and nuns, ignored administrative orders to move outside the Administration Building.

Students were including traditional religious programs in their revolution. Priests were identified with disciplinarians. To combat this, some priests were introducing late night Masses and experimental religious programs in the halls. Any method of measuring student religious involvement was eliminated. Administration and faculty pointed to serious student involvement in social causes as an offset. The faculty panel "Has Change Run Away With the Church?" attracted local club interest. New York, Indianapolis, Boston and Detroit, featured the visiting academic panel.

The unpopular Vietnam War was of course a perennial factor
in most of the campus disturbance. Because it had much sympathy, Father Hesburgh made an extra effort to smooth progress with the creation of the Student Life Council, divided into
three equal groups of faculty, administration and students. To
this writing, it has been assessed on occasion as significant, on
other occasions as useless. The students were now demanding
"parietal hours," hours during which they could entertain girls
in their rooms in their halls. The basis of the complaint was lack
of social space on campus. The trustees said, "The board does
not believe that the only or best or even good solution to this
legitimate desire is to permit visitation to men's dormitory
rooms." As nearly as I can judge, reaction to this principle
among the students has been about the same as the reactions in
the 1920s to the prohibition laws. The promotion of other
students rights, such as the privacy of his room against invasion
by a rector or security guard without the student permission,
has complicated supervision.

Father Hesburgh announced the innovative construction of
two high-rise residence halls on the campus, named Flanner and
Grace after generous contributions from benefactors. And to
recognize both status and need of the faculty, the University
announced the construction of a new University Club building,
the gift of the Robert H. Gore Sr., family, Fort Lauderdale,
whose alumni sons were Robert Jr. '31, Fred '43, George '48,
and Ted '50. The club now contains a magnificent collection of
steins from the Gore family.

The Foundation had reported that in 1954, when the enrollment was 5,401, the operating costs of the University were
$13,000,000. In 1967, enrollment had gone to 7,425 and oper-
ating costs of $36,123,178 were almost triple. The report indi-
cated the need for the new capital campaign in progress. Now,
as Notre Dame's enrollment is around the 9,000 mark, a third
of this graduate students, Father Hesburgh estimates annual
expenditures nearing $50,000,000. To meet this continuous
need for funds, with the Summa program completed, the Foundation has instituted the all-inclusive Annual Fund, based on
the long-established Annual Alumni Fund, whose identity was
retained through the various capital campaigns. During the
Summa campaign 24, 379 alumni gave a total of $25,277,866.
This was a tremendous evidence of loyalty and stature.

Some 1,300 alumni greeted the 1968 innovation of reunion
hats, replacing the long familiar Class caps.

The death of Senator Robert Kennedy saddened the campus and disturbed the students, whose idol he had been.

The Law School announced the creation of a year abroad program of legal study in London.

The Alumni Association made a sorely needed change by revising the 1950 Constitution. The new instrument increased the size of the Alumni Board to 16 members, and created the Alumni Senate to expand and implement stronger board ties with both alumni and University.

President Rosenthal, commenting on the student demonstrations against Dow interviewers, said, "Perhaps what Notre Dame will be may not necessarily be satisfactory to all. Individuals may come and if Notre Dame is consistent with what they are seeking they will be a part of the community. They will be free to go, if what they find is inconsistent with what they are seeking. The University will not get on with its maturity through demonstration and complaint. It will mature through the leadership, interaction and integrity of its membership body."

The Athletic and Convocation Center was opened, with its vast new facilities made known by a week of dedicatory ceremonies and events. These included a high school musical show with 1,000 high school musicians participating; the Andy Williams variety television program; and the Bill Cosby comedy-variety show. The 49th annual football banquet of the Notre Dame Club of the St. Joseph Valley demonstrated the scope and diversity of the new area institution. The Notre Dame-U.C.L.A. basketball game, a Sunday Mass, and the ice rink were enthusiastically received. The Mass, concelebrated by Bishop Leo A. Pursley with 24 diocesan and Holy Cross priests, constituted the formal dedication. I was given a deeply appreciated additional honor by the Alumni Board, as the fourth recipient of the Father Sorin Award.

Leonard Skoglund '38, Chicago business man and another monogram man, succeeded Dick Rosenthal as president of the association. The post, however, was no longer simply a tribute to past athletes. These men possessed competence and experience which the presidency now demanded.

The decision not to move away from the neighborhood of the University has repaid me richly. I am in frequent contact with old friends. And there is the constant stimulation of the continuing kaleidoscope that Notre Dame offers.

New board members on the Skoglund Board were John T. Massman '56, Kansas City, executive of the Massman Construction Co.; Robert A. Erkins '47, president of the Snake River Trout Co., Buhl, Idaho; Frank L. McGinn '52, Florida realtor, Pompano Beach; Robert L. McGoldrick '56, executive Connecticut Genl. Life Ins. Co., West Hartford, and Leonard H. Tose '37, Philadelphia truck executive, present owner of the Philadelphia Eagles.

The Law School announced a symposium to observe its 100th year. Alumni were told that many LL.B. degrees might, by a ruling of the Bar Association, be exchanged for the J.D. degree.

Father Hesburgh appointed a Student Council member to a committee on curriculum revision.

Senator Eugene McCarthy received the Senior Fellow Award, which had succeeded Washington's Birthday and Patriot of the Year programs.

Barat College announced its plans to remain in its present campus.

Father Hesburgh had sent his famous "15 Minute" letter to students, parents and faculty. In a case of a disruptive student force, 15 minutes was to be allowed for meditation, following which, persistence would be followed by suspension of identifiable students, and trespass charges against non-students. The letter brought national praise from the forces of law and order, including a personal letter from President Nixon. It brought doubts from colleagues in higher education, and of course protests from students. The *Alumnus* issued an edition on the theme that "Somewhere A Stand Must be Made." Inklings of a less than utopian campus were implicit in the decision of the Student Honor Council officers to suspend its operations, saying "The current situation makes it apparent that the community is no longer committed to this concept."

With the Athletic and Convocation Center completed, Herb Jones '27, who had postponed retirement to work toward its realization, died suddenly after 47 years at Notre Dame.

Jim Cooney announced the first major national *Alumni Directory* project.

The University announced the provision for an addition to the College of Business Administration, through a $1,000,000 gift from John Healy '30, and his wife, Ramona Hayes Healy, to be known as the Hayes-Healy Center.

The Student Union Academic Commission, operating on a separate budget, began to bring controversial personages to the campus, for "first-hand understanding of public problems." A

Black Power Conference, featuring Dick Gregory, Adam Clayton Powell, James Farmer, Andrew Hatcher and Shirley Chisholm was among the earlier. Gregory had had a younger brother a student on the campus.

The 1968 Alumni Fund, under the Summa program aegis, had produced $1,822,151 from 14,182 alumni, a 49 per cent participation.

Announcement was made jointly by Notre Dame and Saint Mary's of a proposed merger of the two institutions, to effect many changes in the interests of both.

In a move that had merit, but multiplied the machinery of the campus, Father Hesburgh appointed an All-University Forum, to consist of himself, Chairman Ed Stephan of the trustees, the chairman of the Faculty Senate, the president of the Alumni Association, the president of the student body and three democratically elected members of the five constituencies. It was not decision making, but would meet four times yearly to discuss University problems. An intimation of Father Hesburgh's impatience with the constituencies in previous efforts appeared to me in his comment, "It may or may not work, but I can think of no better mechanism to serve our ultimate needs for better community and better communication." The faculty, whose average salaries had been doubled by Father Hesburgh, in addition to improved fringe benefits and self-determination, and the students, whose interests had been championed by Father Hesburgh since his chaplaincy in Vetville, had continued to intensify his problem. His persisting strength was in the support of the trustees in policy, and the Alumni Association in programs.

The Athletic and Convocation Center housed the 1969 commencement, when 1,774 degrees were awarded.

A new shadow was cast when Richard Conklin, of the public information staff, identified the Congregation of Holy Cross as having now only 15 full professors, 20 associates, three instructors, one director, and one assistant dean in the University. The warning was a comment, "While the order has generally favored Notre Dame with its best people, the competition for academic appointment has stiffened, and perhaps even fewer Holy Cross priests will be found on the faculty in the future." Under the new governance, the Provincial of the Congregation no longer has the power of assignment to the University faculty.

Restructuring of staff under Vice President Jim Frick brought James E. Murphy to the assistant vice presidential post;

Frank Kelly, director of development (a post he has just as of this writing relinquished to Brian Regan, to return to the direction of deferred giving); Jim Gibbons, director of special events (following the retirement of J. Arthur Haley '26) and Bruce Harlan as director of photography.

Universal Notre Dame Night met unrest head on with the theme "The Notre Dame Student Today."

The proposed Saint Mary's merger headed the third meeting of the Alumni Senate. Father Hesburgh, and Monsignor Mc-Grath, the president of Saint Mary's, issued a statement affirming the autonomy of both institutions under the proposed merger.

William C. Schmitt '10, died shortly after receiving the fifth Father Sorin Award. Mrs. Armstrong and I hosted an alumni short tour to Rome, the first of five such trips, sponsored by the association, organized by Richard Small '51, Chicago, which have become a part of continuing education efforts for the association.

James Kinnane '57, was appointed to head a University office in Los Angeles, an indication of the University's expanding needs. Gulf Oil made an interesting gift of $100,000 to Father Hesburgh to initiate a study of non-violence.

Father Hesburgh was still trying to empathize with his students. At a Vietnam moratorium Mass on the main campus, civil disobedience and the burning of draft cards were involved. A Notre Dame Resistance was announced. Father Hesburgh had been at the Mass. He predicted some reaction of outrage, and possible prosecution, but added, "What was it Thoreau said? Something like 'in times like these the best men are in jail.'" His patience resulted largely in renewed excesses by the hard core student activists.

The Alumni Board in October of 1969 urged liaison with Saint Mary's; studied the nomination of younger alumni for board membership; urged regular publication of placement opportunities; asked alumni consultantion in curriculum revision; objected to the draft card burning at the campus Mass and accepted the first by-laws for the association, prepared by John Reidy. The board was aware, from the annual briefings, of Father Hesburgh's tolerance for dissent, and his belief that progress was achieved by ferment. But the problems which now confronted each board were becoming increasingly more difficult to translate to the farflung, generous alumni, whose loyalty was vital to University progress. The Alumni Senate was looked to with great hope.

Don O'Brien '42, Houston, was chosen to scuceed Len Skoglund as president of the association. New members of the board were Dr. John C. Lungren '38, Los Angeles; Daniel D. Canale '42, Memphis attorney from a family of Notre Dame alumni; James C. Macdevitt '35, Great Neck, N.Y., attorney; Joseph T. O'Neill '53, St. Paul attorney; John R. Panelli '49, Birmingham, Mich., construction equipment company president and former monogram and pro football player, and Coleman O'Brien '69, McLean, Virginia, elected under a new director-at-large provision. Michael Jordan '68, was appointed assistant alumni secretary. Mike is the son of Cecil Jordan '40, LL.B. '45.

January, 1970, found the non-bowl game tradition which had extended from the Rose Bowl of 1925, broken to permit Notre Dame, with an 8-1-1 season, to play Texas in the Cotton Bowl in Texas. The proceeds from the game were assigned to the pressures of minority scholarships at Notre Dame. Texas was a winner in a close 17-21 game. The experience was constructive, and the University permitted Notre Dame, with a 9-1-0 season, to return to the 1971 Cotton Bowl, where it defeated Texas 24-11. The third bowl game under the relaxed regulations, was the 1973 Orange Bowl game which Nebraska won resoundingly, 6-40, but in all three games the added gate receipts have aided the total funding of a $3,000,000 scholarship fund for minority applicants.

Another Notre Dame first came with the announcement of Bayard Rustin as the first black member of the Board of Trustees.

When Notre Dame student protesters again blocked the path of student interview prospects to the recruiters from Dow and the C.I.A., in the Main Building, the 15-minute rule of Father Hesburgh was invoked. The student newspaper backed the administration. Twelve faculty members signed a paper opposing the administration action.

A proposal to tear down the old Gymnasium was halted by a request from the art department to use the building as a needed art center to encourage all forms of student art. Demolition was deferred. The Alumni Board meetings were now centered on major priorities. Campus ministry, campus security, minority development and post-season bowl games were targeted in January, 1970. The bowl decision was endorsed. The administration was asked to study and up-grade the campus security force. Campus ministry was the area singled out for top priority.

John Macheca '62, was appointed to succeed David Shanahan '58, in the University's Chicago Foundation office. Forty-five

N.D. students helped offset a deteriorating student image when they took part in the Big Brothers program in the South Bend area. A strong tutoring program for area underprivileged children was already popularly recognized. Notre Dame and Saint Mary's students signed a petition asking that Father Hesburgh become chancellor of the University and that Willis Nutting, a lay professor for 35 years, be made University president. More campus and academic rapport seemed to be the motivation, with Father Hesburgh's prestigious involvement in world affairs cited as a handicap to his presidency.

David Krasha became the first black president of the student body. The list of controversial speakers jumped into the national headlines with the campus appearance of Dr. James P. Shannon, Dr. Benjamin Spock and Attorney William Kunstler. Individuals and causes had found the newly affluent society of the campuses, and the crossroads was attracting a different clientele from those who had crossed the bridge for earlier beacons.

Some improvement was noted in student morale when the invasion of Cambodia threatened to be a new torch. Notre Dame reaction was non-violent. Father Hesburgh addressed the students, sympathizing with their opposition to the Vietnam war. The Kent State shootings brought a student strike vote. Separate faculty groups endorsed both the anti-war stand and the opposite action of President Nixon. But there was no real violence during the seven critical days that saw much national campus turbulence. A program of black studies was announced for the Fall of 1970. Tom Sullivan '66, moved from the *Alumnus* to the Foundation staff and was replaced by Timothy Hughes '61, George Scheuer '28, retiring from the South Bend Tribune, became copy editor for Notre Dame publications.

The fourth meeting of the Alumni Senate derived its major significance from the housing of the delegates in the student residence halls. As a result of this close contact with all parties involved, the senate passed an important resolution, "The national Alumni Board and the Alumni Senate in joint session hereby commend the President, the administration, the faculty and students of the University for their deep moral concern at this critical moment in our nation's history, and particularly for their constructive implementation of the concern. We commit ourselves, as alumni of the University, to a heightened understanding of the problems of our attention and to constructive efforts toward achieving peace in our day."

Father James T. Burtchaell, C.S.C. '56, a brilliant young

theologian, was appointed the University's first provost, second in command to the President, and in effect in charge of academic affairs. Father John Walsh was on leave of absence. The 1970 reunions featured a talk by Father Hesburgh at a general alumni luncheon on Friday, and by Ara Parseghian at the traditional alumni banquet. The retirement of Father Louis J. Thornton, C.S.C. '29, who had done outstanding jobs in the critical pressures of the admissions office after World War II, and in the beleaguered Placement Office during the era of student activism, removed a veteran administrator and friend of alumni. He remained on the campus as Infirmary Chaplain. Father William Toohey, C.S.C. '52, became the first director of campus ministry, replacing the University chaplain, who in turn had replaced the last of the prefects of religion.

The alumni office instituted a general class reunion program after each home football game, in the spacious Athletic and Convocation Center.

The Alumni Senate announced regional meetings to stress alumni in community service, continuing education, expanded placement service, and increased cooperation with Saint Mary's alumnae. The communications arts department, which had succeeded the journalism department, was now altered to become a part of the American Studies program. Richard Willemin 42, succeeded Father Thornton as director of placement. Willemin had been in the University areas of testing and guidance.

Controversy continued to offset progress. Jane Fonda was a campus speaker, and Ti-Grace Atkinson brought down intensive criticism, including Our Sunday Visitor. Father Hesburgh defended the right of open speaking on the campus. He commented, in part:

"If I have to take a stand, I will take it here: with the young people who are dedicated, generous, idealistic and who occasionally fall on their faces. . . . The greatest challenge to the Church today is not to discipline and browbeat the young—it is to win young people for the Kingdom of God and His Justice and His Salvation and to do all this in freedom, by manifesting to them His love."

This championing of the young has been consistent. Unfortunately, the valid belief in the majority was often allowed to serve as a sanctuary for a less defensible minority. Unfortunately, too, the students, with a four-year turnover, never experienced the depth of the unfailing loyalty of their champion. Many did not repay it in kind.

William Lawless '44, who had become dean of the Law

School after Joseph O'Meara, resigned to return to New York State, and was in turn succeeded by Thomas Shaffer '61. The Saint Mary's merger progressed, on the basis of the 1,969 students of both institutions who had been active in the co-exchange program. Students confidently announced that the unisex principle of education—separate schools for men and women—was dead.

The incredible paradoxes continued. The Class of 1971 selected the controversial William Kunstler as Senior Fellow. And the Summa Program announced it had achieved its goal of $52,000,000 in less than the allotted five years. It was, in fact, oversubscribed.

It was 1971 before the rising problem of drugs on the American campus was mentioned in the Notre Dame publications.

President Bob Erkins reported an alumni fear of the proposed move toward coeducation and the Saint Mary's merger. This persisted in the face of favorable responses from board and senate meetings after briefings by administrators on the merits. Again, an up-to-date miracle in the old tradition, alumni in 1970 had contributed over $2,000,000, exclusive of honorary alumni, whose gifts added a half million.

On May 14, 1971, the trustees of Notre Dame and Saint Mary's ratified the recommendations of the executive committees of each, for unification of the two schools.

In a story on various religious meetings held on the campus, an interesting comment was made by Richard Conklin, in information services: he suggested that theologians anticipating a Vatican III were beginning to look to Notre Dame as the Vatican II preparations had looked to Louvain "Because Notre Dame has a quality of openness congenial both to varied life-styles and to creative Christian scholarship, and perhaps has the best chance to ride out the polarization storm affecting all established churches."

The Notre Dame trustees expressed dissatisfaction with the student hall administration of parietal hours (which had been granted in modified form) and with alcoholic beverage regulations. The Student Life Council was asked to act. The major result was student demand for the end of the Student Life Council.

In a joint statement signed by Edmund A. Stephan, the Notre Dame Trustees chairman, and Mother M. Olivette of the Saint Mary's Trustees, it was agreed that complete unification at this time is possible. On Nov. 30 the proposed merger was suspended indefinitely. At the same time, Father Hesburgh announced that Notre Dame would accept a limited number of women applicants in its 1972 Freshman class.

The "structure" of Notre Dame was now legally secularized. The all-male University of 130 years was now coeducation.

If I believed that the University of Notre Dame was only the "structure," that it had abandoned the larger and greater "superstructure" of its long history, I would indeed have felt like an alien.

As it stands at this writing, there are sources of even greater hope. The "structure" of Notre Dame, as I have tried to point out, the academic University, can assume many forms, as it did throughout its long history. Even coeducation can find a proper home—women were a part of the Notre Dame pattern from its dedication. It is in the "superstructure," that deeper and richer part of Notre Dame, rooted in the Church and in its magisterium, that the purpose, nature and identity of the University really lie. It is not "school" or "football" which have set Notre Dame apart, even within the framework of other Catholic schools. It is the miracle of a blend of spiritual strength, which has won the respect of non-Catholics and a great public, with the academic achievement which has come from unbelievably modest resources, and with a dynamic drive against all odds, symbolized in its football teams, but inherent in any facet of the institution that may be considered. From its opening, the depth of tradition and the guidance of religion have never closed a door against change or rejected a person or idea without consideration. "Tomorrow" is the keynote of the campus. "Today" has a milling, demanding, controversial citizenry to defend itself. My goal in this chronicle has been to insure that "yesterday," an equally vital segment of Notre Dame, is also and properly recognized.

XXXVIII

Epilogue

I use that word, because there is no conclusion in the chronicle of Notre Dame men—and women.

But I would like to share several of the recent favorable portents of the ongoing success of the University of Notre Dame.

The Alumni Board and the alumni office, augmented by the Alumni Senate, supported by some 200 local alumni clubs, and adding each year a new complement of more than 1500 alumni with the new graduating class, form a structure which has been tested in many earlier eras by many crises, and has remained as strong and vital as the internal structures of the University.

Father James Burtchaell, C.S.C., Notre Dame provost, writes of the controversial doctrine of "in loco parentis" which I believe was one of the keys to the national attraction of Notre Dame.: "The most vociferous dismantlers of the in loco parentis policy, of course, have been the students themselves. Entering into the University often relieves strained relations at home between parental authority and the striving for independence by the child. He does not leave home in pursuit of new authoritarian adults, but to breathe new adult freedom for himself . . .

"Well, despite its unpopularity and untimeliness, the notion of senior members of the University standing in loco parentis to their undergraduate students is one that I should like to sustain . . . Because we accept this larger charge, the natural parents of our students demand much of us . . . desperately hoping that in a few short years we shall somehow be able to undo any negligence or failure they have been guilty of during the past 18 years. . . . But . . with God's grace and our effort we try as parents do to help boys (and now girls) into manhood (and

438

womanhood). This is no small ambition. After having made
even a career out of what is most people's great work in life, we
would not, I believe, choose to stand elsewhere than in loco
parentis. God help us."

And the same young Father Burtchaell, addressing the Notre
Dame faculty during the Mass opening the 1972 academic year,
said in part: " . . . Notre Dame's character is not guaranteed by
its charter, statutes, or bylaws, nor by those who govern it,
despite the assertion of our statutes that it is the stated intention and desire of the Fellows that the University retain in
perpetuality its identity as a Catholic institution. Living traditions live not at all by law and governance if the law and
governance do not find their affirmation in the persons who live
by them. Nor is our tradition preserved, as once it may have
been, by the separatist trends of the American Catholic population . . . To be a Catholic university—and to remain so—was for
the first century and a quarter of Notre Dame's existence
largely assumed by the predominant yearning of the constituency it served: American Catholics. This was a group that was
most identity-conscious, a power-deprived, status-poor, socially
inferior minority, struggling to resist assimilation into the
heathen society, it works and pomps. They prided themselves
on being distinctive.

"We ran before the wind, with the breezes full in our sails.
But now the winds have reversed, and blow against us. The
Catholic community is shy of its tradition. The very forces that
made us distinctive presently bear upon us to make us commonplace and nondescript . . . At Notre Dame we have no task more
important than to recruit and invite into our midst men and
women who, beyond their being rigorously given over to the
profession of learning, are likewise dedicated to life of intelligent belief. If we are to be a Christian University, we must have
a critical mass of Christian teachers. If Notre Dame is to remain
Catholic, the only institutional way for assuring this is to secure
a faculty with prominent representation of committed and
articulate believers who purposefully seek the comradeship of
others to weave their faith into the full fabric of their intellectual life . . . In speaking of our religious commitment I cannot
pass over our special need for Holy Cross religious at Notre
Dame. The school was founded by the Congregation of Holy
Cross and is marked with the seal of that community's spirit
. . . From their graves those dedicated men ordain us all to that
same task. . . . Notre Dame is its people, especially its teachers,

who join in this wonderfully important work of educating, and are sensitive to the long-lived values represented by this 2,000-year-old tradition . . . "

Father Hesburgh, too, has indicated personal effort to withdraw from the maelstrom of outside activities which taxed his talents. Higher education around the world, public service in high office, and the delegation of ecclesiastical responsibilities, almost from the beginning of his long tenure, have compounded the demanding leadership of Notre Dame.

Notre Dame Magazine, the uniperson channel of communication between the University and its alumni and friends, asked administrators very recently for their suggestion for their own epitaphs. Father Hesburgh submitted this one:

> "Here lies Father Ted
>   Often called the Head.
> He preferred at least
>   To be known as Priest.
> When the final trumpet blows
>   Let's hope its the Priest who shows
> —Not the Head.
> He's long dead. R.I.P."

In more serious vein, in the January 8 issue of the New York Times at this beginning of 1973, he is quoted:

"I believed it to be a fairly obvious fact that we have come full circle in our secularized times. Today one hears all too little of intellectual values, and moral values seem to have become a lost cause in the educational process. I know educators of some renown who practically tell their students, 'We don't care what you do around here as long as you do it quietly, avoid blatant scandal, and don't give the institution a bad name.'

"Part of this attitude is an over-reaction to 'in loco parentis,' which goes from eschewing responsibility for students lives to just not caring how they live . . . Moral abdication or valuelessness seems to have become a sign of the times. One might well describe the illness of modern society and its schooling as 'anomie', a rootlessness . . . I have long believed that a Christian university is worthless in our day unless it conveys to all who study within it a deep sense of the dignity of the human person, his nature and high destiny, his opportunities for seeking justice in a very unjust world, his inherent nobility so needing to be achieved by himself or herself, for one's self and for others, whatever the obstacles . . . There is nothing automatic about the liberal education tradition. It can die if not fostered. And if it does die, the values that sustain an individual and a nation are likely to die with it."

I think these excerpts should help you to share my hopes for the future of Notre Dame. The University has always been a school for the future. Notre Dame men have been equipped to meet their future.

In this wholly inadequate chronicle I have sought only to identify the vital relationship of "superstructure" and "structure" of Notre Dame. I have followed the paths of University Presidents, and Alumni Association officers because they have been the central and constant cables of power from which the growing Notre Dame emanated.

There are in these pages most regrettable summaries of great people and events that hopefully suggest books and articles by future writers.

There are segments of Notre Dame life that could produce more colorful treatises—the minor and interhall athletics, the deans and department heads, the musical organizations, the geographical clubs on campus, the literary and debating traditions and the publications—and Notre Dame humor, a sort of verbal acupuncture, with sharp needles but ultimate relief and cure.

I have not dwelt at length on material success of Notre Dame men. There is a rewarding array of churchmen, educators, scientists, engineers, authors, corporate heads, political leaders, coaches and leaders of national organizations of spiritual and social impact.

But when I think of "success" I think of Van Wallace, paralyzed from his sophomore year, an inspirational figure for Notre Dame men, and the mother who never left his side for long and difficult years. I think of Fred Snite, the "Boiler Kid," struck down by polio in China soon after graduation, heir to a fortune, but living the rest of his life in an iron lung, adjusting to his tragedy in the deep religious resignation of the saints and martyrs; of Jack Miles, a buoyant young journalist stricken by polio on the eve of his marriage, whose fiancee insisted on the fulfillment of their dreams, who made a life and career for himself with her encouragement; of Jim McQuaind, a former athlete and coach, stricken by multiple sclerosis, who, with a devoted wife, continued a career increasingly modified by disease but never by loss of faith and spirit. I think of Dr. Tom Dooley, who forfeited a secure career as a doctor to devote his short life to aiding the refugees, the poor and the stricken in far-off Laos. I think of Father Patrick Peyton, C.S.C., priest-alumnus, miraculously brought back from seemingly imminent death, to dedicate his life to the devotion to Our Lady in the Rosary, a crusade world wide in its influence.

That is why, in my interpretation, this chronicle is a story with 50,000 heroes, with 50,000 successes.

Progress has been an uneasy path in many of the periods of history of the University. Today is no exception. Each of the crises of history has found Notre Dame equal to its challenges, and stronger for the struggle.

I hope to enjoy many more years of this continuing story, and to listen and read as others take up the burden of its telling.

The past, present and future of the University contain, as I said at the start, facts and things which defy the analysis of facts. Like her to whom Father Sorin dedicated it, the human and the divine have blended to produce a unique force for good which has spread from a little clearing in pioneer Indiana to the four corners of the world.

There is no farewell, rather an "until tomorrow," with all the faith and hopes of its values, its excitements and its contributions to God, Country and Notre Dame that have brought us to this point.

BIBLIOGRAPHY
APPENDICES

BIBLIOGRAPHY

"Silver Jubilee of the University of Notre Dame" Joseph A. Lyons '58
  1869
"A Brief History of the University of Notre Dame du Lac" Timothy E.
  Howard '64 1895
Notre Dame: One Hundred Years, Rev. Arthur J. Hope, C.S.C. '20 1943
The Catholic Encyclopedia (1st Ed.) Vol. XI 1911
Bound Volumes of *The Scholastic* 1867-1924
Bound Volumes *DOME* 1906-1972
Alumni Directory:
Bound Volumes *The Alumnus* 1923-1972
Alumni Directory: 1908
Alumni Directory: 1943
Alumni Directory: 1970
The Collected Poems of Rev. Charles, L. O'Donnell, C.S.C. '06 1942
Notre Dame: Its People and Its Legends, Francis Wallace '23 1969
Notre Dame's John Zahm, Ralph E. Weber '56 1961
Before Rockne at Notre Dame, D. C. "Chet" Grant '22 1968
Notre Dame: Reminiscences of an Era, Richard T. Sullivan '30 1951
Minutes of the Meetings of the Alumni Association 1908-1924
University of Notre Dame *Bulletins* (Catalogues, Registers) to 1972
Father O'Hara of Notre Dame, Rev. Thomas T. McAvoy C.S.C. '25 1968

PRESIDENTS OF THE
UNIVERSITY OF NOTRE DAME

NOTE: *All of the Presidents of the University, with the exception of Father Colovin and of Father Sorin himself, have been alumni, who have been enrolled in regular courses at the University, varying in lengths of time, but experiencing the student viewpoints of curriculum, housing, food, discipline, and spiritual life.*

Rev. Edward F. Sorin, C.S.C.	1842-1865
Rev. Patrick Dillon, C.S.C.	1865-1866
Rev. William Corby, C.S.C.	1866-1872
Rev. Auguste Lemonnier, C.S.C.	1872-1874
Rev. Patrick Colovin, C.S.C.	1874-1877
Rev. William Corby, C.S.C.	1877-1881
	(second presidency)
Rev. Thomas Walsh, C.S.C.	1881-1893
Rev. Andrew Morrissey, C.S.C.	1893-1905
Rev. John W. Cavanaugh, C.S.C.	1905-1919
Rev. James A. Burns, C.S.C.	1919-1922*
Rev. Matthew Walsh, C.S.C.	1922-1928*
Rev. Charles O'Donnell, C.S.C.	1928-1934*
Rev. John O'Hara, C.S.C.	1934-1940*
Rev. J. Hugh O'Donnell, C.S.C.	1940-1946*
Rev. John J. Cavanaugh, C.S.C.	1946-1952*
Rev. Theodore M. Hesburgh, C.S.C.	1952-

*With the advent of Father Burns' presidency, the Congregation changed its regulations to limit the terms to two three-year segments, not as President, in fact, but as Religious Superior at Notre Dame.

Father Burns retired after his first segment to lead a fund drive.

Father Charles L. O'Donnell died just at the expiration of six years.

Father Hugh O'Donnell died shortly after completing six years.

With the presidency of Father Hesburgh, the technical limitation of six years as Religious Superior and President has been removed by the separation of the presidency from the superiorship of the Notre Dame community.

PROGRAM HIGHLIGHTS
OF THE ALUMNI ASSOCIATION
UNDER THE LEADERSHIP OF THE ALUMNI BOARDS

Following is a summary of such highlights published on the 40th anniversary of the Alumni Board as the Notre Dame Alumni Association's governing body, covering the years from 1924 to 1964.

To these must be added subsequent accomplishments, such as the creation of the Alumni Senate. . . . .

Constant expansion of local alumni clubs and their programs.

Establishment of a student-alumni committee for better liaison. . . . .

Establishment of the Alumni Club for Seniors on the campus.

Intensive cooperation with the Foundation, the alumni-founded arm of the University which has now received over $100,000,000 in gifts and grants since its inception in 1947-48.

Intensive development of activities in conjunction with both placement and admissions office.

HIGHLIGHTS OF
ALUMNI BOARD ACCOMPLISHMENTS,
1924-1964
Taken from THE NOTRE DAME ALUMNUS
April–May, 1964–

I. Alumni office established as a full-time center, 1923-24.

II. Full-time alumni secretary appointed, January, 1926.

III. *Alumnus* magazine established, 1923-24. (Another vital board decision in regard to the *Alumnus* was its continuance during the depression years and during World War II. This preserved the organization and good will and contacts that might have taken years to recover if suspended.)

IV. Universal Notre Dame Night, established in 1924. One of the greatest public relations channels for the University, a key focal point of clubs, and a distinctive and different achievement among colleges and universities.

V. Universal Communion Sunday, established by the New York Club in 1938, and made universal by the board. An increasingly constructive contribution to the broad area of religion and citizenship among alumni, and a basic club program (Events IV and V have increased our clubs from 40 to 181 since 1924).

VI. Placement of graduates. This activity was recommended by the board from the beginning as a service to alumni and a strong tie with new graduates. For years it was a partial function of the alumni office. Ultimately, it was made a full-time University office, under Bill Dooley, and has continued to grow in importance and activity.

VII. Interest in student recruiting. For many years the board fostered alumni activity in recruiting good students, visiting high-school college nights, and talking with parents. The Admissions office has now made this a strong and proper branch of its program, enlisting increasing alumni involvement.

VIII. The biennial Council of Club Presidents has been most effective in reflecting Club thought and development.

IX. A similar biennial Council Class Secretaries has advanced class activity. The separate and cost-covered reunions, with a thousand attending, are typical.

X. The Annual Alumni Fund was first launched by the board in the early thirties, but gave way to a capital gifts campaign.

Reinstituted in 1941, it provided the strong broad base for
the Foundation expansion in 1947.

XI. The Alumni Board co-operated constructively and fully in
the Rockne Memorial campaigns.

XII. Probably the most significant measurable contribution of
the board was the establishment, with the University, of the
Notre Dame Foundation, in 1947, based on the Annual
Alumni Fund and foreseeing the growing need for outside
support. The Foundation, since 1947, has reflected more
than fifty million dollars from alumni and friends as the
twenty-million-dollar Challenge II program opens.

XIII. A major board program, in conjunction with the University, which suffered from a lack of resources of both money
and people, was the anti-Communist movement led by President Arthur Hughes in 1936-1937.

XIV. The Alumni Board has in recent years sponsored the
annual Senior class dinner.

XV. Similarly, the board has encouraged the annual *Senior
Directory* since 1961.

XVI. Alumnae development. For many years, the alumni office,
under the board direction worked with the nuns who attended the Summer Sessions. At one time an active Alumnae
Association was formed, summer picnics were held, and a
directory published. In post World War II years, the University has directly pursued special programs for the sisters.

XVII. The Alumni Board has sanctioned and encouraged the
development of the Law Alumni Association as an affiliated
and supplementary organization.

XVIII. Similarly, the board has worked closely with the National Monogram Club, composed of all letter-winning alumni.

XIX. The board from its beginning has encouraged membership
in the American Alumni Council. This has produced substantial professional progress, and last year resulted in the
Notre Dame representative being the first national president
of A. A. C. from a Catholic college or university.

THE ANNUAL ALUMNI FUND

1941-1972

Year	Number Contributors	Amount Contributed
1941	1,154	$35,808
1942	1,154	35,808
1943	1,154	35,808
1944	3,313	111,342
1945	3,096	94,345
1946	5,885	276,989
1947	7,886	274,913
1948	6,965	350,973
1949	7,508	403,876
1950	7,109	932,112
1951	6,736	323,842
1952	7,000	308,717
1953	9,180	364,093
1954	10,132	481,202
1955	11,298	525,350
1956	10,789	837,199
1957	11,631	565,279
1958	11,677	695,620
1959	11,980	700,420
1960	10,976	625,169
1961	8,424	1,164,215
1962	12,538	1,777,684
1963	11,856	1,258,956
1964	10,794	2,102,299
1965	11,784	1,437,341
1966	13,709	2,165,699
1967	13,456	1,579,765
1968	14,167	1,758,558
1969	14,670	1,810,121
1970	14,201	2,120,284
1971	14,922	2,019,108
	Total	$27,172,907

THE OLD DAYS

by REV. THOMAS E. BURKE, C.S.C. '07

Father Tom Burke, and his brother, Father Eugene Burke, C.S.C. '07, contributed much to the rich humor and literary quality of the Notre Dame campus. Both were at varying times on the editorial staff of the *Ave Maria* magazine. Both brought their talents to campus publications and alumni gatherings. Father Tom was a frequent contributor to the Chicago *Tribune* "Wake of the News" and published a collection of delightful items under the title of his pen identification, T.E.B. The *Alumnus* of 1934 printed this particular contribution to the cause of past, present and future, as featured in a commencement show on the campus in the Fall of 1934. It combines the nostalgia for the rigorous life with the doubts about the modern "softer" life of the student. This was not peculiar to recent thinking at Notre Dame. It was present when Sorin Hall was built in 1899, and even more so when Walsh Hall, long called "The Gold Coast," was erected in 1910. But, as in alumni thinking throughout the lifetime of the University, confidence and optimism overcome doubt and fear—and with them, opposition.

Let me tell you of the old days,
Of the old school and the old ways,
Before men became effeminate and soft:
When the students lived on beefsteak
That would make your heart and teeth ache,
And at every tender delicacy scoffed.

They wore corduroy and jumpers,
And they rode upon the bumpers
When they came here in September to enroll:
And they carried knives and blackjacks,
'Stead of fountain pens and thumbtacks,
For the men of old had spirit in their soul.

Oh, those days are gone forever,
And I fear that they will never
Be repeated on the campus any more:
For the creampuff's silken yellow
Has replaced the iron fellow
Who in past days slept upon the subway floor.

Oh those days are gone forever,
They will come back never, never,
Time has rung the curtain down upon the stage;
All the actors have departed
While we wait here broken hearted,
Out of step and out of concord with the age.

May be when the years have tried them
We may find that we've belied them,
That they'll carry in each fist a double shock;
That though steep the grade, they'll make it;
That they'll stand right up and take it,
Till the world knows they are chips off the old block.

INDEX

INDEX